From: M. Grayken
74 North Main St. #3
Cohasset Ma
Zip: 02025

LIFE FLASHES

a memoir

MERRIE H. REAGAN

First Stillwater River Publications Edition

Library of Congress Control Number: 2022900053
Hardcover ISBN: 978-1-955123-75-4
Paperback ISBN: 978-1-955123-76-1

12345678910
Written by Merrie H. Reagan
Cover Art by Lindsay Whelan
Published by Stillwater River Publications,
Pawtucket, RI, USA.

Publisher's Cataloging-In-Publication Data
(Prepared by The Donohue Group, Inc.)

Names: Reagan, Merrie H., author.
Title: Life flashes / Merrie H. Reagan.
Description: First Stillwater River Publications edition. | Paw-
    tucket, RI, USA : Stillwater River Publications, [2022]
Identifiers: ISBN 9781955123754 (hardcover) | ISBN
    9781955123761 (paperback)
Subjects: LCSH: Reagan, Merrie H. | Cohasset (Mass.)--Biog-
    raphy. | Spiritual life. | LCGFT: Autobiographies. | Diaries.
Classification: LCC F74.C6 R43 2022 | DDC 974.47092--dc23

TABLE OF CONTENTS

INTRODUCTION

Summarizing over 400 pages of content within *Life Flashes: A Memoir* into one sentence was a relatively simple task. Divine love deluges all earthly circumstances. No exceptions. None.

Begun in January of 2007 and completed in February of 2021, the book reveals partial life experiences that I have encountered, and in doing so, it examines personal late mid-life, childhood, adolescence, adulthood, and also early and mid-life years, before I embraced entering senior years. Names in the book have been changed, as a means of offering book subjects additional privacy protection.

A personal, near death, spiritually awakening, and life-changing occurrence opens the memoir. Days, weeks, months, and years beyond the experience found me encountering national, local, personal, and animal figures and regularly revisiting and moving beyond present as well as previous personal and professional relationships. Recorded events and interactions within *Life Flashes: A Memoir* invite readers to re-examine Divine existence and at the same time to reconsider aspects of human relationships, politics, current events, spirituality, religion, psychology, and western as well as alternative medicine.

When the book was nearly finished, several family members had passed away, within a few years. Some longtime challenging matters I was confronting had not been resolved. Meanwhile, remarkable miracles and healing had occurred. Writing the memoir presented another opportunity for me to acknowledge the preciousness of life and consequently to face, address, and move beyond personal issues related with illness, unemployment, relationship challenges, and loss. I hope readers of the work will be similarly affected.

Life Flashes: A Memoir is a testament that demonstrates profound love remains amid as well as beyond all life circumstances. It is hoped that readers of the book will be inspired, informed, and entertained. I hope the book is a work that people want to read today and fifty years from now.

Merrie H. Reagan

FOREWORD

*L*ife Flashes: A Memoir was not initially intended to be published. When I began writing the work, on January 1, 2007, it was solely a diary that I someday wished to bequeath to a family member. Three years later, now eleven years ago, I began to consider publicly sharing the non-fiction work.

Writing, researching, editing, and proofreading the manuscript caused me to realize that writers resemble artists. Writers discover freedom through "throwing" or penning ideas upon paper, as do artists, who utilize paint or pencil strokes, which are drawn or etched upon canvas. While editing, writers perform manuscript revisions; as writing is clarified, words are changed, expanded, removed or left unchanged. Using paint as well as pencil strokes when developing artistic ideas, which are unfolded on canvas or through another artistic medium, artists perform similar editing tasks.

Editing writing resembles panning for gold; it requires sifting completed writing, which allows writers to empty gangue—worthless material, including content, organization, and grammar errors as well as spelling, punctuation, and capitalization flaws, or mechanics mistakes. Sometimes edited material can be recycled or placed in a different manuscript section, giving the revised writing new life. Writing that is properly edited is relevant to the reader and flows evenly. Properly edited copy is neither excessively lengthy nor prohibitively short.

Sufficiently revised writing repeatedly solicits the interest of the reader. Perfectly revised writing, like panned gold, has been edited until solid gold writing remains.

Writing a book resembles penning poetry or prose. Each word, each sentence, and each paragraph demonstrates a particular rhythm, reason, and meaning. Each writing part or segment influences the development of completed writing.

Proofreading resembles editing, without being editing. Proofreading involves making final spelling, capitalization, and punctuation changes. Proofreading involves re-examining the layout of the manuscript. Proper page numbering, page spacing, spacing between words, and tab spacing are also important.

A writer is a person who utilizes as few words as possible to convey clear and concise thoughts as well as to stimulate new thinking. The writing style of *Life Flashes: A Memoir* respects existing grammatical rules; it also challenges some of the rules. Why? As an author, I want to energize and empower readers in new ways. Doing so was accomplished in a number of ways.

First, balancing the use of first-person active voice and third-person passive voice is intended to provide writing equilibrium. When writing is essentially personally focused, through continual employment of the first person tense or possessives, growth of the writer is delayed. Connection between the writer and readers is delayed.

Second, infrequently using possessives and not continually using articles or prepositions was employed as a means of moving readers away from observing relationships with persons, places, or things as being primarily equated with personal possession or connection; not focusing primarily on possession enlivens interactions with these entities.

As a means of intellectually stimulating readers, prepositions and articles, which are connecting words, were intermittently omitted. Readers are regularly encouraged to connect words without these grammatical aids, and in doing so, to be intellectually challenged as well as physically invigorated. From time to time, improper nouns were converted into proper nouns as a means of animating a person or animal and giving the person or animal equal representation with additional subjects in an anecdote.

The writing style of *Life Flashes: A Memoir* was modified, yet not fully omitted, after I consulted with several professional editors and proofreaders. Unanimously, the wordsmiths respected the unusual style of the memoir manuscript. The literary professionals also advised me, that when a writer initiates significant writing style changes, it is important that the changes are introduced in small doses, as instituting writing style changes without properly discerning what level of writing style change potential readers are ready to accept is a perfect recipe for literary failure. At the same time, being a successful writer involves accepting risk—acknowledging the possibility of failure as well as success. Experiencing contentment as a writer also means accepting that responsibility for the quality of writing rests primarily on the shoulders of the writer, not an editor or proofreader.

Writing, editing, and proofreading found me remembering words someone, whose name I cannot remember, uttered. "Do not ever write anything that you would not want to read on the front page of a newspaper." This is sage advice. A writer who seeks excellence regularly re-examines personal writings because written material that he or she wrote may later be found to be immaterial, inaccurate, or inappropriate. Published or not, writing which does not demonstrate literary limits damages author credibility as well as the relationship between the author and readers.

Writing is not an essentially solitary process. While writing, an author is continually interacting with people, places, animals, and things that he or she is examining. After writing for several hours, writers generally experience considerable physical as well as emotional fatigue. Why? While writing, authors privately engage with people, places, and things, sometimes as intensely as in person. During the past fourteen years, I have consistently discovered social life I have missed while I have been living alone and have been writing, rewriting, or editing for much of the day—mostly at home or in libraries or coffee shops—has been active, within me. Solitary and social interactions are remarkably similar; the two communication methods are not mutually exclusive.

No endeavor, including writing, is conflict-free. As a rookie laptop computer user, I lost sections of the manuscript on several occasions, without warning. The manuscript text could not be rewritten; passing time can render a writer unable to recreate experience, mood, and atmosphere. Authors continually learn how to grieve and move beyond literary losses.

Writing *Life Flashes: A Memoir* reignited passion for living within me. I have again embraced the belief that acceptance of uncertainty and loss is fundamentally connected with being fully alive. Writing the book has enabled me to become grounded, through realizing employment, financial, educational, or relationship status, or any worldly standing is not essentially what defines success. Exuding contentment amidst regularly changing life circumstances exemplifies true success.

ACKNOWLEDGEMENTS

*L*ife Flashes: A Memoir* is a literary surprise party; words celebrate the festivity. Guests of the party are people, animals, places, and things, named, as well as unnamed, having given me and others life-changing inspiration. Emerging through Divine inspiration, the work was carefully guided, as it evolved from the beginning to the end. Innumerable occasions found me wondering where words I was writing, changing, or rewriting originated; I regularly experienced noticeable and unexplainable spiritual energy resembling electrical energy, running through the arm and fingers that I was using to write or to compose.

Authors as well as book producers, Dawn and Steven Porter, of Stillwater River Publications assisted me with preparing the book for distribution and in doing so, provided me with final copyediting and proofreading assistance and formatting and production services. Editor and author Lydia Redwine and I were successful partners, during two editing stages. Working with several professional people who can serve as what is termed in the publishing business as another set of eyes is highly advisable, whether a writer decides to work with an editor while developing a manuscript or to do so when a manuscript has been completed. Delighting me, I discovered that in turn, working with literary professionals to prepare a book for publication gives an author another set of eyes while the author is reviewing an edited or proofread manuscript.

Visiting Hingham Public Library (HPL), Paul Pratt Library in Cohasset and Scituate Public Library allowed me to use any available desktop computer for countless hours and also enabled me to receive welcomed library staff advice. Anna Byrne, HPL Director of Technology Services gave me several hours of assistance, aiding me with formatting the Table of Contents page. HPL technicians Alex Gomez as well as Robbie St. John also aided me with resolving additional manuscript-related issues.

Longtime historian and biographer David McCullough read the first four chapters of *Life Flashes: A Memoir*. He encouraged me to move the writing project toward fruition in a response letter he sent me. I received the correspondence two days before Christmas, in 2016. Mr. McCullough wrote, "In the work I do, I am ever dependent on letters, diaries, unpublished memoirs, etc. I often think that future historians and biographers are going to have little or nothing to work with, since nobody writes letters or keeps a diary anymore."

In recent world history, people have nearly stopped writing letters and keeping journals; this cultural trend has been continuing since the early 1990s. This means that for a generation—generally considered to be about thirty years—society has become increasingly unable to connect with present as well as past and future generations through letters, journals, and diaries.

Privacy losses associated with email messaging and other social media forms as well as virtual worldwide covert acceptance of the contents of social media forms as not truly being private, have crippled but not crushed the development of genuine, confidential, and intimate communications, which letter, diary, and journal writing fosters. The letter Mr. McCullough wrote to me on personal stationary while using a manual typewriter reminded me of the timeless value of dignified, thoughtful, and internally stirring writing, which Mr. McCullough has created for decades.

The late Casey Kasem, an actor and a disc jockey, created and hosted a number of radio countdown programs, including "American Top 40," which featured the top forty songs of the day. Active as a disc jockey for over fifty years until shortly before he died in 2014, Mr. Kasem often read letters on air that listeners and had sent him. The radio show "American Top 40" continues to air today on Sunday mornings from coast to coast in the United States.

Profoundly moving was recently hearing the recorded voice of Casey Kasem as he read a letter an immigrant to America sent him, depicting triumphs and trials involved in resettling in the United States. The missive included a request to hear the song "Coming to America," written and first recorded by singer and musician Neil Diamond in 1980. Mr. Kasem played the tune after reading the letter. Hearing thoughts, feelings, and beliefs expressed in the letter deepened the appreciation of the letter writing I experienced when hearing the song.

Dr. Vincent Panetta, PhD., was a trusted confidante for nearly all the years that I was writing the book. Having been a practicing psychologist for thirty six-years, Mr. Panetta has treated numerous clients, including patients who were diagnosed as schizophrenic. Remarkably, some schizophrenic patients that Dr. Panetta has treated, who were formerly institutionalized, are now living and working independently. Psychologists do not prescribe medication and are not licensed to do so. Dr. Panetta believes that the healing of mental and emotional illnesses primarily occurs through treating an ill person with dignity, which allows a patient to truly be heard.

Steve Bekarian and Dorothy Matthews are trusted business persons who aided me with home improvement projects, house work, and yard work during the months that *Life Flashes: A Memoir* was being prepared for production. Without Steve or Dot helping me to maintain domestic and extra-domestic order, the manuscript would not have been properly completed.

Thank you, each and all.

LIFE FLASHES

2007

CHAPTER ONE

AWAKENING

Monday, January 1, 2007

Donning a white turtleneck jersey, black pants, and light orange, waist-length spring jacket, I stepped outside an apartment I am sharing in Weymouth, Massachusetts. Winter morning darkness surrounded me. The time was 5:00 a.m. Walking upon sidewalks aside Commercial Street and then High Street in Hingham, Massachusetts, caused me to again consider and face reality. Having experienced many years of job dissatisfaction, having drifted from job to job and having been socially isolated and financially unstable for many years, I was engulfed with emotion. Darkness resembling a level of internal dread I have undergone few times in life overcame me.

Chances are, I will probably leaving the world being emotionally ill, homeless, or both, I was thinking. Amidst facing overwhelming personal failure, I solemnly chose not to leave this world in a despondent state, while at the same time not knowing how to move beyond experiencing massive internal darkness. When one truly experiences mortal fear, there is no questioning Divine existence or human and Divine connection. None.

I began praying. Utilizing simple non-verbal conversation enabled me to express personal wrongdoing for which I had been experiencing longtime remorse and to convey accompanying feelings of hopelessness. Within seconds, a supernatural being, emanating unimaginable love and hope, emerging through suddenly and naturally appearing spiritually intense Bright White Light, surrounded me. I heard a non-human voice that I recognized as the voice of God. God said, *"Merrie, You were forgiven for these wrongdoings many years ago; you are forgiven for all of the wrongdoing you have committed."* Experiencing profound joy, humility, and gratitude, as tears were falling from my eyes, I said, "Thank you, Lord," adding, "God, I don't know how to begin again. I do not know Step One."

"Come, I will show you how to live again," God said. Profound, humbling, and calming contentment entered me. Renewed hope awakened me. Today, I stopped ingesting antidepressant medication which had been prescribed for me for two years. Serenity has re-surged within me; I am confident that genuinely and slowly re-establishing a trusting, respectful and cooperative relationship with God, no matter how weak belief in God is, is the primary reason healing or miracles happen. I am also generally certain that I will not seek or consume prescription medication again.

Saturday, January 13, 2007

After awakening this morning, I showered in cool water. Initially being shocked with chilly water falling upon me rendered me being filled with contentment, seconds later. Today I decided to recommence walking, eating nutritious food, and engaging in desired purposeful pursuits, including daytime as well as evening informal prayer. I remembered savoring and regularly engaging in the disciplines before becoming emotionally ill. Having again become quietly enthused with embracing these and additional empowering regimens, I am rediscovering that passion is a powerful painkiller.

Today found me strolling for two-and-a-half hours amidst rain, all the while experiencing inner peace. As does any physical activity, walking lifts human spirits. While sauntering in residential areas, and while doing so, passing homes and yards of varying sizes and observing dormant grass and trees waiting to be reborn, I viewed another woman who was pushing a baby carriage in which an infant, partially covered with blankets, was facing her. I smiled at the woman and child; passing them found me crying softly, as re-emerging emotional losses came to mind.

Additional activities I performed this day included praying, fingernail painting, reading, and eating pizza. Today found me also considering being a doggie daycare business employee, possibly working as a dog care giver— a dog supervisor, walker, and playmate. Having pondered the role awhile, I reconsidered, deciding hmm.., this is probably not going to happen.

Thursday, January 18, 2007

Outdoor temperature this morning is thirteen degrees Fahrenheit. Brrr… Until two days ago, the 2007 winter season had brought record-breaking warmth. This year on some days in December, the weather temperature was nearly sixty degrees. Winter chill has surely descended upon us.

Walking several miles shortly before sunrise found me recalling love remaining amid personal and professional relationships mutually established with people whom I have not seen or shared any communication except goodwill, for decades. I also thought about loved ones who are residing physically near me. Interestingly, although physically distant and physically close relationships differ, the partnerships are remarkably similar; neither is superior nor inferior to the other.

Acceptance is helping me to embrace universal truth. All relationships are valuable. All relationships are limited. All relationships change. All relationships end. All relationships endure. Newly accepting mortality and preciousness of life since the New Year began has assured me any prayer form validates that all love is eternal and accepts division. Love unites far beyond separation.

Friday, February 9, 2007

Weather this month is good and cool; daytime temperatures are low, fluctuating in the mid-twenties. Sometimes there is accompanying wind chill. One reputed New England weather-related saying is, "if you do not like the weather here, wait five minutes." The aphorism can also be applied to life circumstances.

Wishing to work again, I am seeking assistance with preparing to work in an office position that requires good communication skills, including up-to-date computer skills. Following waking, showering, dressing, and eating breakfast, I have been walking one-and-a-half hours daily, during weekdays, beginning at 5:30 a.m.

When completing these activities, I leave the apartment and drive to a train station. After entering a train station and later riding on a train, I arrive in downtown Boston. Then I walk three or four blocks, before arriving at an adult learning center which is currently offering classes providing instruction in developing job market re-entry skills. Teacher-led instruction includes computer proficiency retraining.

Each session of the six-weeks-long course begins at 9:00 a.m. and ends at 3:30 p.m.; thirteen students are enrolled in the class. We are learning how to proficiently utilize, Word, Excel, Outlook, and PowerPoint. We are being

3

taught how to write polished cover letters and how to tailor these cover letters and accompanying resumes to mock job advertisements as well as advertisements for currently available positions.

We are consistently discussing employment-related issues in small groups. Class students are performing individual on-the-spot oral presentations surrounding personal job qualifications and experiences, as a means of preparing for interviews. Students are also participating in mock job interviews, in which the class teacher imitates an employer who is currently hiring. Sometimes a student acts as an employer. The teacher and class students offer constructive feedback about the simulated job interviews, so that when a student officially applies for available positions, he or she is aware of the interview process, not only from the perspective of the potential employee, but also from the point of view of an employer who is hiring.

At noon, we break for forty minutes, which allows class members time to eat lunch, recreate, or do both. While strolling about Boston Common environs and momentarily stopping to feed birds and squirrels during the lunch break today, I viewed a medium-tall brawny man wearing an overcoat which almost covered the business suit he was wearing, including a vest, dress shirt, tie, and pants. He was feeding pigeons that wander about Boston Common; observing the scene was simultaneously stunning and delightful.

When nearly six hours of instruction and discussion surrounding job re-entry skills ends, I remain seated aside a classroom desk; the work surface supports one computer. Working here enables me to complete assigned homework before leaving the classroom, between 5:00 p.m. and 5:30 p.m., in order to enter an underground MBTA (Massachusetts Bay Transportation Authority) train station on Park Street. After standing on the train platform area here for between five and fifteen minutes, I board an arriving Red Line southbound subway train. Thirty minutes hence, the commuter train enters one Quincy, Massachusetts train stop-named Wollaston.

When departing Wollaston station and thereby directly accessing the parking lot, I find and then slip into the car I drive before motoring for about twenty-three minutes, and then arriving at Hingham Public Library. Staff working at Hingham Public Library (HPL) and neighboring Paul Pratt Library in Cohasset allow library patrons to use desktop computers, which can generally be used without time limits. Wishing to continue diary writing and wanting to write cover letters and to revise personal resumes in accordance with jobs currently being advertised, I visit either of the libraries most weekdays either until 8:00 p.m. when the Paul Pratt Library closes or 9:00 p.m., when Hingham Public Library closes.

Having numerous times failed smoking cessation attempts, I stopped smoking several weeks ago. For the past year or so, I had been smoking a pack of cigarettes a day and in doing so, primarily desiring to relieve emotional pain and at the same time wishing to experience a sense of being mentally and emotionally stable. Smoking accomplished the imagined personal victory, for very short time periods.

This time, when I had chosen not to smoke for one, two, and then three consecutive days, smoking mysteriously and fully ceased interesting me. Having jogged or strolled for sixty to ninety minutes for several days and having consistently inhaled generally clean air, I was afterwards thinking, *Do you really want to smoke now...?* Daily inhalation of fresh outdoor air while walking is healing and humbling me. Performing regular physical exercise is motivating me to realize the value of good health as well as the truly sickening, dirty, and offensive nature of smoking.

Also wishing to discontinue drinking coffee, I am discovering that drinking steadily increasing water amounts diminishes coffee drinking desires. While hoping someday soon to be able to drink eight glasses or sixty-four ounces of water daily, which public health officials as well as medical personnel recommend, I have meanwhile found that gradually increasing daily water consumption promotes internal serenity. Why? Drinking water, which is bodily hydrating, also diminishes mood swings. A mood swing is a sharp and sometimes sudden vacillation in emotional state.

When one undergoes a mood swing, one generally experiences an artificially increased metabolic rate accompanied by a false sense of euphoria, before the mood spirals downward, which generates a negative outlook and noticeable fatigue. Mood swings are often, though not always, induced through eating food or drinking fluid that contains unhealthy chemicals. Increasing water intake has caused me to experience naturally increased and relaxed mental, physical, emotional, and spiritual energy. Water moistens, nourishes, and heals every body part, including the soul.

Frankly, the fact that I have experienced longtime generally good physical health defies logic, as for nearly thirty years, I drank between one and six cups of coffee daily, smoked from time to time, regularly consumed unhealthy foods, beverages, and candies, and rarely drank water. During these years, consistently jogging or walking about five miles daily probably mitigated some of the unfavorable effects that these eating habits generated. Earthly human and animal life, beginning with gestation, during which water plays an active role, identifies one of many significant life purposes that water fulfills.

Friday, March 16, 2007

Outside air temperature reached sixty degrees yesterday. The sign of newly and slowly emerging spring weather is welcome. I sent nephew Rylan Reagan a birthday card.

A son of my brother Jared Reagan and sister-in-law Elissa Dickson Reagan, Rylan became one year old today. Jared and Elissa are also parents of nephew Jamus, who is five years old and niece Brynn, who is three years old. All are currently Scotland residents.

Monday, March 19, 2007

Today marks the fourth anniversary of the United States militarily entering the Iraq war, in 2003. Wishing to increasingly understand involvement of America in the Iraq war and wanting to know what circumstances surrounded the September 11, 2001 American tragedy, I researched the happenings today.

American military troops entered Iraq in March 2003, nearly nineteen months following 9/11. About mid-morning, on September 11, 2001, two passenger-carrying airplanes that had been hijacked by terrorists, had departed from Logan Airport in Boston, Massachusetts, and were headed to New York City, one after another, crashed into the former Twin Towers buildings, which were located in Lower Manhattan, a section of New York City. Both of the planes had been headed to Los Angeles, California from Logan International Airport in Boston, Massachusetts. Each of the Twin Towers skyscrapers was one hundred and ten stories high and both contained large and small businesses.

The first terrorist-manned plane hit the North Twin Tower at 8:46 a.m. Seventeen minutes later the second hijacked plane struck the South Twin Tower at 9:03 a.m. Within ninety minutes, the two edifices imploded. Two thousand seven hundred people died instantly or near instantly and were buried under massive debris. All of the passengers and crew members in the hijacked planes were among the deceased.

At 9:37 a.m., a third hijacked passenger-carrying aircraft which had departed from Dulles Airport in Dulles, Virginia and was also headed toward Los Angeles, California, struck the Pentagon in Washington. D.C. The building houses United States Department of Defense offices. One-hundred eighty-nine people, including military and civilian personnel and plane crew and passengers, were killed in the incident. The fourth and final terrorist-manned passenger plane which had departed from Newark, New Jersey and was headed to San Francisco, California, crashed in a field near Shanksville, Pennsylvania at 10:07 a.m.

News reports indicated that the last hijacked aircraft was initially destined to destroy the U.S. Capitol building in Washington, D.C. Shortly before the airliner crashed, passengers aboard the plane valiantly attempted to overcome terrorists who were manning the aircraft. There were also no survivors among the forty-four occupants of the flight from Newark.

Heroic actions of passengers on the flight probably saved the lives of many people working in Washington, D.C. who had initially been targeted by plane hijackers. Media outlet news reports indicated that nearly three thousand terrorist victims died on 9/11/2001. Since the fateful day, eight hundred thirty-six first responders, including firefighters and police personnel, have also succumbed.

During the evening of 9/11, U.S. President George W. Bush spoke with Americans via television communication saying, "Today, thousands of lives were suddenly ended by evil despicable acts of terror. These acts have filled Americans with disbelief, profound sadness, and anger. These acts of mass destruction were intended to frighten this nation into chaos and defeat, but they have failed."

Continuing, President Bush said, "Our country is strong. Terrorist attacks can shake the foundations of our biggest buildings, but they cannot shake the foundation of America." Mr. Bush confidently stated that America was attacked because this country represents an exceedingly bright beacon of light representing freedom and opportunity. Commander-in-chief Bush asserted no person or persons can or will ever stop this light from shining.

U.S. military troops entered Afghanistan, October 7, 2001, less than one month after the events of September 11, 2001 unfolded. American servicemen stationed here attempted to depose the Taliban government. Since 1995, for about seven years, the Taliban government militia was controlling much of Afghanistan.

Including members who have been referenced as being rigidly religious, Taliban affiliates were suspected of harboring terrorists who participated in attacks on America on 9/11. Motives that Afghan terrorists asserted for the 9/11 attacks were: protesting an increased U.S. military presence in Saudi Arabia, opposing American support of Israel, and denouncing US sanctions that punished Iraq.

American military forces invaded Iraq on March 19, 2003, a little over eighteen months after the devastating events of September 11, 2001 happened. Motives reported to have influenced American government leadership to authorize employing military forces to attacking Iraq included seeking the disarmament of weapons capable of mass destruction that were allegedly being hidden in Iraq, wanting to dismantle alleged links between Iraqis and Al Qaeda—a now twenty-year-old terrorist group that was also being held responsible for involvement in the September 11, 2001 tragedy—and wanting to depose Iraqi ruler Saddam Hussein. Iraqi President Hussein was viewed as a tyrannical ruler who supported terrorist acts. He is the first modern-day world leader known to have advocated utilizing chemical weapons to kill Iraqi people who criticized him unfavorably.

American oil interests in Iraq were also considered to be motivation for the U.S. government to approve attacking Iraq. Statements made by officials of the United States government, asserting that Iraq was hiding weapons capable of mass destruction were ultimately proven to be false. When the regime of Iraqi leader Saddam Hussein toppled in April of 2003, U.S. military forces entered Baghdad, the capital city of Iraq. The fallen leader, who had gone into hiding, was captured in December of 2003 by American military forces, approximately eight months later.

Simply stated, the outcome of two Iraqi trials, one conducted in 2005 and another held in 2006, in which President Hussein was charged with numerous humanitarian crimes, was that Saddam Hussein was convicted and sentenced to death. A hanging sentence was effectuated December 30, 2006. Today, President George W. Bush said U.S. military presence in Iraq will end when the currently ongoing insurgency threat here dissipates.

Having today briefly researched September 11, 2001 American tragedy and its aftermath has given me increased mental clarity regarding the events. Investigating the occurrences did not initially find me experiencing resolve. While re-examining what happened, I have been slowly and steadily reassured that each and all persons are capable of accepting and moving through difficult life circumstances, with Divine guidance. Human beings are innately resilient and optimistic. Stunningly, primarily triumphant as well tragic experiences, although not identical, are similar; both involve losses as well as gains and are therefore, processed in a remarkably comparable manner.

Monday, April 9, 2007

Reading *In an Instant: A Family's Journey of Love and Healing,* authored by Lee Woodruff touched and humbled me. Perusing the work has reminded me that everyone everywhere experiences life circumstances as regularly and unexpectedly changing. Triumphs and tragedies of small, medium and large nature regularly occur, without any warning.

Bob Woodruff, an ABC television news reporter for the past eleven years, who is also a husband and father of three children, suffered severe brain injury when in an instant, on January 29, 2006, an IED (improvised explosive device) hit an armored tank in which he was traveling, while he was accompanying U.S. Marines stationed in Iraq. The vehicle was immediately thereafter subjected to enemy fire, on all four sides.

Mr. Woodruff survived fatal injury, underwent brain surgery and subsequently remained unconscious for thirty-six days. Continuing to receive rehabilitation services, he is learning to walk and to talk again. Observing Woodruff family happenings has found me admiring and respecting the Woodruffs and observing the family members as inspirational. For even five minutes, I could not handle the circumstances that they have courageously faced.

Lee and Bob Woodruff have been married for nineteen years; they are the parents of four children. Bob hopes he will be returning to ABC network as a news reporter.

As the world turns, I believe Mr. Woodruff will be reporting news again. He recently indicated that he wants to document as well as aid soldiers who have suffered brain injury in the Iraq war.

Tuesday, April 10, 2007

Through the years, experiencing separation and conflict in relationships whether or not the partnerships are physically distant has naturally been personally challenging. Daily prayer, which promotes positive realistic thinking, is allowing me to confidently form, re-establish, and nurture personal and professional relationships, whether the relationships involve physical distance. Prayer in any form transforms anger and disappointment into renewed calm.

In fact, utilizing informal and formal prayer or a combination of both is teaching me that the foundation of all relationships is goodwill; in other words, the basis of each and every relationship is not how often people visit or see one another, not compatibility, not depth of shared love, or readiness for love. All relationships are influenced by these circumstances or accidents. When goodwill—kindness, respect, and cooperation—is present within a relationship, amidst any situation, the relationship grows and flourishes. Goodwill is fundamental; it is grounding and guiding.

Mysteriously, prayer improves relationships through converting negative life attitudes into affirming life outlooks. Prayer turns confusion into understanding. Prayer changes impatience into tolerance. Tolerance may or may not include acceptance. Any prayer form supports developing relationships, especially when division is occurring in relationships.

Praying every day, formally or informally, is teaching me that life is not essentially about any earthly person, place or thing; life includes all creation. Every day, every hour, and every moment that I spend in prayer affirms in me one universal truth; all life is essentially in the hands of God. Experiencing earthly contentment includes the work of human hands, cooperating with God, individually and communally assisting the fulfillment of Divine worldly purposes. Simply stated, this means that God is the benevolent non-bullying car driver; humans are the car passengers. Acknowledging this reality enables me to experience utter relief and pure joy.

Not seeking discord, yet accepting that division regularly occurs in each and all relationships and is intrinsic to relationship growth is cathartic. When a person affected by human limitations as well as human failings utilizes prayer in any form, he or she is able to remain generally serene, civil, and non-judgmental when division occurs. Often times, simply offering another person encouragement in the form of saying words such as, "Good day" or "Thank you" or "Good wishes" represents sufficient conversation, whether or not two or more people are experiencing harmony. Prayer promotes relationship re-engagement as renewed trust, respect, and understanding are developed.

When one admits to having committed wrongdoing, the confession of wrongdoing immediately begins to offer healing to any person one has injured, whether one is physically facing an injured person or whether or not an injured person or persons accept such healing. There are times when directly addressing a wronged person or persons is generally harmful; an apology in prayer form is advisable in these instances. Employing prayer aids someone who is discerning whether or not facing an injured person or persons is warranted.

Wednesday, April 11, 2007

Good and certain is this. A continued self-diminishing, self-defeating attitude, not chemical imbalance in the brain, induces depression in large case numbers, though perhaps not all. When someone repeatedly internally voices thoughts such as *I am a failure, I can't do anything well, or. it is too late to change,* mind, body and soul functions readily respond, voicing agreement.

A person who privately or publicly verbalizes these or similar self-defeating thoughts on a regular basis will likely wish to lie down soon thereafter, and when doing so, possibly demonstrate a fetal position. As cerebral thoughts become increasingly negative, brain chemicals become imbalanced. Mind, body, and spirit functions correspondingly regress.

Every day after December 31, 2006 has found me re-discovering that daily prayer, cool showers, exercise, healthy eating and drinking habits, and engaging in purposeful activities overturn psychological negativity. Formal or informal personal and communal prayers—whether or not said in a church—promote purposeful positive-minded living, which in turn, largely decreases negative or self-defeating thoughts. Side effects of depression medication involve highly questionable risk; these include possibly experiencing suicidal thoughts.

While consuming prescribed anti-depression medication for nearly two years, I not only experienced circumstances surrounding depression symptoms occurring within me being mentally and emotionally blurred, I also sustained a loss of interest in being physically active, which is key to recovering from any emotional or physical illness. Talk therapy can curb but does not cancel side effects that anti-depression medications present. And yes, sadly, before I stopped ingesting anti-depression medication, on the first day of this New Year, I had experienced deadly thoughts.

I can now increasingly and compassionately acknowledge the twisted or demented thinking that accompanies suicidal thoughts and deeds; one

11

who is considering such thoughts and actions falsely rationalizes the measures as being reasonable, or in other words, a logical way to end feeling worthless and therefore being a burden to others. Recent days have also found me re-discovering that experiencing feelings of hopelessness, sorrow, and pain present a person with an opportunity to learn and therefore, to develop a renewed and formerly unimaginable understanding of God, fellow humanity and self, as does experiencing feelings of hope, love, and joy.

Having been recovering beyond emotional illness for three months now, I find that trusting God through engaging in daily prayer and while doing so, regularly performing personally desired healthy daily activities, has not only enabled me to address and overcome harbored longtime sadness and discouragement but has also motivated me to cease smoking and ingesting antidepressants. Divine relationship is truly curing me. Faith is truth. Truth is healing. Healing is empowering. What truth, what purpose is served when someone who is experiencing mental illness is prescribed anti-depression medication that dulls the symptoms of depression and generates side effects including a loss of interest in physical activity and thoughts of self-harm which are potentially perilous?

CHAPTER TWO

REFLECTING AND RECONNECTING

Thursday, April 19, 2007

This evening, Emmanuel College, located in Boston, Massachusetts hosted a previously advertised lecture event. I graduated from Emmanuel College in May 1975, four years after I graduated from high school. Before attending the scheduled lecture in the library auditorium, I entered Cardinal Cushing Library, located on the college campus. Being here caused me to wonder whether revisiting the reading and studying place would evoke any personal memories.

Slowly, I visually panned the library environment. While doing so, and looking through a very large, long, two story high, paned library window facing The Fenway—a downtown Boston neighborhood located near Kenmore Square that includes walking-accessible beautified parks and adjacent attractive medium-tall professional and residential buildings—I observed religious as well as lay professors individually tutoring students; both were seated aside library study tables or sitting near desktop computers. Unaccompanied students, who were reading or studying, were also present in the library.

Wondrous was seeing many computer devices, which became widely used in the mainstream of society the 1990s. Neither desktop nor laptop computers were present on college campuses in the 1970s, except those having been installed in small numbers within large universities. Tonight, while standing inside Cushing library, I recalled meeting the honoree of Cardinal Cushing Library, the late Archbishop of Boston, Cardinal Richard Cushing, on Easter Sunday, in 1961. I was seven years old. Unexpectedly, the memory of encountering a former senior leader in the Catholic Church, who presided over the diocese of Boston, re-ignited me.

Easter Sunday morning, in 1961, after driving into Boston, Massachusetts, Reagan family attended the 9:00 A.M. service at St. Anthony Shrine, which was a high mass. The primary celebrant, Cardinal Richard Cushing, clerically led the full ceremonial service, which included music, incense, and assistance from fellow priests. Several deacons assisted Cardinal Cushing. As Reagan family members entered the cathedral, there were no accessible seats; only standing room was available. Mom was probably holding one-year-old infant Valerie, as she accompanied Dad, my sister Lizzie, then eight-years-old, brother Jared, then four-years-old, and me.

After Easter Sunday mass celebration, Cardinal Cushing and fellow mass celebrants, who were walking behind him, proceeded toward the entrance of St. Anthony Shrine. As Cardinal Cushing and I greeted one another, he extended his left hand toward me. I bent slightly forward and kissed a large solid gold ring he was wearing, which had been placed on his left hand ring finger. Exhibiting a square shaped setting, the noticeable ring contained red ruby gemstones.

In the 1950s, kissing a ring that a Cardinal was wearing, which identified a Cardinal as such, was a Catholic tradition; performing the gesture was viewed as a symbol of trusting and respecting Catholic Church values and leadership of the church. When the tradition was ended, I do not know. Before I kissed the ring Father Cushing was wearing, I looked upward and toward him. He was smiling. Profound kindness, compassion, and mercy he emanated touched me. Instantly, I was pierced, with holy fear. Experiencing intense uncertainty, I trusted that no harm would befall me. This exemplifies true holy fear. Holy fear is also known as true love.

Fr. Cushing radiated love. Meeting him once, for a few moments, has enlivened me for over fifty years. He loved children. Catholic Church officials supported the efforts of Father Cushing to establish St. Coletta by the Sea, the first northeastern United States-situated school founded to serve special needs children. Opened in 1947, St. Coletta by the Sea school, including classrooms and residences, initially served thirty-five students. Cardinal Cushing called the students exceptional children.

Initially, St. Coletta by the Sea school administrators and teachers were five Sisters of St. Francis of Assisi, who specialized in educating exceptional children. Originally based in Milwaukee, Wisconsin, the sisters willingly relocated; they accepted residing in Hanover, Massachusetts, at the St. Coletta by the Sea school site. Three additional school personnel assisted the nuns with operating the school. The school curriculum included academic studies and life skills training. In the early 1950s, St. Coletta by the Sea school chapel - named Portiuncula Chapel of St. Francis - nearby dormitories and an indoor swimming pool were constructed. The educational complex was subsequently renamed Cardinal Cushing Centers.

St. Coletta Day School, in Braintree, Massachusetts was opened in 1957, ten years following the opening of St. Coletta by the Sea. Both of the schools are continuing to operate successfully. Cardinal Cushing Centers now serves approximately one hundred forty-four students. St. Coletta Day School, solely offering day classes, currently serves twenty-nine pupils.

Cardinal Richard J. Cushing was born August 24, 1895. Thirty-six years later, in 1921, he was ordained as a Catholic priest. Father Cushing was appointed as Archbishop of Boston in 1944. He was actively engaged in the role for twenty-three years, until shortly before he died, November 2, 1970. He was then seventy-five years old. Cardinal Cushing was buried on the grounds of St. Coletta School Portiuncula Chapel.

Tonight, while standing amidst Emmanuel College Cardinal Cushing Library, and waiting to attend the lecture I discovered a biographical book I was holding was slipping through my left hand, before it fell abruptly upon the library floor. The book depicts a renowned person, whose mother conducted in-home abortions that were performed in a basement. Now recalling the incident and at the same time, remembering the love of children as well as the non-judgmental nature that Cardinal Cushing demonstrated, gives me shivers, moving up and down the spine.

Friday, May 4, 2007

Longtime successful mortgage company owner and broker John (Jack) McGill and I talked this afternoon; we met inside the mortgage company which Jack owns and operates.

We had previously conversed here for beyond one hour on two occasions. One week ago today, Jack hired me to fill a vacant part-time administrative assistant position.

Jack owns several cars and residences. Today, while we were working together, Jack asked to see the ten-year-old car I drive. Jack and I exited office space, entered the office building parking lot, and accessed the almost eggplant colored mini-SUV.

Having entered the car driver seat, Jack described the automobile as intriguing. He requested and was granted driving permission. Facing the car steering wheel and having placed both hands upon the mechanism, Jack became enthusiastic and child-like. He resembled a young boy in a candy shop, who was viewing varieties of sweets and treats inside a glass-covered counter.

On another workday afternoon, while he was looking through an office window, Jack suddenly observed a colorful feathered peacock, standing alone in the woods, outside the office building. Immediately ending what he was doing, he exited the building and retrieved a personal camera, which had been stored in his car trunk. He then walked briskly behind the rear entrance of the office building. Mylie McGill, the wife of Jack, who had been visiting him at the office, followed Jack, as did I. Holding a thirty-five-millimeter camera, Jack gingerly approached Peacock. For several minutes, he repeatedly shot pictures of Peacock. Peacock barely moved. Mutually established boundaries between Jack and Peacock were respected and upheld as the large, elegant and multicolored creature was being photographed.

Sunday, May 27, 2007

This morning I visited French Memories, a café, located in Cohasset Village. Shortly after sitting down aside a small table here, I observed my brother, Jared and Elissa, the wife of Jared, and their three children. All were entering the charming, small bakery and bistro. Having ended residing in Scotland, Jared and Elissa have decided to inhabit Cohasset for several years, before residing in England, where Elissa was born and reared. Jared has not resided in Cohasset since leaving here after he graduated from high school; he has regularly visited Cohasset during holidays. Unexpectedly seeing Jared and Elissa and also greeting, hugging, and kissing five-year-old nephew Jamus, three-year-old niece Brynn, and one-year-old Rylan was contenting.

While I was sitting inside French Memories café, I was wearing spectacles, which enabled me to read the Sunday newspaper. Alternately, I drank herbal tea and ate a blueberry scone. When I suddenly heard noise, which prompted me to look upward, I saw and addressed a former longtime Cohasset resident, Norrie Edwards. Norrie was seated aside a table that was near me. She was waiting for fellow Sunday morning church goers, who were meeting her at French Memories; the weekly churchgoers include a sister of Norrie, named Addie Simons.

As Norrie and I talked cheerfully for a few moments, I quietly recalled being a high school freshman. Ellen Edwards, a daughter of Norrie and her late husband, Bill Edwards, married her high school sweetheart, Mitch Harrison, sometime in the early 1970s. Mitch and I had dated for several months before he and Ellen met; a relationship with Mitch was the first boyfriend and girlfriend experience I underwent.

Mitch and I were close when he was a tenth-grade Cohasset High School (CHS) student and I was a ninth grade student who also attended the high school. The "first love" relationship did not physically survive, beyond six months. Mitch and I have not seen one another, except for a few times, in passing, since we parted. Mitch and Ellen began dating shortly after Mitch and I broke up. They were married shortly after graduating from colleges they attended.

When Mitch and I were dating, one day I made him a chocolate birthday cake, which I covered with vanilla frosting, before placing it upon two paper plates and covering it with aluminum foil. I carried the present to school and directly thereafter, I carefully placed it in the high school locker that was assigned to me when the school year began. Not wanting him to dislike eating a piece of the cake, I was hesitant about giving Mitch the homemade birthday present. This is probably why I stored the baked good in a locker for nearly three full days. One afternoon, near or following the birthday of Mitch, I offered him a slice of the cake. He had not been informed that the treat had been sitting in a locker for almost seventy-two hours. Accepting and then eating a cake portion, he critiqued the food gift as being "delicious" and then said, "Thank you," before he finished fully consuming the slice.

I was not anywhere near ready for a steady romantic relationship when Mitch and I were dating. If I was ready for such a relationship, would I have given Mitch an unrefrigerated, almost three-day-old slice of frosted birthday cake? I think not. I would have at least known how to pack it with ice.

Fellow Cohasset resident, Kate Campbell arrived at French Memories after she attended a church service. She addressed me sometime after and Norrie Edwards and I had ended conversing. Today, Kate recalled me babysitting Campbell children, including Jill, Willie, Lily, and Stevie. When I was a high school freshman, I babysat these kids one or two days a week, during school summer vacation months. Larry, the fifth and final Campbell family child, was not yet born, when Kate and her husband, John Campbell were employing me.

As Kate and I talked, she became mortified, upon hearing that near the end of one babysitting job, Willie and Stevie had tied me to a chair, using rope. When I assured her that the boys were primarily performing healthy mischief, she expressed relief. Babysitting Campbell kids was a "cushy" summer job. Driving a few miles beyond the Campbell family home in Cohasset, Kate transported a chosen baby sitter and the Campbell children to a yacht club located in Scituate, Massachusetts.

Summer babysitters that Kate and John Campbell hired enjoyed some yacht club membership privileges, including being permitted to swim in an outdoor pool and being given ample spending money for food. Campbell family summer babysitters were appreciated and well compensated. Although Kate and I rarely see one another anymore, when we do run into one another, we share heartening conversation, which is consistently punctuated with laughter.

Brielle Morgan was also a Campbell family babysitter. Brielle and I met at Cohasset High School in September of 1967, on the first day that school was in session; we were then ninth grade students. Morgan family began residing in Cohasset prior to the beginning of the 1967–1968 school year. In many states in the U.S., including Massachusetts, the school year begins on the first Tuesday morning in September, following a three-day weekend ending on Monday, Labor Day.

Brielle and I joined the same five fellow ninth-grade girls who ate lunch together during nearly every school day. We girls sat together aside a cafeteria table and talked while we ate school lunches or homemade bagged lunches. We attended sleep overs for girls only and coed parties. We talked using language which was popular amongst adolescents during the 1960s.

For example, if we really liked someone or something, we might say, "I dig him or her," or "I dig it." If we were not interested in or enthusiastic about something we might say, "That's not my bag," "That's a drag." When we encountered disappointing situations, we would say, "What a bummer."

When we were interested in sharing intimate conversation with someone, we might say, "Lay it on me," or "sock it to me." When we enjoyed some activity or event, we would say, "It was a gas." We referred to money as "bread."

We called interesting people, places and things "groovy," "wicked good," "wicked neat" or "far out." We termed people who were fashionably dressed as "spiffy dressers." We defined unbelievable statements as "bogus." We referenced fellow adolescents who falsely inflated stories as "ravers." We characterized embellished stories including good humor and not intending harm as "good raves." When it was time to leave someone or somewhere, we would say it was "time to split."

Accompanying their mother and father, Brielle and her three sisters moved from Cohasset to Connecticut when she was entering the tenth grade. Heartbroken when Brielle had moved considerable distance beyond Cohasset, I was elated when the Morgan family moved back to Cohasset, nearly two years after leaving here. Brielle and I were now car-driving Cohasset High School seniors. When school classes ended, we completed Morgan as well as Reagan family errands, while utilizing a Morgan or Reagan family car, all the while discussing family, boys, and school-related matters. While undertaking these small tasks and sharing ebullient or quiet conversations, we were as content as world travelers.

Since she graduated from college, Brielle has been employed as a legal administrator for many years. She and I last shared a phone conversation many years ago. Now named Brielle Morgan Bosted, she became a wife and mother. Longtime residing on the North Shore of Massachusetts, she has been administratively assisting two attorneys whose practice is based in Boston.

Tuesday, June 5, 2007

Starting at 9:30 a.m. this morning, inside Atlantica restaurant, Buttonwood Books in Cohasset hosted a Breakfast with the Authors event. Atlantica restaurant guests can view scenic Cohasset Harbor; various types of boats are moored here. Hank Phillippi Ryan, one of the authors featured today, has also been a longtime reporter for Channel 7 television station, which is located in Boston. *Prime Time* is the first published novel she wrote. It is being serialized. Before discussing the mystery book, Mrs. Ryan related how she evolved as a journalist during the last four decades.

When she was employed in 1970 in an ongoing local political campaign, Hank was traversing Indiana. Indiana was then the home state of Ms. Ryan. When the political campaign ended, Hank decided to consider radio work. Entering a local radio station, she succeeded in meeting a radio station executive. While she informally interviewed the executive, she stated she wanted to be hired there as a radio station news reporter.

The executive responded, "You can't be a radio station reporter, you don't have any reporting experience." Ms. Ryan lobbied, verbally detailing political campaign work she had recently completed, including interviewing political figures, writing press releases, and preparing press conference material. She ended the employment appeal, coyly saying, "Besides, the FCC (Federal Communications Commission) license for this radio station is being reviewed soon and…, there aren't any women on staff here… are there?"

Audience members gushed forth laughter. They laughed even more when Ms. Ryan said the radio station executive hired her shortly after the impromptu interview. Since then, Hank Phillipi Ryan has been a journalist for over thirty years. Suspense novel *Prime Time* depicts a leading television reporter who believes spam email clogging a personal computer he uses contains secret coded messages which reveal that big business insiders are mysteriously being sent large and illegitimate money amounts. The last person who sought to unlock the code and went missing and was later found, in a morgue.

Sunday, June 17, 2007

Prayer, housecleaning, writing, polishing fingernails and toenails, walking, visiting nearby Cohasset-located Sandy Beach and wading in ocean waters there, were among activities that I enjoyed today. Glorious, sunny, and nearly cloudless weather allowed afternoon socializing outdoors; Mom, brother Jared, sister-in-law, Elissa, nephews Jamus and Rylan, niece Brynn, my sister Lizzie, nephew Rhett, and I shared lunch. We were seated at a long wooden table inside a screened porch. Overlooking ocean, the eating and relaxing area adjoins the Reagan family home.

During lunch, I related a joke depicting a bachelor whose male friends requested that he write a living will. Bachelor is initially enthused, and considers writing a living will.

Moments later, he realizes he possesses two worldly items, namely, a George Foreman grill and a DVD player. Suddenly, the writing a living will idea that Bachelor was considering had become a penning a dying IOU reality. Ba da bum.

Friday, August 10, 2007

Today found me visiting Boston, Massachusetts, Museum of Fine Arts (MFA). The museum is currently showcasing the work of artist Edward Hopper. Initially traveling here via car, I subsequently parked the car in an MBTA (Massachusetts Bay Transportation Authority) public parking lot, entered and later departed a public transit train, and then walked for several minutes, before entering the museum.

Some watercolor and oil portraits created by Edward Hopper portray seaside homes. Lighthouses are connected with some of the houses he painted that are located in Cape Cod and Gloucester, Massachusetts. Although not being featured today, rural vistas, urban scenes and portraits of people were also amongst chosen subjects of Mr. Hopper.

Edward Hopper was born on July 22, 1882 in Nyack, New York. Nyack is located beside the Hudson River and slightly over twenty-nine miles north of New York City. The village was a reputed yacht building center in the 18th and 19th centuries. Mr. Hopper lived in Nyack until he was twenty-eight years old; for decades, he also resided about an hour away from Nyack, in New York City. These circumstances understandably influenced the development of artistic works that he created.

Painter and printmaker Edward Hopper is also referenced as having worked and lived in Europe and particularly in Paris, France. The artist painted people situated in public as well as private settings. Profiling Mr. Hopper in an online publication named *Thought Co.*, writer Jackie Craven stated that he often changed the faces and blurred the details of people he painted in order to create fictional characters.

What an interesting comment. I was not aware of this characteristic of the works of Mr. Hopper. Ms. Craven also stated that works of artist Hopper that portrayed people evoked dark psychological traits; this is true. Paintings Edward Hopper crafted are distinctive; subjects portrayed in these works do express differing reflective, solitary and disillusioned moods.

The irreplaceably tender, precious, and poignant nature of artistic work Mr. Hopper developed is unmistakable, notwithstanding emotional overtones of the work. Not among works of Mr. Hopper which were presented today is the famous oil on canvas painting entitled *Nighthawks*. Edward Hopper completed the work in 1942. I observed an online copy of the painting late today; the picture portrays four persons; three people are seated inside an all-night diner aside a triangular-shaped wooden counter.

Two of the people, a man and a woman, are sitting together. A third unaccompanied person is seated on the opposite side of the counter. As it is dark outside and inside the diner there are few diner customers; it is possible that the time is near or after midnight. The fourth person represented in the painting is a diner employee. He is standing behind an elongated diner counter.

He is wearing an all-white work uniform, including straight legged pants, a short-sleeve shirt, and a full-length bib apron. He is also wearing a uniform hat which resembles a sailor hat. Not visible is the task the diner employee is performing; perhaps he is washing dishes and utensils that were placed in a bar sink below the counter. *Nighthawks* deftly examines four people, who are displaying pronounced, thought provoking, and varied human temperaments.

Artist Hopper also painted ocean side scenes; some were displayed inside MFA today. These artistic works suggest that Edward Hopper was inwardly serene, when he was composing seaside landscapes in which people were not portrayed. Someone observing ocean side paintings that Mr. Hopper created might reasonably surmise that he savored solitude, particularly when he was experiencing personal conflicts.

Specific lighting clarified subject and object definition, and mood emanation distinguish the creative work of Mr. Hopper. Realism is an artistic movement which involved portraying artistic subjects naturally; the movement began in the late 1850s and ended around 1915. Surrealism is an artistic movement which explored and sought to expose the unconscious mind; it began around 1920 and ended in the late 1960s.

As he was born in 1882 and was eighty-five-years-old when he died in 1967, painter Edward Hopper was clearly influenced by the two creative movements. He ingeniously combined realistic as well as surrealistic elements in paintings he originated. One real-life Cape Cod, Massachusetts scene Mr. Hopper painted depicts a large lighthouse overlooking ocean waters. Observing the painting can leave someone being internally and mysteriously transported beyond the true-life scenario.

While walking toward the Boston Museum of Fine Art's front door late this afternoon, preparing to exit the gallery, I blew kisses toward a baby situated in a stroller being pushed past me. After leaving the galley, I walked to an outdoor subway station near the museum and then stood on a platform, while waiting to board a subway train. Suddenly, I spotted an elderly woman standing on a train platform on the other side of me.

Standing near fellow train riders, she was seeking to travel in the opposite direction. Attired in ragged clothing, the woman was either looking directly toward me or viewing someone who was standing behind me. Suddenly, evidencing sassy and childish behavior, she thrust her tongue forward. Immediately responding, I laughed good-heartedly, while being utterly stunned.

Tuesday, August 16, 2007

Today, I finished reading a book entitled, *His Way: An Unauthorized Biography of Frank Sinatra,* which discusses former world renowned beloved and deceased singer Frank Sinatra (1915-1998). The author of the book is Kitty Kelley. A former researcher for the Washington Post editorial page, Ms. Kelley wrote two previous books, *Jackie Oh!* (Jackie Kennedy Onassis) which was published in 1978 and *Elizabeth Taylor: The Last Star,* which was published in 1981. None of subjects of the books agreed to be interviewed. Subjects of the books neither approved of the writing nor consented to the publication of the works. This is why the books are termed unauthorized.

In *His Way: An Unauthorized Biography of Frank Sinatra,* Ms. Kelley suggests that Frank Sinatra associated with late President John F. Kennedy and that the late U.S. Attorney General, Robert F. Kennedy, brother of President Kennedy. The book also contends that Mr. Sinatra was connected with Chicago crime boss Sam Giancana as well as New Jersey crime boss Willie Moretti. Frank Sinatra publicly denounced *His Way: An Unauthorized Biography of Frank Sinatra,* before it was published. He asserted that the book contains inaccurate information.

In fact, Mr. Sinatra sued Ms. Kelley as soon as he found out that she intended to write a book about him. The lawsuit failed; the non-fiction work was published in1986. One sentimental book paragraph highlights a letter Frank composed for his parents, Dolly and Martin Sinatra. Frank presented the letter to Dolly and Martin during a fiftieth wedding anniversary party given for them, which Frank organized.

A former Pope, John Paul II, had blessed the letter. Mr. Sinatra had written, "The sands of time have turned to gold. Love continues to unfold, like the petals of a rose, in God's garden of life. May God love you through all

Eternity." Few dispute the legendary singing ability of Frank Sinatra. Who knew Frank Sinatra was also an eloquent writer? Wow.

Thursday, August 18, 2007

Jack McGill, who recently employed me as a part-time mortgage business administrative assistant, received a hilarious email today entitled, Bad Hallmark Cards. He sent me a copy of the email, while we were working together. One card message stated, "You brought me back into religion; I stopped believing in Hell—until I met you."

Another card sentiment was, "When we were together you said you'd die for me. Now that we're not together anymore, it's time for you make good on this promise, especially since you didn't do this when we were together." The third and final greeting card stated, "Congratulations, I heard you were promoted. Before you go, would you remove this knife from my back? You might need it again."

Thursday, September 6, 2007

Now having lived in Weymouth, Massachusetts for three years, I have recently considered moving back to Cohasset. Meanwhile, living in Weymouth has found me learning invaluable life lessons. Here are three such lessons.

Distinctly different are taking care of people and giving people care. Giving people genuine care indicates that one is offering mutually warranted, wanted, and respected care.

Someone who is taking care of a person or persons is often denying the care recipient(s) full aid; he or she is neither allowing the recipient or recipients to perform tasks independently nor to execute tasks while being assisted by another designated or non-designated care giver. One who is taking care is taking, not essentially giving care. Taking, not giving is also called stealing.

Another lesson I am again learning is what God wills, amid any earthly situations or circumstances is what humans truly desire. Trusting Divine love heals in a manner that no medicine can; healing may also include medicine. The third life lesson repeatedly reinvigorating me is realizing that relationship involvement, home or car ownership, employment status, formal education completion, financial stability, or similar attributes characterizing humans do not necessarily indicate that one is successful. Each and all standings may or may not contribute to successful circumstances.

On many occasions seeking Divine counsel through prayer has found me quietly saying, "God, this does not look good, being financially unstable, being unemployed and not being in a relationship." God has calmly and consistently responded, advising me that life is not essentially about how people look. I have been duly and consistently reassured that remaining content while experiencing consistently changing life situations and circumstances exemplifies true success.

Sunday, September 9, 2007

Brother Jared and I talked this afternoon. Maddie Robinson, an administrative assistant, who is managing the Cohasset office of the investment business that Jared owns and operates, has decided she wishes to rent a home. Jared offered to sublease the apartment that Maddie has been renting to me; he and I mutually agreed upon subleasing terms.

Tuesday, September 14, 2007

Effective October 1, I will resign from the mortgage company administrative assistant position in which I have been employed for about five months. Today, I presented work supervisor John (Jack) McGill a privately composed letter, indicating that I am leaving the position, in two weeks. Jack and I previously discussed the matter.

Mr. McGill and I now agree that I am not called or gifted with being able to perform financial services work. Retaining complex financial concepts such as mortgage financing and refinancing, which requires an understanding of money operations and stock market matters, is personally overwhelming and confounding; I have neither been nor will be at any time in the future, grasping the concepts.

While leisurely driving home from work this evening, I recalled driving to work this morning and suddenly being drawn toward observing two nearly still swans. The creatures were gracefully resting upon peaceful pond waters. Remembering the sight enables me to be mysteriously and contentedly serene.

CHAPTER THREE

MOVING

Monday, October 1, 2007

Today, after moving to a new address in Cohasset, I admiringly surveyed high ceilings and furnishings of a second-floor apartment in a single-family home, where I will now be living. A loveseat couch and an opposing oversized chair, both covered with dual dark and light pink striped upholstery fabric, are situated in the living room. Manicured hardwood flooring underlies a living room Oriental area rug, which exhibits a dark red flower pattern surrounded with a soft golden hue. A glass top coffee table is centered between the loveseat couch and oversized chair. Complementing the living room décor is a large attractive framed floral painting, set above the fireplace. Opposing the oversized chair, the living room love-seat couch faces a large window overlooking a sizeable backyard and nearby woods, which are a short distance from the town commons.

A tall reading lamp is situated beside the oversized living room chair, which is located near an equally tall wooden book case. A proximate glass door leads toward a tiny wooden enclosed deck with adjacent rust iron stairs and railings—painted black—that spirally descend toward back yard. An antique stationery desk and accompanying chair are set slightly beyond the right side of the glass door. The apartment front door, which was fashioned with four sections of paned glass inlaid in the upper half of the wooden door, is beside a mahogany stationery desk and near a tall deep storage closet.

A fully equipped galley kitchen adjoins the living room. White paned glass doors with knobs cover the interiors of storage cabinets which are above the kitchen counters. Slightly above floor-level cupboard space is on either side of the dishwasher, sink, and stove. Hardwood flooring in the living room extends into the kitchen. Two chairs face a round, solid oak small table, also called a Pembroke table, at which four people can sit and whose two folded leaves can be extended. The kitchen table nearly abuts the love-seat couch in the living room.

Walls of the apartment were painted off-white; ceilings and wood work moldings were painted white. Carpeted, the master bedroom also contains ample closet and storage space. Moving one or both doors of one or both sets of louver doors aside opens the closet area. The full size master-bed and an accompanying headboard slat are near a French provincial design night table, upon which a lamp rests, alone. An antique oak bureau and a neighboring upholstered, small, and armless high back chair directly face the master bed and are properly set apart from it.

I packed filled moving boxes into the mini-SUV I own, before driving from the apartment in Weymouth to the Cohasset apartment. After arriving here, I cleaned woodwork, hardwood floors, and the bathroom in the new living space, before unpacking and settling clothes and sundries into appropriate places. Tonight, I used a hand-held push button flame thrower to ignite newspaper stashed between store bought fireplace logs. Store-bought logs can burn for nearly three hours.

Imagining and truly hearing crackling living room firelight delighted me this evening, as I remained in bed, awake and supine. Moving to a new home has enabled me to re-discover and embrace stability, uncertainty, and contentment. Amid imperfections of earthly living, peace abounds.

Friday, October 5, 2007

Curiously, I was waiting to see the first of a number of Greenbush line trains which started running daily today; sunshine dominated the clear and crisp October morning. The Greenbush line is a branch of the Massachusetts Bay Transportation Authority (MBTA) system, which is serving the South Shore region of Massachusetts. Moving above and below ground, the commuter train departs from the Greenbush station in Scituate, stops briefly to pick up passengers waiting at train stops in Cohasset, Hingham, Weymouth, Quincy, and Dorchester, and shortly thereafter, arrives at South Station, which is in downtown Boston. Commuters wishing to enter a Greenbush line train that is at another time, departing from South Station, traveling to points south, and later arriving in Greenbush, can do so.

One of the train routes of the Old Colony Railroad, a division of the New Haven Railroad, which formerly served southeastern Massachusetts and Rhode Island, operated on the same tracks as the newly created Greenbush line and one of the train stops was in Cohasset, near where Reagan family members lived. Mom, Dad, sister Lizzie, brother Jared, and I moved to Cohasset in 1958 and resided near the Gillies, Freitas, Atkins, Remiah, Stahl, Wood, and Langoni families. Before we moved to Cohasset, we had lived in Roslindale as well as Jamaica Plain, urban neighborhoods surrounding Boston.

My sister Lizzie was six-years-old, brother Jared was two-years-old, and I was almost five-years-old when we moved to Cohasset. My sister Valerie was born one year later, in 1959. A small, bucolic, coastal, and suburban town with a current population of about eight thousand people, Cohasset is located twenty-seven miles southeast of Boston.

While the car I drive was being repaired this morning at nearby Riggins Garage, I was standing near the former Old Colony Railroad train stop where Mom used to board a Boston-bound train. The train stop is near the car repair shop; the stop is now a railroad crossing on the Greenbush line. The Old Colony Railroad was opened in 1872. Passenger service on the train line continued for eighty-seven years, until it ended in southeastern Massachusetts and parts of Rhode Island, in 1959. Amtrak and the MBTA continue to use the main line of the former Old Colony Railroad for passenger service from Boston to Providence, Rhode Island.

While waiting to see a Greenbush line train, I recalled Mom leaving the Reagan family home and traveling on an Old Colony Railroad train into Boston on Saturday mornings, forty-seven years ago. Walking a short distance, Mom arrived at the nearby train stop, where she waited until a train arrived, and then she boarded it. After making additional stops, the train arrived in Boston, nearly an hour later. She was seeking R and R, also called rest and recreation, which for her included shopping in downtown Boston stores and eating out, allowing her to be free for several hours from domestic duties, including child care, housecleaning, cooking, bookkeeping, and laundry—washing clothes in a washing machine, hanging them on a clothes line to dry, and later, depending upon the weather, removing the clothes, folding them, and ironing most of them, before putting them away.

Having given us kids care on weekdays during morning, afternoon, early evening, and sometimes mid-evening hours, while Dad was working,

Mom relished leaving home for most of the day, on as many Saturdays as possible. Having grown up in Boston and Quincy, Mom initially struggled with living in suburbia, mothering four young children and being without car transportation during the week, while Dad was working in Boston. Dad was a salesman for an insurance company. He commuted to work driving the Reagan family automobile; he often worked long and late hours and he also used the car while he was greeting and meeting with potential new and existing company clients.

Saturday mornings, afternoons, and early evenings when Mom was enjoying R and R, Lizzie, Jared, Valerie, and I remained at home. Dad supervised us. On these days, as on many days in childhood years, Lizzie, Valerie, Jared, and I often played outside, in back yard, when weather permitted outdoor recreation. Sometimes on the weekends, Dad joined us in the backyard. He enjoyed teaching us softball skills.

While Mom was away on Saturday, we kids often played in the finished basement of the house, which served as a playroom. Sometimes we concocted short skits in addition to songs and dances resembling a partial lineup of the *Community Auditions* television show and we performed the homemade version of the talent show when Mom returned home from Boston on Saturday afternoons or early evenings, or on Sunday mornings, before or after we watched *Community Auditions.* Aired in Boston for forty years, the television show featured singers, dancers, comedians, magicians, and impersonators in addition to contestants displaying a variety of unusual talents.

Beginning in 1950, the first *Community Auditions* television program host was Gene Burns. Starting in 1965, Dave Maynard was the second host of the show, for twenty-five years. When each or all Reagan children finished performing acts, including solos and duets, tap dances, and skits simulating talent featured on the *Community Auditions* show, sole show audience members, Mom and Dad, clapped in a manner which manifested support, ranging between strong enthusiasm and simple goodwill.

Being patient, we kids tolerated and accepted substitute cook skills that Dad employed, while Mom was off-duty on Saturdays. I recall eating unappetizing fish chowder that Dad had laboriously prepared for us on one Saturday evening. He was also able to make an unrivaled mouthwatering meal that he served us, featuring plated comingled steamed hot dogs and hot dog rolls. Dad put mustard, relish, or both on top of the boiled hotdogs in the rolls, depending upon whether each of us desired one or both of the condiments. Warm Boston baked beans were set beside the hot dogs.

As the use of automobiles, buses, and trucks increased significantly in the first half of the twentieth century, so did the construction of major highways. Therefore, over time, train ridership seriously declined. In 1959, one year after the Reagan family moved to Cohasset, Mom could no longer rely on train service for weekend jaunts into the city, as Old Colony Railroad train service in southeastern Massachusetts and most of Rhode Island had ended. She was deeply disappointed.

Fortunately, the Southeast Expressway (I-93), an interstate highway which connects Boston with points south, was completed in the same year. Delighted, Mom was eventually able to obtain a driving license and again commute into Boston once a week. When doing so, she parked the family car in a high rise garage located near where she wished to shop, allowing her to be worry-free, while she enjoyed a break from family life-related duties.

As the first Greenbush line commuter train whizzed past me this morning, the conductor of the train sounded a blaring horn, announcing the Grand Opening of the Greenbush-South Station commuter service. Watching the scene, I realized that Cohasset has not had commuter train service since Old Colony Railroad service stopped, nearly fifty years ago. Viewing the new Greenbush line train and waving toward passengers seated inside the train excited me, while I considered riding in the new commuter rail. Greenbush line trains running twelve times a day will offer commuters round-trip service. The sound of the train is definitive; it is boisterous.

The new commuter rail passes directly behind the home in which Mom and Dad have lived for forty-nine years. Since they do not intend to sell the house, they hired a landscaper to place natural fencing—tall and wide bushes or hedges which are placed on the borders of a private or public space—which serves as a partition or an enclosure. Natural fencing will also modify the noticeable sound of the train. The newly planted natural fence abuts tall protective fencing made of galvanized steel which was grounded beside Greenbush line railroad tracks.

Saturday, October 20, 2007

Having courted for two years, my niece Kristin Jenkins and Payden Sullivan, the fiancé of Kristin, were wed this evening. Kristin and Payden smiled and kissed one another several times during the wedding ceremony, which was held inside the home of brother Jared and sister-in-law Elissa, the wife of Jared. Kristin and Payden exuded excitement, innocence, and uncertainty.

My sister Lizzie Jenkins, mother of Kristin, and brother Jared led Kristin up an L-shaped staircase below a balcony; they stopped mid-way, when reaching a platform on the staircase which is beside a very large radius window that overlooks Cohasset Harbor. Wedding guests were standing in a decorated sizeable hallway near the staircase.

Minister Maryellen Snowdon, the wife of George Snowdon, and a friend of the Jenkins family, performed the wedding rite, while one hundred invited guests observed. Due to illness, Ron Jenkins, the father of Kristin, and nephews Rhett and Jonas Jenkins, were unable to attend. Also unable to be present was Jenny Romney, a step-sister of Mom, and Tim Romney, the husband of Jenny.

My nieces Grace and Myla Watson and nephew Matthew (Matt) Watson attended the wedding ceremony, accompanying their mother and father, Valerie (Reagan) Watson and Grant Watson. All traveled here via airplane, initially departing from Jacksonville, Florida.

After arriving in Boston three hours later, they disembarked the plane and later entered a livery vehicle which transported them to a guest house. During the late afternoon wedding service, twelve-year-old Grace was the honor maid. Ten-year-old Myla was the flower girl and six-year-old Matthew was the ring bearer.

Facing Cohasset Harbor, Atlantica restaurant was the wedding reception site. Chosen Best Man, Rhett Jenkins, brother of Kristin, toasted and roasted the bride and groom, minutes before the wedding reception dinner began. Dancing started after dessert service. Encircled by wedding guests, Kristin and Payden danced a first dance as husband and wife, before requesting wedding company to join them on the dance floor.

As Kristin and Payden exited the dance floor, wedding guests surrounded Jonas Jenkins, brother of Kristin and Rhett. When he momentarily left his wedding guest and longtime companion, Liane Lindon, Jonas slowly infiltrated a circle of guests surrounding the dance floor. Following another dancer who was exiting the center of the circle, he entered the center and performed stunning musically accompanied dance moves, including Moonwalk dance steps; entertainer Michael Jackson originally created and has performed the movements. Wedding guests responded to Jonas. First, they generated rousing applause, praising the showmanship he displayed. Then, having been duly motivated, wedding invitees continued to dance until midnight. Around 10:00 p.m. I viewed six-year-old Matthew Watson. Lying across three wedding reception room chairs, he was sleeping soundly.

Uncle Jim Fannon as well as Uncle John Barnard invited me to dance. Uncle Jimmy as well as Uncle John—both septuagenarians—are able to dance like teenagers do. Both are good conversationalists who are also jokers. Being seated near Aunt June Barnard and Uncle John Barnard, Uncle Jimmy Fannon and Aunt Anne Reagan Fannon. Cousin Bridget Fannon McGregor and Dan McGregor, the husband of Bridget, was heartwarming.

All of the wedding guests were seated beside round tables covered with pressed white tablecloths. Elegantly simple dinner settings and centered vases filled with fresh cut flowers and water adorned the tables. Cousin Jeff Fannon and Nancy Soudoukas Fannon, the wife of Jeff, cousin Patrick Fannon and Laurie Fannon, the wife of Patrick, Dan and Laura Fannon, son and daughter of Laurie and Pat, cousin Paul Fannon and Deanna Fannon the wife of Paul, cousin Maureen Fannon McRoven and Reed McRoven, husband of Maureen and cousin Kathy Fannon Lymen, and Lyn Lymen, husband of Kathy, also attended the wedding service as well as the reception. Are these descriptions beginning to sound like the lineage passage in the first chapter of the Bible?

For a few moments, while being encircled by wedding guests who had been dancing alone and with partners, I commemorated the evening, before it was nearly ended. Dancing solo and simulating a ballerina, I bent slightly backwards, and while twirling, I gently extended both arms and then gradually unfolded fingers on each of both hands, one after another, from pinky to thumb. I was reaching toward sky, toward Heaven.

Saturday, October 27, 2007

Today, dog Jura and I walked for nearly three hours; we strolled about Nantasket Beach in Hull, Massachusetts. When they were living in Scotland, brother Jared and Elissa, the wife of Jared, adopted Jura in January 2001. I remember meeting Jura for the first time, probably three years ago, when I visited John, Elissa and nephew Jamus in Scotland. Moments later, I thought, *Cute dog, I don't want a dog.*

Now six years old, Jura is as content living in America as he was when he resided in Scotland, for the previous five years. He demonstrates virtually no sense of possession. Jura came to America this summer via transatlantic flight. If he had been born in America and was visiting Europe or relocating here, Jura would initially have been quarantined for six months, per European regulations.

Emigrating from Scotland and immigrating to America in June of this year, Jura was set inside a pet cage and later placed inside an airplane cargo section. He remained there during a transatlantic flight which ascended from a Scotland airport and descended roughly six-and-one-half hours later, at Logan Airport in Boston. After being released from the pet cage, when the plane landed, Jura, accompanying brother Jared and family, entered a livery automobile and around one hour later, he was roaming back yard outside the new home of Jared, Elissa, and their children. Shortly thereafter, Jura transited the electric fence in the backyard, leaped beyond adjacent shore rocks, and probably entered ocean waters while he was belly flopping. Finding Jura wandering on land three hours hence, a kind Cohasset resident returned him home, via automobile.

Thursday, November 1, 2007

Walking along coastal Jerusalem Road in Cohasset on this brilliantly sunny day found me serenely observing nearly one hundred small birds standing side by side upon large tree limbs and tweeting or conversing. The bird gathering was curious. It came across as resembling an aviary convention. Birds were chirping, and while doing so were communicating in primarily high tones. The birds came across as being content.

The creatures were probably giving one another good news gossip about current events in the bird world. One possible reason for the aviary convention is that daytime-occurring weather temperatures, generally registering in the sixties in the fall, are now nearly gone. Birds are beginning to or have already begun migrating southward; New England winter 2007–2008 is drawing near.

The fifth birthday of nephew Jamus Reagan, generally observed today, was honored two days ago, this year. Celebrated inside the new home of Elissa and Jared, the late afternoon party was elaborate. Invited family, parents, nannies, and babysitters accompanied approximately twenty school chums of Jamus. Forty birthday party guests were offered a buffet of pizza and salad for dinner. Games as well as unusual birthday entertainment followed.

Jared and Elissa hired an entertainer named Creature Man, who provided live birthday amusement—an extra-large, wing-flailing bird. Creature man had attached a safety rope to the collar the creature was wearing, in order to be able to release and retract the sizeable and wondrous bird of prey, whose name I cannot remember. A tarantula, large spider, and several additional small and distinctive animals were also presented and welcomed as birthday party entertainment.

Jamus generally enjoyed the party; sometimes he exuded bewilderment with being among many people. Three-year-old Brynn, sister of Jamus, navigated the event with relative ease; when she became uninterested in the multi-sensory, action-packed birthday party, she simply exited the festivity and rode a plastic bicycle inside the kitchen-adjacent screened porch, which is a part of the home. One-year-old Rylan was content with being passed among able party guests, who held him gently and tenderly.

Elissa organized the lovely party for Jamus, as Jared is traveling abroad this week and addressing business matters. Elissa is an England native. Residing in America for the first time, not knowing many people here, and being a wife whose husband is regularly required to travel, due to international as well as national business concerns, has understandably challenged her considerably.

Early this morning, Jura and I were again walking in Hull, along Nantasket Beach. With a population of about ten thousand persons, the town of Hull is a peninsula which borders the neighboring towns of Cohasset and Hingham. When he is running, Jura often resembles a race horse. He consistently increases speed while he trots and then gallops upon beach sand. When he enters the sea, he wades or swims there for several minutes. After he emerges from ocean waters and is again grounded on beach shore, Jura socializes briefly and respectfully with passing dogs, dog owners, and beachgoers.

Jared and Elissa named Jura after the island Jura; the rugged sparsely populated isle is situated one hundred thirty-seven miles west of the mainland of Scotland. Approximately five thousand red deer are living here. Red deer outnumber the inhabitants of Jura by about seventy-five percent. The current population of Jura has been calculated to be below two hundred persons. On the isle there is one church, one hotel and one retail shop. Bus as well as ferry services are available. Truthfully, if I lived here, regularly drinking alcohol would be very attractive.

Before Reagan family arrived in America, dogs Jura and Harris were separated. Harris is a yellow Labrador retriever that Jared and Elissa also adopted when they lived in Scotland for a short time. Jura and Harris lived and played together for several years. I do not know why Harris was ultimately reunited with the breeders from whom Jared and Elissa purchased Harris and Jura. Jared and Elissa appreciate that I volunteered to walk with Jura almost daily; they are finding that while it is rewarding, rearing three children who are under six-years-old, nurturing individual careers, and giving dog Jura care is regularly good and challenging.

As Jared owns and manages an international investment company, while also being a husband, father and parent, he travels regularly, sometimes for up to fourteen days. While being a wife, mother and parent, Elissa is a freelance writer as well. She also teaches a Shakespearean play-acting class two evenings a week. Doing so, she commutes to and from a university extension school located in Cambridge, Massachusetts.

Now having walked with Jura several times a week for approximately four months has found me experiencing renewed self-confidence. Seeing Eye dogs guide blind persons. Jura can also be aptly described as a Seeing Eye dog or guide dog. I believe he has been divinely designated to heal sighted people. Jura is playful, sociable, humble, obedient, and occasionally noticeably stubborn. He is in many ways evolved far beyond me.

Jura offers the world unconditional love, exemplifying near boundless patience, humility, and good humor. Sometimes I address Jura, saying, "You little rascal," when he suddenly gleefully demonstrates behavior that is noticeably inconveniencing.

One illustration of this is that sometimes he quickly exits the mini-SUV I drive and runs over to open backyard, in order to romp in grass, when I have moments ago completed errands and shopping tasks that required several hours of time commitment, and I am responsible for carrying numerous shopping bags up three flights of stairs leading into the apartment in which Jura and I reside. Such animal behavior, which can certainly be applied to human behavior, is also known as Holy mischief.

Tuesday, November 6, 2007

Saudi Arabia native Dr. Kayem, a Boston University Dental School student, and I shared conversation today during a routine dental visit. Momentarily diverted from discussing dental matters, we began exchanging

35

passionate conversation surrounding conflicts occurring in the Middle East. As the interchange ended, Dr. Kayem and I slapped respective left and right hand palms together, before mutually grasping respective palms. For one brief mysterious moment, I figuratively experienced blood within arm veins in Dr. Kayem running into arm veins within me. This manner of international interrelation gave me spine chills—energy resembling electrical current rapidly moving up and down the spine.

Wednesday, November 28, 2007

Five-year-old nephew Jamus, three-year-old niece Brynn, one-year-old nephew Rylan, and I shared dinner this evening. Neighbors of the Reagan children, Mary Summer, who is five-years-old and one-year-old Carena Summer, joined us. We were seated around the Reagan home dinner table. Rylan and Carena were sitting in booster seats. While we were eating plated macaroni and cheese as well as bowled fruit, Jamus began demonstrating visible non-verbal anxiety. Suddenly he declared to Mary—who had finished eating and had expressed a desire to eat dessert—that she was not allowed to eat any dessert, until everyone had been served after-dinner sweet treats.

Deciding to play Hide and Seek after dinner, we all entered a playroom; soon afterwards Jamus questioned fairness of rules of the Hide and Seek game. He disputed who had been designated to hide as well as who had been assigned to seek. Having become distressed and confused, and then weeping, he raised both arms about me, almost reaching waist level.

Jamus asked me, "Why isn't everything fair?" Amid shared profound silence, heartbreak, and tears, Jamus was hugged firmly and gently.

Friday, November 30, 2007

Today I finished reading *His Way; An Unauthorized Biography of Frank Sinatra*. Frank Sinatra and Nancy Barbato were wed in 1939. Nancy and Frank parented three children: Nancy, Frank Jr., and Tina. Frank and Nancy were divorced in 1951. Frank wed actress Ava Gardner, in the same year. Ms. Gardner and Mr. Sinatra were divorced in 1957.

Mr. Sinatra wed Mia Farrow in 1966; Frank and Mia were divorced in 1968. Frank married model Barbara Marx in 1976. Frank and Barbara Sinatra remained together until Frank died in 1998. Mr. Sinatra, who was often referenced as being "a ladies man," is also quoted as having said, "I love women; I don't understand them." Whoa.

This is interesting. Then again, the remark is good and reasonable; it is probably reflective of how women feel about men. Maybe love is important in a way that understanding is not.

Saturday, December 1, 2007

After purchasing The Boston Globe newspaper Saturday edition, I read a feature article about Emmanuel College. The news article stated that Emmanuel College was near financial collapse in 1999, when then twenty-seven-year Emmanuel College president, Sister Janet Eisner, SND (Sisters of Notre Dame) and Merck Pharmaceutical Company brokered an enormous real estate deal. The colossal contract miraculously ended dire circumstances Emmanuel College was facing.

For eight years now, over one-hundred-years old Merck Pharmaceutical Company, based in Kenilworth, New Jersey, has been leasing land on the Emmanuel College campus. The lease duration is seventy-five years; the lease price tag was fifty million dollars.

Doors of the fully constructed Merck research laboratory in Boston were opened on the college campus three years ago, in 2004; scientists working there are conducting research surrounding causes of cancer and neurodegenerative diseases in addition to developing cures for these illnesses. Since the real estate deal between President Janet Eisner and Merck Pharmaceutical Company was negotiated, Emmanuel College student enrollment has almost tripled.

In 2001, following a rising national trend, the college, which had formerly accepted only female students, began accepting male students. Sister Janet is pictured in the news article which appeared in *The Boston Globe* today. She exudes kindness, common sense, and compassion. Not previously having observed nuns as brokers of multi-million-dollar business deals, I found the newspaper story intriguing.

Tuesday, December 11, 2007

Six-years-old, dog Jura has been missing since yesterday. I am wondering if he is dead. Nephew Rhett Jenkins and his mother, Lizzie Reagan Jenkins, who is my sister, have been dog-sitting Jura, while brother Jared and family have been vacationing in Vermont. Rhett and Lizzie reside in Scituate, Massachusetts.

Rhett discovered that Jura was missing when he returned home last night, after leaving the construction work site where he is employed. When he telephoned me yesterday, he asked me whether I had seen Jura wandering around in Cohasset; Cohasset and Scituate are neighboring towns. Sadly, I advised Rhett that unfortunately, Jura had not been discovered roaming about Cohasset, by anyone.

Yesterday morning, before he left the home in which he is currently living with Lizzie, Rhett closed all of the doors facing the front, side, and back entrances of the home and then he headed toward the main office of the construction company that employs him. Lizzie had already begun the weekday, rising early and then driving into Winchester, Massachusetts. Employed as a nursing supervisor, she works at a nursing home. I wonder if it is possible that one or both of the doors of the bulkhead in the basement of the Jenkins home were accidentally left open yesterday morning.

A few months ago, a kitten that Rhett had adopted, an outdoor cat who freely entered as well as exited the home by walking outside opened basement bulkhead doors, was found dead outside the house. One or more coyotes had attacked and killed him. Coyotes roam woods of Scituate and neighboring towns. Rhett initially discovered the cat when he was living in East Boston, Massachusetts.

One fall day, the abandoned kitten had walked underneath a car engine and then crawled up and inside it, seeking shelter. Hearing meowing as he was strolling past the vehicle, Rhett slithered underneath it and found an abandoned, deaf, and shivering kitty. He retrieved the innocent animal, brought him home, cleaned him, and named him Jesse.

Cat fur on Jesse, though covered with engine grease and exhaust, initially appeared to be pure black. When bathing the animal for the first time, Rhett was astonished when he discovered that fur on Jesse was pure white. For nearly a year, Rhett gave Jesse daily loving care. I cannot recall Rhett previously crying in the way that he did, when he informed me that Jesse had been found dead. Tonight, memories of Jura comfort and sustain me. Sleep came unusually early this evening. Sleep lasted unusually long tonight.

Thursday, December 13, 2007

Jura was found. He had been missing for nearly two days. Rhett called me. He said Jura was found. Where was Jura found? I cannot remember.

Does this matter? Comforting and contenting was hearing the voice of Rhett; he reassured me that Jura is now good and safe.

Today I finished reading *Memoirs of a Geisha*, a novel by Arthur Golden. Unsettling, the book depicts two girls, Chiyo and the elder sister of Chiyo, named Satsu, who in the 1920s, resided in an impoverished Japanese fishing village, with both parents. The mother of Chiyo and Satsu is dying, due to cancer illness. The father of the two girls, who is unable to give them care, decides to sell them. Satsu is forced into a life of prostitution; Chiyo becomes a Japanese geisha, an escort who is trained to entertain men with dance, conversation, and song. Novel *Memoirs of a Geisha* mainly addresses experiences of young Chiyo.

As the story progresses, Geisha house owner and head geisha, Hatsumono, is brutally mistreating nine-year-old Chiyo. Mahema, another head geisha, rescues Chiyo. Mahema renames her Sayuri and then begins to teach her how geisha women entertain wealthy men; doing so, Mahema utilizes specified language as well as lessons in song and dance. When World War II occurs, Japanese cities Nagasaki and Hiroshima suffer horrific nuclear bombings. Many geisha friends of Sayuri are killed while attempting to flee cities.

Sayuri surely leaves *Memoirs of a Geisha* readers experiencing wonderment and bewilderment, as when as one is almost finished reading the work, Sayuri says, "Adversity is like wind; it tears you apart from everything, except who you truly are." Contemplating the character of Sayuri, I was stupefied and puzzled, when I read what she said. Sayuri lost both parents and a sister in youth, was sold into slavery, was brutally treated and then was employed as high society escort. Miraculously, throughout these life situations and circumstances, she retained composure, dignity, and serenity.

Friday, December 14, 2007

At approximately eight o'clock this evening, a good-looking man approached me, as I was seated inside a local pizza house, alternately eating pizza slices and writing. The man had previously attended an investment company Christmas party; clients as well as company employees were party guests. Investment company salespeople are often required to work long and late hours. Shortly after we began conversing, I asked the man if he dislikes working late. "Yes," he said, "I do mind working late."

Married, a father of young children and regularly working overtime, the man admitted that he experiences career anxiety. Aloud, he questioned whether or not he is able to successfully continue supporting a wife and children, financially. In fact, he was "feeling the Cheerios," which also means he was mildly inebriated. Suddenly he said, "Do you want to have sex with me?"

"Whaat?" I replied. Initially shocked with the query, I was also fleetingly flattered. Seconds later, recovering clarity and hearing the question being posed for a second time, I began laughing ridiculously, shocking him. He was then firmly and tenderly slapped, on a cheek.

"No, I do not want to have sex with you. Go home, be with family and share the pizza you have bought," I said. Wishing to reassure him, I added. "All is well." Surprisingly, I realized the man did not truly want indiscriminate relations; he clearly wished to relieve considerable tension he was experiencing, surrounding work as well as family issues. Facial as well as verbal expressions he was exuding illuminated the reality.

"You're not mad at me, are you?" he suddenly squealed, now nearing sobriety and at the same time exhibiting genuine remorse. Smiling, I said, "Go home. The matter is forgiven and forgotten." This story represents an interesting observation of the male psyche. Wait one minute. This is 2007. This anecdote demonstrates an interesting male psyche perspective, which is applicable to the female psyche.

Tuesday, December 25, 2007

Last night, I watched a television documentary which honors military men and women. The program was focused on U.S armed forces members who have been serving in Iraq. While watching the documentary, I recalled a heated argument among family members that occurred one year ago, today.

Late Christmas morning, four family members and I were seated inside a sport utility vehicle (SUV). Headed down a highway toward a restaurant inside a large Boston hotel, we intended to share Christmas dinner here with additional family members. Nephew Jonas Jenkins was driving. Stationed in Iraq during 2005 and 2006, Jonas served aside fellow National Guardsmen for twelve months.

Jonas, who returned to America from Iraq a little over one year ago, was becoming visibly and increasingly agitated, while he heard the additional four car occupants arguing and yelling, while debating inconsequential matters, as we were neared the hotel. Suddenly, he erupted, saying, "This is ridiculous. We live in paradise in this country. Every day, Iraq is being bombed. Children, women, and men are being killed. Some are losing limbs. Some are being decapitated. Stop arguing; let's be grateful with what we have been given, and move on." Profound, humbling Christmas Day silence promptly followed.

Saturday, December 29, 2007

Tonight, sister Valerie, Jura, and I shared pleasurable evening walking. Valerie is visiting Cohasset this week; Accompanying her are her husband, Grant as well as their daughters, Grace and Myla, and son Matthew. Florida residing Watson family members have for the last few years, spent Christmas Day visiting a sister of Mom, Aunt Nancy Burkhardt, Uncle Harold Burkhardt, her husband, and Burkhardt family.

Valerie informed me that she is struggling internally; as a management level employee at an international shipping company, Grant is required to travel regularly; the occurrence leaves Vicki routinely resembling a single mother. Passion and dreamy-eyed illusions in any relationship fade quickly, as the work of facing reality and meanwhile, maintaining goodwill, continues.

Mid-afternoon today, six-year-old nephew Matt and his five-year-old cousin, Jamus Reagan, sitting in the second back seat of a large sport utility vehicle, were wrestling while they were seated aside Brynn, a sister of Jamus. Brother Jared was driving; Jared, Elissa, Valerie, Grace, Myla, Brynn, Jamus, Rylan, and I were returning home after having eaten lunch inside Paparazzi restaurant in Hanover, Massachusetts. Jamus, wishing to end rough housing, was heard saying, dramatically, "Matt, stop, I'm going to die." Matt retorted, "You're not going to die. Pull yourself together." Laughter erupted among all of the car occupants.

Almost immediately, Jamus smiled demurely. Then he addressed his aunt, Valerie, enthusiastically saying, "A boy in class named Jason, is a bully. He bullies everyone." Valerie, now teaching kindergarten, directly and firmly replied, "What does the class teacher do?" Jamus replied, "She says if she sees Jason bullying anyone, she is going to swat him. Then, we all eat a snack."

2008

CHAPTER FOUR

READING, *THE BUCKET LIST,* SOUL FAMILY, THEFT

Monday, January 1, 2008

Good morning. Happy New Year. I have finished reading a biography of actor Jimmy Stewart (1908-1997). The acting career of Mr. Stewart spanned nearly seventy years. Jimmy is viewed as having handled professional as well as personal matters with impartiality, generosity, and good humor.

Mr. Stewart was the headlining star in twenty films. Versatile is one word that can be used to describe the acting career of James Stewart; movie goers found the name Jimmy Stewart headlining western, suspense, family, biographical, and comedy films. Mr. Stewart starred in acclaimed films, including *It's A Wonderful Life, Mr. Smith Goes to Washington, Rear Window, The Philadelphia Story,* and *Vertigo.* Jimmy Stewart received five Academy Award nominations. In 1941, he won an Academy Award acclaiming the role that he played in *The Philadelphia Story.* Jimmy Stewart accepted acting awards for Lifetime Achievement in 1968 and 1980.

The professional resume of Jimmy Stewart included military service. Having earned private as well as commercial pilot licenses before entering military service, Mr. Stewart entered the U.S. Air Force Reserve. He subsequently became certified as a pilot instructor. He served during World War II and the Vietnam War.

Jimmy Stewart flew during WWII European combat missions. In 1966, the final military role he played involved being an Air Force non-active duty Observing Officer. He participated in a Vietnam War covert bombing mission involving B-52 airplane. When ending military service, Jimmy Stewart was a Brigadier General.

Actors Henry Fonda and Jimmy Stewart were lifetime friends. Jimmy and Henry rented an apartment together when both were single. Mr. Fonda also entered military service. He was a Quartermaster on the *USS Satterlee* naval destroyer during World War II.

He was later employed as a Naval Air Combat Intelligence Junior Grade Lieutenant, when he was stationed on a ship positioned in Pacific Ocean waters, which was probably commissioned to watch out for potential military attacks on America. It is written that conservative Republican Jimmy Stewart and liberal Democrat Henry Fonda once argued publicly and bitterly about political matters and thereafter agreed not to publicly discuss politics again.

Jimmy Stewart was forty-one years-old when he and model Gloria Hatrick McLean were wed; Gloria subsequently bore the couple two children. Before being married, Gloria and Jimmy agreed to continue parenting two children Ms. McLean was rearing after a former relationship in which she was involved ended. Gloria and Jimmy had been married for forty-five years when Gloria died, in February of 1994. Jimmy was eighty-nine when he died in July of 1997.

In addition to being a highly admired and respected actor and veteran, Mr. Stewart was a longtime philanthropist and poet. He strongly supported the Boy Scouts organization. When in 1981 he was a guest on *The Tonight Show,* sitting alongside late night show host, Johnny Carson, Jimmy read aloud a touching poem that he wrote, honoring the Stewart family dog Beau, who had passed away. As he read the tender, touching, and heartbreaking verses, he depicted Beau as having been as playful as he was mischievous. Beau loved walking and running after tennis balls. He bit people. Once he caused a house in which Jimmy and Gloria were living to catch fire.

Continuing to read the poem aloud, Mr. Stewart indicated there were nights when Beau would sometimes rise from his dog bed and then jump onto the bed in which Jimmy and Gloria were sleeping. Beau would then stare at Jimmy or Gloria, indicating that he wanted to sleep between them. He was seeking to give and receive affection and comfort. When he had nearly ended reciting the self-composed poem, Jimmy suddenly became emotional and faltered, as he read the stanza lines, "There are nights when I reach out to stroke his hair and then I realize—he's not there. Oh, how I wish that wasn't so. I'll always love a dog named Beau".

Following several seconds of profound silence, *Tonight Show* audience members began steadfastly clapping. Longtime beloved late night comedy show host, Johnny Carson wiped away tears. Demonstrating support, he gently and firmly placed his right arm around the back of Jimmy Stewart, for several moments. *Tonight Show* television show viewers, including me, had also become sentimental.

Jimmy Stewart is remembered as being an outstanding actor, gentleman, and patriot. Confidently masculine, Mr. Stewart was also a reputed practical joker. It is written that one evening, when Jimmy and Gloria were attending a party, a male friend of Jimmy who was also a party guest, jokingly kissed Jimmy on the lips. Jesting, Jimmy immediately returned the kiss. When Jimmy momentarily thrust his tongue into the mouth of the man, partygoers evoked boisterous laughter; this was the response that Mr. Stewart desired.

Wednesday, January 16, 2008

Today found me watching a memorable television program interview. A television reporter was interviewing a woman who was newlywed less than two years ago. The woman and her husband, a U.S. Marine, had become first-time parents. Shortly thereafter, he was deployed to Iraq, to serve in the ongoing war here. Before the couple parted, the trembling wife asked her husband, "Are you in peace with God?"

Solemnly, he answered, "Yes."

Shortly after entering the battlefield, he was killed. Reflecting upon the near-final conversation the wedded couple shared allows one to witness stunning bravery the man and woman exuded, as a couple and as individuals, loving God, one another, and fellow humanity. Having been single for a long time, I confess that I have from time to time falsely and naively viewed being coupled as exemplifying consummate happiness. No coupling of any kind eradicates experiencing division, separation, loss, or death.

Saturday, January 19, 2008

This early morning, while lying in bed with a warm blanket and underlying sheet covering me, I was looking outside a bedroom window, observing small birds standing on tree limbs and chirping, while at the same time, enduring subfreezing temperatures. Knowing neither where food nor rest will be found, the tiny cheerful creatures demonstrate no concern. Although

I will not ever be evolved in the same manner as any wildlife, I do want to emulate the wondrous, sacrificial love that these unworried creatures faithfully exude, each and every day.

Tuesday, January 22, 2008

A fantastic, huge, round, and full moon was facing me this mid-evening, as the car I was driving idled. I had momentarily stopped at the intersection of Cushing and Main streets in Hingham, Massachusetts, while I was returning home after having viewed a film called *The Bucket List*. Cameo Theatre in Weymouth, Massachusetts is currently featuring the over ninety minutes–long movie. Veteran actors Morgan Freeman and Jack Nicholson are the headlining stars of *The Bucket List*. The story depicts two men; each has been diagnosed with terminal cancer; each is now recovering, after having undergone lengthy surgical procedures.

As the film begins, millionaire bachelor Edward Cole, (Jack Nicholson) and married mechanic Carter Chambers (Morgan Freeman) are virtual strangers, who are lying upon nearby-situated hospital beds. Having undergone cancer surgeries, both are supine. Initially appearing to share little compatibility beyond goodwill, both men gradually discover that they wish to fulfill similar dreams which have been unexpressed for a long time.

Having retrieved a blank sheet of paper and a pen, Carter begins writing a bucket list, which details unfulfilled personal desires and dreams that he wants to realize before kicking the bucket, or dying. While Carter has been recovering from surgery, the physician who operated on him informs Carter that his medical prognosis is six months to live. Recalling the projection, while he is writing the bucket list, deeply discouraged Carter wads paper on which he has been writing the list into a ball and he throws it into the air before it drops onto hospital flooring, near the bed of Edward Cole. Disheartened and mournful, Carter sighs.

Leaning over, Edward Cole retrieves the crumpled record. After opening the paper, he begins reading the list and at the same time, he encourages Carter to pursue dreams he has written about on paper. Retrieving a pen, Mr. Cole adds new wishes to the list. Sweetening the bucket list fantasy, Edward says he will join Carter Chambers and in addition, he promises that the two men can fulfill personal privately-harbored lifelong dreams together. In fact, Edward says he will provide financing for the bucket list. The relationship between Edward and Carter, the newly developed duo, has begun in earnest.

Shortly thereafter, the dynamic twosome begins three months of world-wide travel. The two men embrace adventuresome experiences including skydiving, race car driving, joining an African lion safari, motorcycling across the Great Wall of China, visiting the Taj Mahal mausoleum in India, and climbing the Egyptian pyramids. At one point, the two men discuss faith, family, and mortality. Carter informs Edward that he believes that when one dies, one is asked two questions: Did you enjoy life? Did you give others joy? Being seated in the movie theatre and hearing Carter say this found me wondering: can one truly enjoy life without simultaneously giving others joy?

Wednesday, January 23, 2008

Considering cat adoption, I visited a nearby cat shelter last weekend, after having previously made an appointment with the shelter director. When I exited the shelter after touring the environs and viewing cats available for adoption, I had resolved a personal issue surrounding cat adoption. I was also bewildered.

As we walked about the shelter, the manager of the temporary cat home and I shared conversation about shelter procedures and cat adoption regulations. During the discussion, we briefly referenced personal living situations. The manager was informed that I am currently single and living alone. Characterizing self as married, the shelter manager referenced self as the spouse of a same sex partner.

"Why do people refer to same-sex domestic partnerships as spousal relationships, when for thousands of years, females, males or males and females who are not biologically related, who are in love and may or may not be living together, have been honorably, publicly and privately been proclaimed as soul family?" I asked. Soul family is defined as non-biologically related soul brothers, soul sisters or soul brothers and soul sisters etc., who are in love, who are family, and who may live together, in a manner which resembles but is not a spousal relationship. "Oh, that's different," the shelter manager said, while at the same time, clearly displaying a desire to quickly end conversation about the matter. Soul family discussion was then promptly, mutually, and respectfully ended.

Cat adoption conversation between us naturally followed. Brief dialogue between the shelter manager and me concerning cat adoption also enabled me to realize I am not currently able to give any cat or dog home-based care. This experience also helped me to realize loving dogs or cats or both animals does not automatically mean one is compatible with cat or dog adoption.

Wednesday, January 30, 2008

Being good and discouraged about not having worked for over a year and having sought hundreds of education and business related positions, I entered a coffee shop. Acquainted with the owner, I inquired about the availability of a counter server position. While talking with the owner, for some unknown reason, I suddenly turned halfway around and glanced toward the table where I had previously been sitting. The pocketbook that I had brought with me and had left on a guest table a few moments ago was missing.

The shoulder bag, containing two cherished diary notebooks, a set of car and apartment keys, and a small amount of cash had been stolen. Shocked and disillusioned, I walked sluggishly, as I exited the shop and entered the parking lot. Lamenting losing the handbag, I was grateful, when I realized that a spare set of car and apartment keys were inside the glove compartment of the car I drive.

Entering and driving the mini-SUV, I arrived twenty minutes later in the parking lot outside a consignment shop. Tearful while entering the resale shop, and at the same time, wishing to shop here and to find a replacement for the stolen pocketbook—also known as undergoing retail therapy—I faced shop owner Raquelle Vachris, who greeted me, professionally and warmly. Speaking slowly and stuttering, I informed Raquelle that the shoulder bag that I had been using and had left upon a coffee shop table had been stolen.

Raquelle replied, "Stealing is mean." Wanting to encourage me, she also indicated that the stolen pocketbook is replaceable. "No," I mournfully asserted, "the pocketbook cannot be replaced; the diary notebooks inside the purse cannot be replaced either." Continuing to grieve aloud, I lamented, "I loved the pocketbook and the diary notebooks inside it."

Tears fell from my eyes. While believing that what I was saying was true, I suddenly recognized that I had become maudlin, self-centered, and short sighted. I offered Ms. Vachris an apology. Having previously become overly emotional, I had not realized that "retail therapist" Raquelle had been offering me compassion and comfort and was about to give me an unexpected gift.

Facing me, standing in the back of a jewelry showcase, she said, "I will be right back," before she left the counter area. Moments later Rachel returned. She was holding a pocketbook; the purse remarkably resembled the stolen pocketbook. Raquelle said, "This is for you. You are not buying this. It is a gift." When I began writing a check in order to pay her for the item, she firmly and gently advised me, "I do not want the check. The check will not be cashed. Tear it up."

After arriving home tonight, I glanced at the telephone answering machine, which is set upon a stationery desk. The number one was flashing on the answering machine screen. After I pressed the play button, I heard a message which indicated that a Department of Public Works (DPW) employee had discovered the stolen pocketbook, which had been discarded in an alley. The purse contained diary notebooks, personal identifications, car and apartment keys and no cash. No cash. No problem.

CHAPTER FIVE

HEAVEN, OVERAGE FLIRTING, *DEAD MAN WALKING,* *YOUNG AT HEART,* NEW DOG

Thursday, February 21, 2008

Hoping to enter Heaven someday, I am wishing, when doing thus to soon thereafter learn how to blow bubble gum. Blowing bubble gum involves chewing and softening bubble gum, and then blowing into it and filling it with breath, which forms a bubble gum balloon, before air pressure pops or bursts the sticky, generally round mass, or it sags into a prune-like shape, due to lack of air pressure. Blowing bubble gum is an activity I have not been able to perform thus far; I will probably not master the activity while living on earth. It has been said that when you are in Heaven, you can do anything you were unable to do on earth. I am also hoping to find a sunny beach resort overlooking miles of soft sand and refreshing ocean waters up there. Ha-ha.

These days living in a manner exemplifying life in colonial America, I interact with people on a regular basis solely when walking about Cohasset, Hull, or Hingham. I rarely call anyone, except when I want to discuss employment matters. Living in this manner is personally contenting. Experiencing little telephone communication and therefore, not knowing when one will connect socially, presents an opportunity for personal growth, that can, in turn, generate heightened satisfaction when one meets people spontaneously.

This morning several orange-and-black-spotted lady-bugs have been visiting the apartment in which I reside; insect travel here is slow and deliberate. Bugs stop intermittently while moving along ceiling molding as well as woodwork around windows. Traversing window or door frames, the attractive insects will eventually move outside, as happened last year. Male as well as female lady-bug tourists are welcome here, anytime.

Monday, March 17, 2008

Today found me honoring St. Patrick Day, and in doing so, I experienced gratitude, while laughing and joking when conversing with people. I relished eating a baked potato. I savored wearing a green shirt with three-quarter-length-sleeves and chosen black pants. Interestingly, the color blue was initially worn on St. Patrick Day. Irish mythology probably influenced the occurrence, as lore depicts ancient Ireland female Sovereign Flaitheas Eireann as having worn a blue robe.

Roman government officials occupied Great Britain when St. Patrick was born here, in 387 A.D. When he was born, Patrick was named Maewyn Succat. The first family of St. Patrick was Romano-British and wealthy. The father and the grandfather of Patrick were Irishmen who were Christian church deacons. When he was sixteen years old, in 403 A.D., Patrick was kidnapped. Irish raiders who seized him subsequently re-inhabited an Irish island where the teenager was enslaved. Folklore indicates that God inspired Patrick to escape captivity and that God assisted him in doing so. Patrick returned to Great Britain and subsequently became a priest.

Later he returned to Ireland. In 432 A.D., he became a Christian Bishop. Father Patrick was then forty-five years old. As an evangelist, spreading Christian beliefs and values, he is reported to have utilized a shamrock plant, exhibiting three shamrock-shaped leaves, when he was demonstrating the Christian Trinitarian concept. When he had been evangelizing for nearly thirty years and was seventy-four years old, Patrick died on March 17, 461 A.D.

Patrick was longtime observed by many as being a virtuous, upright, and honest man. He was a faithful church servant for decades. The reason he was not officially canonized or recognized as a saint is because the process of official canonization did not begin in Christian churches until 933 A.D.

St. Patrick Day was officially celebrated for the first time in Ireland in the 1700s. By then, inhabitants of Ireland had been celebrating the occasion for several hundred years, since the ninth and tenth centuries. Since then, many countries around the world have joined Ireland, in celebrating St. Patrick Day, including the United States, Great Britain, Canada, Argentina, Australia, New Zealand, Japan, South Korea, and Switzerland. International St. Patrick Day festivities include churchgoing, baking and eating soda bread, and attending sporting events, parades, and parties. Customs of observing the day include wearing some or all green clothing. Before the 1970's, Ireland did not allow restaurants or bars to serve alcohol on the feast day.

Researching the life of St. Patrick and how St. Patrick Day celebrations came to be intrigued me for several reasons. First of all, I did not know the familial roots of St. Patrick were Romano-British. Second, I was not aware that he lived before the church practice of canonization was instituted. Third, I did not realize St. Patrick Day is celebrated worldwide, in such countries as Japan, South Korea, Argentina, and Switzerland.

Finally, I was unaware that Ireland did not allow restaurants or bars to serve patrons alcohol on St. Patrick Day, until the early 1970's. Doing so was viewed as a mark of respect for St. Patrick. It was also then believed that allowing bars to remain open on St. Patrick day during the Christian Lenten season would encourage drunkenness and possibly incite disorderliness.

Wednesday, March 18, 2008

An elderly man I met today informed me that he had been given many high blood pressure medications and that these medications had not been generally effective. He also said a man who befriended him advised him to utilize an "English high blood pressure remedy," which the elderly man accepted. The natural medicine is a combination of apple cider vinegar and water. One drinks a combination of eight ounces of water and one teaspoon of apple cider vinegar on the first day. On the second day, one drinks a combination of eight ounces of water and one tablespoon of apple cider vinegar. On the third day and every day thereafter, one drinks a combination of eight ounces of water and two tablespoons of apple cider vinegar.

Shortly after beginning to employ the remedy, the elderly gentleman revisited the physician who diagnosed him. When the elderly man was given a blood pressure test, the medical device being employed indicated that his systolic blood pressure reading, which was initially two hundred, had fallen precipitously to one hundred twenty-five. Systolic pressure is the maximum amount of pressure the heart exerts while beating. A normal systolic pressure level is one hundred and twenty. A normal blood pressure reading is one hundred twenty over eighty. The number eighty represents diastolic pressure, or the amount of pressure occurring in heart arteries, when the heart is between beats.

I want to experiment with the English blood pressure remedy, whose demonstrable effects are remarkable. Although I do not suffer with blood pressure-related medical issues, I have heard that diluting apple cider vinegar with water also aids people who are experiencing digestive issues. People have advised me to begin employing the remedy using small amounts of apple cider vinegar and one cup of water and then gradually increasing the apple cider vinegar amount to up to two tablespoons a day. In years past, I repeatedly dismissed the value of natural medicine. Events of the past year have influenced me to embrace natural medicine as a genuine means of treating many ailments.

Thursday, March 19, 2008

Having formerly been an elementary school tutor, I decided to attend an early evening discussion forum, promoted as "The State of the Boston School System." The event was held tonight, inside John F. Kennedy Library in Boston, Massachusetts, inside an auditorium annex. Being nearly full in attendance, this forum featured Dr. Carol Johnson, newly appointed Superintendent of the Boston Public Schools. In August 2007, Mrs. Johnson began performing the role of Superintendent.

She was previously the Superintendent of the Memphis, Tennessee Public Schools. City public schools here serve 119,000 students. Carol Johnson is credited with having helped one hundred Memphis public schools become re-invigorated, sparing the educational institutions from being determined "at risk schools," per Tennessee public schools' "No Child Left Behind" guidelines. The Memphis Parent Teacher Association once named Dr. Johnson Superintendent of the Year.

Former Channel 5-WCVB Boston correspondent, now WBUR-Boston radio talk show host, David Boeri, interviewed Mrs. Johnson today. Mr. Boeri presented her with precise, tactful, and humorous inquiries and comments. Mr. Boeri and Mrs. Johnson were seated in upholstered chairs set near one another upon the JFK library stage. A round table, upon which two royal blue nearly-filled water goblets had been set, was between them. Superintendent Johnson and Mr. Boeri were facing approximately five hundred library forum guests.

Now having been employed as Boston Public Schools Superintendent for twenty-four weeks, Dr. Johnson indicated that thus far, she has met administrators and staff at seventy Boston Public Schools. The achievement is admirable. The number of Boston Public Schools is presently one hundred forty-three; the total student body of Boston Public Schools is fifty-six thousand. Dr. Johnson commented that charter school and pilot school movements within the Boston Public School system are growing; she said both movements incorporate differing not dissimilar educational desires of Boston Public School system students and their parents.

Before the forum started, I found an empty auditorium chair and had sat beside an elderly gentleman. Observing the man nodding off several times near the end of the forum, I extended my right hand behind his back and began massaging him, hoping to gently nudge him awake. "Are you well?" he was asked, when he awoke.

"Yes, I am well," he replied, while also definitively declaring "I am seventy-nine years, nine months, and twenty days old."

The elderly gentleman informed me that his only sister died two months ago; he said she was nearly ninety years old. He commented that he had traveled to the JFK Library late this afternoon via subway train. After he exited the train station, he had walked nearly three miles before entering the one-hundred-twenty-five feet high library. Comprising nine stories, the structure faces Boston Harbor.

Following the forum, I offered the gentleman a car ride to a nearby subway train station, so that rather than walking to the train station entrance, he could immediately enter it, after exiting the car. He accepted. Considering him negotiating nighttime darkness while walking toward the subway station, I had been skeptical, wondering if he would be safe. As we neared the subway train station entrance, I offered to escort the gentleman down the entrance stairs, before leaving him.

Politely, he refused. Then he asked me if he could kiss me before he departed. Unnerved, I quietly and firmly replied, "No." Stormily exiting the car, the nearly eighty-year-old man was clearly furious. Disconcerted, I decided that any octogenarian man who boldly solicits a kiss from a woman who is almost thirty years junior can certainly handle going home via subway train. Humph…

Thursday, March 26, 2008

Sister Helen Prejean, a Louisiana native, who is also a Medaille, Louisiana-based Sister of St. Joseph, spoke this evening inside a crowded Glastonbury Abbey conference center in Hingham, Massachusetts. Glastonbury

Abbey is a Catholic monastic center comprised of three residences, a church and conference center. Sister Helen entered the Meadville, Louisiana based Sisters of St. Joseph convent in 1957, when she was eighteen-years-old. She has been a nun for fifty-one years. Intrigued with persons who have embraced religious life, I wanted to attend the presentation. I was also interested in hearing about a book Sr. Helen wrote entitled, *Dead Man Walking.*

Standing front and center in the conference room, which was nearly overflowing with seated and standing guests, Sister Helen used a hand-held microphone, while she discussed the book. Published in 1993, *Dead Man Walking* has been widely read and praised. Based on a true story, the novel observes Sister Helen pastorally counseling a fictional convicted murderer, who is facing execution. The book was converted into a movie, which was shown for the first time in 1995; movie goers and film critics acclaimed the motion picture.

The book as well as the movie exemplifies real life brothers, Patrick and Eddie Sonnier, who were convicted of murder. In November 1977, using a dated security guard badge and two twenty-two caliber guns, the men approached an eighteen-year-old Louisianan girl and the seventeen-year-old boyfriend of the Louisianan girl; the young couple was sitting in the wide front seat of a car, which was parked in an isolated area, including a spot named "Lovers Lane". The time was 1:00 a.m.

Speaking with the couple, the Sonnier brothers, impersonating policemen, falsely indicated that the two young people were trespassing on private property. Patrick and Eddie then arrested the couple, forcibly entered the car, and while doing so, coerced the two adolescents into the car back seat. One of the two brothers then drove toward a remote Louisiana area.

The young man was handcuffed and then tied to a tree trunk; the young lady was immorally assaulted. Fearing police action, Patrick and Eddie untied the young man and demanded that the boy and girl lay face-down in the grass. Thrice shot, the two young people were instantly murdered. Both Sonnier brothers were indicted on two counts of first-degree murder and subsequently faced a jury trial. Patrick and Eddie Sonnier were convicted of the charges and were later sentenced to death by execution.

Sr. Helen has counseled many imprisoned death-row inmates; she has observed the executions of inmates who were formerly on death row. She has offered spiritual counsel to families of victims, inmates, and family members of inmates. When offered counseling, parents of one victim agreed and parents of the second victim refused. One Sonnier parent consented to pastoral counseling and the other refused. The objecting parents protested against Sr. Helen giving pastoral assistance to persons who are convicted of murder. Admitting that she has struggled from time to time with giving spiritual support to convicted carnal abuse offenders and murderers, Sister Helen says she upholds and will continue to perform the work.

The Catholic pastoral counseling process utilizes universally embraced Christian principles, she stated. She referenced Christian values as encouraging people to emulate the way in which Jesus lived and loved. Sr. Helen stated Christianity does not condone, justify, or excuse wrongdoing in any situation.

Paradoxically, Sr. Helen professed that Christian values neither demean dignity nor withhold compassion in any life circumstances. Hearing Sr. Helen restate the values found me later recalling a Bible verse in the New Testament, in the gospel of Luke, chapter 7, verse 47, which states, "Whoever has been forgiven little, loves little." Equally true is the maxim, "One who forgives little, loves little."

Patrick Sonnier was executed in 1984. No Sonnier family member, friend, or loved one was present. Mr. Sonnier was the first death row inmate that Sister Helen Prejean counseled pastorally. Sister Helen was the only person who witnessed the execution of Patrick Sonnier. Sr. Helen said she wanted to face Patrick as he was being executed; she wanted to emulate Jesus being present in the circumstance. She believes Jesus was truly present when Patrick Sonnier died. As of this date, Eddie Sonnier remains incarcerated.

Dead Man Walking examines capital punishment. While writing the work, Sr. Prejean noted the work of French early twentieth century journalist, novelist, and philosopher, Albert Camus (1913-1960). During the presentation she gave tonight, she restated the views of Mr. Camus regarding capital punishment, indicating that one who endorses capital punishment supports murdering persons who have been convicted of murder. Sr. Helen said that Albert Camus viewed capital punishment as egregious; she said, "Mr. Camus wrote that execution, which is planned, is premeditated murder."

Uplifting as well as bewildering is considering pastoral work that Sr. Helen has humbly performed for decades. I can confidently assert that it is nearly impossible to leave a presentation she has given without being moved or without considering who one truly is, inwardly as well as outwardly. It is gratifying to hear Sr. Prejean talk about relevant societal matters; lectures she gives are often standing room only events. Witnessing the Southern drawl, good humor, and compassionate demeanor she demonstrated as she discussed inmate pastoral care and religious life was humbling, stimulating, and in several moments downright hilarious. P.S. Sr. Helen also confessed she is a scofflaw; sometimes she speeds willfully while driving. She has been given speeding citations. How few or how many? Shhh...

Friday, March 28, 2008

This day found me reading material detailing campaign promises presidential candidate Senator Barack Obama has made thus far. Commitments he has made include removing U.S. military troops from Iraq; U.S. military involvement in the Iraq war has been ongoing for the last five years. As a war-deterring strategy, Mr. Obama said he wants America to continue developing military strength. Senator Obama has stated that he also wants all Americans to be able to receive affordable health care. Offering every American child who is attending elementary, junior high, and high school a refined public education is another presidential plan the senator has proposed.

Candidate Obama has been a U.S. Senator representing the state of Illinois since January 2005. He was a state senator for Illinois from 1997 to 2004. Democratic presidential nomination challenger, Hillary Rodham Clinton, was First Lady, from 1993 to 2001. Since 2001, Senator Hillary Clinton has been a U.S. Senator representing the state of New York. Thus far, the nomination of Senator Obama as the official presidential candidate of the Democratic party looms large.

Friday, April 4, 2008

One gallon of gas is now around three dollars and nine cents; by this summer, the cost of a gallon of gas has been forecasted to rise to four dollars per gallon. At this time last year, gas was priced at nearly two dollars per gallon. This gas price surge is wondrous.

Wednesday, April 30, 2008

Tonight, listening to a living room-style conversation shared between Massachusetts U.S Congressman Barney Frank and a chosen John F. Kennedy Library forum moderator, New York Times columnist, Paul Krugman, was interesting educational experience. Generally not enthused about political discussion, I have ironically been drawn toward observing as well as meeting political personalities from time to time and understanding how and why they endorse or oppose political ideas. This evening, while sitting in chairs set upon a stage facing seated as well as standing guests in the main auditorium of the JFK Library, Congressman Frank and Mr. Krugman discussed current economic conditions Americans are experiencing.

Congressman Frank admits improper bank loans have caused the American economy to become weak. He said bank representatives who have knowingly finalized loans that borrowers cannot repay are culpable. Mr. Frank said twenty or even fifteen years ago, predatory lending generally did not happen. He indicated bank deregulation, beginning in the late 1980s and early 1990s, allowed fraudulent loan practices to accelerate.

Mr. Frank said that an increasing number of homeowners who have stopped paying mortgage bills and who have entered home foreclosure status as a result are also partially responsible for the downturn in the American economy. "Years ago, people did not suddenly walk away from making regular mortgage payments," Congressman Frank said. Mom also recently verified this truth. Mr. Frank commented that this circumstance is now happening with increasing frequency.

Congressman Frank informed the five hundred members of the library audience that another factor which is influencing the present American economic crisis is that many American homeowners who have accepted low interest, variable or adjustable-rate mortgage (ARM) programs have discovered that their loan payments have suddenly "ballooned" or substantially increased. ARM or variable rate mortgages (VRM) initially relieve fixed-rate mortgage payment amounts. However, economic indicators can suddenly and significantly raise the mortgage payment amount.

Economic indicators are defined as statistical information released by governments, non-profit organizations, and private companies that communicate information about economic health, business cycles, and consumer status within the economy as well as the economic forecast. When released, these stats can cause ARM or VRM interest rates to "balloon" or to rise rapidly. Many American homeowners facing these economic circumstances have been financially unable to handle the occurrence.

Understanding this reality caused me to think that accepting an adjustable or variable rate mortgage resembles investing money. If one chooses to invest funds which are not government supported, then one also accepts the reality of losing investment funds when economic conditions deteriorate, just as if one accepts an ARM or VRM loan, one also accepts incurring suddenly increasing interest rates associated with the loans, amid changing economic circumstances.

Thursday, May 1, 2008

Late night political talk show host Jon Stewart interviewed Senator Barack Obama. Jokingly, Mr. Stewart respectfully commanded Mr. Obama, "Say when you become U. S. President, you will not be using bait and switch tactics and enslaving the white race." Good natured Senator Obama, the late show audience, and late show television show watchers, including me, laughed uproariously.

Humor presents an opportunity for people to make challenging, critiquing, or uncomfortable statements in a comic manner, which clarifies matters being raised. Humor also provides a safe emotional atmosphere for addressing the matters. A person who exhibits either little or excessive humor is a person who is not well, indeed.

Wednesday, May 7, 2008

Waking near 4:00 am this morning, lying supine in a master, bed found me considering God, people, places, and things. Near 5:00 a.m., I noticed emerging light in the sky as well as flowering trees and bushes outside the bedroom window in the apartment. Last night, I watched a documentary film which was made public in 2007. *Young@ Heart* is being shown in Loring Hall Theatre, in Hingham, Massachusetts for the next two weeks.

First opened in 1936, the Main Street situated theatre is seventy-two-years-old. When walking just beyond doors of the entrance to the cinema, moviegoers can view and may or may not pass a counter area where candy on sale is stored in a glass counter and where popcorn, soft drinks, and water can be purchased. The interior of the movie house is an auditorium comprised of about four hundred and fifty theatre seats which face a sizeable single movie screen that hangs down from an arch on the stage.

Young@Heart, a documentary, portrays an actual Northampton, Massachusetts singing group named *Young at Heart*, comprised of twenty-two real-life members; ages of the group members range between eighty-one and ninety-two. The director of the group is Bob Cilman. None of the men or women in the ensemble is an actor or actress. Mr. Cilman founded *Young at Heart* twenty-six years ago, in 1982. Initially, the vocalists generally sang vaudeville musical selections.

When Mr. Cilman introduced rock and roll, rhythm and blues, and punk rock singing selections, group members were initially unenthused. Rebellious, some resisted rehearsing. The popularity of the *Young at Heart* chorus skyrocketed almost instantly when the group began publicly performing music that Director Cilman had recommended. It began to draw international and national audiences.

One concert audience portrayed during the *Young@Heart* film included inmates confined in a high-security-level prison. A tall chain-link fence, with barbed wire atop, secures the prison outdoor environs. Before beginning the concert, Director Cilman advised *Young at Heart* group members that inmates residing within a high-security-level prison might not be receptive concertgoers. Expecting the concert viewers to be enthusiastic might be unrealistic, he cautioned.

While watching the film, being shown today inside a sparsely populated movie theatre, I silently supported the advice of the director. However, while the concert was ongoing, viewing the prisoners as video cameras panned the *Young at Heart* audience, which included professional staff and inmates, left me stunned and shaken. The convicts came across as being eerily gentle, humble, and innocent, as I observed them sitting outdoors, quietly and respectfully watching the show.

Inmates there did not overtly evidence bitterness, disrespect, or hardened hearts—personality characteristics which have been assigned to prison populations. Distinct differences between prison staff and the prison population were not noticeable. If surrounding chain-link fencing, barbed wire, and prison security staff were not present here, inmates would not be recognizable as prisoners. Teary-eyed and near sobbing when *Young @ Heart* film ended, I joined nearly one hundred steadfastly clapping fellow Loring Hall Theatre moviegoers. I do not remember the last time I heard moviegoers applauding in this manner.

Tuesday, May 20, 2008

This morning ABC television news correspondent Diane Sawyer interviewed Senator Barack Obama, Democratic presidential candidate. Michelle Obama, the wife of Barack, was sitting beside him. Suddenly the interview focus was changed, when Michelle mentioned, "By the way, we're getting a dog."

Barack immediately became defensive, thwarting Michelle, saying firmly, "We're not getting a dog, unless we're sure our kids (two girls, Malia, 9, and Sasha, 6) are also able to help us with dog care." Continuing to view Michelle, Barack sternly said, "You may want a dog, but we want to be sure someone is going to bring this puppy outside, in the middle of the night."

Unmoved, Michelle, looked directly at Barack and expressed resolve, saying, "We're getting a dog." Barack smirked and became visibly uncomfortable and embarrassed, before he directly inquired, "We're getting a dog?"

Grinning, Mrs. Obama responded gently and firmly, "Yes, we are getting a dog." Reporter Diane Sawyer, *Good Morning America* television production crew, and nationwide television viewing audience members were unexpectedly, respectfully, and unanimously amused. It was gratifying to not only view presidential candidate Barack Obama discussing pertinent political issues, but also to observe how he handles suddenly changing circumstances.

CHAPTER SIX

ARRANGED MARRIAGE, SPRING TEA, SUMMER ADVENTURES, CANDIDATE OBAMA, RAKAN HASSAN

Friday, May 23, 2008

Tomorrow evening, Jonas Jenkins, a son of sister Lizzie Jenkins, will wed Liane Lindon. Jonas and Liane have been committed companions for several years. The wedding location is in Maryland. The ceremony setting will be near the Lindon family home. Wedding attendees will number thirty people, including friends and family. Minister officiated nuptials will proceed before the wedding reception dinner, which will be accompanied with live classical music. After departing Maryland on Sunday, Jonas and Liane will live in New York City, where Jonas is employed as a financial adviser.

Today, an eye and ear specialist who examined me diagnosed me with an ear infection. Because the doctor asked me not to travel via airplane, I am unable to attend the wedding of Jonas and Liane. The ear specialist advised me that when one is experiencing an inner ear infection, air travel can cause the inner ear to rupture, inducing possible permanent hearing loss.

Saturday, May 24, 2008

This past Wednesday evening found me watching *Arranged* (2007). Having received a four out of five stars internet rating, the film was shown inside a library meeting room. The movie begins, depicting two girls, one Jewish and one Muslim, whose marriages are in the process of being arranged. Ninety minutes long, *Arranged* portrays the matchmaking custom as effective when it progresses naturally and unsuccessful when unjust pressure is exercised during the process.

Asian, African, Middle Eastern, Latin American, and Japanese cultures currently continue to employ arranged marriage customs. Natural arranged marriages are not forced. Relationships are generally developed through trust as well as time and involve family input, including guidance from the person whose marriage is being arranged. Generally, family member-employed matchmakers contribute substantial marriage advice, which resembles networking with additional families who are also considering arranged marriage.

An arranged marriage that is developed naturally fosters the union of a man and a woman who share mutual marital aspirations and acceptance of the responsibilities of marital life; an improperly arranged marriage promotes a marriage relationship which is based on unhealthy obligation, or an "I owe you" sense of partnership. Truthfully, young men and women who are not ready to marry or are not interested in marriage have been pressured into accepting arranged marriages. *Arranged* examines unhealthy family pressure that is exercised while marriages are being arranged. The film also observes the beginnings of successful arranged marriages.

Having been matched with an incompatible suitor, the Muslim girl in the film is considerably discouraged; she wants to leave home. Eschewing parental advice, the young woman attends a party given by a cousin living in a distant American city. Entering the home of the relative, she greets her cousin. As the young girl wanders tentatively about apartment rooms, she observes fellow young adults drinking alcohol, smoking marijuana, and exhibiting inappropriate and overtly intimate behavior. Disillusioned, she leaves the gathering and returns home.

The Muslim girl previously met a Jewish girl; the two girls discovered they are attending the same college. They develop a friendship. The Jewish girl has also been matched with an incompatible suitor. She is currently unenthusiastically dating a prospective husband. Without her friend knowing, the Muslim girl secretly and bravely offered the matchmaker employed by the family of the Jewish girl a photograph picturing a boy that the Jewish girl genuinely admires.

Parents of the Muslim and Jewish girls, initially resisting the development of any relationship beyond goodwill between Jews and Muslims, gradually accept that the two girls have become friends and consent to sharing mutually helpful matchmaking information, as this arranged marriage process unfolds. Soon after, the Muslim girl is introduced with another suitor; shortly thereafter, she realizes that the relationship between her and the prospective partner goes beyond what has been referenced as "puppy love," or love that has not matured.

Watching *Arranged* was a personally enlightening experience; the custom of arranging marriages resembles what Americans call professional networking. Whether or not a matchmaker is employed in a coupling process, relationships developed naturally, through word of mouth, have repeatedly been demonstrated as being successful in a different manner than pairings that are developed through singles websites. Coupling or dating sites do allow users to publicly acknowledge a desire to meet new people. The sites do facilitate the development of conversational skills.

In contrast to the individualized arranged marriage process, singles websites offer people seeking a new relationship dozens of matching options, which are not selective. There is little sense of fate or community involved in online matchmaking. One picks a potential match or possible matches after viewing large numbers of candidates. Profiles of match candidates on the website often present no photograph and a peripheral profile, a photograph and a peripheral profile, or no profile.

Ample social research indicates that people who do not believe that profile information on singles websites is truly private do not post profiles along with personal photographs, do not post photographs with personal profiles, or write misleading information contained within personal descriptions accompanying photos. Many studies of matchmaking websites have indicated that the development of a steady relationship through meeting on a singles websites generally does not happen.

Is this impossible? No. It is not impossible; this is probably one of the reasons why singles websites were born. In the meantime, enjoying life each day and at the same time welcoming new experiences, whether the experiences include meeting a prospective partner, generally does work, no matter how little or how long one waits.

Dad was a successful businessman. Mom was a successful homemaker. When my sisters Lizzie and Valerie, brother Jared and I were growing up, Mom as well as Dad taught us that developing personal or professional relationships through word of mouth, patience, respect, and good humor is important. I treasure sage advice that Mom and Dave gave us.

Sunday, May 25, 2008

Today found me delightfully licking and swallowing soft serve vanilla ice cream before chewing the cone supporting it, until the cone also disappeared. I purchased the treat while standing outside JJ's, an ice cream hut, located near Route 3A in Cohasset. Open between April and October, JJ's has been in business for over fifty years.

During spring summer and early fall months, ice cream as well as sandwich and soft drink seekers regularly crowd JJ's, standing in lines formed outside two serving windows.

On some days and a number of nights, adults and children can be seen standing in two lines of at least ten people. Many are waiting for ice cream; some are waiting for sandwiches and soft drinks. In recent years, JJ's has also begun selling frozen yogurt.

JJ's customers generally drive there and park in the ice cream stand parking lot. When customers see a full parking lot, they park along the roadside of Route 3A. JJ's is a Cohasset hot spot that sister Lizzie, brother Jared, sister Valerie, and I visited regularly during spring as well as summer months in childhood and teenage years. I can also confidently state that all Reagan family nieces, nephews, great-nieces, and great-nephews have been introduced to JJ's and have repeatedly revisited the ice cream hut.

This afternoon, after leaving JJ's and driving southward for two miles, I parked the car in a lot and then entered a consignment shop. While browsing in the small well organized Cohasset shop offering attractive displays of apparel and home goods, I suddenly spotted two ceramic tea mugs with ceramic handles and tea bag holders. Observing the items prompted me to remember one Christmas Day many years ago, when Valerie and I were opening Christmas presents that Aunt Alva, a sister of Mom, had sent us.

The gifts were ceramic tea mugs which resembled the tea mugs I was viewing today, inside the boutique. The mugs had centered flower designs on the front and back sides. The name Valerie was printed on one mug; the name Merrie was printed on the second mug, below the flowers. Demonstrating Old English font, the printed names were situated below the painted colorful flowers. Not having ever seen ceramic mugs with attached tea bag holders before, Valerie and I found the design concept intriguing.

Most likely, Valerie was sixteen-years-old and I was probably twenty-two-years old, when we were sent the Christmas presents. She and I were excited, as we considered using the medium-sized mugs. One afternoon, while Vallie— as I sometimes call her—and I were talking at home in the living room, she put tap water into a tea kettle, boiled it on the kitchen stove, and then she poured the hot water into the two mugs. Tea bags were dunked below the hot tea water. Milk and sugar were poured into the mugs.

When the tea was brewed, each of us removed a wet teabag from each of the two mugs. Additional tea was squeezed out of the hot teabags into the mugs; the shriveled teabags were placed inside the designated ceramic tea bag holders. Being generally sure the hot soaked tea bags would remain inside the teabag holders while we were drinking hot tea, Vallie and I began consuming the steaming beverage.

Almost immediately, hot tea water and a hot soaked teabag dropped out of each ceramic tea bag holder, wetting as well as staining shirts Vallie and I were wearing, before each teabag somehow dropped onto the off-white living room carpet. "What stupid mugs," she shouted, as she and I nearly fell off living room chairs, while laughing recklessly.

Having retrieved the two fallen teabags, Valerie walked toward a dark wooden cabinet under the kitchen sink, pulled the cabinet doorknob open, and then tossed the two teabags inside the wastebasket. Each of us, one after the other, used a small soft cloth that Valerie had moistened with cold water to absorb tea stains on the living room carpet— officially ending the failed experiment with the tea bag holders. I wrote that Vallie and I laughed recklessly, when the hot soaked teabags fell swiftly onto the cream-colored living room carpet. —Recklessly? Hmm…Maybe we had become dizzied tea drinkers.

Sunday, June 1, 2008

Having been offered and having accepted a political invitation, last night I attended a political meeting; the meeting purpose was to examine the written campaign platform presented by presidential candidate Senator Barack Obama. The home of a Hull, Massachusetts resident was the setting for the discussion. As I drove here and entered a condominium development parking lot, I suddenly became nostalgic, remembering the summer of '73, when I worked inside Paragon Park.

Paragon Park was formerly located where the large condominium development site is now situated. Paragon Park was closed in 1984. The family who owned and wanted to sell the amusement park was unable to find an interested buyer. Auctioned Paragon Park was later dismantled and then underwent condominium conversion.

Opened in 1908, historic Paragon Park offered Boston residents as well as North and South Shore Massachusetts dwellers, vacationers, and tourists beachside summer recreation and food refreshment. For seventy-five years, each of the front entrance gates of the park, facing Nantasket Beach, and the rear entrance gates of the park, overlooking Nantasket Bay, were opened, allowing millions of park goers into the theme park. Offering multiple sites where food and drink could be purchased, the recreation site and tourist attraction also offered numerous rides.

Rides included the Giant Roller Coaster, a ninety-eight-foot-high, over one quarter of a mile-long amusement attraction, made with a curving light railroad track on which cars carried coaster riders while moving at speeds of up to fifty-three miles an hour, the Crazy Teacups, large, turning, multi-colored teacups with varying colors and designs, and the Congo Cruise, a canoe cruise along water inside a darkened and enclosed cruise route, incorporating various inlaid dioramas of colorful tropical scenes and sounds. As the cruise was ending, the canoe ascended and then descended rail tracks before splashing into water, which gushed over cruise participants.

Additional rides included Bumper Cars, mini self-driven electric cars with flat rubber undercarriages which allowed car drivers to safely crash into one another and then continue to drive about a surrounding enclosed area, The Kooky Kastle—riders sitting in coffin-shaped cars traveled through the castle, while they passed eerie plywood cutouts on springs and hinges, and the High Striker, a game which tested physical strength and was played with a mallet and puck.

Using the mallet—a type of hammer comprised of a long wooden handle and an attached large rounded wooden or rubber head—the High Striker contestant struck one end of a lever, a wooden bar resting on a pivot located in the base of the striker machine. The other end of the lever contained a puck attached to a tower. Depending on the amount of force utilized by the striker when he or she struck one end of the lever, the opposite end of the lever drove the puck upward. If the puck reached the peak of the machine, a bell located here was sounded. The contestant won one of several available prizes.

Brother Jared as well as sisters Lizzie and Valerie and I were Paragon Park employees, for one or two summers in the mid-1970s. Joining fellow Paragon Park co-workers, we stood behind food and drink stands, while we prepared and then served hamburgers, pizza, ice cream, cotton candy, fried clams, French fries, and sodas. In the summer of 1973, Liz turned twenty-one years old, I was nineteen-years-old, Jared was seventeen-years-old and Vallie was thirteen-years-old.

One work day, a fellow Paragon Park co-worker offered me an amusing Paragon Park customer service story. The fellow employee said that one workday afternoon, Jared was serving a food stand customer a box of French fries. The customer rudely said, "Are the French fries hot?" Jared immediately removed one boxed French fry. Chewing the deep fried potato, he immediately exclaimed, "Yes, the French fries are hot, delicious, and cost fifty cents. Thank you."

On many workdays, Paragon Park employees Brielle Morgan, Patty Devaney, Mary Ellen Devaney, Kelly Roleman, Liz, and I commuted to and from work together; one of us drove. When we exited the employee parking lot after work, especially on hot and humid nights, the designated car driver generally drove along shoreline adjoining Atlantic Avenue in Hull with Jerusalem Road in Cohasset; the driver continued driving on seaside Atlantic Avenue in Cohasset until we arrived at Sandy Beach. All of us were intending to share a midnight or near midnight dip, before returning home.

After we exited the parked car, we removed work sneakers and socks we were wearing. Moments later, while holding hands and not having removed casual clothing we were wearing, we walked and then ran toward the seashore. We were jubilant. We expressed mixed delight and uncertainty as we neared ocean waters. Suddenly, running ceased; laughing and screaming became moaning and then silence, as we entered chilly ocean waters and sank below the surface. Experiencing complete darkness, we were far away from distant powered street lights. After emerging above and exiting ocean waters, each and all of us were serene. We were experiencing bliss...

Seven nights a week, the "Roaring 20s" restaurant and bar, featuring nightly bands and dancing, attracted Paragon Park patrons. Paragon Park co-workers frequented the club when we desired late night socializing, approximately once every two weeks. "Roaring 20s" music featured rock and roll as well as disco selections. When I recall meeting and dancing with fellow Paragon Park employee, William (Will) Powell I am calm and content.

William inspires people; he demonstrates consistent faith, intellect, and enthusiasm. He is gifted with a good sense of humor. I remember talking and working with him one day, when standing beside me and facing me directly, he confidently and gently said, "People can change, at any age, at any time." William helped me to realize and believe that one cannot experience true fulfillment in life without embracing connection with God and in turn, growing in relationship with fellow creation as well as self. This is not judgment. It is truth. Without acknowledged continuing Divine partnership, human beings cannot fully develop.

In the summer of 1973, William Powell was preparing to be a high school senior. Rick and Maria Kriddick Powell, the father and mother of William, Cassie, Amy, Missy, Luke, Tom and Ed Powell, vacationed in Hull with their four sons and three daughters for a number of years, from the end of May until Labor Day or almost until Labor Day weekend, when they returned to the home the home in which they lived in a Boston neighborhood. Except for running into one another three or four times, decades ago, William and I have neither seen one another nor talked, since the summer of '73.

Now having been married for many years, William and Miah Witten Powell, the wife of William, are residing outside Massachusetts. Family of William and Miah Witten Powell includes their five children, who are by now, probably adults or nearing adulthood. I heard that William is now employed as a computer company vice-president.

One Sunday morning over twenty years ago, sometime between 1981 and 1985, I was living in Washington, D. C., and reading The Washington Post newspaper, Sunday edition, when I observed a wedding announcement in the newspaper. The wedding of William Patrick Powell and Miah Witten Powell had been posted in the Weddings section.

Viewing the announcement found me smiling softly. The wedding day of William and Miah Carol Witten was July third, one day before Independence Day. The wedding photograph pictured Mary Witten Powell attired in a wedding gown and wearing a wedding veil with a shoulder length—or longer—flowing train. She was gazing upward, internally emanating profound love, deep commitment, and acceptance of uncertainty. Viewing the picture found me being good and certain that the relationship of William and Miah Powell, which clearly began in Heaven, is also ending here.

Monday, June 16, 2008

This past weekend, I attended South Shore Arts Festival (SSAF), sponsored by the South Shore Arts Center, (SSAC). The fair happens annually on Father Day weekend. Now fifty-three years old, the event, held on Cohasset Commons, began Friday evening and ended early Sunday evening. Many

71

juried fine arts works, including paintings, sketches, and sculptures were displayed inside an enormous tent; some were able to be purchased.

Artworks hung upon panels placed inside the tent. Sculptures rested upon wooden podiums there. Both waited to be seen by arts lovers. Security personnel watched the art-work during daytime, evening, and overnight hours, while the South Shore Arts Festival event was ongoing.

Additional SSAF participants, who owned or rented small collapsible tents, assembled the tents. First, they secured tent poles four-square into the ground and then they covered the poles with tent tops. The sheltering tents were used as marketplaces that artisans created to display and sell hand-crafted jewelry, photographs, clothing, and home décor. South Shore Arts Center provided an additional erected large tent in which tables and chairs are placed, so that South Shore Arts Festival volunteer staff, who were equipped with art-making supplies, which include drawing paper, pencils, crayons, paints, paintbrushes, art bibs, and additional craft-making items, were able to work with children who visited for a short time inside the tent.

Sitting at tables covered with disposable plastic table cloths, children performed arts and crafts activities while being supervised by volunteer child care staff. Parents or child care givers visiting the fairgrounds were able to temporarily leave children with the volunteer staff while they meandered about festival grounds, interacted with artisans, vendors, or fellow fair goers, and were also able to purchase a variety of art, crafted goods, foods, and beverages. Thousands of fair goers visited the South Shore Arts Festival; the event continues, throughout Father Day weekend, unless forecasters from local television and radio stations predict serious weather advisories, or seriously inclement weather suddenly appears.

Musical groups performed throughout the weekend, offering festival goers a variety of musical selections, including rock and roll, country, blues, gospel, military, bluegrass, and jazz tunes. Each scheduled band performance was nearly one hour long. Festival goers who wished to view a concert or simply rest were allowed to sit in chairs facing tables situated in front of the festival band stage. Festival attendees purchased and enjoyed food which festival venders offered or they brought and ate homemade food. Additional concert goers sat on lounge chairs on the grass or stood aside trees.

By mid-morning today, tents and craft booths used during the South Shore Arts Festival were dismantled and removed. The band stand was deconstructed and withdrawn. Food trucks that had closed operations Sunday evening had moved on. Human activity on the Cohasset Common temporarily came to a near standstill. No visible proof of the previously ongoing festival remains. For an unspecified number of days after the event, many former festival goers, including me, when passing the Cohasset Commons, suddenly become teary-eyed; we are missing the South Shore Arts Festival.

Viewing professional art and craft work as well as hearing seasoned musicians perform stimulates human creative as well as transcendent senses. Being among thousands of people, including artists, sculptors, artisans, merchants, and fellow fair goers, even when one is not directly interacting with people can be curiously connecting and contenting. Eating healthy food and occasionally consuming food which is not especially healthy, is something people also generally enjoy doing.

Tonight, a restaurant was offering karaoke. Karaoke entertainment, featuring amateur as well as amateur professional singers, occurs there on Saturday evenings and it generally begins at 8:30 p.m. While facing a karaoke audience, karaoke performers sing music lyrics that audience members cannot see. Words are displayed on an elevated karaoke machine, which resembles a small to mid-sized television. Voices of karaoke singers can be aptly described as ranging between sublime and *whoa, hearing this is good and embarrassing.*

While sitting at the restaurant bar, I ordered a strawberry margarita sans alcohol; the beverage was poured into a chilled martini glass and then served. While I was waiting to sing and intermittently drinking the mocktail, I approached the karaoke director and handed him a song request. When the director later summoned me, I walked toward the hardwood platform, accepted the microphone he handed me, and then turned around and directly faced the quietly conversing audience. Confidently and nonchalantly, I said. "Yes, everyone, I admit that I have been sitting at the bar for a while drinking a strawberry margarita sans alcohol and I am now going to sing a really depressing love song, "How Do You Mend a Broken Heart?" What is wrong with this picture?"

Numbering nearly thirty people, the karaoke audience members laughed out loud, almost fully removing stage fright occurring within me and empowering me to sing. "How Do You Mend a Broken Heart?" Utilizing minor dance moves enabled me to later zestfully sing a second, final chosen song, "Dancing in the Street." Audience members who wished to dance then entered the hardwood dance floor. When I finished singing, I thanked the karaoke audience members as well as the karaoke director and then jokingly commented, "Mom probably thinks I am home alone, reading a book and doing laundry."

Wednesday, June 18, 2008

Dog Jura was nearly killed. Since last summer, Jura and I have been walking together nearly every day. Today, while we were walking upon sidewalk on Hull Street in Cohasset, Jura suddenly darted across the street; he wanted to interact with a barking Irish setter standing in the fenced-in front yard of a home.

"Jura, no!" I screamed, as I viewed a middle-aged man driving an eighteen-wheeler truck headed directly toward Jura as the driver attempted to stomp on the truck brake. Seeing Jura near death, I immediately closed both eyelids and then seconds later, opened them, as the eighteen-wheeler truck swerved from one side of the road to the other before it stopped moving. Looking toward me, Truck Driver displayed exhausted relief.

Somehow, he successfully avoided hitting nearby trees. Amazingly, he was not harmed. Jura was not struck. Truck Driver and I were viscerally shaken; we had witnessed the near sudden death of Jura. For timeless moments, I observed Truck Driver with gratitude, as well as bewilderment and sorrow.

Sitting and facing the steering wheel in the truck, he was visibly pale and speechless. "Am sorry," I said, contritely, while I looked toward him and remained standing on the edge of a sidewalk. Having acknowledged and accepted the confession, Truck Driver re-commenced driving. Having played with the Irish setter while Truck Driver and I non-verbally conversed, Jura returned to walking with me shortly thereafter.

Jura had been leashed before we began walking outside this morning. When he saw the barking Irish setter, he ran beyond me, defying leash restraint. Jura does not enjoy being confined by a leash. While we are walking, Jura often vigorously pulls the leash that was attached to his dog collar. Once, while we were running across beach sand, he pulled the leash so hard that I momentarily became airborne, before belly flopping.

Weighing seventy-five pounds, Jura occasionally sits down and will not move, when he wants to change the direction in which he is walking and I resist changing direction. Having observed Jura nearly being killed today, I decided that when Jura and I are walking together, we will be walking on wooded or concrete park trails where dog leash removal is generally safe. Otherwise, sadly, Jura and I will not be walking together.

This afternoon, five-year-old nephew Jamus, three-year-old niece Brynn, and two-year-old nephew Rylan and I played together; we frolicked in a saltwater heated pool located outside home in which the Reagan children live. Jamus and Brynn had arrived at home after school, after attending respective elementary and preschool classes in which they are enrolled at a private school. Brother Jared, sister-in-law Elissa, or a Reagan family employee performs weekday round-trip driving to and from the educational institution.

While they jumped into the pool, one following another, Jamus and Brynn laughed, screamed without fear, and sometimes requested that I catch them. Jamus was not wearing a life jacket; he swims almost as fast as a tadpole. While Jamus and Brynn recreated in pool waters, Rylan enjoyed hot tub relaxation.

When playtime in the pool ended, Rylan and Jamus were floating face up. Each had extended both arms horizontally; their eyes were closed. Brynn, also supine had stretched out both of her arms. Both feet of Brynn were facing both feet of Jamus and Rylan. Brynn was resting upon the partially saltwater pool waters with both eyes closed. Viewing the scene left me still, serene, and sensing peace on Earth.

Sunday, July 20, 2008

Having previously vacationed in New Hampshire, sister Valerie and her husband, Grant Watson, have arrived in Cohasset, accompanied by their children, Grace and Myla, respectively twelve-years-old, and ten-years-old, and nine-year-old Matthew.

All will remain here for one week. Grant will then fly back to Florida, allowing him to return to a working as a manager with a shipping company. Valerie and the children will return to Florida via van, after visiting a family who in recent times befriended the Watsons; the family lives in Maryland. The visit will be brief, as the first session of school in Florida public schools begins in early August.

Last Thursday brother Jared extended fishing trip invitations. He asked his son Jamus, daughter Brynn, sister Valerie, nieces Grace and Myla, nephew Matthew, and me if we wished to join him. All except Grace and Myla enthusiastically accepted. Derek Griffin, the property manager for

Jared and Elissa, who also owns and manages a construction company in Cohasset, joined us. Before we embarked on the fishing trip, Jared asked Derek to teach Jamus and Matt fishing techniques, allowing Jared to steer the boat and navigate ocean waters.

After boarding the Reagan family yacht, we were approximately thirty minutes beyond shore when Derek, Jamus, and Matthew began fishing. Fish weren't jumping. When Derek did catch one small fish, Matt and Jamus observed blood pouring out of its mouth, before the fish was thrown back into the water.

Five-year-old Jamus, whose facial coloring suddenly became as white as a sheet, decided right then and there that he was done with fishing. Meanwhile, three-year-old Brynn, who had previously begged Mummy and Daddy to allow her to join Jamus and Matthew as an equal fishing trip partner, now considered the fishing venture to be a bore. Sobbing, she clearly vocalized wanting to go home.

Near the end of the trip, when the yacht was moored near land, we hot and frustrated boat trip participants agreed to jump into the ocean, one at a time. Wearing a bathing suit underneath shorts and a shirt and also being intensely shy about being observed while solely wearing a bathing suit prompted me to quickly remove shorts and a shirt that I was wearing and then to jump beyond the boat. Instantly plummeting into the sea, into approximately fifty-eight-degree water and then surfacing seconds later, I said, "Whoa."

Derek jumped off next, wearing shorts and no shirt. He leisurely treaded ocean waters for several minutes, before he swam toward a ladder and then climbed into the boat. Moments later, Valerie performed a cannon ball jump into the water; I had aided her by jokingly pushing her off the backside of the boat, called the stern. Jared was not wearing swimming attire; he was donning dungarees. When he suddenly emerged beyond the yacht cabin area—dressed solely in boxer shorts—and then he speedily jumped off the stern, all present were cheerfully aghast.

Many years ago, Mom informed me that during a family vacation, Jared skied downhill for the first time when he was eight-years-old. Before he performed the ski run, Jared had accompanied Mom as both entered a large ski chair operated by a mechanical chairlift. The aerial apparatus consisted of continuously moving steel wire strung between two terminals which contained a number of cable-connected chairs that transported skiers toward the mountain summit, and then stopped briefly, as up to three skiers exited the chairlift and entered nearby designated ski trails. The lift subsequently reversed direction, and later re-entered the mountain base, where it retrieved additional skiers.

During the decades old family vacation, when eight-year-old Jared exited the ride, he immediately skied straight down one trail beginning on the summit of a mountain—alone. An avid skier might call the behavior *schuss booming*. Perhaps enjoying risky behavior influenced Jared when he was considering a stock market-related career.

A few days ago, during the boat trip, three-year-old Brynn jumped beyond the yacht and entered the sea, after Jared, her Dad. She was not afraid. Moments later, rising above sea water, reversing direction, and dog padding, she swam toward the boat and then re-entered it. Wearing cute goggles, five-year-old Jamus imitated Brynn, first jumping off the yacht and then utilizing similar confident swimming skills.

Nephew Matthew jumped overboard last and returned to the yacht shortly thereafter. Ending the outing, all of the fishing trip participants boarded the dingy moored aside the anchored yacht. Jared extended an arm around Matt to support him as Matt steered us toward shore.

Thursday, July 24, 2008

Three women were unofficially ordained Catholic priests; a woman was unofficially ordained a Catholic deacon. The ceremony was conducted inside a Protestant church in Boston, Massachusetts. One unofficially ordained priest said she has wanted to be a priest since she was five-years-old. Another informally ordained woman was formerly employed by the Catholic Archdiocese of Boston. The development is stunning.

This morning, I watched a news program host on a Boston television station interviewing two of the three recently unofficially ordained women as well as a woman who officially represented the Archdiocese of Boston; they discussed unofficial ordination.

Many years ago, someone I met said that there were women priests in the early Christian Church. A website titled, "A Brief History of Celibacy in the Catholic Church" includes information that indicates that this is true, although I do not understand why the website was given the headline that it was given.

In the fourth century in 325 A.D. a ruling body called Council of Laodicea, located in present day Turkey, decreed women are not to be ordained. The website indicates that this historical fact signifies that it is good and possible that before 325 A.D., women were ordained as priests. The webpage also indicates that in the fourteenth century Bishop Pelagio complained that women were still being ordained and hearing confessions.

What about allowing women and men to be what each truly believes he or she is called to be, in any profession, notwithstanding being male or female or notwithstanding whether a person wishes to be married or whether a person wants to raise children?

Sunday, July 27, 2008

Great nephew Zachariah Jenkins Sullivan was born inside Brigham and Women's Hospital this morning. Doctors and nurses assisted niece Kristin, mother of Zachariah, as he was delivered. Payden Sullivan, husband of Kristin was present and later admitted that when he was becoming a father for the first time, he experienced considerable uncertainty.

Monday, July 28, 2008

Tonight, hundreds of invited guests attended a fundraiser and subsequent reception presenting and honoring presidential candidate Barack Obama. Held inside a State Street office building in Boston, in two very large conference rooms, one that was comprised of two stories, the early evening event was a political rally as well as a birthday celebration. Seven hundred and fifty Obama campaign supporters were present.

Former Channel–4 Boston news anchor Liz Walker and Massachusetts Senator John Kerry hosted the event. Rousing speeches introducing Obama summarized genuine admiration and praise for the candidate. When most of the guests, including enthusiastic participants who were standing on the second story of the large conference room, began echoing support for Mr. Obama, a sudden frenzy and momentary near mass hysteria permeated the atmosphere.

Thankfully, common sense prevailed. Pandemonium was avoided. The gathering was not only a political rally and fundraiser. It was also a surprise birthday celebration; Mr. Obama will be forty-seven years old on Monday, August 4, 2008.

Upon entering a makeshift rally stage, standing aside a podium and anticipating speaking, Senator Obama was serenaded with a "Happy Birthday" chorus. Singer Harry Connick, Jr. and a daughter of Harry, Sarah Kate Connick, led the tribute. Audience members accompanied the performers, singing, clapping, and cheering. When the song ended, Senator Obama thanked invited guests and complimented Harry as well as Sarah Kate. He hugged Sarah Kate, gently and tenderly.

An Arlington, Massachusetts-based bakery owner and manager then presented candidate Obama with a large, donated, and decorated, and frosted birthday cake that she had made. Frosting on top of the cake included a replicated Obama campaign insignia. After thanking the bakery owner and blowing out the candles, Senator Obama opened two birthday presents, one after another. Withdrawing tissue paper from the first gift bag, Senator Obama pulled out and displayed a Red Sox baseball shirt.

Holding the bright, red–white–and–blue shirt displaying the Red Sox insignia, Mr. Obama exhibited gratitude, laughter, and sudden visible bodily discomfort. Humbly, he commented, "I do appreciate this, even though I am a White Sox fan." Many fundraiser guests laughed; more fundraising rally attendees noticeably booed. No laughter followed. Sudden tension among seven hundred and fifty fundraising guests became palpable.

Seconds later, Barack Obama removed tissue paper from the second gift bag, allowing him to pull out and present an official White Sox shirt. Goodwill prevailed. Rigidity was wondrously relieved. Relatively easily, the U.S. senator from Illinois segued into briefly discussing what he wishes to accomplish if he is elected President of the United States. Remarks Mr. Obama made included continuing the withdrawal of American troops stationed in Iraq, increasing American military presence in Afghanistan, and focusing directly on strengthening the economy of the country.

Mr. Obama indicated that he wants to implement specific economic measures; these included preventing foreclosures on homes and small businesses, addressing exploding college student loan costs, curtailing American dependence on foreign oil, and promoting alternative fuel sources. He said he also wants to offer Americans who are unable to afford health care insurance affordable insurance options and he wants to offer Americans who are presently enrolled in health care insurance plans new and improved health care options.

Having been campaigning for nearly two years, Senator Obama has given thousands of speeches. Words he spoke late this afternoon were genuine and informatively repetitive. At times, remarks he made were understandably robotic. Presidential candidate Obama comes across as not essentially being defined by political party, race, religion, marital status, economic standing, or related attributes. Barack Obama demonstrates an ability to offer thoughtful, cooperative, and consistent political leadership surrounding political issues that all Americans share.

Sunday, August 3, 2008

Boston Globe columnist, Kevin Cullen wrote an article about an Iraqi boy named Rakan Hassan. Today, the newspaper featured the published story. More than 200,000 *Boston Globe* readers were invited to peruse the tender, heart-wrenching column.

Rakan Hassan was situated in a car, with family, as the vehicle was being driven about Iraq, when U.S. soldiers mistakenly bombed the automobile. As the parents of Rakan lay near him dying, blood spilled upon Rakan. He was paralyzed, fully unable to move; he survived, as did his infant brother and his two teenage sisters.

U.S. soldiers stationed in Iraq brought Rakan into America. Hospitalized here for more than one year, Rakan recuperated, as doctors, nurses, and physical therapists continued to treat him. He was revered amongst hospital staff and fellow patients. During the time that he was hospitalized, Rakan befriended many people, including a son of *Globe columnist* Kevin Cullen.

The son of Mr. Cullen regularly visited Rakan. The young boy, who was around the same age as Rakan, would sometimes move Rakan about a hospital hallway, while Rakan was sitting in a wheelchair. When the two boys reached a nursing station, Rakan then arose from the wheelchair, using crutches. Standing in place, Rakan and the son of Kevin Cullen teased nurses posted at the nursing station, sometimes until Rakan, laughing boisterously, involuntarily released crutches he was using and fell down onto a hospital floor, while he continued to laugh.

While he was hospitalized, Rakan met one young girl; these two young people were reported as having been mutually fond of one another. When he had been recuperating for over one year, Rakan said he wanted to go home. Hospital doctors, nurses and fellow staff who were giving Rakan care discouraged him from leaving; the caregivers indicated full accident recovery involved receiving additional treatment.

Rakan was unmoved; he insisted that he wanted to return to Iraq. Eventually, hospital personnel relented. When he arrived home in Iraq, Rakan was re-united and living with a brother-in-law and family. Shortly thereafter, amid the continuing Iraq war, the home in which Rakan and family were living was bombed; all living there were killed.

Rakan was fourteen-years-old. This account depicts another example of life circumstances which uncover the inherent goodness and bravery of human beings and the devastating, tragic, and traumatizing consequences of war. Meanwhile, there is no substitute for a life exemplifying child-like innocence, kindness, and cooperation. None.

CHAPTER SEVEN

BIRTH, NIECES AND NEPHEWS, GRATITUDE, PRESIDENT OBAMA, SUMMER-LIKE WINTER WARMTH

Wednesday, August 5, 2008

As she and I conversed via telephone, niece Kristin Jenkins Sullivan said she and nearly one-month-old baby Zachariah are good and well. Kristin and husband Payden agreed that Kristin will not work outside the home until Zach and any additional children she and Payden welcome are attending kindergarten classes. An employee of a utility company subcontracting firm, Payden savors the challenge of working with utility team members in urban and suburban areas, installing, repairing, and replacing utility lines. Payden, Kristin, and Zach are now residing in Hull, a town which borders Cohasset and Hingham; all of the towns are seaside.

My sister, Lizzie Reagan Jenkins, a nurse and the mother of Kristin, coached Kristin through baby delivery; Liz has advised Kristin that engaging in regular purposeful pursuits, including outdoor activities, prevents post-partum "blues" symptoms from developing after birth. Kristin said she has found the advice useful; she and Payden are realizing that first-time parents regularly become fatigued, as they experience suddenly occurring and rapidly increasing childcare and parenting responsibilities.

Via telephone, Liz recently informed me her daughter-in-law, Liane, is pregnant. Nephew Jonas Jenkins and Liane Jenkins, the wife of Jonas, are enjoying city living. They reside in New York City, near Central Park. Jonas works at a nearby company, serving as a financial adviser. About to become a grandmother for a second time, Liz said she wants to be called Mimi, a name which is synonymous with Grandmother.

Friday, August 6, 2008

Kristin introduced me and great nephew Zachariah Jenkins Sullivan. Enjoyable was holding Zach, sharing lunch with her, and watching her giving him care. Kristin savors motherhood.

Saturday, August 7, 2008

Today I visited nephews Jamus and Rylan, niece Brynn, Brother Jared, sister-in-law Elissa, and Reagan family invited guests—Mark O'Donovan, who befriended Jared when Jared and Mark were in elementary school, and Reena O'Donovan, the wife of Mark, and also a longtime friend of Jared. Addressing Reena and me, Elissa said, "Do you know what Brynn said, the other day?" Suspenseful, Reena and I said, "No, what?" Elissa replied that three-year-old, Brynn dramatically commented, "Mummy, I don't like having brothers. I wish Jamus and Rylan would both die and I would be the only one." Elissa, Reena and I erupted, chuckling boisterously.

This sunny afternoon, Brynn, Jamus, Rylan, and I played in yard overlooking Cohasset Harbor, outside the home where the children now live. Being unable to climb a heavy-duty plastic circular slide situated there, as Jamus can, Brynn became frustrated and then upset; she began crying. Consoling her, I reassured her that sisters who cannot do something brothers can do are not inferior. Brynn was unconvinced.

When seeing tears falling down her face, I perceived another maneuver; I thought perhaps Brynn could climb the slide if she removed the sox and shoes she was wearing. After removing her sox and shoes, with assistance from me, Brynn walked up the slide. This time she reached the slide apex, directly across from the stairs leading to the slide. Cheerfully and joyously Brynn announced, "Merrie, I made it."

As Brynn was descending the stairs, we congratulated one another, mutually touching our right hand forefingers. The touching gesture found me recalling the 1982 movie, *ET*. Meaning extra-terrestrial, the film depicted interaction between humans and aliens. Love developed between a young boy and an alien ET, who was pure, kind, and gentle. At one point, ET and the young boy mutually touched forefingers, exemplifying reciprocal lasting, love, respect, and acceptance.

Soon Jared, Elissa, Jamus, Brynn and Rylan will be Boston residents. Jared and Elissa purchased a condominium located in Boston, as Jamus, who is now nearly six-years-old and Brynn, who will be four-years-old in

October, were consistently overtired after commuting nearly two hours during every school day to an international private school they are currently attending. Round trip driving time to the school will be significantly lessened, as the elementary school the children attend is located fifteen minutes from the condominium address.

Elissa will also be able to enjoy significantly shortened commuting time; she is currently teaching a Shakespearean play acting class at a university extension school in Cambridge, Massachusetts. Jared, self-employed as an investment business owner, will be near Logan Airport, when business travel is necessary. Jared recently asked me if I am interested in giving dog Jura weekday overnight care, while Jared, Elissa, and Reagan children are residing in Boston during weekdays. I agreed to return Jura to the Reagan family on weekends, when they are in Cohasset. Quietly considering Jura and I living together has found me experiencing enthusiasm as well as uncertainty.

Saturday, August 23, 2008

On this brilliantly sunny morning, while Jura and I were walking about Cohasset environs and strolling near Atlantic Avenue shoreline, I spotted Derek Griffin, the property manager who works with Jared and Elissa. He was driving a mid-sized truck. Dayea Valencia, a Reagan family housekeeper and babysitter, was sitting on the passenger side of the front seat and holding two-year-old Rylan Entering the side of the road, Derek slowly and steadily stopped the truck, aside Jura and me.

Smiling and rolling down the right-side window in the front seat of the truck, Dayea raised Rylan toward me and greeted me. He was holding a naked Barbie doll in one hand; he does this regularly. Sometimes Rylan holds two naked Barbie dolls, one is in each hand. Derek suddenly said, "I think I'm going to buy him a GI Joe doll soon." Dayea and I burst into laughter.

As Ms. Valencia lifted and passed Rylan to me, he grasped me firmly and gently around the neck, using both arms. Holding him for several minutes before returning him to Dayea was delightful. Two-year-old Rylan is joyful, good-humored, and thoughtful. He regularly expresses gratitude, saying "Thank you."

Wednesday, August 27, 2008

This morning found me visiting a former student, named Brain Halloran. Brian and I worked together for six weeks, while he was a student at special education school and I was on a winter break from college and was a volunteer teacher aide for one month in the classroom in which he was enrolled. When he and I worked together, Brian was around seventeen years old.

Brian is now fifty-years-old. A U.S. postal service employee, he has worked for nearly twenty years at the Boston, Massachusetts U.S. post office as a mail clerk. Thinking of someone working anywhere for twenty consecutive years leaves me bewildered, as I have not ever worked anywhere for two decades. The positive attitude Brian has exuded throughout the years, while facing lifelong challenges, has endeared him to many, including me.

While driving and then nearing the summer cottage of the Halloran family in Hull, Massachusetts, I viewed Brian, Eileen, the mother of Brian, and a young woman that I did not recognize. All were stationed on the front porch of a single-story cottage. Eileen was comfortably seated on a wooden Adirondack chair; Brian and the woman I did not yet know were standing aside a wooden front porch railing.

After Jura and I exited the car, I ascended cottage front stairs, entered the porch, and greeted Brian and Eileen. Brian introduced me and Gail Cafaro; Gail and I shook respective right and left hands. Visiting Brian, Eileen, and Gail was rejuvenating, as Brian discussed developing friendship between him and Gail. The visit was also saddening. Eileen informed me that Frank Halloran, her husband, died two years ago. Having been together for many years, Eileen and Frank Halloran evidenced a loving relationship. Brian remains single and is living with Eileen. Paula and Patrick Halloran, respective elder sister and brother of Brian, are married. Both are living near Boston, Massachusetts.

Dog Jura was delighted, as he explored outdoor environs of the summer cottage and later gave and received human attention. When returning home with Jura after visiting with Brian, Gail, and Eileen, I was profoundly content, while driving serenely and leisurely along seaside roads. Eileen and Brian Halloran are beautiful, gentle people, who have confronted and overcome challenges I will not ever face. Inner peace that Brian and Eileen exude, borne from accepting, addressing, and moving beyond joy and suffering entered me quietly, gently, and deeply, this day.

Tuesday, September 16, 2008

Now six-years-old dog Jura has been remaining overnight with me from Sunday afternoon through Friday afternoon. The dog bed on which he sleeps in the living room is the love seat couch there, covered with a blanket. Initially, I wondered if giving Jura overnight care for five days a week is personally workable.

Having left the home in which I grew up many years ago, I have not lived with another person or an animal since then. Feelings of anxiety that surfaced within me from time to time vanished, the morning after Jura remained with me overnight for the first time. Jura is wonderful company. When near him, I am free in an inexplicable and unrepeatable manner.

Jared asked me to watch Jura this past weekend. When I awoke Saturday morning and looked outside the bedroom window, I viewed steadily falling heavy rain, which had been forecasted. One hour later, as Jura and I walked together on Beach Street near Atlantic Avenue, rain was ceasing. Sun suddenly burst forth, from behind the clouds. Air temperatures rose, reaching a high of sixty degrees.

Shortly after we entered Sandy Beach, I removed shorts and a shirt covering a tank-suit I was wearing and then removed socks and sneakers on my feet, before setting the removed items upon dry rocks, near the ocean. I walked beside Jura, as we entered refreshing Atlantic Ocean waters; the water temperature was warm, approximately sixty-four degrees.

As Jura waded beside me, I spotted a dog accompanying a couple. The couple and the canine were standing on beach sand, as they played ball. The dog was retrieving a ball that each of the two people was repeatedly throwing into the ocean. The canine brought it back to the couple. The man and woman and I began cordially conversing, from a distance. Moments later, coming out of the ocean and stepping onto shore allowed me to continue conversing with the couple, while walking toward and then joining them. Minutes later, I called Jura; he was eating a large dead fish. Jura had previously been prancing upon beach sand, while he proudly paraded the deceased amphibian.

After leaving the expired fish, Jura ambled closely toward the couple and me. He humbly greeted the couple and then gingerly sniffed outside and inside the near hip-level pockets of pants that each of the new acquaintances was wearing. Yes, Jura was seeking dog treats. Scientific research indicates that Labrador retrievers are genetically prone to food obsession and obesity.

A few moments later, the dog of the couple was eager to share the activity of chasing and retrieving a ball with Jura; Jura enthusiastically accepted. All at once, while the two dogs were playing, Jura began regurgitating the expired fish he had been eating. When he finished doing so, he commenced re-ingesting the moribund fish. Witnessing the occurrence, I was aghast and embarrassed. Scurrying to the scene, I enfolded the dead fish remains into sand, put the garbage into a small plastic bag, knotted the bag, and then discarded it in a nearby trash bin.

Thursday, October 9, 2008

Gas prices, having reached four dollars and twenty cents per gallon during the summer months, have been steadily falling since then. Locally, one gallon of gas now costs three dollars and nine cents. Southeastern parts of the United States continue to battle high gasoline costs. Media reports indicate that Nashville, Tennessee gas price signs are showing one gallon of gas as costing three dollars and eighty cents. Declining gas prices are naturally welcome; such prices also raise curiosity.

Driving past a local station, posting a price of three dollars and nine cents per gallon of regular gas, I suddenly veered left, enabling me to enter a side street beyond the gas station.

Then I turned left again, entered the station, and stopped beside one of the pumps. After a station attendant filled the gas tank of the car, the nearby pump displayed a price of thirty-four dollars and sixty-seven cents. A little over seven days ago, filling the tank at the same gas station cost nearly forty-eight dollars. A local newspaper reporter, who was touring the gas station and soliciting comments and opinions regarding fluctuating gas prices amid the current economic recession, approached and then questioned me.

"Saving almost fourteen dollars in gasoline charges is exciting, and encouraging," I responded casually. Being asked if I believe the recession is near ending found me expressing reasonable doubt. "An economic recession which formally began nine months ago that has resulted in abnormal job losses, home foreclosures, and noticeably fluctuating food and gas prices is probably not ending any time soon. Meanwhile, economic recessions allow people to rediscover essential living practices," I advised the competent reporter.

"When shopping these days, if I forget to buy one or more items, I wait for a week before shopping again and then buying forgotten items, versus returning to the grocery store in the next day or two to purchase forgotten items, as I have previously done. Personal dining out, movie going, and vacationing are now rare occurrences. Meanwhile, facing economic challenges is teaching me how to effectively limit spending, how to use personal imagination related with cooking, and how to enjoy both of these challenges," I commented quietly.

Continuing, I said, "Regularly making meals at home enhances the experience of occasionally eating out. Homemade food nutrition often equals and sometimes exceeds restaurant or fast-food nourishment. I have become aware of types of fruits and vegetables of which I was formerly unaware, since beginning to purchase produce with reduced prices. For example, I have bought mango fruit, which is delicious," I said.

"Is the recession discouraging?" the reporter asked me. "It is what it is. People everywhere, everyday choose to face and move beyond challenges or to allow difficulties to be defeating," I responded. As the impromptu interview was ending, the newspaper reporter indicated she appreciated comments she received from me. She also said she observes me as being someone who really enjoys conversation which left me delighted, contented and slightly abashed.

Sunday, October 19, 2008

Sister Valerie sent me an email indicating thirteen-year-old Grace is now a lead singer in a high school rock band that she and fellow high school students formed. Eleven-year-old Myla has been cast as Dorothy in a local Wizard of Oz musical production and nine-year-old Matthew is continuing to play baseball. She also wrote that the Watson family puppy Sasha sits, rolls over and is, well… not housebroken, yet.

Through word of mouth, Jura and I discovered an entrance to Wompatuck State Park in Cohasset. Curiously, though having lived in Cohasset for over fifty years, I did not realize the Cohasset entrance existed. Hingham and Norwell, two towns neighboring Cohasset, also offer entrances to the park. Before discovering the woodlands, Jura and I had tiffs nearly every day, as Jura prefers not to be leashed. Having often been unleashed while we were walking outdoors, Jura temporarily disappeared from view or entered a street several times a day, while he and I were strolling about Cohasset, Hingham, Hull, or Scituate environs.

Before realizing the Cohasset entrance of Wompatuck exists, I had been questioning whether I can continue giving Jura care. Regularly viewing Jura unexpectedly running, chasing squirrels, dogs, or cats, and while doing so, entering a street with oncoming traffic, had become unbearable. Regularly discovering that Jura was missing after realizing I had become distracted while he and I were walking together had also become unacceptable. Having discovered the Cohasset entrance to Wompatuck State Park, I am now generally confident that I can continue to give Jura good care.

The main entrance of Wompatuck State Park is in Hingham. Park lands cover three-thousand-five hundred and twenty-six acres and offer numerous wooded or paved trails. Without worry or monetary charge, cars can be left safely inside the park parking lot. Park management permits walking, running, or bicycling in the park on paved or wooded trails, during summer, spring, and fall months as well as cross country skiing, mountain biking, snowmobiling, or snow shoeing, on snow-covered winter days.

Walking and running in the park during winter months is also possible, unless sufficient snowfall delays plowing of the paved trails. Wompatuck State Park regulations permit walking with unleashed dogs. Dogs can wade or swim in water bodies within the park, until consistent thirty-two degrees and below freezing temperatures solidify the reservoirs.

Driving home last night, near 10:00 p.m., I viewed a beautiful handsome deer. Handsome Deer was crossing the street on which I was driving. Walking directly in front of and beyond me, he or she entered adjacent woods. The scene rendered me wondering, is Handsome Deer up late? Suburban residents generally refer to being outside or continuing to socialize near or after ten o'clock p.m. on Monday through Thursday nights or Sunday nights, as being out late.

If I was living in Boston or Cambridge, Massachusetts, I might not be driving a car, because public transportation is readily available in cities as well as large towns. Ten o'clock p.m. or near ten o'clock p.m.is the time when Boston or Cambridge nightlife is often beginning. By ten o'clock p.m., lights in suburban homes and businesses are generally out, excepting those in restaurants, small night clubs, convenience stores, and movie theatres. —Hmm, maybe city and suburban living, although not the same living experience, are not essentially dissimilar.

Monday, October 20, 2008

Wanting to work again, I do not desire to work more than thirty hours weekly. I also do not want to begin working until late morning. Giving Jura care finds me treasuring morning, afternoon, and evening walks as well as car rides we share. Working thirty hours a week would allow me to balance professional as well as personal life.

Tuesday, October 21, 2008

Personally beloved Bible passages follow.

Old Testament Isaiah 55:10-11
For just as from heaven, rain and snow come down,
Not returning until earth is watered, leaving it fertile, fruitful,
Giving one who sows, seed, giving one who eats, bread,
So shall be word going forth from me,
This shall not return void.

Old Testament Isaiah 45:3
Thus says God,
You will be given treasures, bursting through darkness,
Riches that have been hidden away,
You will see I am Lord, God
calling you and naming you.

Old Testament Isaiah 43: (1-2, 4, 18-19)
Now says the Lord, who created and formed you,
Fear not, for I have called you in name, you are mine.
When you pass through water, I will be with you, in rivers you shall not drown.
When you walk through fire you shall not be burned, flames will not consume you.
Because you are precious, because I love you,
Remember not events past; things long ago, consider not,
See I am doing something new.
Now it springs forth, do you perceive this?

Whether one reads Bible stories and passages often, seldom or not at all, there is inspiration, teaching, and wisdom in holy books that is precious, timeless and unique.

Wednesday, November 5, 2008

A few moments before 11:00 p.m., last night, Illinois Senator Barack Obama was elected the President of the United States. He defeated the nominee of the opposing party, John McCain, who spoke shortly after media outlets announced the results of the election. Senator McCain gave a grace filled concession speech, and while doing so, he humbly acknowledged and respected newly elected President Barack Obama.

President-elect Obama delivered a brief, genuine and low-key acceptance speech. The incoming U.S. President exuded contentment, gratitude, and humility. Words he spoke and facial expressions he displayed indicated that he is also experiencing profound loss. Awareness of the senses is heightened, after undergoing any triumphant or tragic event.

While making the acceptance speech, Mr. Obama stated he intends to fulfill election promises he made. Obama family daughters, Malia, ten-years-old, and Sasha, seven-years-old, were included in the campaign covenants. President-elect Obama said Malia and Sasha will be able to help Mom and Dad find and raise a new puppy. He stated that Malia and Sasha suffered bravely during the past two years, while he was on the road, campaigning. As he was near daily traveling to multiple locations and speaking events, he was rarely able to return home.

Thursday, November 27, 2008

Jura and I remained home today, Thanksgiving Day. Jura is now permanently living with me. Having observed me as growing in love with Jura, being good and compatible with Jura, and being able to give him full-time care, Jared, Elissa, and family recently surrendered Jura to me, allowing me to officially adopt him.

Generally, I find being unaccompanied during holidays manageable. Being social does not mean that one is not alone. Being solitary does not mean one is alone. Experiencing solitude allows a person to quietly connect with God, people, places, and things in an essentially spiritual manner.

Socializing also enables a person to connect with God, through physical interaction with people, places, and things. As does social interaction, solitude naturally and regularly becomes internally challenging. The activities of prayer, hearing music, cooking, reading, and interacting with Jura have allowed me to move through difficult moments that have occurred today.

Prayer in the form of silent or verbal conversation with God brings acceptance, hope, and contentment each and every day.

Jura and I went walking in the woods for three hours this morning. After we came home, I decided to prepare and then bake some casseroles and quick bread, while playing and listening to music CDs as well as radio music. This afternoon, I prepared roasted red pepper hummus spread and green bean casserole. Tasting the hummus spread was a satisfactory experience.

The baked green bean casserole, made with cream of mushroom soup, milk, crispy fried onions and green beans was, well, one sloppy mess, when it had been baked. Ingredients in the casserole did not congeal; the finished product bore virtually no resemblance to the green bean casseroles that Mom used to make. I believe I accurately followed the green bean casserole recipe directions listed on the back of the can containing the green beans. Perhaps this asserted belief is really denial.

This evening found me watching and appreciating two television magazine stories being aired for the first-time today. The first story featured a young boy whose left leg was amputated when he was nearly two-years-old, due to illness or an accident. As the leg was severed directly below the waist, prosthetics was not a treatment option. Utilizing one leg, the remarkable boy, who is now probably eight or nine-years-old and attending elementary school, plays three sports.

The second television magazine segment featured a construction worker and his companion, a duck. Duck sits aside Construction Worker while the two friends are in a truck and headed toward and leaving job sites. Duck rests on top of the truck roof while the duck owner is working. The owner of Duck is a former duck hunter.

No animal is ever going to know how to send a man or woman to the moon. In the meantime, animals are evolved far beyond humans in numerous ways. Animals can and do give humans instruction in near boundless life and love lessons, including the value of humility, the wisdom of accepting uncertainty, and the wonderment of discovering every moment of life as being precious, purposeful, and promising.

Sunday, December 1, 2008

Brother Jared and Reagan children, Jamus, Rylan, and Brynn visited Jura and me at home today, during mid-morning. Jamus and Brynn assisted me as one after another, each using a push-button flame thrower, ignited balled-up newspaper, which had been stashed between three stacked wood logs in the fireplace. Jamus, Brynn, Rylan, and I then sat near one another on the living room love-seat couch.

Drawing a throw toward us, we set the warming mini-blanket down, at waist level. The temperature regularly displayed on the apartment thermostat is fifty-eight degrees. Brynn, Jamus, and Rylan alternately turned the pages of *Maisy's Snowy Christmas,* as I read the book by Lucy Cousins aloud. Jared, sitting a few feet from us in an upholstered chair and listening, was shown book illustrations. Sitting aside Jamus, Brynn, and Rylan while I was reading them a Christmas story was pure delight.

Saturday, December 20, 2008

Entering a mall in Hanover, Massachusetts I sought to do some Christmas shopping. Retail stores are barely busy this Christmas season, as in years past. News reports say unemployment is reaching a level not seen, in the past thirty-three years.

Thursday, December 25, 2008

Christmas Day. Jura and I went walking through Wompatuck State Park after accessing the Cohasset entrance to the park. Fortunately, when snow falls in the park, at some point, snowmobile riders drive over some snow-covered paved and wooded trails, making the flattened trails clearly visible and relatively easy to navigate on foot. A buck, crossing the trail on which Jura and I were walking faced us. In fleeting moments after this, Buck began sauntering and then fled. Buck did not come near me or Jura, who was standing near the wondrous animal.

When I returned home, I removed a glass casserole dish from the refrigerator and put the dish—containing prepared vegetarian lasagna—into the oven. Then I put split pea soup ingredients, including water, vegetable bouillon, split peas, carrots, small portabella mushrooms, onions, and garlic into a stock pot, placed the pot on top of a kitchen stove burner, and turned the corresponding knob on the stove to medium-high heat. Family members will soon receive three banana breads that I made today.

The flat screen TV in the apartment was operating while I was performing casserole preparations, making breads, and waiting for these to be fully cooked. When wishing to recall programs that were being aired this afternoon, I become hazy. Research studies of television viewers indicate that people who are not partnered watch above average amounts of television. As I am single and do not regularly watch TV, I do not agree with these research results. I do believe that from time to time, watching stimulating television programs offers people who are not partnered and people who are partnered a means of engaging in simulated relationships.

Late this afternoon, when Jura and I were seated in the eggplant colored mini-SUV that I drive, I was traveling on Atlantic Avenue in Cohasset, on the right side of the road, and while doing so, driving on Cunningham Bridge, which is set above Little Harbor. Atlantic Ocean waters flow horizontally below the bridge. Suddenly turning my head and shoulders leftward, I observed the sun, as it was beginning to set. Today the sun appeared to be very large and round. Sun displayed varying orange and yellow shades, as it began to fade below the horizon, mesmerizing me. Luckily, I was only momentarily turned toward the sight, as when I again faced forward, I realized the car had drifted slightly onto the left side of Atlantic Avenue; cars were moving forward—toward me—and were close to crashing into the mini-SUV.

Entering Sandy Beach parking lot prompted me to pray before stepping outside. This late afternoon, the weather temperature was approximately thirty degrees; strong winds accompanied cold air. When I opened the mini-SUV right back door, Jura hastily exited the car, joyfully entered the parking lot, and then galloped upon beach sand, as he headed toward ocean waters. After splashing into sea water, he began dog paddling, or using all four paws to push against water, enabling him to move forward. After he emerged from ocean waters, he sauntered toward a woman walking aside two Siberian Husky dogs. As she and I exchanged greetings from afar, Danielle indicated she owns the thick-furred, wolf-like, athletic, and intelligent dogs.

As we walked toward and then stood beside one another, we continued conversing. Danielle said she had recently temporarily relocated to Cohasset, as her mother is seriously ill and family members are sharing the responsibilities of supportive care. A certified nurse, Danielle also sought and found temporary employment at a nearby hospital. Danielle demonstrated ease, acceptance, and optimism, as she discussed the advanced Cancer diagnosis that Mum was recently presented.

While Danielle and I were conversing, warm flowing air had suddenly appeared; she and I noticed the appearance of summer-like weather temperatures, although brisk winter winds, accompanying temperatures registering around thirty-three degrees Fahrenheit had not changed. Unexpectedly, I recalled attending college and viewing an illustrated poster appearing on a bulletin board. A message on the poster quoted philosopher Albert Camus, who wrote, "In the midst of winter, I found within me an invincible summer."

Remembering the occurrence brought me serenity, humility, and quiet amusement. When I initially observed the poster, decades ago, I was experiencing a different mindset. When I read the words, "In the midst of winter, I found within me an invincible summer," for the first time, I silently and arrogantly thought, *What stupid words; what the heck does this mean?"*

2009

CHAPTER EIGHT

CASTING CALL, INAUGURAL BALL,
LIFE FLASHES, DANCING

Thursday, January 1, 2009

After awakening this morning, I groggily entered the living room and activated the television set remote. I viewed a TV weatherman airing a report; temperatures are forecasted to register in the teens and there will be wind gusts measuring around fifty miles per hour, he indicated. The report left me wondering if I am really living in Minnesota.

While Jura and I were walking outdoors this morning, he was clearly delighted, as he wondrously romped about in snow that had fallen overnight. Later, supine, he rolled in near-frozen snow, all the while pointing all four paws toward the sky. Jura is childlike. Jura is kind. Clearly not wanting to do this, he agreed to return inside the apartment, after walking about the town common for about ten to fifteen minutes during morning, afternoon, and evening hours today.

In the neighboring town of Hingham, Hingham Community Center (HCC) is the setting for Hingham *Cabaret* auditions. Singing tryouts are generally held annually inside the center on New Year day, January 1, beginning at 2:00 p.m. Dance auditions follow, for several days, after the singing tryouts have been completed. Forty-seven-years-old, the Hingham *Cabaret* production presents an opportunity to raise funds for Hingham Community Center educational programs. In recent years, a small group of *Cabaret* cast members has begun directing, choreographing, and producing the two-hour-long singing, dancing, and comedy show. A production company formerly managed the extravaganza.

Incorporating nearly one hundred cast members, *Cabaret* show practices are held on weeknights for four weeks before the show runs on Wednesday through Saturday evenings during the last week in January, Hingham Armory, with its large six-hundred-and-fifty-person seating capacity, is where the *Cabaret* performance happens. One week before the show opens, *Cabaret* crew members convert the Armory auditorium into a theatre, setting up lighting, stage sets, and props in addition to making temporary male and female dressing rooms. Beverage and snack stands are also placed near doors opening into the performance space.

During the week of the show, show goers can attend the Wednesday night dress rehearsal and purchase reduced price tickets. Many seniors attend the Thursday evening show, which begins at 7:00 p.m. *Cabaret* Friday and Saturday evening shows start at 8:00 p.m. Doors open sixty minutes before the performance begins. A number of show goers bring dinners or snacks and beverages; these are set upon folding tables which have been covered with tablecloths, each one seating twelve people. Some show guests, who bring battery-operated candles or standing candelabras, place these upon a table. Fire regulations prohibit live candles in the building.

Some show watchers bring balloons and tape them to the ends of tables. Individual raffle tickets and packets of the tickets offering a vacation trip—three days and two nights to destinations such as Las Vegas, Nevada, an entertainment hot spot in the western part of the United States—are sold during show intermissions. Raffle winners are announced on Saturday evening, during the intermission of the final show. Running four consecutive nights, Hingham *Cabaret* features professional, semi-professional, and amateur singers, musicians, dancers, and comedians, who volunteer to prepare for and promote the show.

This New Year Day, nearly thirty singers signed up to audition for the show. Audition spectators seated in a meeting room of the community center amounted to about fifty. Observing vocalists, musicians, and comedians displaying individual and group talents was stunning, exciting, and uplifting. Show stopping professional singer and *Cabaret* show veteran, Laurie Gilson Battiglia, was among soloists who performed today. Laurie and Brian Battiglia, the husband of Laurie and a physician, are former clients with whom I worked, when I operated and managed a small business for ten years.

This afternoon, Hingham *Cabaret* singing audition entries included rock and roll, country, gospel, and barbershop song selections. A semi-professional singer, nicknamed RP, role played renowned vocalist Tina Turner, singing the 1969 hit tune that the Creedence Clearwater Revival band originated and performed, named "Proud Mary". Provocatively attired, RP wore a Tina Turner-style dress. She was also wearing stiletto high heels and a Tina Turner-style wig, with spiked hair. Petite, dramatic, and feisty RP is talented and humorous. She brought the house down, as she professionally performed the feisty, fast-paced, and rambunctious act.

When asked to perform, I rose from a foldable chair and walked toward the front of the audition room. Suddenly I was almost unable to move, feeling as though I was walking with heavy lead weights instead of legs. No rational reason supported what I was sensing; I had rehearsed singing the "Beauty and the Beast" tune nearly forty times.

I remembered someone many years ago saying that fear is an acronym for False Evidence Appearing to be Real. Somehow moving to the front of the room and then facing the audition audience, I announced that I had chosen the theme song from the 1991 Disney movie production, *Beauty and the Beast*. Then I confessed that dog Jura, who had been lying down, raised his head and looked at me while I was singing, and then almost immediately, he lowered his head and fell asleep. I was hoping the admission would help me build rapport with the audience and relieve stage fright I was feeling. This happened.

While singing, I forgot one line of "Beauty and the Beast" lyrics. Mysteriously, I continued performing. When the audition was completed, I curtseyed and expressed audience appreciation. Receiving rousing applause was humbling and uplifting. This first singing audition experience was gratifying. Sadly, I did not make the cut; I was not among the chosen 2009 Hingham *Cabaret* show soloists.

Friday January 16, 2009

Air temperatures continue to register in the teens during daytime hours and then fall into single digits during nighttime hours. Temperatures in Midwestern America have been dropping to and below minus fifty degrees, according to weather reports. Not repeatedly viewing televised weather reports detailing frigid New England weather has enabled me to calmly venture outdoors and to walk with Jura. Recently, Cohasset postal service mail deliverer, Lanie Franklin, has been spotted wearing a Santa Claus hat, while she is delivering mail.

Wednesday, January 21, 2009

Today I viewed President Obama, as he was inaugurated; he officially became the forty-fourth president of the United States. Supreme Court Justice, John Roberts, officiated the proceeding, which was set upon a temporary outdoor stage, in front of the U.S. Capitol building.

While Justice Roberts recited, and President Obama repeated the presidential oath of office, Mrs. Michelle Obama, seven-year-old Sasha Obama and ten-year-old Malia Obama stood beside the president. Vice-President Joe Biden, former political campaign partner of Barack Obama, who also represented the state of Delaware as a United States senator for over three decades, was also sworn into office today.

Dignitaries seated behind the Obama family were among more than one million people attending the inaugural festivities; Washington Mall was fully opened for the first time during an inauguration, allowing hundreds of thousands of spectators to be present during the event. Ten of the presidential inaugural balls that were held this evening were televised.

Around 8:15 p.m., while sitting upon the living room couch, I retrieved a remote control device. After powering the television set, which rests upon a small stand, I pressed one channel number indicator on the remote and unexpectedly selected the channel on which the inaugural neighborhood ball was being televised. As hundreds of inaugural ball guests surrounded them, President Barack Obama and Michelle Obama, the wife of Barack, danced the first dance as President and First Lady, while vocalist Beyoncé (Beyoncé Giselle Knowles) crooned the famous rhythm and blues song made famous in the 1960s by singer Etta James, called "At Last." Sultry, romantic, and intimate music lyrics surrounded gentle smiles and soft embraces that the President and the First Lady exchanged. Neither the ball gown that First Lady Michelle Obama was wearing nor the tuxedo that President Obama was wearing this evening appeared to be exceedingly high-fashion garments. Subtle attire that Michelle as well as Barack wore highlighted the ordinary, respectful, wondrous and uncertain relationship the new First Couple shares.

Later, during another televised inaugural ball, President Obama was videoed while he was standing next to someone outside one of the ballrooms; he was conversing with ABC television network news reporter, Robin Roberts. Observing the manner in which Ms. Roberts and Mr. Obama were talking prompted me to wonder if they are developing a newly discovered friendship. Composed, outgoing, and good humored, Robin Roberts has worked in the television broadcast television business for nearly twenty years. She was an ESPN television network sportscaster from 1990 to 2005. Since 2005, Robin has been an ABC television network news reporter. Exuding joy, grace, and dignity she embraces single life.

Tuesday, February 17, 2009

Today found me thinking especially about Patsy, a Labrador retriever dog that Mom and Dad rescued and adopted, who lived for seventeen years. When I was about thirty-five years old and had returned to the home in which I grew up, after residing in Washington, D.C. for five years, in the early 1980s, I asked Mom and Dad if I could live at home for a while; they graciously accepted me.

Almost daily, twelve-year-old Patsy jogged near me. She and I generally ran together during daylight hours; sometimes we jogged together in the dark of night. One evening, while we were running, Patsy darted beyond me and entered the middle of a road; cars were coming toward us. A driver, not seeing Patsy in the darkness, hit her. The driver stopped, emerged from the vehicle, and apologized. Patsy was seriously injured.

Miraculously she survived. Embracing life, Patsy lived five years beyond the tragedy. As is Jura, Patsy was good and joyful. She enjoyed people as well as fellow dogs. She loved walking and swimming. She enjoyed car rides. At night, sometimes, Patsy slithered down to the foot of the bed in which I slept; following lying down, she fell asleep in an embryonic position.

Virtually every morning, Patsy cheerfully greeted a new day with gentility, humility, and acceptance. During the final two years that she was alive, Patsy bravely battled a canine illness called Cushing Disease. The congenital disease eventually leaves a dog fully or near fully immobile.

Two days before she died, she suddenly closed her mouth and would not open it. Patsy was unwilling to eat.

Experiencing denial, I thought "this circumstance will not last." The last Friday night she was alive, Patsy was lying near me, on an area rug set on top of living room carpet. I hoped that when Monday arrived, Patsy would be fully recovered.

On Saturday morning, I realized denying that Patsy was gravely ill, was selfish, although understandable. Thinking about the possibility of losing self-control and crying uncontrollably when Patsy died and not wanting to do so, I was intensely uncertain. I brought Patsy into Hingham Animal Clinic, where she had been examined and treated for many years. Veterinarian Dr. Charles Simmons confirmed that Patsy was gravely ill; he stated that when an animal no longer wants to eat and consequently firmly closes its mouth and will not open it, the circumstance is not temporary; the animal is dying.

A wool blanket was set atop a stainless-steel veterinary examining table; Patsy was placed here. Moments from death, seventeen-year-old Patsy looked up toward me; she exuded profound love, gratitude, and humility. Looking upon her and becoming tearful, I whispered, "We love you Patsy," as tears filled my eyes. Dr. Simmons administered a euthanizing shot; Patsy succumbed instantly.

Bewildering self-composure outweighed sadness I was experiencing, when I left the veterinary office. Profound inner peace confirming truth arose within me. Patsy is now truly Home. All creation, regardless of form, longs to experience eternal peace. Eternal peace, or unending love and contentment, is also known as Heaven. There is Heaven on earth; Heaven on earth resembles and yet is not synonymous with Heaven after life.

Sunday, March 1, 2009

This afternoon, I was one of several volunteers who prepared dinner and served the meal to Atlantic Symphony Orchestra (ASO) musicians before they performed a concert at a venue outside of Boston. ASO was initially formed in 1945. Then a quartet, Atlantic Symphony was originally named Hingham Civic Orchestra. Having grown over the years, the sixty-four-year-old community orchestra now comprises about sixty professional musicians; some of the musicians attend conservatories. Internationally recognized Atlantic Symphony conductor Jin Kim has led the orchestra for twelve years, since 1997.

Before the concert began, I unwittingly sat near Ellie Scanlan as well as Beth Scanlan, a daughter of Ellie and John Scanlan. John Scanlan, the husband of Ellie, was unable to attend the concert. John and I were introduced to one another during college years; a handful of times we attended the same parties or church services. Longtime married, John and Ellie are the parents of four children. This afternoon, while Ellie and I were sharing conversation, Ellie introduced me and Beth, who was sitting beside her.

I recounted meeting John and a friend of John, Stephen Dillon, during a party I attended in the fall of 1971. Patty Devaney, who was a personal childhood friend, fellow high school class member, and then fellow college commuter, hosted the evening gathering. Steve and John were hilariously enchanting. Shortly after the party started, while standing alongside male friends who were initially standing on one side of the living room in the home of the Devaney family, a group of about ten to twelve boys, including John and Steve, were singing and dancing enthusiastically. They accompanied musical selections such as "Dance to the Music" and "Everybody Stand;" these were some of the hit songs of the 1970s singing group Sly and the Family Stone.

About the same number of girls, who were initially interacting on the opposite side of the room, fully enjoyed and appreciated the performance. Being socially shy, I shared brief conversation with one or two boys afterwards. During the gathering, I intermittently drank one drink containing a very small amount of wine and considerable ginger ale. Ellie Scanlan was not informed about what happened after the party.

After leaving the gathering at around 1:00 a.m., I entered the family Volkswagen Beetle and began to drive home. Though not speeding, I suddenly lost control of the car, when heavy steady rain began falling. The VW smacked into a deep large and wide rain puddle, jolted me, and then continued moving directly toward a telephone pole. I became resigned with dying. Then there was blackness.

Suddenly incredible, unimaginably benevolent and welcoming Bright White Light appeared, as I experienced Life Flashes—while being in an unconscious state, re-uniting with and making amends with people one has loved throughout life and at the same time discovering undeniable universal connection with God and attendant unexpected, incomprehensible, and unimaginable contentment. I was fully at peace.

Intensifying, Bright White Light, radiating inexplicable love, compassion, and forgiveness continued to move me forward and draw me close. I observed the risen Jesus. Radiant, he was cloaked in a flowing stainless garment. Then I heard a voice, I heard God calling me by name and saying, "I want you to come Home; the day has not arrived, yet."

Consciousness suddenly awakened me. Becoming fully alert and passionately desiring to re-enter Bright White Light found me experiencing Holy fury or peaceful anger, due to wanting to be and not yet being in Heaven. Amid alternately crying and sobbing, I was experiencing wondrous inner serenity. Moments later, Cohasset Police, ambulance personnel, and Mom and Dad arrived.

A man driving a tow truck came afterwards. The totaled Volkswagen Beetle was towed away. No serious injury afflicted me. Police and rescue personnel requested Mom and Dad to bring me to a local hospital emergency room; Mom and Dad complied with the suggestion. Dad drove. A hospital emergency room doctor examined me, diagnosed me with slight concussion symptoms, and then requested that I return home and rest for a couple of days.

This afternoon, while watching the ASO concert with Ellie and Beth, I did mention to Ellie that I had seen John as well as Steve at one or two parties held sometime after the party Patty Devaney hosted. I commented that one party going girl, named Mary Pat McAllister and I agreed that Steve was intriguing. When Steve realized Mary Pat and I were competing for attention from him, he decided not to ask either Mary Pat or me to go out with him. To this day, the recollection leaves me chuckling. Ellie said that Steve Dillon is married, a father, and a psychologist working at Boston hospital. John Scanlan is a court judge.

Wednesday, April 8, 2009

Two days ago, a massive earthquake devastated Italy. Today, a ninety-year-old woman was found sitting under quake rubble. She was knitting. True story.

On some recent winter and spring evenings, Jura and I have been walking in Brewster Woods, which is located behind the apartment living quarters we share, not far from Cohasset Village. One entrance to Brewster Woods is within walking distance from the apartment. Last night, observing moonlight brilliance spanning the woods was mystifying, humbling, and steadying. Flashlight assistance was not necessary.

Spring weather has been cool this year. Weather temperatures, which generally run in the low-to mid-fifties this time of the year, have been stuck in the forties; cloudy days have been dominant. One day last week, the weather temperature in Iowa reached seventy degrees. Two days later, the state received eighteen inches of snow.

Saturday, April 25, 2009

DanceSport Boston staff hosted an open house this afternoon. The fifteen-year-old ballroom dance teaching school offers beginner, intermediate, and advanced level students a number of choices surrounding group dance instruction and private ballroom dance lessons tailored for individuals and couples. Husband and wife, Jayson and Alia Marie Palmer, who have been teaching ballroom dance classes since the early 1980s, own and manage the school. Located in Weymouth, Massachusetts, the business was founded five years ago, in 2004.

Seasoned professional teachers as well as dance competitors, Jayson and Alia Marie also train and perform with DanceSport Boston students who are or want to be individual competitors partnered with a dance instructor or students who want enter dance competitions as a couple. In addition, Jayson and Alia Marie teach ballroom dance classes at a large university in Boston.

The open house was welcoming, warm, and masterful. Jayson and Alia Marie greeted attendees and then explained and demonstrated steps of some of the basic ballroom dances, without and then with musical accompaniment. Basic ballroom dances are waltz, tango, foxtrot, rhumba cha-cha, and swing. After Jayson and Alia Marie introduced and performed each of the dances, an enrolled DanceSport Boston student was asked to demonstrate the dance, joining Jayson, Alia Marie, a fellow DSB student, or a personal dance partner. Whether or not they brought dance partners, open house attendees were urged to select dance partners and to practice introduced dances. After an hour-long dance lesson, open house participants were offered bottled water and tasty desserts.

Intriguing was watching Jayson and Alia Marie dance. Not communicating verbally, the couple moved together lovingly, precisely, and cooperatively, while each exuded dignity, passion, and respect. The DanceSport Boston open house was individually as well as communally challenging. I have decided to attend a beginner waltz class.

Monday, April 27, 2009

Yesterday morning, around 10:00 a.m., while driving on King Street in Cohasset and then slowing down and braking, before turning right onto

Route 3A and proceeding northward, I viewed a single rooster marching slowly, steadily, and proudly across the two lane highway, with unusually little traffic. An antique car was moving southward, toward Rooster; the car driver squeezed the car horn. Stunned, Rooster scurried toward the opposite side of the road.

Observing the scene found me momentarily imagining being alive in the early 1900s; American cars were invented and regularly improved upon during the first fifty years of the twentieth century. The time machine experience was delightful.

Last Saturday, I sent sister Valerie and her daughter Grace belated birthday cards. The inscribed cards were inserted into envelopes, sealed, and then deposited inside a post office mailbox. Last night, while performing routine evening activities, I suddenly realized I had not addressed the birthday card that Grace is intended to receive. This morning, after entering the Cohasset Post Office, I faced and greeted a postal clerk standing at the front desk. I asked, "Is finding an unaddressed greeting card possible?"

"Yes, this is possible," the clerk pleasantly indicated, directing me toward the administrative office, where undeliverable mail had been placed in an open cardboard box, which had been placed on office flooring, near a partially opened door. Discovering the birthday card I had sent Grace in the box, I retrieved it, addressed it, and then re-inserted it into a mail slot inside the post office. One benefit many small-town post offices offer customers is being able to reclaim unaddressed or unstamped mail, if the sender returns to the post office within a reasonable time period, usually within one week or so. I am not sure whether the service is possible if one is living in, for example, New York City, Charleston, South Carolina, or Boston.

Today I also bought Mother Day greeting cards for Mom, niece Kristin, sister-in-law Elissa, sister Lizzie, and sister Valerie. The card being sent to Valerie pictures an elderly grandmotherly woman. Gramma is wearing construction clothes and an accompanying construction helmet. Employing a jackhammer, Gramma is breaking pavement. Inside the salutary card is the message—"Motherhood is not for sissies."

Tuesday, April 28, 2009

Today, *Good Morning America,* an ABC network television program, featured a man who has been training grizzly bears for twenty years. While being interviewed, the animal trainer said, "Grizzly bears are eighty percent vegetarian." Hearing this, I shrieked, vocalizing disbelief. The news also left me inspired, as I considered large wooly bears not often eating meat, chicken, or fish.

Sunday, May 4, 2009

Watching an animated television sitcom this afternoon, nephew Rhett and I viewed a hospital physician, facing a patient sitting in a hospital bed. The doctor became visibly uncomfortable when he began informing the patient that he is seriously ill. Suddenly, a barbershop quartet, comprised of four burly men wearing red and white striped shirts, bow ties, white pants, and top hats entered the hospital room, while singing, "You have cancer, you have cancer, you have full blown cancer and the prognosis isn't very good."

The vocal group ended the chant singing, "We're sorry it's not less serious," as all of the performers smiled, while displaying horizontally outstretched arms, torsos curving left, straightened left legs, bent right knees, and slanted right feet, pointing upward. Rhett and I responded in kind, gushing forth laughter.

After being diagnosed with cancer fifteen years ago, I received excellent medical care from Dr. Maureen Killion and her colleagues, Dr. Andrew Baldini and Dr. Callie Lamori, as well as additional staff members of a Boston hospital. Except for the time when I woke up after the operation and some times during the rehabilitation process, I felt as though I was on vacation in a sunny resort while I was being treated by medical professionals and supporting staff at the hospital. The experience has inspired me to continue emulating dignity, humility, competence, and compassion that these professionals exemplified and to uphold these values in every professional as well as personal relationship that I enter.

Wednesday, May 7, 2009

During telephone conversation that she and I recently shared, Mom, who is now five feet and four inches tall, small boned, and nearly eighty-years-old, remarked that she recently replaced a home toilet seat and toilet tank handle. "I'll be seeking a plumbing license soon," she chuckled.

Brother Jared and I visited briefly today. We met inside the Cohasset Village investment business office that he currently utilizes. Jared introduced me to Maddie Robinson, an office assistant who works with him.

When Jared and I finished conversing, he returned to work. Ms. Robinson and I continued discussion that we briefly began before Jared and I started talking. She related an interesting tale regarding Harris, a dog that Jared and Elissa also adopted. They found both dogs after seeking a breeder. Jura and Harris are both Labrador Retrievers, not from the same litter.

When Jared and Elissa were living in Scotland, in the early 2000s, Ms. Robinson began assisting Jared administratively; Jared had begun regularly working from home, as he wanted to give Elissa additional assistance with childcare and dog care. He also wanted to decrease the amount of time he was traveling, for business reasons.

Employing a thick British accent, Maddie informed me that while she and Jared were working together, she regularly observed Harris master-minding home escape plans; he wanted to include Jura in the schemes. Being naïve, adventurous, and naturally cooperative, Jura enthusiastically participated, joining the runaway games, until Jura and Harris returned home, where they sought and found human love, dog food, water, and rest on dog beds.

"You see," Ms. Robinson continued, "Harris would ask Jura to wait near the double front doors of the home, until a delivery person opened the doors. Maddie said that before the two dogs departed from the house, she sometimes viewed Harris and perceived him as non-verbally saying something, such as, "C'mon Jura, the door is open, let's run outside into the woods." When a delivery person opened the doors, the two canines escaped; they ran through the double doors, entered the back yard and then moved into a wooded area directly behind the home.

Harris also taught Jura to jump through an invisible electric fence, above a wooden fence, located behind the home in which Jared, Elissa, and baby Jamus lived. Ms. Robinson explained that Harris, while wagging his tail and looking toward Jura, often silently said words such as, "Yes Jura, there is an electric fence out there, but think, for one or two seconds of pain, we can be running, sniffing, playing, and exploring the woods all day long. What do you say?"

Jura, pausing for one second, would then eagerly follow Harris, as both dogs darted outside the large opened front doors, jumped above the wooden fence and through the electrical fence, and moments later, were roaming freely in adjacent woods. Having encountered and survived momentary electric shock, Jura and Harris entered open woodlands and discovered new freedom.

CHAPTER NINE

MOTHER DAY, HOMELESSNESS, UNEMPLOYMENT, ETHICS

Sunday, May 10, 2009

Mother Day. I found a curious pinkish looking mass on the left hind leg of Jura. Initially believing the mass was a tick manifestation, I pulled it several times, wishing to remove it. It did not move. Suddenly, I realized it is a growth. Veterinary advice will be sought as soon as possible.

Tuesday, May 12, 2009

I attended a 6:30 p.m. waltz class, as a new student. Instructor Jayson Palmer teaches the weekly class. Jayson exudes competence, discipline, and humor. Fifteen students are attending the class; all are partnered, excepting three single women, including me. Jayson presented basic steps of the dance and then asked students to practice the steps, while he alternately observed and guided coupled as well as unaccompanied students. As he and I were dancing, Jayson advised me that eye contact and maintaining proper spacing between partners is important. Consistent eye contact and proper body spacing develop trust and respect between partners, allowing dance communication and performance to become unified, flowing, and mutually gratifying, he assured me.

Two fellow class members are septuagenarians. Connie, who dances fluidly, attends DanceSport Boston (DSB) classes once or twice weekly; she also regularly attends ballroom dances which happen outside the studio. This evening, I observed another class member, named Cary, when he entered DSB studio parking lot. Cary is about seventy-years-old. He drives a shiny Volvo sedan. He uses a smartphone.

I do not own or know how to use a cell phone. I drive a ten-year-old car with back seat windows that are partially covered with dog slobber. Observing Cary, who is at least ten years older than me, caused me to wonder if I am still living in the Stone Age period.

Fellow class member Melody King and I are similar ages. Melody has danced since she was five years old. A Dominican Republic native, she says dance is incorporated into the enculturation process of the Dominican Republic, which begins in early childhood. When a dance partner was not available, Melody and I used poles extending from the studio hardwood floor to the ceiling as substitute dance partners. While doing this, we laughed regularly and heartily.

Thursday, May 14, 2009

Belatedly honoring the day that annually honors mothers, celebrated May 10 this year, sister Lizzie, niece Kristin, and I bought Mom lunch. All of us had previously decided to meet outside the recently opened Five South Main café in Cohasset Village and then to eat lunch inside the bistro. Moments before arriving here, while driving, I suddenly viewed another car driver entering the parking space that I wanted. After mumbling unrepeatable words, I immediately became sorrowful, as I observed someone emerging from the now-parked car she had been driving. The driver was Lizzie. Today, she is using a rental car as a temporary substitute for the sport utility vehicle she owns, which is currently being repaired. Oops.

Mom was standing outside the café for twenty minutes after the time Lizzie, Kristin, and I had agreed to meet her; she was understandably disappointed. Lizzie, Kristin, and I offered Mom individual as well as collective apologies. Mom accepted each and all of the apologies and forgave us. After we were seated inside the café and were given menus, we discussed family matters as well as current events and continued to do so, in between ordering and being served food. We mixed good humor and constructive criticism into the conversation. We were efficiently and politely served fresh, appetizing and wholesome meals.

Kristin delighted us; she brought eight-month-old Zachariah with her. All of us enjoyed Zach; he is endearing as well as enthusiastic. He enjoys trucks and dancing. Holding him while sauntering about the café environs, and intermittently stopping while show him pictures hanging on café walls, gave me contentment.

After lunch, Mom, Kristin, Lizzie, Zachariah, and I exited Five South Main. All except Zach, of course, had arrived here driving separate cars. We departed in the same manner, signaling that each and all of us are true American suburbanites. Five South Main café is about a five-minute walk from the apartment in which I live. Yes, I confess that I drove to Five South Main Cafe. How good and pathetic is this? Only God knows. Actually, God is not the sole being who knows.

Friday, May 15, 2009

Jura visited Hingham Animal Clinic today. Veterinarian Dr. Charles Simmons examined him. Observing the pinkish color growth on the left hind leg of Jura, Dr. Simmons said he believes the protruding mass is benign. He believes the lump will probably remain non-cancerous. He asked me to regularly observe the mass and wash it with warm soapy water. He also suggested applying Neosporin antibacterial ointment to the mass, as Jura has been discovered licking the mass, or using his teeth to scratch it.

Sunday, May 17, 2009

Amid an overcast and rainy morning, nephews Jamus and Rylan, as well as niece Brynn urged me to go swimming with them today. They had decided to go into the outdoor pool, outside the Reagan home. Any divergent suggestions I offered, non-verbally or verbally, fell upon the selectively deaf ears of the children. Surrendering, I drove home and retrieved a tank-style bathing suit. Previously, I decided to leave Jura at home today, while I was visiting with Jamus, Brynn, and Rylan. When Jamus, Rylan, Brynn, their babysitter, Julia, and I individually stepped into the salt water pool, it was raining; noticeable wind accompanied the weather temperature, which was about fifty degrees. Rylan, Brynn, and Jamus remained unfazed.

The salt water pool is thankfully partially heated. Six-year-old Jamus was chosen to tag or tap four-year-old Brynn, or me, while we all were swimming, as we boisterously played the game, Tag, You're It. Recreation time included good-natured hollering and full-blown laughter. While Jamus, Brynn, and I were playing Tag in the pool, three-year-old Rylan decided to float face up above the pool entrance steps. He politely refused several requests to exit the pool. This is why the color of his lips was blue and purple, by the time recreation period ended.

Monday, May 25, 2009

Memorial Day, commemorated the last Monday in May, was celebrated throughout America today. I did not attend the annual Cohasset Memorial Day parade. Instead, after driving for a while and arriving at the parking lot outside the Cohasset entrance of Wompatuck State Park, I chose to mark the holiday while momentarily remaining in the mini-SUV driver seat and listening to patriotic music emanating from the car radio.

One vocalist sang "America the Beautiful". For several moments during and after the performance, I was solemn and tearful. Privately or publicly honoring Memorial Day gives Americans an opportunity to reflect upon and appreciate wondrous physical beauty of America and to recall American military members who have aided Americans in times of crisis and national disasters, while providing essential services in addition to protection from harm. Memorial Day encourages Americans to consider servicemen and women who have courageously served and died during wartimes.

Honoring Memorial Day is also a way to pay tribute to servicemen and women who survived wartime service. Celebrating this holiday as well as additional national holidays offers Americans an opportunity to appreciate being connected with one another, not only from coast to coast, but also from and around the world, every day. When engaged in day-to-day activities, Americans understandably lose sight of this reality, from time to time, which is precisely what leads them to regain appreciation of being connected as countrymen and women of fifty united states and also being related as neighbors of cities and towns.

Jura and Buddy, dog of sister Lizzie, accompanied me today. When we entered Wompatuck State Park, around noon, I was stunned, when I observed three wondrously large yellow-and-black fluttering butterflies, momentarily remaining still, in air, before flying away. Walking with Buddy and Jura in woods was quieting.

Returning home allowed me to experience continued quiet satisfaction, while I organized, dusted, and then vacuumed rooms in the apartment. Meanwhile, Jura and Buddy were lying down in the living room. Kindly, they temporarily moved from spots where they were resting, enabling me to vacuum here.

Afterwards, I carried the vacuum down the hallway stairs and outside, before returning upstairs, plugging an extension cord connected to the vacuum cord into an outlet, walking down the stairs and outside, and restarting the vacuum. Doing so allowed me to clean the mini-SUV. I had driven it up to the entrance of the apartment. After cleaning the car, I laundered some clothes. Reading several book chapters after dinner and walking with Jura one more time before each of us retired was satisfying.

Friday, May 29, 2009

Today I assisted Mom, who had asked me to help her clean the inside panes of windows in the home in which she and Dad live. When Mom and I finished the task, we rested, while we sat upon living room chairs, sipped hot tea in mugs, and shared family news and additional light conversation. As I was leaving the house, Mom suddenly said, "Your father wants you to have this book." Mom was holding a medium-size, hardbound picture book entitled, *A Year in the Life,* which she had retrieved from a book-case in the living room.

The book contains over one-hundred photographs of Boston. Reputable former *Boston Globe* photographer Bill Brett, who retired in 2001, is the photographer who shot the pictures. When offered the book, I remembered meeting Jim Brett. Bill Brett and Jim Brett are brothers. Former Boston City Council member James Brett sought and won a seat on the Boston City Council in the early 1970s.

Receiving the book curiously found me remembering a childhood family vacation which was spent on Nantucket Island. While nearly all Reagan family members were relaxing on beach sand, Dad suddenly entered the ocean. Swimming toward and then reaching me, he grabbed me by the waist with one arm and pulled me out of a treacherous ocean undertow, and then, using the other arm, swam toward shore using one arm.

Resembling water moving in an operating washing machine, rising ocean water had enfolded me and seconds later, had thrust me down onto the ocean floor, before repeating the cycle. Before Dad saved me, I had been resigned with drowning. When each of us emerged beyond ocean waters, I was stunned and deeply grateful. Minutes later, I viewed the bottom half of the red two-piece bathing suit I was wearing; it was practically filled with wet sand.

For many years, Dad has been instrumental in teaching me that remaining faithful with single life values, whether or not one is eventually married, is good and noble. He has encouraged me to reflect beyond personal circumstances I face, whether the circumstances are good or ill. When I was nearly a teenager, Dad gave me waltz dance lessons at home in the living room. At the beginning of the lesson, he opened the lid of a dark brown wooden stereo cabinet.

Backing a wall in between two windows partially covered with long sheer curtains, the cabinet faced the center of the room. Gold colored mesh covered the speaker. Dad opened the cover of the cabinet, retrieved one of a number of vinyl records filed in the cabinet next to the turntable, and then he removed the record from its covering, also known as a jacket. He turned on the power dial on the turntable and placed a chosen record on the spindle of the medium-sized turntable.

Seconds later, he released the metal arm on the base of the turntable. The arm contained a stylus or needle. When he placed the metal arm on the circulating vinyl record, the needle moved up and down grooves in the record. Audible, sweet, and inspirational music entered and began permeating the living room and nearby kitchen and dining room. Moments later, Dad commenced teaching me the 1-2-3 counts and accompanying steps of the waltz and the rise and fall actions associated with the smooth dance.

Monday June 5, 2009

Resembling a homeless person, I am as of late, around mid-morning, leaving the shelter of home, bringing Jura with me almost everywhere I go, and returning during early evening hours. After feeding Jura each morning and preparing for the activities of the day, I tidy up the apartment. Leaving the apartment during mid-morning hours generally finds me driving; Jura accompanies me and we usually arrive either at the Cohasset entrance of Wompatuck State Park or neighboring Bare Cove Park in Hingham.

After the car is parked, Jura and I generally walk for two hours in either of the parks.

During spring, summer, and fall months, while we are walking in one of the parks, Jura intermittently enters waters abutting the dog-friendly parks. He wades briefly, before he continues strolling. When we finish walking, Jura is rinsed and dried with a towel and given water to drink, before he re-enters the passenger seat or the back seat of the car. When leaving

Wompatuck or Bare Cove Park, Jura and I usually travel either to Paul Pratt Library in Cohasset or to Hingham Public Library.

When Jura exits the car and he cannot accompany me, I generally attach one end of a lead—a long and flexible wire coated with plastic with fasteners attached at each end—to the dog collar Jura wears. The opposite end of the lead is wrapped around a nearby tree trunk or tree limb and then secured. Doing this allows Jura to rest upon green grass or cool dirt, to chew a frozen marrow bone when I offer him one, before leaving him, and to wander short distances or change sitting as well as lying positions, while he is outside and I am not able to be near him.

After entering either Paul Pratt Library or Hingham Public Library, I generally sit in one of many chairs facing desktop computers and work with one of the computers or I sit at a study desk and then set my laptop computer upon the desk. While I continue to write and edit the diary, I perform fact-checking and research activities. Library available computer internet services also allow me to explore potential employers and then email the employers cover letters and attached resumes. Employing longhand cursive penmanship, I also write thank-you notes. I send the notes to company representatives, after we have met during informational or formal interviews.

Jura and I re-visit Wompatuck State Park or Bare Cove Park between 4:00 p.m. and 6:00 p.m. We walk here, for forty to sixty minutes. When we return home, I prepare respective dinners that Jura and I eat. Each of us dines in separate kitchen spots. After dinner, Jura generally sits or lies upon the living room rug, while I sit upon the living room love-seat couch, alternately reading and viewing nightly television news and sometimes watching sitcoms.

When reading or writing in the evening, I often listen to a music-only program which television channel 548 offers, allowing one to hear easy listening music. Wikipedia defines easy listening music as mood music. The internet encyclopedia states that "initially becoming popular between the 1950s and 1970s, instrumental music, without accompanying lyrics, incorporates standards, hit songs, non-rock vocals, and instrumental covers of selected rock songs."

Jura and I complete one final fifteen minute outdoor walk, before 9:00 p.m., when retiring time is near. When blanketed, the living room love-seat serves as a pet bed. Once each night, before retiring, Jura enters the master bedroom, jumps upon the bed, rests near me awhile, and then he returns to the living room, climbs upon the blanketed love-seat couch and falls asleep. Quieting, humbling, and soothing is being near Jura, whether he is awake or asleep.

No alarm clock is necessary when I am sleeping. Each morning, Jura enters the master bedroom and stands beside the bed; seeing me generally in a near facedown position and semi-awake, he wags his tail and at the same time, moves toward me as closely as he can. First, he nuzzles me, on the face. Next, he repeatedly prods any additional part of me that he can reach, until I am fully awake. Then Jura jumps upon the master bed, lies beside me, and extends his right front paw across my back and onto my right shoulder. He is encouraging me to rise up and walk. Early morning behavior that Jura displays, summoning me, is a sufficient wake-up call.

Thursday, June 4, 2009

As Jura and I were walking this evening, we approached the Cohasset Town Hall, which was built in 1857. Although I am not sure why, I stopped, bent over, stooped, lowered the spectacles I was wearing, and then peered through the basement window of the building. I believed an ongoing town board meeting was happening here. Town board members were sitting aside a semi-circular table situated near the meeting room entrance. Two board members were also wearing spectacles. One board member was speaking.

Participating in the meeting, town residents were sitting in varying spots within several rows of chairs, which faced the town board members. Suddenly, one board member glanced directly toward me. Immediately looking away from him, I viewed audience members, generally town citizens, who were seated a few feet beyond the town board members. One spectator was writing notes, using a spiral notebook, paper, and a pen. I perceived that he was probably a local newspaper company reporter, who covers town government affairs. Board members and meeting attendees were bodily expressing differing levels of interest in what was being discussed.

Subsequently rising and resuming walking with Jura found me amusedly smiling. Twentieth-century renowned artist, illustrator, and author, Norman Rockwell, (1894–1978), illustrated reputed *Saturday Evening Post* magazine covers for forty-seven years. Portraying American culture as he did, with his well-known sense of artistic realism, good humor, and emotionalism, found me believing that Mr. Rockwell might have enjoyed painting the scene having occurred late this afternoon inside and outside Co-hasset Town Hall.

Monday, June 15, 2009

For two years, I have been seeking employment. Although having previously been employed as an educational tutor, a substitute teacher, GED teacher, and educational learning center manager, I have recently decided to discontinue pursuing any position in the education field. Although the choice saddens me, it is also ironically freeing.

I am re-discovering that passion one experiences surrounding work that one does, which may or may not include having had direct experience in a chosen work field, significantly influences job-seeking success as well as job fulfillment. Accepting that I will not ever be suited to the education profession, I realize that having formerly been employed as an elementary school educator allowed me to discover that I love children. Having worked in the education profession also enabled me to gradually accept that experiencing a love of children does not mean one is automatically suited to being a teacher, mother, father, or childcare giver.

Not fully sure why or how this occurred, for decades I secretly thought there was something wrong with me, a woman who was not working with children as a mother, full-time teacher, or child care giver. Quietly, I falsely believed that whether or not a woman is married, a woman who is not a teacher, a mother or working with kids in some manner is not truly a woman. In fact, I feared that a woman who is not a mother or a teacher or a child care provider is a woman who is selfish.

Equally unsure as to how or why this personal circumstance ended, at some point I trusted that being a woman who is not teacher or a mother or a childcare giver does not mean that a woman is not truly a woman. I realized that forsaking any or all of these callings, or occupations, when one realizes that one is not ready to be a mother, teacher or childcare giver, is virtuous. No matter what choices one makes in life, from time to time, it is as natural and normal to grieve losses associated with choices one has made as it is to regularly celebrate choices one has made. If one is continually grieving a choice one has made, it is time to make new decisions surrounding the choice.

For many years, when people asked me why I pursued college-level elementary education studies and subsequently sought to be employed as a teacher, I enthusiastically said, "I love helping people." Today, if any college-going student informs me that he or she wishes to teach essentially because he or she loves helping people, I immediately see a large red flag. No job or career essentially involves helping people. Every job includes helping people, while at the same time being passionate about the profession in which one is working.

Friday, June 12, 2009

This morning, after exiting the apartment in which Jura and I live, we continued strolling on North Main Street for about one and a half miles, until we arrived at the home in which I grew up. We came here today intending to visit Mom and Winston, the dog of Mom and Dad. While Mom and I were conversing, Mom requested assistance, as her hands and fingers have become arthritic.

Mom asked me to help her re-cover square-shaped sofa cushions with recently cleaned cushion covers. She also wished aid with zipping the covers as well as refitting cleaned arm rest slip covers onto the arm rests of the sofa. Two decades young, the sofa cushions and arm rests, made of heavy cotton fabric and imprinted with beautiful dark flowers, have remarkably endured.

When we finished the task, Mom and I decided to drink herbal tea and eat cookies, while sharing conversation and being seated in living room chairs. Two hours later, Mom was driving me and Jura home, as the car I drive is being repaired. Looking toward Mom, who is now seventy-nine-years-old, I experienced deep heartbreaking love, as I suddenly and silently uttered, "Where did years, where did this relationship go?"

Tuesday, June 23, 2009

This afternoon, while driving home from Boston, I spotted an injured seagull that was sitting in the middle of a city road. Car drivers traveling on the two-lane road were practically speeding, in one not two directions, only a few inches from the plump bird. The gull was flailing its damaged wings. Veering off the road, onto the roadside, I turned off the car ignition and darted outside the car. After jogging for a few seconds, I stopped, bent down, extended both arms, and enfolded the creature that I silently named Seagull. Seagull did not protest; the large creature was experiencing injury-associated shock.

After placing Seagull on the car back seat, I drove at a moderate speed, while I also looked for a nearby wildlife medical facility. Viewing a policeman, and then signaling the officer, I slowed down and then stopped the car when it was near him. Speaking with him, I requested information about nearby animal shelters. He directed me to South Boston Animal Shelter.

Because I worked in South Boston many years ago I found the shelter within ten or fifteen minutes.

For two years, between 1977 and 1979, I was a South Boston Boys Club (SBBC) afternoon education program assistant, aiding the director of the SBBC education program. Located in an urban neighborhood, SBBC served elementary, junior high, and high school-age youth.

While being an SBBC employee, I enjoyed mentoring elementary school children as well as offering the kids after school homework assistance. Club-going boys and girls and I also originated South Boston Boys Club News. The newspaper contained several double-sided pages of news and feature stories that elementary school going boys and girls had written on notebook paper. After the stories had been typed onto mimeograph paper and then printed, copies of SBBC News were stapled, before being distributed club-wide.

SBBC Christmas parties were also memorable. Since I stopped working here, in 1979, SBBC has changed. Part of a national organization, SBBC was renamed in 1990. It is now known as South Boston Boys and Girls Club.

South Boston Animal Shelter (SBAS), located on Silver Street, faces a very narrow side street. Arriving here and then entering SBAS, I was informed that the small animal shelter, clearly operating with a skeletal staff, is unable to offer wildlife care services. Staff working here referred me to Boston Animal Rescue League, (BARL). The non-profit organization is located on Tremont Street in Boston.

Arriving at BARL, forty minutes after discovering Seagull, I reached inside the car back seat where the seriously wounded bird lay. Placing both hands underneath the waist of Seagull, I attempted to retrieve the wild bird. No longer in shock, Seagull began again flailing his wings and at the same time began biting me. Frightened, as probably was this bird, I screamed, "Stop!" several times. Somehow pulling away, shutting the car door, and then walking hastily, I entered Boston Animal Rescue League office building and requested assistance.

The mini-sport utility vehicle in which Seagull and I had arrived was parked outside BARL, where a "No Parking Zone" sign is posted. Absent-mindedly, I left my pocketbook inside the car, on the front passenger seat, before entering BARL. Seeing me enter the shelter, an additional staff member, who heard me discussing Seagull with a receptionist, offered me immediate aid; she said she was ready and able to assist me with bringing the bird inside the shelter. She also said she wanted to help me right away, because she did not want me to receive a parking ticket.

The Boston Animal Rescue League staff member sought and found a large open box that would allow us to confine Seagull. We walked outside together. I slowly opened the rear left side door of the car. Not fully being sure of what happened next, I remember the shelter staff member and I somehow safely placed Seagull inside the box, which I carried as we re-entered the shelter reception area. The BARL staff member assisting me was reassuring and competent. She advised me that telephoning her late in the afternoon and seeking information regarding the welfare of Seagull was acceptable and welcome.

Arriving home approximately one hour after I had left BARL, I was thankful that Jura had not accompanied me today, sitting on the mini-SUV back seat, as he generally does. When I called the Boston Animal Rescue League, the shelter staff member who had aided me quietly and solemnly said that Seagull was examined by a veterinarian and was diagnosed as being gravely injured. Sadly, medical procedures were deemed unable to save the creature, she added.

Seagull was euthanized. Being able to give Seagull one hour of care was precious and memorable experience. Honestly, I sometimes wonder whether having left Seagull upon the city road where he was found, in the middle of ongoing traffic, might have minimized suffering the wild bird endured. Truthfully, I cannot bear the thought of having left Seagull in the middle of a road with oncoming traffic.

CHAPTER TEN

CONVERSIONS, REUNIONS, MIRACLES

Tuesday, October 13, 2009

Beginning today, this diary, having thus far been recorded in longhand, in medium-size composition notebooks, is being transferred into a laptop computer that a family member gave me. I realized that continuing to manually write and edit the journal is generally inefficient. White correction liquid that is used to erase unwanted handwriting requires several minutes of drying time. If the liquid is not spread evenly on paper while using a spreading brush, when it is drying, it will do so unevenly and it may accumulate, making rewriting over it frustrating.

These circumstances make reading re-written words as well as sentences challenging. Using correction liquid, I have revised nearly one thousand pages of the diary, written in a composition notebook. What is a saying that I have heard? Now I remember it. "Don't want to do this anymore." Defending transferring diary material into the laptop computer now rests.

Wednesday, October 14, 2009

Spending a week in Wolfeboro, New Hampshire with my sister Valerie and her children this past summer was good and fantastic experience. Grant Watson, husband of Valerie, had departed Wolfeboro the day before Jura and I arrived. The home that the Watson family rents for three weeks in the summer is a two-story house, situated in a wooded area; it is directly adjacent to Lake Winnipesauke. Now that three months have passed since July, I can barely remember any additional summer occurrences beyond vacationing with the Watsons.

After entering the rustic summer house, which displayed ample wood paneling and spartan furniture, I tentatively approached an extension of the kitchen counter that resembled a small, curved bar table. At the same time, I viewed twelve-year-old niece Myla, who was clothed in dungaree pants and a slightly above-waist-level sleeveless tee shirt. Standing aside the kitchen sink, in between counters which are situated directly in front of the bar table, she was washing a tall, slender, glass mug, while she was holding its handle. Myla suddenly turned toward me. Greeting me cheerfully and employing redneck language, she said, "Welcome to the Soda Shack, where we put everythang in a mug."

"I'm Myla and this is my assistant, Valerie," (mother Valerie) she added. This manner of talking stunned and bewildered me; fatigue surely contributed. Having ended a five-hour long drive, Jura and I had arrived here late on a Saturday afternoon. At one point during the road trip, I became lost. We entered the Watson vacation cottage an hour after the estimated arrival time. Watson family members and I had not seen one another for over one year.

Bending, I slowly sat down upon a comfortable kitchen bar stool. Valerie offered me a drink that included ginger ale, fruit juice, and well...yes, one speck of alcohol. What kind of alcohol it was, I do not remember. Maybe it was vodka. Lifting the beverage glass, I began sipping the concocted drink. Shortly thereafter, I was using the same redneck language Valerie and Myla were employing.

Suddenly speaking language I had moments ago deemed as being generally improper was unexpectedly amusing, thrilling, and downright hilarious. Being handed the fruity drink that Valerie had made, whose name now escapes me, is not the sole reason I began laughing and participating in redneck conversation. I am here honestly and yes, cowardly admitting that social anxiety occurring within me, considering I had not visited Valerie and her children in the previous twelve months, was partially relieved, while I was imbibing the bubbly beverage.

Family conflicts were addressed and resolved this afternoon, when Valerie and I later sat down together at small round wooden table and talked for a while. Renewed trust overcame feelings of fear and sadness. There are no difficult life circumstances which cannot be tolerated and eventually overcome when mutual honesty, respect, patience, and good humor are employed. Valerie confessed that she experienced a similar revelation today; we agreed that Angels had visited the summer home.

Saturday evening, a few hours after dinner, my fourteen-year-old niece Grace offered to perform a stand-up comedy routine for Valerie, Myla, Matthew, and me. Accepting the offer, we chosen and enthusiastic audience members sat down. A few moments later, while she stood in the living room of the vacation home, Grace performed an almost thirty-minute-long monologue, which was scintillating. She started the comedic routine, explaining that she intended to imitate a counter server working in a fictional franchise which resembles a well-known fast-food chain. Employing a sultry accent and a distinctive southern drawl, Grace began, saying enthusiastically, "Welcome to Fast Food Palace, where you can have it your way, but don't go crazy on us."

Continuing the charade, she pretended a Fast Food Palace customer was facing her; the customer was leaning toward the make-believe ordering counter, asking for a make- believe something. Grace approached the ordering counter microphone, looking bewildered and then said, "You want whaat?"

"Girl," she continued, "do you see this machine here and that machine over there? Do you see these *gorgeous, long, manicured, and polished pink finger nails*? If I give you what you want, I'm gonna have to push this button on this machine over here and then I'm gonna have to push that button on that machine over there. Oh, no girl, you gonna have a Coke." She added, "And girl, don't you give me any backtalk, 'cause if you do, I will definitely call your parents."

Valerie, Myla, Matt, and I gushed forth laughter; Grace, harboring hilarity, tottered. Momentarily struggling and then regaining composure, she maintained character, while she continued the pretense of being a fast-food worker, as she neared the climax of the standup comedy routine. Meanwhile, m Fastake-believe Food Palace General Manager approached Grace, appearing calm, resolute, and stern.

Addressing her, Mr. Manager immediately advised Grace of complaints he received from customers who were unhappy with unsatisfactory customer service she offered.

When he firmly reminded Grace of the high level of service standards Fast Food Palace promotes, Grace suddenly exclaimed, "Oh, is that what you had said, Mr. Manager?"

Mr. Manager responded affirmatively, firmly, and compassionately. Coyly and submissively Grace added, "Well sure thing, Mr. Manager, anything you want, Mister Manager." Satisfied, faux Mr. Fast Food Palace GM left the ordering area.

Grace then headed straight toward the make-believe fast-food ordering counter. Hand-holding a stationary microphone and smiling, she again ardently states, "Welcome to Fast Food Palace, where You can have it your way, but don't go crazy on us."

As Valerie, Myla, Matthew, and I roared with laughter; our bellies ached. All of us, including Grace, while mimicking the completed comedy routine for another hour, were near tears as well as hysterics. When we were emotionally exhausted, we entered respective cottage bedrooms at around 10:00 p.m.

Eight-year-old-Jura, who earlier had been lying near us in the living room, had retired to the guest bedroom, while the charade was ongoing. Entering the guest bedroom found me viewing Jura resting upon an area rug that covered hardwood flooring below two twin beds that were separated by a night table. Having previously heard boisterous sounds during the comedic routine, Jura may have become overwhelmed.

During the Wolfeboro vacation, nine-year-old Matthew Watson found a new friend named Alec Romero. Alec is twelve-years-old and lives year round in a home near the summer home that the Watson family currently rents in July. Romero family members include Alec, the mother and father of Alec, an elder brother whose name I do not recall, and five-year-old Derek Romero.

Matt and Alec became delighted and enthusiastic, as the two boys realized that they share several individual interests. The boys went fishing and boating, enjoyed playing with Legos, and savored "boys only" activities, some days, until 11:00 p.m. Now and then, twelve-year-old Myla was invited to share in activities Matt and Alec had chosen. Sister Valerie speculated that Alec might be developing an interest in Myla. Naïve, Myla did not notice this.

I did not observe this either; maybe I am naïve as well. Myla is maternal. She has indicated that one day she wants to be married and to be a mother. Several years ago, her sister Grace declared that when she becomes an adult, she wants to "be a doctor, to be married and not have any kids." Nine-years-old, Matthew is not expressing any interest in marriage or a career. He enjoys playing baseball and other games, fishing, and being involved in school as well as after-school activities.

One morning, I observed Myla while she was preparing to play the role of an elementary school teacher. As Matt, Derek, and Alec, the students in the class, had not yet arrived, Miss Watson continued to set up a makeshift classroom inside the screened porch attached to the summer home. The classroom included collapsible chairs facing an easel that supported poster-size writing paper and writing implements.

When the vacation summer school was in session, students of Miss Watson were clearly mesmerized, as they observed intellectual, comedic, and organizational senses she displayed. The pupils did not overtly acknowledge the professional qualities of the class teacher. Matthew, Alec, and Derek listened carefully and embraced the teachings of Miss Watson, while each and all of the boys followed her educational requests, demonstrating perfect obedience.

In the middle of one afternoon, Valerie, Matt, Alec, and I boarded a Whaler-like small motorboat. Valerie wished to show me a tiny island located somewhere in Lake Winnipesauke; Matt enjoys fishing here. Jura as well as the Watson family dog, Sasha, joined us; the canines sat on flat wooden seats in the mid-section of the boat. Valerie was the self-designated motorboat captain; the reason for the wise decision later became evident.

Sunny sky evidenced few clouds, as we entered the small craft, moored near Winnipesauke Lake shoreline, behind the vacation home. Valerie wrapped a starter rope around a flywheel on the outboard motor secured to the boat. She set the throttle and choke, and then, holding the handle of the motor with one hand, and at the same time pulling the rope attached to the flywheel with the other hand, she started the motor. Continuing to hold the handle of the outboard motor, she steered the boat backwards, away from shore, and then she turned the handle roughly ninety degrees, heading it toward open lake.

Vallie and I had been conversing for almost twenty minutes, when we began to observe increasing winds, developing white caps, and darkening sky and clouds.

Having been self-designated as the captain, she decided to press onward. Forty minutes after venturing out, we reached a tiny island, significantly covered with brush and rocks.

Unrecognizable from afar, the land mass measures approximately twenty feet in length and seventeen feet in width. After we pulled the motorboat ashore, beyond rocks situated below lake water, Matt and Andy went fishing. Vallie and I talked as we walked and surveyed the mini-island. Jura and Sasha, while wandering together, explored and smelled island terrain. Suddenly, torrential rain began falling.

Within minutes, Matthew ran toward Valerie, exclaiming, "Mom, the boat is flooding." Valerie was unconcerned; she encouraged Matt to remain calm. Returning to the boat, Vallie and I discovered the skiff was nearly half full of rainwater. Heavy rain had begun to move the small boat away from the shore; the outboard motor was beginning to be fully submerged in lake waters.

"Everybody bails," Vallie screamed almost frantically, after we had pulled the boat closer to shore. Valerie, Matthew, and Alec nervously lifted the bail buckets set inside the boat and began bailing. Almost instantly, she grabbed the bail bucket Matt was using, and yelled, "You're not bailing fast enough." Standing nearby and being in shock, realizing that we could be stranded indefinitely in the middle of pouring rain and high winds, I resisted bailing.

Wearing a three-quarter-length, white-and-blue stripe, A-line, sleeveless sundress with a four-inch-long vertical slit on the left side, above the hem, I was thinking, hmm…the boat *is* sinking…we could be stranded here long-term, but… I love this beautiful sundress and I really don't want this fashionable, ankle-length dress, or me, to be soaking wet. Seconds later, after being stricken by reality, I became fully conscious and responsible. Rushing toward the boat, I began assisting the bailing endeavor, joining Alec, Matt and Valerie.

Valerie remained unsettled. Matt and Alec were also visibly shaken. Continuing to oversee "Operation Bailout", Valerie requested each boat trip participant to re-enter the skiff, one by one, when bailing activity was completed. All participants complied. Then, standing in almost neck-deep, rising water, she began maneuvering the passenger-filled boat backwards, past large rocks slightly below the lake water surface. Losing footing, she was submerged underneath water a few times; each time she resurfaced above the water, gasping as she recovered breath, while rain poured down on her.

Valerie persevered.

After moving the boat beyond rocks, she crawled into the boat. She was physically weakened, fatigued, and chilled. Slowly rising and then standing, she again wrapped the starter rope around the flywheel on the outboard motor, set the throttle and choke, and then holding the handle of the motor with one hand, she pulled the starter rope with the other hand, until the motor came to life. Continuing to hold the handle of the outboard motor, she reversed the direction of the skiff and began to steer it toward the mainland, which was nearly forty minutes away. Valerie, Matt, Alec and I shared quiet, respectful, and humble conversation during the return trip. Sasha and Jura remained still. Both were again seated on the second of three flat seats in the boat; they were shivering.

Remorseful, I did not mention thoughts I had previously entertained of not wanting the sundress I was wearing to become wet, until all boat trip participants were safely back on shore and wearing dry clothes. Jura and Sasha had been dried with towels and had been fed. Holding a cup of soothing herbal tea, I recited the sundress confession aloud and then contritely apologized. Valerie grinned. As she expressed forgiving me for the behavior, she also rolled her eyes heavenward, before she lowered them.

Recalling that she had been screaming orders while managing the flooding incident, Valerie apologized for the action and requested forgiveness. Matt, Alec, and I re-assured her that she was also forgiven. Confidence, courage, and capability that she summoned while we were in peril far outmeasured any disappointing behavior that she displayed.

Torrential rain, which occurred that afternoon, was potentially able to leave Valerie, Matthew, Alec and me and dogs Sasha and Jura stranded indefinitely on a teeny tiny island. As we uniformly agreed that being caught in steadily down pouring heavy rain, observing the boat being nearly flooded, and seeing Valerie being in danger was sufficiently challenging, no additional boat excursions happened this week. Matt and Alec did venture out on one or two extra short fishing trips. While doing so, they remained within visible distance from shore.

During the summer respite that Watson family members undertook, lasting three weeks, fourteen-year-old Grace remained generally content, spending many hours alternately reading and texting her Jacksonville, Florida residing friends, while she used a cell phone. Sometimes she continued the activities until nearly 2:00 a.m. Grace enjoys cooking; that week she prepared several delicious family meals.

Grant Watson had returned to Florida, when Jura and I arrived in Wolfeboro. Doris Watson, the mother of Grant and Brett Watson, who lives in Wolfeboro year-round, joined us nearly every evening around dinnertime, and when doing so, she remained with us for a short time thereafter. Brett Watson and Ellie Watson, the wife of Brett, who reside primarily on the West Coast, and were visiting Grant and Doris, also joined us on several evenings during dinner-time hours.

While vacationing, Myla was generally occupied with reading, preparing and cooking meals, and attending sailing and tennis lessons. She frequently joined Matt and Alec while the two boys were playing. Matthew was also enrolled in sailing and tennis lessons. While vacationing in Wolfeboro, Grace and Myla, respective teenager and borderline-teenager, began expressing boredom.

Having repeatedly heard the two girls bemoaning not having met kids who are the same or similar age and who also vacation or reside nearby, Valerie suggested, "Well, why don't we go visit some nearby summer camps? If you do not want to accompany your father and me when we vacation in Wolfeboro next year, maybe you can attend a summer camp for girls," she added. Valerie and Grace responded, non-verbally, showing little enthusiasm.

Later Valerie went to the Wolfeboro Public Library and after researching nearby summer camps for girls she contacted persons overseeing the operations of the camps and made two touring appointments. Valerie invited me to accompany her, Grace, and Myla when she and her daughters traveled to the camps in the family van. I accepted the invite. Grace and Myla also consented to touring the camps, after being promised that they would be allowed to order breakfast bagels and beverages at a drive-thru coffee shop, at the beginning of the drive. Both camps are located about forty miles beyond Wolfeboro and serve pre-teenage as well as teenage girls.

During one camp visit, we viewed many campers attired in swimsuits and standing upon a lakeside dock. Daily scheduled swimming lessons were ongoing. Both all-female summer camp sites we visited were comprised of compact rustic cabins. Each cabin contained two sets of bunk beds, sleeping arrangements for four campers. Packed clothes and sundries were stored beneath and slightly beyond the foot of the bunk bed. During one campsite tour, the director of the camp advised us that morning, afternoon, and early evening camp activities mainly involved group ventures and some personal free time.

"*Where are the shopping malls?*" Myla cried, after one camp visit, as she and Grace were re-entering the green van in which we had arrived at the camp. Grace echoed the sentiment. Vallie and I burst out laughing. Grace and Myla remained good and respectful during the guided camp tours; the girls did occasionally mumble, nervously.

During the ride home, Vallie, Grace and Myla initially agreed that high-level organized activity within the summer camps is good and admirable. Meanwhile, good-natured camp going resistance soon became overt objection, as the girls continued to consider attending the camps next summer. For understandable reasons, Grace and Myla do not enjoy highly organized summer activities.

Throughout the school year, Grace, Myla, and Matthew attend school classes on weekday mornings and early afternoons. They participate in sports activities after school and during early evenings. When returning home in the evening, the siblings do homework assignments and sometimes attend church group meetings. As Valerie drives Grace, Matthew, and Myla to differing and tightly scheduled weekday activities and meetings, she regularly stops at one point at a drive-through restaurant and purchases dinner, which she and the children eat while sitting in the van. Valerie, Grace, Myla, and Matthew do not return home, until 9: 00 p.m., on many school-day evenings.

Touring the summer camps served a unique purpose. After the visits, each time Grace and Myla began to re-issue boredom grievances, Valerie said, "Well, applications for the next session of summer camp are on the kitchen table. I am willing and able to fill out the camp forms, right now." Grace and Myla immediately protested, in unison, saying, "*No!*" Alternately aired ennui (boredom) grievances and camp-going proposals continued, until the complaints substantially dwindled and then suddenly died.

Wednesday morning, the day before Valerie, Grace, Myla and I visited the summer camps for girls, Valerie and I observed a new sign that Myla will be a teenager next year. A few hours before attending a scheduled summer vacation sailing lesson, Myla argued, "Mom, I don't want to go. I'm not learning anything; don't ask me to go."

Valerie responded, "Your father and I paid for the sailing lessons; we are hoping that you will finish them."

"I don't want to do this," Myla firmly retorted.

Remaining calm and collected, Valerie said, "Myla, you and I will compromise. Go to the sailing lesson today. If you truly do not enjoy it, you can skip the last lesson, which is tomorrow."

Moments later, at approximately 12:45 p.m., an unappeased Myla stormed outside the house, slamming the screened front door, behind her.

Valerie, facing me and imitating someone who speaks with a thick British accent, suddenly said, "Well, I do believe Myla has had her first major tantrum; she is officially on the road to becoming a teenager." When Myla returned at approximately 3:45 p.m., Valerie politely and tentatively asked her, "How was sailing class?"

"Good," Myla answered, abruptly.

"Are you going tomorrow?" Vallie softly queried.

"Of course," Myla replied, as she definitively stomped up stairs leading to the second story of the summer home. Vallie and I smirked simultaneously.

I do not know whether Jura and I will be visiting with the Watsons next summer. I recall a precious conversation that Valerie and I shared on the final day that we were vacationing together. She and I were standing in the summer home kitchen, mutually expressing appreciation for family healing having occurred, through shared prayer, purposeful activity, and honest conversations, punctuated with laughter. Quietly and humbly Valerie said, "The week was magical. It was miraculous." She was smiling peacefully. "Yes, the week was miraculous," was replied.

2010

CHAPTER ELEVEN

GREEN RIVER, HAITI, HEALTH CARE, MIND GAMES, JOB SEEKING

Friday, January 1, 2010

No memory. Squat. Nada. Happy New Year.

Tuesday, March 16, 2010

Wikipedia, the internet encyclopedia, declares and affirms that tomorrow, March 17, is St. Patrick Day. The internet information source also pictures the Chicago River, which is annually dyed green just before St. Patrick Day. A photograph of the emerald Chicago River accompanies the Wikipedia description and history of St. Patrick Day. Employing a laptop computer, while being seated aside the kitchen table, I finished editing and revising a new draft of the diary one hour ago. Interestingly, laptop computer users who wish to employ internet service outside the home can now access the global computer network in public places, when they enter businesses such as libraries, restaurants, bakeries, gyms, and coffee shops.

The service is called Wi-Fi, or wireless fidelity. Connecting a modem with a telephone is not necessary, as is often required when internet services are being used inside a home. Internet services involve the use of search engines, email, and other services. When Wi-Fi service is available, as the laptop user employs Wi-Fi service directives, extra-domestic internet service magically becomes available. One can use a laptop for about three hours, until re-charging the computer with a battery cord is required. Now having been using a laptop for a little over a year and having recently begun using Wi-Fi service has been curious, exciting, and bewildering personal experience. Innovation is intriguing, challenging, and stimulating.

Thursday, March 18, 2010

Viewing the New England Cable News (NECN) documentary, entitled "The Heart of Haiti," was gripping. NECN longtime news anchor, R.D. Sahl, hosted the hour-long program, as television cameras visually depicted devastation that Haiti suffered on January 12 this year, when a severe earthquake literally tore Haiti apart. Haiti is situated approximately eight hundred miles southeast of central Florida, in the Caribbean Sea, near Cuba and the Caribbean Islands. The mid-January seism was centered west of Port-Au-Prince, which is the capital of Haiti. The population of the country is currently estimated to be around ten million people. Haiti is nearly the same size as the U.S. state of Maryland. As about seven hundred people reside in each square mile of the country, the nation is a renowned world leader in population density.

Published reports indicate that the early evening earthquake registered 7.0 on the Richter scale. The internet Britannica Encyclopedia indicates that the Richter scale, which measures earthquake intensity, begins at 1.0 and ends at 10.0. A 1.0 measurement indicates a low intensity seism, which people may not notice, though the weather event can be recorded on meteorological instruments. Any Richter scale measurement indicating 8.0 or above signifies severe destruction over large areas and high numbers of deaths.

However, there is little difference between the devastating 7.0 seism Haiti experienced and what is termed an 8.0 or above occurring earthquake, except that an 8.0 measurement probably affects an increasingly large land area. The January 12, 2009 Haitian tremor left over 200,000 people dead, over 300,000 injured, and over one million people homeless. This is massive destruction.

Traveling throughout Haiti, a little over two months following the natural disaster, Mr. Sahl reported that Haitians, being given international humanitarian and monetary assistance, almost immediately began and are currently continuing to build and to operate makeshift hospitals, shelters, and schools. Tents sufficing as homes are being erected; tent cities are being formed. In the middle of quake rubble, huts made with scrap metal, wood, and plastic sheets are being erected. Haitians have assumed the challenge while at the same time burying deceased loved ones. Witnessing courage Haitian people exemplify is profoundly humbling.

Tuesday, March 23, 2010

A televised special report that I watched late this morning depicted President Barack Obama signing the Patient Affordable Care (PAC) legislation into law. For two years prior to the signing, President Obama promoted the bill, which has now become law, after having been congressionally endorsed and then signed by the president. Believing that Mr. Obama has exhibited a genuine desire to work cooperatively with congressional members on political issues, including developing affordable and sound health care options for every American, I watched the signing event. Late Sunday night, congressional members voted on the bill, when it was passed. Tallied vote results indicate that two hundred members of Congress voted yes and two hundred twelve members voted no for the proposed legislation.

Present among three hundred people attending the bill-signing ceremony in the White House East Room were Victoria (Vicki) Reggie Kennedy, the widow of the late Senator Edward M. Kennedy, and Rhode Island senator, Patrick Kennedy, a son of the late Senator Ted Kennedy. Edward (Ted) Kennedy was a United States senator for forty-seven years, between 1962 and 2009. After battling brain cancer, for fifteen months, Senator Kennedy succumbed, on August 25, 2009. He was seventy-seven years old.

During the bill-signing ceremony, Patrick Kennedy, a longtime supporter of national health care, and Vicki Reggie Kennedy presented President Obama with the original, copied, national health care legislation that late Senator Kennedy first presented in August 1970, as he stood and spoke in the chamber of the U.S. House of Representatives. Patrick Kennedy was quoted as saying, "No memorial oration or eulogy could honor his (Senator Kennedy) name more than the earliest possible passage of this bill, a bill for which he long fought. His heart and soul are in this bill."

Yearlong legislative debate preceded the passage of the PAC act, also known as the Patient Protection and Affordable Care bill. Today, the atmosphere in the White House East Room was a mixture of sheer delight and utter relief. Advancement of the legislation was threatened until two days ago, when it was approved on Sunday evening at 10:47 p.m., little more than one hour before the midnight deadline for passage. As television viewers observed participants in the bill-signing ceremony, they were also able to witness palpable mixed emotions circulating throughout the atmosphere in the East Room.

For the first time, Patient Protection and Affordable Care Code provisions insure people who were previously denied health care coverage, due to a pre-existing condition. This means that persons having been previously diagnosed, for example, with cancer or heart disease, cannot be denied insurance coverage, as has previously happened. Having become law, Patient Affordable Care legislation is expected to engender millions of new health insurance customers. Health insurance companies have been given an adjustment period, which allows the companies to prepare for major business surges that will occur when the PAC act is enacted two years from now.

PAC code mandates full coverage of preventative care. Preventative care includes routine vaccinations as well as specified screenings, tests, and shots. The new national health care plan requires new private health insurance plans to cover preventative services, without seeking co-payments. Health insurance companies cannot charge for the services, under any newly created health insurance plans.

In view of challenging economic circumstances that young adults are facing, nationwide health insurance plans, effectively beginning on or following September 23, 2010, are required to allow young people who are currently incorporated into a parental health care plan to continue being covered in the plan until reaching the age of twenty-six. The previous cut-off age for young people who are health care dependents was twenty-one. Young persons who have become legal adults and are unable to access employer funded health insurance plans are now eligible for coverage for an additional five years.

United States Health and Human Services (HHS) offices will also soon offer a health care insurance plan to persons who have been denied health care-coverage, due to a pre-existing condition. Compatible with the Patient Affordable Care law, the plans will serve as temporary health care coverage options, until PAC code is implemented. HHS insurance plans will offer consumers with pre-existing conditions medical coverage when they have been without insurance for six months or more, when no additional health insurance plan resources are available, and if persons are legal United States residents.

The Patient Affordable Care law does entail a questionable provision. Consumers who are eligible for Patient Affordable Care, who do not purchase PAC-compatible insurance, will receive a tax penalty, when the bill is enacted. This provision of the law causes me to wonder if constitutionally supported, congressionally formulated, and presidentially approved legislation is not intended to be based on free will or freedom to choose?

It is also curious that not one of the congressional members of the political party that opposed the PAC bill voted for the bill, which has now become law. The framework of the Patient Affordable Care legislation comes across as addressing some important issues within the American health care system issues and in doing so, demonstrating goodwill toward all Americans. Although not without imperfection, the Patient Affordable Care code presents a perfectly valid means of improving American health care systems. Amid earthly imperfection, perfection exists. Imperfection can be individually and communally amended.

Thursday, April 29, 2010

Mom, wearing socks and no shoes when entering her home laundry room, slid onto linoleum flooring, and then she slipped further, falling face forward. Dad, sitting in a living room chair, immediately arose, intending to aid Mom. Then he also fell down and landed upon living room carpeting. Moments later, stunned, yet not seriously injured, Dad rose again, and walked slowly toward Mom. Her lower right leg was seriously bruised. Dad helped her to rise.

Mom has not sought medical attention. While she is recovering, she is conducting normal daily activities, slowing the pace at which she moves, avoiding bending, and consuming aspirin with water, in order to relieve pain. Realizing Mom and Dad are aging again reminds me that embracing abiding love means accepting uncertainty.

Friday, May 7, 2010

Today, Mom assisted me as we washed windows, while we alternately stood still and moved about outside the home of Mom and Dad. Mom and I wore rubber raincoats, perfect waterproof window-washing apparel. We used a new window cleaning invention that Mom recently purchased. It is a plastic spray bottle with a removable nozzle which includes a spray tip. The bottle is nearly filled with window cleaning solution.

To begin the window cleaning process, one screws the nozzle on one end of a hose into threads of an outdoor spigot; then one screws the threads in the opposite end of the hose into a nozzle on the back of the spray bottle. Turning on the spigot allows tap water to run through the hose and into the plastic bottle, diluting and pushing the window cleaning solution in the base of the bottle into the adjustable spray tip, which is on the front end of the nozzle attachment.

A thin plastic knob on the spray tip is turned to the rinse position, generating tap water, when one wishes to remove window debris before cleaning windows or when one desires to rinse washed windows. The knob is turned to the on position, when one wants to clean windows, and it is turned to the off position, when one completes window washing. Two-story-high residential or office windows can be reached and cleaned, while using the newly available window cleaning gizmo.

Instantly, I loved the new cleaning toy, which considerably lessens cleaning time. The window washing tool is safe as well as effective. Today, Mom insisted on helping me to clean exterior windows; we took turns doing this. Her lower right leg remains noticeably black and blue, since little more than one week ago she stepped off the laundry room threshold, suddenly slipped, and immediately fell onto linoleum flooring.

When we finished cleaning windows today, Mom and I continued to work outdoors, sweeping and gathering sand in a descending driveway beside the house. Three hours after we started the cleaning projects, she and I were seated on living room wingback chairs.

We were sipping hot herbal tea that Mom had made and had poured into thick mugs with handles, while I shared stories from a televised version of the *Blue Collar Comedy Tour* that I recently watched. The show features stand-up comedians Jeff Foxworthy, Bill Engvall, Ron White, and Daniel Whitney. At some point, Daniel Whitney was nicknamed Larry the Cable Guy.

The four seasoned funny men toured the United States for six years, starting in Omaha, Nebraska in 2000 and ending in Washington, D.C in 2006. Talking with Mom about the *Blue Collar Comedy Tour* was contenting. Relating stories shared during the show surely relieved physical discomfort Mom and I were experiencing after cleaning for several hours.

Shortly after the tour arrived in Washington, D.C., Mr. Foxworthy, Mr. Engvall, Mr. White and Mr. Whitney decided to tour the Lincoln Monument. When Daniel Whitney was looking at the statue of President Lincoln, he said, "Wow, I had no idea he (Lincoln) was that big." Jeff Foxworthy looked at Larry and said, *"You didn't think he was that big? He's not even standing up."*

During one performance on the tour, comedian Ron White, said, "De-Beers Company recently came out with some new advertising. The new slogan of the jewelry company is—Diamonds are forever." While smoking a lit cigar, Mr. White then nonchalantly said, "DeBeers slogan used to be—Diamonds are a girl's best friend."

Ron suddenly remarked, "Why doesn't DeBeers Company say it the way it really is— *Diamonds, yeah, that'll shut her up… for a minute."* Mom and I loved this one; we laughed about it for several minutes. Then I related another matter that Bill Engvall discussed on stage during the tour. Shortly after he began performing, he commented, "The wife and I had an argument that was so stupid, it bears repeating. By the way, she collects twist ties."

"Yeah, welcome to my world," he said, to a laughing audience, before continuing. "Last week, I wanted to make a sandwich. So, I took the bread down. I took the twist tie off and I made a sandwich. Did I put the twist tie back on the bread? No, I did not." (Male audience members voiced agreement.) "I did what every man in America does. I spun the loaf of bread and tucked it underneath." (Rousing applause came from the audience.) *"Apparently, this is where I went wrong folks,"* he lamented casually.

Mom allowed me to relate a final anecdote about the televised version of *Blue Collar Comedy Tour.* As Daniel Whitney or Larry The Cable Guy, was performing a final bit during the show, one female spectator, sitting among five hundred fellow show goers suddenly shouted, "I love you, Larry." Larry hollered back, *"I asked you to wait outside, in the truck."* Standing, Mr. Whitney immediately genuflected, looked skyward, and said, *"Lord, I apologize for that."* Roaring, cheering audience members echoed Divine forgiveness, Holy humor.

Saturday, May 8, 2010

Early this evening, Jared, Brynn, Jamus, Rylan and I shared dinner; an Italian restaurant in Cohasset was the chosen dining place. Sister-in-law Elissa was not able to join us; she is currently in England, visiting Martha and Ron Dickson, the parents of Elissa, Sally Dickson Rumford and Catherine Dickson Bravers.

Although not having been together often during the previous twelve months, Rylan and Jamus, Brynn and I almost immediately began recalling Nancy Pini stories and formulating new ones. We invented Nancy Pini one night, when Jared and Elissa were out socializing, and I was babysitting. Remembering and creating Nancy Pini stores is enjoyable.

Why? Nancy Pini can be or do anything. For example, Nancy Pini can be described as a mermaid who submerges below sea water, surfaces, and then swims. She can be depicted as a four-eyed monster with six legs. Nancy Pini can be categorized as a debutante who is preparing to enter a grand ballroom, as hundreds of guests are waiting to see her. Meanwhile, Nancy does not realize that the bodice of the strapless, full-length, and not fully zippered evening ballroom gown she is wearing is slowly falling down, to waist level, as she dreamily tiptoes down wide marble stairs leading into the ballroom and sashays across the ballroom dance floor, wearing stiletto high heel flip flops.

One boundary is set, when one is concocting Nancy Pini stories; the condition is that each successive story is required to demonstrate increasing ridiculousness. As Jared witnessed Rylan, Jamus, Brynn, and I laughing heartily, while we were reliving and reinventing Nancy Pini escapades, he was clearly feeling excluded. Becoming visibly anxious he suddenly said, "Who the heck is Nancy Pini?" Once he was given Nancy Pini tutelage, Jared was fully calm.

Additional dinner conversation generally revolved around the private school Jamus, Brynn, and Rylan attend. We discussed school activities as well as classmates and friends with whom the children interact. Conversation among us continued, as we were served and shared five plated dinner entrees: penne with pesto sauce, spaghetti marinara, pizza, chicken cacciatore, and chicken marsala. We also drank varied beverages.

As we exited the restaurant, Jamus, Brynn, Rylan and Jared greeted and patted Jura. He was sitting and waiting in the back seat of the mini-SUV. When we will be together again is uncertain. Jared, Elissa, Jamus, Rylan, and Brynn will be living abroad again, in Geneva, Switzerland, two months hence, in late July.

Late tonight, winds were blowing and howling. Heavy rain and thunder sounds awakened me. The time was 3:00 a.m. I heard sound resembling an operating lawn mower.

Considering someone operating a lawnmower in the dark after midnight as not being probable, I was also unable to discern the true nature of the sound. As moments passed, thoughts swirling about my brain became sinister. I was wondering if someone may have murdered a fellow human being and was slicing the body of the deceased victim with an electric chainsaw. Furthermore, I pondered, is the murderer intending to store the severed, bloody body parts somewhere?

Pensive, I arose from the bed to investigate the eerie sound. Seconds later, macabre thoughts swirling about my brain subsided. I entered the apartment bathroom and spotted the electric toothbrush that I use. Stationed in a charger on top of the bathroom sink, beside a ceramic soap holder, it was operating and vibrating. The suddenly functioning battery-charged toothbrush had previously been inoperable, for several months. No kidding.

True story.

Tuesday, May 11, 2010

I temporarily experienced emotional near-delirium, considering that for over three years, while writing a diary, I have also been steadily searching for a job and failing to find employment. Having initially considered re-entering the education field; I now accept that I am not suited to working permanently in the education business. Having been employed in the education field as a tutor, substitute teacher, after-school program assistant, and learning center manager enabled me to develop refined interpersonal relations, organizational, supervisory, and communications skills and talents. I continue to admire and respect people who have experienced job or career fulfillment, while being employed in the education field.

Having owned and managed a small residential and commercial cleaning company for over ten years gave me an opportunity to appreciate the business world, and I enjoyed cleaning and organizing homes as well as offices. When ending the proprietary experience, I decided not to pursue self-employment again, as I am not internally entrepreneurial. Meanwhile, I had begun to experience an emerging interest in the legal profession.

I entered a part-time paralegal certificate program being offered at a nearby college. Participation in the paralegal studies program involved two years of part-time study, two nights weekly, for two years. Criminal Law class instructor, Attorney Paul Shanahan and Civil Litigations class teacher, Attorney Beth Cossick, are mentors I remember as having regularly delivered stimulating class lectures, facilitated thought-provoking class discussions, and assigned challenging homework. Each distributed fair exams which were quickly and thoughtfully corrected. Mr. Shanahan and Ms. Cossick encouraged me to grow, persevere, and excel academically as well as personally.

When I completed the paralegal certificate program, I received a high grade point average score. I was sent an awards ceremony invitation which was sincerely declined. A paralegal certificate was mailed to me.

Later, when I was employed in a temporary position within a law office, I was regularly restless and fidgeting. Shortly thereafter, I resigned the position. Desiring to work in a profession involving a high level of physical activity and intellectual stimulation is one of the primary reasons that I realized that performing legal administrative work is unworkable for me.

I have recently experienced a re-awakened passion for the restaurant business. I recalled having been employed in a Washington, D.C. restaurant when I lived in the city for five years, beginning in 1980 and ending in 1985. During that time, I was employed as a waitress or server for approximately two years at an Italian bistro, named Adriatico. Offering welcoming, refined, and intimate dining atmosphere and providing dining customers with delectable Italian and American food choices combined with satisfying beverages, the small restaurant, seating approximately forty guests, was open nightly, except on Sundays.

Shortly after I started working there, I found a stray kitten outside the restaurant and for short time, was feeding the animal. Later, I named the cat Tica and brought her home. Unfortunately, Tica was not well. She died from jaundice, a few days later.

The general manager of Adriatico, Reesa El-Ferris, was competent, prompt, and jovial. Reesa did not hold official staff meetings. The management style that Reesa employed made official staff meetings unnecessary. Each night, after meeting with Adriatico kitchen staff, comprising two or three people, she also met with restaurant servers or wait staff; we sat in the dining room, before the restaurant was opened. Reesa offered on-duty kitchen and wait staff one gratis meal that was to be eaten before the beginning of the shift.

Adriatico staff members were allowed to choose one of three menu selections, which competent kitchen staff here prepared. All of the on-duty wait staff ate dinner together in the dining room, where Reesa conversed with us nightly about pertinent guest service matters and dining room set-up and break down matters. Most of the time, Reesa sat at a four top—table seating four persons—next to us during the pre-shift meeting.

Sometimes she also ate dinner during the approximately thirty minutes long meeting. Adriatico service staff included Ginger Nielson, Patty Nielson, a daughter of Ginger, Jofur Ahmadi, Sharuk Hosseini and me. Beautiful and gentle people, Iran natives, Jofur and Sharuk were working here and at the same time attending a Washington D. C. university during the then-ongoing Iranian Revolution.

In addition to allowing restaurant staff one gratis meal for each shift, Ms. El-Ferris occasionally made delicious homemade meals and served the food to on-duty staff. Because she held regular unofficial staff meetings, which included initiating morale building and strengthening practices, Ms. El-Ferris was able not only to motivate Adriatico employees but also to boost restaurant profits.

Five years of previous restaurant and catering business experience, including executing hostess, server, and temporary dining room supervisor positions, has found me again wanting to explore restaurant employment. I hope to soon be employed in an entry-level restaurant management position that does not involve more than thirty hours of work each week. I enjoy work requiring a high level of physical activity as well as the use of supervisory, interpersonal, organizational, and communications skills.

Thus far, seeking to be employed as a manager or assistant manager in a restaurant has been challenging, as I have not been previously employed in the role. Recent years have found me not wanting to work more than thirty hours a week. To be honest, I have not ever truly wanted to work outside home, for more than thirty hours. Many restaurant management positions require working at least forty hours per week.

Wednesday, May 12, 2010

Two online book self-publishing company representatives called me. Publishing this diary is not necessary. Until now I had not thought about making the work public.

If it is not intended to be published in book form when it is completed, bequeathing it will be sufficient. As of today, the memoir has officially become a book manuscript. Exploring traditional book publishing as well as self-publishing ideas is exciting.

CHAPTER TWELVE

SENIOR COUPLES, BEACHED WHALES,
UNREQUITED YOUNG LOVE, RESURRECTION

Thursday, May 13, 2010

Below is a rephrased comedic script which appeared in a local newspaper today.

SENIOR COUPLES REGISTRY

Jacob, age 92, and Rebecca, age 89, both living near one another in Florida, have recently begun a personal relationship and are considering permanent commitment. One day, as they are strolling, they pass a local drug store. Jacob suggests going inside. When they are inside, he addresses a man standing behind the counter.

Jacob: "Are you the owner of the drug store?"

Pharmacist answers, "Yes."

Jacob: "Do you sell heart medication?"

Pharmacist: "Of course."

Jacob: "Circulation medicine?"

Pharmacist: "Many kinds."

Jacob: "Rheumatism medicine?"

Pharmacist: "Definitely."

Jacob: "Medicine addressing memory problems, arthritis, and Alzheimer disease?"

Pharmacist: "Oh yes, a large variety."

Jacob: "Vitamins, sleeping pills, Geritol and Parkinson's disease antidotes?"

Pharmacist: "Absolutely."

Jacob: "Do you sell wheelchairs, walkers, and canes?"

Pharmacist: "All speeds and sizes."

Jacob: "We'd like to call this store the Committed Senior Couples Registry."

Monday May 24, 2010

Niece Kristin and her husband Payden are now living in Cohasset. Last week, Kristin and I worked for eight hours, organizing and deep-cleaning first-floor rooms inside the Sullivan family two-story ranch-style new home. Kristin and I were elated when we finished the project, as we initially perceived the spring cleaning project as requiring several days of work.

This past Saturday evening, Kristin, nearly two-year-old Zachariah and I dined together; we shared food Kristin had prepared. Following the meal, Kristin placed Zach in the baby room crib mattress and gave him a small bottle, which was nearly filled with warm milk. He grasped and began sucking the bottle nipple. He was soon sleeping. Moments later, Kristin and I were sharing good news gossip as we were seated upon the living room couch, each of us was holding and drinking from large wine glasses containing apple juice and alternately using forks and knives as well as napkins, while eating plated circular and spongy strawberry shortcake pieces, topped with whipped cream and strawberries that she had prepared.

A friend of Kristin, named Carmella, recently called her. Carmella asked Kristin to go out to lunch sometime soon; Carmella is also a young wife and mother of two young children. Kristin is pregnant again; she and Payden are expecting a second son; she is due in October. While she and I were sharing conversation, she reminisced about conversation that she had recently shared with Carmella. She said she and Carmella began giggling as both of the girls remembered days when they were single, entering night clubs, and when doing so were wearing make-up, nail polish, attractive dresses, and nylons, as well as stiletto high heels complementing the apparel.

Giggling, Kristin suddenly asked Carmella, "What the heck happened? Now, we're both married, wearing tee shirts and sweat pants, not using make-up, and hardly ever thinking about hairstyling. We're running around, following kids all day and half of the night. I feel like a beached whale, with a bad back. What about you, Carmella?"

Friday, May 28, 2010

After returning home via mini-SUV around 5:00 p.m. and backing into a driveway parking space tonight, I rolled down a car window near the driver seat. I greeted Lance Callighan, son of landlady and landlord Mary Rita and Paul Callighan. Lance was seated in a shiny black sedan facing in the opposite direction. The driver side window of the car was open as he was backing out of an adjacent parking space.

After Lance greeted me, he indicated that he and two male buddies and his sister, Faith, also seated in the car, were embarking on an evening of club-going from one nightclub to another. Lance said the activity might last until early tomorrow morning. Gael Callighan, junior sister of Lance and Faith, was otherwise occupied this evening.

One young man sitting in passenger seat of the shiny sedan suddenly asked me, "Why don't you come out with us?" Immediately I quipped, "Do not even think about asking me out; I am old enough to be your second mother." The young man snickered at me and then visibly gagged; he was probably visualizing dating a woman who is old enough to be mothering him. Suddenly embarrassed and defensive, the young man countered, "Well then, what are you doing tonight?"

"Dating a couple of good books and then eating a sizzling hot slice o' pizza" I said, smirking, leaving all four car occupants giggling. Wouldn't you know, a few days following the encounter, while turning on the apartment living room television, I was suddenly watching a rolling sitcom, featuring five single people, seated upon a living room couch as well as two chairs, who were sharing several pickup lines. The first one is, "Did I feel an earthquake or did you just rock this world?" The second pickup line is, "Is that sunburn, or are you always this hot?"

"Were you named Magician, because whenever I look at you, everyone else disappears," is a third opposite sex teasing approach. "I don't own a library card, so can I check you out?' is the fourth suggested flirting format. The final pickup line recorded here is, "Are you going to kiss me, or will I be lying in my memoir?" Ba da bum. We're done. No more pickup lines.

After sharing conversation with Lance and company, I re-entered the apartment and afterwards decided to delay feeding Jura, who was resting on the living room floor. I left the apartment and walked toward Cohasset Town Hall. A large crowd was gathering there.

People were hoping to see Cohasset High School seniors who accompanied an invited guest to the CHS senior prom tonight. When announced, each couple, wearing formal attire, exited the Town Hall entrance, stepped down onto a stairway and then entered a temporary red carpeted runway, which lead toward Cohasset Common.

The runway was lined with two railings decorated with flowers and bows. As the prom couple strolled toward the Common, media members, family, friends, companions and relatives photographed them. Being among the spectators, I recalled attending the Cohasset High Senior Prom held in May of 1971. Then a college student, CHS 1970 graduate, Mark Miller, escorted me. The setting of the CHS Class of 1971 prom dinner dance was the former Kimball's restaurant, which was located beside Cohasset Harbor.

Near the end of the dinner dance, I entered a powder room and asked someone to help me pull down a zipper on the back of the prom dress I was wearing. The A-line design, ankle length satin dress was pale yellow. Yellow chiffon covered the satin. The empire waist bodice, also covered with chiffon, was embroidered with small delicate pink and white flowers. Long chiffon sleeves of the dress were intended to be buttoned at the wrist. A lengthy yellow satin ribbon below the bodice which was stitched to the gown was also sewn into each side of the zipper in the back of the dress and was intended to be tied into a bow, allowing the remaining bow strings to fall below the bow.

Emerging from the powder room, wearing casual clothes, I accompanied Mark as he drove us to the prom after-party. The party setting was a donated, furnished and large seaside Cohasset home. Attending the 1971 CHS Senior Prom allowed me to fully realize that going to a high school prom or after prom party, or anywhere, primarily because one wants to be seen, is inadvisable.

Mark and I had been seeing one another for two months before attending the prom. During the after-prom party we were barely communicating. At some point, he clearly wanted to fully join after-prom party guests with whom he had been interacting for a while. This was not truly bothersome; Mark and I admire and respect one another. We are friends who resemble a brother and sister. He and I have recently reconnected. These days, when we run into one another, we talk. We laugh. We do not mention the 1971 Cohasset High School Senior Prom.

When during the Cohasset High School Class of '71 prom night-time had become the following day, the time was 5:15 a.m., and daylight was appearing, Mark and I had decided to part company. I began walking home, strolling along Atlantic Avenue. The road connects with Jerusalem Road; both roads adjoin coastline. While watching the sun rising and slowly walking upon Jerusalem Road and beside Rocky Beach, I discovered two people, a boy and a girl, who were sitting very closely together on the beach upon a large blanket. Heartbreak surged and lodged inside of me.

Brody McLaughlin is the name of the boy who was sitting on the beach. Brody and I first became acquainted, when we were assigned to the same CHS ninth-grade homeroom class. When I was a CHS high school junior and then again when I was a senior, I again considered Brody. During senior-year school days, Brody and I conversed a few times. He is generally outgoing and calm. He is gifted with a good sense of humor. Brody was recognized as having been an adept high school football player.

After being asked to hold a football resting on a tee until seconds before a girl kicked it, in a fourth down play in the November 1969 annual CHS Powder-puff football game, during which two teams of girls who are junior class members play football in a way that does not require wearing safety equipment, yet each team wants to win, I was permanently removed from the game. Why? Beats me. What error I made remains, unto this day unknown to me.

One year hence, in the fall of 1970 and then in the spring of 1971, as a CHS senior, I continued to be intensely shy and quiet, while I remained interested in Brody. Hoping to see and talk with him during the senior prom, I wanted to attend the event. When I saw Brody and a girl he had been dating for a while at the prom dinner dance, I was very bashful and therefore unable to talk with or even approach him and the girl who accompanied him to the prom.

Following the after-prom party, when I saw Brody and the girl he brought to the prom sitting together on Rocky Beach sand and was crushed, I lowered my head and sighed. Continuing to walk home, I turned left onto Forest Avenue. Later, turning right allowed me to enter upper North Main Street, where I lived then. Arriving home at 6:45 a.m., I was grateful that awakened family members had not heard me moving into the den and dining room and then ascending the hallway stairs.

After entering the second-floor bedroom that I shared with sister Lizzie, who was either asleep or downstairs, I began to cry. Then, without changing the after-prom clothes I was wearing, I slumped head-first down onto one of two twin beds and landed upon the mattress and pillow. I wept and wiped tears running down my face until I fell into a deep, long lasting sleep.

Brody McLaughlin and I recently became reacquainted. He is employed in the deep-sea fishing business. He is also self-employed. He has owned and managed a painting company for many years. Brody is the dad of three daughters. He is now single. Time has relieved former insecurities within me regarding developing relationships with people. I accept the reality that many relationships do not ever develop beyond goodwill. Luckily, goodwill is what begins and maintains a relationship, regardless of how much or how little the relationship develops.

Saturday, June 5, 2010

Not complaining, I am wondering where the ticks are this year. Summer-like, unusually warm and humid weather has arrived early. Generally, ticks thrive in warm and humid weather. This spring, I have not found any ticks on Jura. Curious and delightful is this. Vegetation is lush this year; beyond average rainfall which occurred this past winter and has continued into the spring is said to be attributing to the diminished presence of ticks this year. Many people have noticed little tick activity this spring season.

Ticks are not often present on Jura, as Jura swims in ocean waters, near daily, during spring, summer, and fall months. Someone recently informed me that ticks do not like salt water. Whoopee. Dogs, as well as humans, who are bitten by a tick, can contract Lyme disease, an illness which can potentially cause arthritis, neurological disorders, and heart disease. Last year, canine and feline vaccinations for Lyme disease became available for the first time.

Liquid Lyme disease-fighting medications were available before Lyme disease vaccinations became obtainable. A dog or cat owner administers liquid Lyme disease prevention medications monthly; the dog or cat is given a measured amount of medication, which is placed on the neck of the dog or cat, under fur. Veterinarians request that dog as well as cat owners neither bathe the animals nor allow them to enter water, for a minimum of twenty-four hours, so that the medication can be effective.

Last summer, while Jura and I were walking in Bare Cove Park in Hingham, I temporarily joined a lady who was walking with her dog in the park. The lady informed me that she knows someone whose dog was not only vaccinated for Lyme disease, but was also administered monthly Lyme disease medication. The dog contracted Lyme disease. Hearing the story found me wondering whether giving a dog or a cat a yearly Lyme disease vaccination in addition to giving a dog or cat a monthly flea and tick-killing liquid medication may overmedicate the animal.

I surmised that overmedication threatens the immune system of the animal, thereby limiting its ability to fight Lyme disease as well as other illnesses. Confidently, I decided that Jura will not be given a monthly flea and tick killing medication. Instead, he will receive an annual Lyme disease vaccination, and meanwhile, will continue to eat healthy food, drink satisfactory amounts of water, and exercise daily.

Sunday, June 6, 2010

This morning I read an article appearing in the June 2010 edition of *Yankee* magazine. The piece relates the story of a young girl, who following Sunday Mass, accompanied her familial grandmother, Mama Rose and her Uncle Rum, a cousin of Mama Rose, when the relatives visited the gravesites of deceased family members; the graves are situated on two sites in a cemetery. Uncle Rum drove and assisted Rose, as she gave the gravesites care, once a month.

Sitting in the back seat of the car, the young child accompanied her two relatives. Generally remaining silent when exiting the car in which all had arrived at cemetery, she walked and then stood aside Mama Rose and Uncle Rum, as the three relatives "visited the dead." The former young girl, now an adult, wrote the article which appeared in the monthly magazine. The writer is author Ann Hood.

As a young girl, Ann tolerated commuting to the cemetery; actually the car rides were not long, though the driving time appeared to be endless in the mind of young Ann. She also did not relish visiting the gravesites of family members. In fact, she dreaded the unwanted obligation. Being afraid to verbally protest the gravesite visits that Mama Rose mandated, Ann tolerated the activity; she remained silent before, during, and after the cemetery visits.

When the outing was completed, Mama Rose and Ann entered a local bakery. For remaining silent during the sojourn, Ann received a material reward, one sugar cookie. She chose the treat while she was standing beside Mama Rose, as Rose purchased a dozen pastries as well as sugar cookies that she and Ann chose.

Ann wrote that when Mama Rose, arrived at the cemetery and occasionally forgot Ann, who was sitting in the back seat of the car, Ann felt fortunate. She listened "to a local AM pop radio station, turned on low." As Mama Rose and Uncle Rum "marched forward" toward the gravesites, Uncle Rum carried plants, while Rose was holding a gardening spade and grasping a flower watering can.

One gravesite displays the name of the deceased husband of Mama Rose. The inscription on the second memorial monument identifies the deceased mother of Mama Rose. Two remaining engraved gravestones reveal the names of two deceased children of Rose. Rose bore ten children, including seven girls and three boys. When she was twenty-three, one of the daughters of Rose died, while she was undergoing routine dental surgery. One of the sons of Rose suffered a fatal heart attack which occurred one year on St. Valentine Day. The fatalities occurred when Ann was around three-years-old.

Ms. Hood wrote that when Mama Rose remembered Ann was sitting in the back seat of the car at the cemetery, she asked Ann to follow her and Uncle Rum to the gravestones. Ann admitted she was barely able to watch Mama Rose, while she was tending to the family internment sites. Her grandmother sobbed, when she initially faced the monuments of each of her two deceased children.

Rose slumped upon the burial site of one child, then arose and kneeled near the grave, and then traced the name of the departed child. She repeated the actions when she had moved to the gravesite of the second deceased child. When the gravesites of the two expired children had been given proper care, Rose arose. Ann Hood wrote that as Mama Rose was standing on two feet, she exposed hands "lined with dirt." Soil had collected compactly underneath her fingernails. Ann also recalled viewing noticeably wrinkled skin on both hands of her grandmother.

Ann commented that Mama Rose displayed "efficiency and stoicism," when she was tending to the gravesites of her husband and mother. When having finished caring for the burial places, Rose momentarily remained kneeling, as she faced the designated gravesite. After praying silently for a few moments, she stood up and slowly walked forward.

The sole brother of Ann Hood, Skip Hood, died in 1985; he succumbed during a household accident. Since attending the funeral service memorializing Skip, Ann has not visited his gravesite. She wrote that her mother visits and tends to the monument, daily.

Lloyd Hood, the father of Ann Hood, died in 1997. Grace Adrain, a daughter of Ann Hood, passed away when she was five-years-old. Grace had contracted the bacterial disease, streptococcus, in 2002. She died shortly thereafter.

The article Ms. Hood penned is entitled, "Finding Grace in a Cemetery." Ann visits the grave of Grace annually. In the magazine piece, Ann revealed why she does not more than once a year visit the gravesite where her daughter is buried. She wrote that she does not experience the spirit of Grace as being essentially here, no matter how beautiful the memorial is or no matter how abundant or how fragrant the blossoms surrounding the gravestone are. She stated that she believes Grace is now "in no place in particular." Continuing she wrote, "She (Grace) is everywhere."

Moments after reading the magazine article, I recalled a Biblical account which states that awhile after Jesus was crucified, the body of Jesus was discovered missing from the place where he had been buried. The spirit of Grace Adrain, resembling the spirit of Jesus, is in no place particular; the spirit of Grace, resembling the spirit of Jesus, is everywhere. Not being a regular magazine reader or subscriber, I do not fully know why, when visiting a nearby library mid-morning yesterday, I unexpectedly retrieved an issue of *Yankee* magazine, featuring the memorable article by Ann Hood.

CHAPTER THIRTEEN

SUMMER 2010, ECCENTRIC DOG OWNERS CLUB, *BEING CATHOLIC NOW,* DUMP CONFESSION

Sunday, July 4, 2010

Having chosen to sit on a hillside outside the Hingham Square Historical Society building, which faces Hingham Square, I asked Jura to sit beside me, while I unfolded a beach chair, enabling me to watch the Hingham Independence Day parade, which starts at 10:00 a.m at Hingham High School and ends over an hour later in Hingham Square on Main Street. Attracting spectators in the thousands, the Hingham Fourth of July parade features marching bands, moving floats, and antique cars as well as walking, waving military veterans, civic groups, and local politicians.

While settling into a beach chair, I encountered Jean Cassini, who was sitting near me. Jean and I worked together, during the 1975 through 1976 school years; we were then fellow Deer Hill School employees. Deer Hill School is the public school in Cohasset that enrolls students in grades four through six. Jean, who was a fifth-grade teacher at Deer Hill School when we met, informed me that she is now retired and a self-employed tutor. While I was a Deer Hill School employee from September of 1975 to June of 1977, I tutored students who were chosen for participation in the Title I academic improvement program, in the areas of Reading and Mathematics. Reconnecting with Jean invigorated me.

Independence Day has been steamy hot. Outdoor temperatures reached nearly 100 degrees Fahrenheit; humidity level was high. When the parade ended, Jura and I walked on several crowded street sidewalks before each of us re-entered the used car that I was recently gifted; the vehicle is a ten-year-old luxury station wagon with very low mileage, a sizeable back seat, and a large cargo area. While driving and merging into Hingham Square traffic, I was not surprised to see automobiles advancing at a pace resembling the movement of tortoises, in both northward and southward directions.

Seeking relief from traffic congestion, I entered Bare Cove Park; the park is located a few minutes beyond Hingham Square. When I had parked the car inside the parking area directly outside the park, I exited the front seat, let Jura out of the back seat, and together, seeking heat relief, we entered the park and began walking on a wooded trail leading to Back River, which contains salt water. Before wading in an area far beyond where dogs enter the river, I partially removed clothing I was wearing, which covered a one-piece bathing suit.

Honestly, humans are asked not to wade in Back River, probably because many dogs wade and swim in it and motorboats as well as cruise boats regularly navigate the river in spring, summer, and early fall months. After Jura and I went wading, he joined fellow dogs and frolicked with them in another part of the river, as dog caregivers, including me, encouraged, praised, and disciplined the respective dogs, while we stood nearby, on park grass or rocky shore. Jura played with fellow canines for over sixty minutes. Meanwhile, gravitating toward a wooden bench and then sitting there allowed me to remain nearby, observant, and serene.

Again having accepted an invitation from my sister Valerie Watson to spend time with her as well as her daughter Myla and son Matthew, I visited Wolfeboro, New Hampshire for several days after the Fourth of July weekend. Myla is now thirteen-years-old and Matthew is now ten-years-old. Her daughter Grace, who is fifteen-years-old this year is visiting with my sister Lizzie. As he did last year, Jura traveled with me to Wolfeboro. If Jura cannot accompany me somewhere, I generally do not go somewhere.

Remaining with Valerie, Myla, and Matt for four days this summer contrasted as well as compared with the vacation time we shared together last year. Except occasionally, we found that referencing the house that the Watson family rents annually for two weeks in the summer as "The Soda Shack," and alternately employing redneck and aristocratic English dialects—which we did last year—was generally unsatisfying. Visiting Valerie, Myla and Matthew this summer invoked a quiet atmosphere, which differed from vacation time we shared last year. The respite resembled a family retreat; Valerie and I talked quietly, honestly, and sometimes jokingly for many hours, concerning family and work matters.

Not as many vacation LOL (laugh out loud) moments occurred this year, as happened last year. However, lively moments were not excluded from the family reunion. Entering a diner in the center of Wolfeboro allowed Valerie, Myla, Matthew, and me to share an especially heartwarming late afternoon lunch. The eating establishment was fashioned with 1950s era design, including shiny stainless-steel appliances, Formica counters with stainless-steel edges, and bold paint colors on the walls. Former Boston Red Sox team member pictures are hung upon walls on all four sides of the diner.

Stunning us, we discovered that among these black-and-white images is a mid-sized framed photograph of a former Red Sox pitcher and Baseball Hall of Fame (2000) inductee, William (Bill) Monbouquette. Now seventy-five-years-old, Mr. Monbouquette and Mom are distant relatives. Nearly eleven-years-old, Matthew, who loves baseball and is currently a baseball team member, used a digital camera to repeatedly shoot images of the framed photograph. He said he hopes to give Gramma (Reagan) copies of pictures that he decides to print.

Valerie, Matt, and I as well as brothers Alec and Derek Romero, friends of Matthew and Myla, held some late-night disco dancing contests, which began around 10:00 p.m. While displaying sensual disco dance movements, each contestant, who clearly enjoyed executing free style dance patterns, laughed regularly. Audience members experienced natural contentment as well as organic embarrassment, while observing contestants performing unusual body gyrations.

While sitting upon grass one afternoon and watching Matthew and Myla participating in lessons given at adjoined tennis courts, I became overheated, fatigued, and disheartened. Sunny, very hot, and humid weather had become nearly overbearing. Radio weather forecasters had advised listeners that relief was not anticipated in upcoming days. Suddenly, calling me from one of the courts, Myla addressed me. She requested that I join her, playing singles tennis, when the lesson which she was attending was completed. Though I was experiencing heat frustration and had not played tennis for over forty years, I consented reluctantly, yet cooperatively.

Retrieving a tennis racket that was stored in the car I drive, I entered one of the fenced-in tennis courts. After grasping a tennis ball with my right hand, I vertically raised the tennis racket I was holding in the left hand, threw the borrowed tennis ball slightly above the racket with the right hand, and then hit the falling ball with the tennis racket. Shockingly, I served the ball correctly, diagonally into the opposing court. Myla was standing here with a racket. Her knees were slightly bent; she was ready and waiting to rally. While we lobbied several times, she encouraged me.

Tennis playing tips she gave me before, during, and after the game were as gratifying as playing the game with her. After the match, while I briefly considered re-enrolling in tennis lessons, I put the idea on a mental Bucket List. A Bucket List is generally defined as a list indicating something(s) one wishes to do prior to "kicking the bucket," aka dying.

Sunday, July 18, 2010

Late this morning, via automobile, Jura and I departed the Watson family summer vacation home. We returned to Cohasset four hours hence. Suitcases were unpacked. Apartment cleaning responsibilities as well as laundry and ironing duties were performed. Jura was fed and given water. I prepared and ate a late lunch.

Late this afternoon as Jura and I were walking together, we strolled along Cohasset sidewalks, traversed Cohasset Village and then turned left onto Summer Street. We stopped outside the George H. Mealy American Legion Post, which faces Cohasset Harbor. Hearing a human voice greeting me caused me to suddenly turn sideways, leftward, and while doing so, I recognized an extended family member, Johnny Fannon, who was standing outside the veterans post. We began talking and joking. When the conversation ended, Johnny re-entered the post. I called Jura, not realizing he had jumped into James Brook.

A canal-like body, James Brook is situated beside the Legion, a gathering place for military veterans. The brook enters Cohasset Harbor. Caught in a high tide current, Jura was struggling to maintain equilibrium; a metal grate connected with the underpass of James Brook was preventing the fast-moving brook current from submerging Jura and carrying him into the harbor. I removed the wrist watch I was wearing, placed it on nearby grass, and prepared to enter the brook and to retrieve Jura, when I heard a bystander declare, "Miss, jumping into the water is not a good idea; debris, rocks, and glass are in the bottom of the brook."

Sadly, I surmised that whether or not the brook contained, rocks, debris or glass, fighting the brook current while wading or swimming and then retrieving and lifting Jura—who weighs seventy-four pounds when he is not soaking wet—onto the high embankment was not personally possible. After deciding not to enter the water body, I addressed Bystander, saying, "Well, what can we do? Can you call the police?" With both front paws, eight-year-old Jura continued to hold onto the brook grate, while he fought forward-moving current, by paddling against it with his rear paws. Bystander asked me to remain calm and to continue reassuring Jura, until rescue personnel arrived.

Doing as Bystander asked immediately relieved anxiety which had surfaced within me; experiencing acceptance and surrender allowed me to continue comforting Jura, whose eyes were reflecting internal longing, fatigue, and pain. Jura had been struggling with the moving current for ten minutes. The arrival of rescue personnel was not immediate.

The first responders were probably answering another local distress call. While remaining seated on the stone embankment and facing Jura, I suddenly heard sirens. Quickly, I turned sideways, this time rightward.

A Cohasset fire truck, police cruiser and ambulance appeared. *Whoa,* I thought. Three firemen, including a personal acquaintance, Cohasset Fire Department Sergeant, Mark Trask, approached and comforted me. Then Mark began directing fellow firemen.

The lower part of a several feet high stainless steel fire truck ladder was grounded below the surface of the canal waters. The upper portion of the ladder was slanted against a fence on the sidewalk bordering the canal, above the underpass. Two firemen held and steadied the ladder apex. From the sidewalk above the canal, another fireman coached and encouraged Jura, as he requested him to climb the ladder. Jura joyfully enters subfreezing temperature sea water and plays here in the middle of winter. Ladders scare him.

Seeing Jura stepping onto the ladder and immediately faltering, Coaching Fireman climbed onto and descended the ladder and then jumped into the brook. Standing in near waist deep water and at the same time facing the ladder, he cradled the backside of Jura, using his left arm; he set the right arm upon the ladder right column. As Jura ascended the ladder steps, Coaching Fireman also climbed the ladder, giving Jura support. He used simple, soft-spoken, and firm commands as well as comforting words.

Standing on a sidewalk above the brook pass, two firemen continued to steady the ladder that was placed into the canal. While observing two

Cohasset policemen, firefighters, and various passersby who were present at the scene, eagerly cheering and earnestly encouraging Jura to ascend the ladder and then to emerge onto the sidewalk, I suddenly imagined being amongst thousands of enthusiastic cheering spectators who had risen from stadium seats while they were watching Jura and Coaching Fireman climb the several foot high ladder. During the adrenalin rush-causing moments, I was joyfully tearful and humbled.

When Jura stepped off the ladder and onto the sidewalk and we were re-united, I repeatedly kissed him on the left cheek and nose and then thanked all of the Cohasset firemen who saved him from grave peril, including Coaching Fireman. Ambulance service personnel, having assessed the accident scene before Jura was rescued, conferred with firemen and then departed. A fireman who assisted the rescue effort offered me a long, thick, and coiled rope. He said that the rope could be used to make a dog leash; he was non-verbally and respectfully requesting me to leash Jura, when Jura and I departed the scene.

Moments after Jura and I started to walk home, I recalled the rescue effort and immediately burst out laughing. I was imagining a fireman who participated in the rescue returning home and non-verbally saying, "I want the woman I love to kiss me like the lady who owns the dog that nearly drowned kissed her dog." Then I pictured an imaginary woman who is the partner of the fireman, who upon hearing the request, addresses the fireman, saying "Finish this 'to-do list' and I will kiss you like the lady who owns the dog that nearly drowned kissed her dog."

Sunday, August 1, 2010

Sister Valerie, nieces Grace and Myla, and nephew Matthew have returned to Jacksonville, Florida. They had remained in Cohasset for ten days. Brother Jared, Elissa, the wife of Jared, niece Brynn, and nephews Jamus and Rylan, who had also been vacationing in Cohasset since June, returned to Europe. Jared and family will soon be residing in Geneva, Switzerland. No goodbyes were said among us.

The circumstances initially left me bewildered. Later, I remembered a time when I taught a college level course entitled Effective Business Communication. As an adjunct instructor, I taught the course for one school semester. One statement in the primary textbook that was used in the class indicates that 93.3 percent of the meaning of what people are truly communicating with one another is derived from non-verbal cues, not verbal messages. Another statement in the researched-based book stipulated that when one is questioning the veracity of what another person or persons is saying one relies on non-verbal, not verbal cues.

Reconsidering the textbook material found me re-acknowledging that on a regular basis, people stop talking with one another for unspecified amounts of time. Generally what is being communicated when people cease conversing with one another is that a relationship has undeniably changed. In other words, the previous manner of accepted interaction and communication manner within the relationship is dying or is passing away. As this is happening, a new way of relating is slowly and steadily emerging.

While a new relationship style is growing, remaining detached or objective encourages the maintenance of goodwill, whether or not detachment requires physical separation. This is what is intended to happen in relationships around the world. Goodwill is the expression of consistent kindness, respect, and cooperation within any type of relationship. Goodwill unites each and all relationships, in all circumstances. No worries.

All forms of communication naturally flow and ebb; this is not problematic. Viewing the stopping or slowing of communication as solely abnormal is not reasonable. When one or both persons in a relationship repeatedly experiences a sense of not being allowed to leave the relationship or not being allowed to change the manner in which the relationship is expressed, the relationship becomes unhealthy.

Whether people live together, people regularly meet and form new relationships with new people, throughout life. This reality does not give any person permission to dishonor the boundaries of an existing relationship or the limitations of a new association.

All relationships are valuable. All relationships involve boundaries. All relationships involve intimacy, which is expressed in innumerable ways. Newly formed sound relationships with properly established boundaries, have also been called holy affairs. These associations enliven previously established holy or healthy relationships.

Tuesday, August 17, 2010

Entering a fast-food restaurant at around noon today, I spotted Cohasset Middle School sixth grade special needs teacher, Julie Rimens, and Glenn Rimens, husband of Julie, and longtime Senior Minister of Second

Congregational Church in Cohasset, who were sitting in the dining room of the eating establishment.

Julie and I became acquainted during years we were Cohasset Public Schools employees. Church services and evening programs Second Congregational Church has hosted have intermittently drawn me here.

After ordering and receiving food, entering the restaurant dining room and then sitting aside a table, near where Julie and Glenn were sitting, I heard Julie asking me what brought me into the eatery. Socially nervous and at the same time chuckling, I responded, "I am buying Jura and me lunch. Jura is in the back seat of the car, probably hoping to eat a double hamburger. I am splurging on a hot apple pie." Joking, I added, "Let's see you equal this story."

This happened. While they were eating lunch, Judy and Glenn admitted having experienced difficulty with re-naming the Rimens family dog, after they adopted the animal, a retriever, I believe. Judy and Glenn then confessed to having looked through a book containing Baby Names, until they discovered the name Finian.

"Welcome, you are now officially recognized as being new members of the Eccentric Dog Owners Club," I gleefully replied. Dog Finian is now seven-years-old.

Monday, September 7, 2010

Sun is shining; air temperatures are registering about eighty degrees. Many people experience summer as being over when Labor Day arrives the first week in September. However, fall does not officially begin until September 22 or September 23, depending on the occurrence of the autumnal equinox.

Today, mid-morning, while strolling in Bare Cove Park with Jura, I glanced beyond land and viewed five anchored and tethered, medium-sized yachts, situated in one section of the Back River, a saltwater river bordering Bare Cove Park. Totaling an estimated sixty persons, occupants of the yachts, including adults and children, were merrymaking. Boisterous and enthusiastic, a number of partygoers were playing the game of Trivia. Someone, shouting as though he or she was using a megaphone, asked, "What well-known seabird generally inhabits the Pacific Ocean area?"

Standing on shore, while Jura played with fellow dogs, I responded, muffling, "Ah... I don't know." I could not hear the answer that was given to the question.

The correct answer may be albatross. Yes, I am confessing to having sought "Google" aid to answer the question. Continuing to view people who were standing in as well as moving about these boats left me intrigued and somewhat bewildered, while I imagined socializing among nearly sixty people, while partying and intermittently traversing several anchored yachts connected with thick marine rope.

Thursday September 23, 2010

Today is day two of fall 2010. Air temperatures continue to be good and mild, in the middle eighties, during daylight hours. The atmosphere was also unusually warm last night. The moon was especially large, full, and nearly orange in color; thin cloud patches passed by.

Is this moon called a harvest moon, I wondered. Yes, this is true. Internet research indicates that a harvest moon occurs twice annually, first on March 20 or March 21, also known as the spring equinox, and again on September 22nd or September 23rd, which is also known as the autumnal equinox. Each of the two equinoxes happen every year, when the sun crosses the celestial equator. The celestial equator is formed when the tilting of the equator causes an abstract or imaginary projection of the equator into space. A celestial equinox causes the length of day and night to be equal. A harvest moon appears enormous, solely because the sun, while crossing the celestial equator is illuminating the moon. Actually, this gigantic lunar appearance is an optical illusion.

Last night, while driving along coastal road and viewing a harvest moon from a considerable distance, I imagined a witch riding a broom, wearing a witch hat, and flying directly in front of and past the moon, as one might picture on Halloween Eve. The fanciful peaceful moment ended almost instantly, when I unexpectedly realized that Halloween is more than one month away.

Friday, September 24, 2010

Being Catholic Now upholds the value of truth as well as humor. The author of the book is Kerry Kennedy. She is a daughter of the late Senator Robert Kennedy and Ethel Kennedy, the widow of Senator Kennedy. Published in 2008, *Being Catholic Now* features excerpts from interviews that Ms.

Kennedy conducted with widely known Americans surrounding faith and Catholicism.

As we stood outside the Cohasset home that Neamh Babineau Ramsay shares with Andy Ramsay, husband of Neamh, she and I were intending to eat lunch together. Before we departed, I read an excerpt from *Being Catholic Now* aloud. Neamh and I howled with laughter, as we were huddled together, while I read the book passage.

Pulitzer Prize-winning author and Newsweek columnist, Anna Quindlen, is the first featured interviewee in the book. On page five, it is written Ms. Quindlen stated "As a child, I internalized the sense that I didn't need to feel that bad about anything, because I could make it better on a Saturday afternoon, in a dark place. When we first started going to confession, we really had nothing to confess; that is why we made everything up. And by the time we really had things to confess, either they were things the Church had taught us were so shameful, that we didn't want to confess them, or they seemed too amorphous to be confessable."

Longtime Cohasset residents, Neamh and I were both reared Catholic. She accompanied me as I drove to a new healthy food and pizza restaurant, where we talked while we shared a vegetarian pizza. Jura was outside the eatery sitting in nearby yard and eating a marrow bone. I had attached a lead to the dog collar Jura wears and after uncoiling it, had wrapped it around a nearby tree trunk and then secured it.

When we finished sharing lunch, Neamh and I decided to walk in nearby Wompatuck State Park. We continued conversing while I drove and Jura was situated in the back seat. When the car was parked in the park parking lot, we decided to walk in wooded versus paved park trails; both of these types of trails are present in the park. While walking with us, Jura periodically wandered beyond us, before he returned.

After walking for nearly forty-five minutes, Neamh and I stopped beside a park bench, intending to rest and at the same time wanting to stretch. While we were performing stretching exercises for ten minutes, we agreed that stretching is as beneficial as walking.

We both confessed to feeling as light as air, when we finished this activity, before we continued to stroll back toward the parking lot. After retrieving her cellphone and viewing the time displayed on the device, Neamh informed me that two hours had elapsed, when we had finished walking.

We decided to purchase and eat small soft-serve ice cream cones available at an ice cream shop in Cohasset Center. The sweet spot is beside a train stop which is about a seven-minute drive from Wompatuck State Park. A few weeks ago, niece Kristin, great nephew Zachariah, and I visited the same ice cream and sandwich shop. We traveled here on foot, walking for about thirty minutes; Kristin brought a stroller, so that Zach could sit in it, when we were returning home. When we three had finished eating respective ice cream and ice cream cones, we headed back to the Sullivan house; Kristin was pushing a stroller in which Zachariah was sitting. Along the way, we passed Greenbush line commuter train tracks; some of the tracks distantly parallel North Main Street.

Shortly thereafter, we entered the split-level design house that Kristin and her husband Payden and two-year-old Zachariah, now inhabit. Later, standing aside a railing in the living room of the home, Zach called me, as I was stepping down front hall stairway stairs near the railing, preparing to depart. He was radiant, smiling with glowing eyes.

He had clenched his right hand into a fist; the right-hand forefinger was pointed straight up, toward sky, toward Heaven. Silently drawing me near, Zach non-verbally asked me, "Do you hear train? Train is coming." As the heart within me spiritually melted into a million pieces, I became tearful.

This afternoon, Neamh Ramsay and I shared conversation mixed with laughter that lasted nearly five hours. We agreed this conversation will sustain us for a long time. After Neamh and I parted, I returned home and slipped into a summer dress, nylons, and shoes. An hour later, I entered DanceSport Boston (DSB) studio, exchanged street shoes for dance shoes, stepped onto the studio dance floor, and entered an ongoing dance class.

Lead DSB instructor Pace Lomacki is teaching the Hustle dance. Popular in nightclubs and discotheques in the 1970s, the Hustle is a fast-moving energetic dance, which involves quick, flowing, and wide sweeping movements and turns. The disco dance was gradually modified and incorporated into ballroom dance school syllabuses. The acclaimed 1977 film *Saturday Night Fever* starred John Travolta, who portrayed Tony Manero, a nineteen-year-old young man whose home and work life was difficult. Tony developed an increasingly positive attitude about life when he began going to nightclubs in Brooklyn, New York on weekends and he learned to dance. With other night club goers in the film, he performed the famed Hustle dance.

Saturday, September 25, 2010

While he was talking with me this afternoon, a Cohasset Recycling Transfer Center (CRTC) employee was unknowingly playing the role of confessor. Having grown up referencing the recently newly named recycling center as The Dump, I now find not calling the center The dump feels, well, uncomfortable. Truthfully, sometimes saying The Dump evokes laughter and a little embarrassment. Likewise, sometimes saying The Recycling Transfer Center comes across as overtly intense, or excessively serious.

Wearing a red shirt and blue jeans, the dump employee may have seen me throwing three plastic bags filled with household trash into a dumpster; the trash bags had not been covered with a large town-identifying and officially mandated plastic trash bag. Each town trash bag costs $1.50; a pack of ten costs fifteen dollars. Having seen household trash bags which had not been covered with a town mandated trash bag appearing in one dumpster, I felt weakly justified; I pitched the three plastic bags filled with household trash that I brought here from home into the dumpster.

Minutes later, a transfer center employee walked past me. Remorse invaded me. Intentionally and immediately I walked straight toward the man, and when I was near reaching him, he suddenly turned toward me, while I was saying, "Ah…, pardon me, I want to confess something." Facing me, he viewed me calmly and then quizzically.

Then he heard me nervously say, "I put three trash-filled plastic bags into a dumpster without covering them with mandated Town of Cohasset trash bags." Instantly becoming defensive found me also being unreasonably assertive. "I think covering plastic trash bags, using another plastic trash bag, costing a dollar-fifty per bag, is silly," I stated. The dump employee was advised that I, the dump regulations offender had previously addressed the Cohasset Town Manager and had politely expressed opposition to being required to cover plastic bags filled with household trash with another mandated plastic trash bag.

Extending me understanding and compassion, the Cohasset Town Manager, sitting at a desk in the office of the town manager explained, "Selling the bags does generate town revenue and the bags are recycled."

Climaxing the confession monologue and continuing to address the Dump employee, I solemnly admitted to loving Cohasset and wanting to respect Cohasset trash bag regulations, whether or not I like the rules. Then I apologized. "I am sorry for having done this and will not do it again," I said quietly. While cautiously raising my lowered head, I viewed the employee who had suddenly become a confessor. He observed me, emanating kindness, compassion, and respect.

"Good deal," he humbly responded. The spiritual judge then walked past me.

What? I thought. *No lecture? No condescending attitude?* Interacting with the gentleman left me wondering, was he ever a priest? Whether or not this is so, this fellow human being is clearly a true and admirable confessor. One Sunday morning following the encounter, while attending a local 9:30 a.m. church service and standing in a communion line, I discovered the kind, gentle, and forgiving dump employee is also a Eucharistic minister.

CHAPTER FOURTEEN

BEING CATHOLIC REVISITED, CONDOLEEZZA RICE, WAR LESSONS ROSALYNN CARTER, WANDERING EYES

Tuesday, September 28, 2010

Today I finished reading *Being Catholic Now*. Pages of the book contain recorded interviews that author Kerry Kennedy conducted with thirty-seven widely-known Americans who are Catholic. The conversations allowed interviewees to share personal faith journeys and enabled Ms. Kennedy to illuminate universally shared ideas about religion and spirituality. Previously noted author Anna Quindlen offered candid, humorous, and respectful personal reflections. Contributions that interviewees author James Carroll and actor Martin Sheen made to the work were intriguing as well.

A former priest, James Carroll is quoted in *Being Catholic Now* on page sixty-one, as saying, "We really never know for sure who God is, or what God means; we really don't know for sure who Jesus was, or what Jesus meant." Mr. Carroll says he continues to experience connection with God. As do many, he believes that the relationship between God and humanity cannot be broken, in life or in death. *Being Catholic Now* also quotes James Carroll as saying, "God is unknown. God is beyond the horizon. What I know about God, I know from Jesus and the community that remembers him."

On page two-hundred thirty-five of the book, seventy-year-old actor Martin Sheen is quoted as saying, "I had May 1, 1981 off. In Europe, of course, it was a national holiday, so I went to church." In Europe, May 1 is also referenced as May Day. On this day, springtime soil, livestock, and fertility are celebrated. Village and community festivities accompany the holiday. Sometimes May Day festivities include crowning a May Queen.

Martin Sheen was residing in Paris, France, in the spring of 1981. Mr. Sheen indicated that he believes May Day, 1981 imitated a day that one arises, decides to do something, and is not deterred from doing something in any way. "I decided I would come back to the Church," he said. Mr. Sheen related arriving outside a Parisian cathedral and knocking upon the large heavy front doors. Receiving no reply, he then rang the church doorbell.

No response followed.

He wondered whether he was truly meant to go to church again. As he turned around and was walking down front steps of the cathedral, he suddenly heard sound signaling that the front doors of the hundreds-years-old sanctuary were swinging wide open. Instantly turning around again and facing the doors, Mr. Sheen discovered a priest was standing inside the church entrance. The reverend was eating food. Looking toward Martin Sheen, the clergyman said, "What is it?"

Turning toward the priest, Mr. Sheen replied, "Father, I've been away from the church for many, many years and I'd like to come back; I'd like to go to confession." Martin Sheen commented that the spiritual Father, glancing toward him, was clearly moved.

The reverend said, "You came to the right place."

Mr. Sheen commented that while he was making confession, he trusted the reverend, even though the two men had not met before. He said that during the process, brokenness flowed through him. As confession ended, the reverend looked upon him kindly. Then he simply and quietly said, "Welcome back."

Mr. Sheen indicated that he was overjoyed as he realized that he had begun a renewed relationship with God, fellow humanity, and self, and that he had been motivated to do so through love, not through fear or guilt. He is quoted on page two-hundred thirty-six of *Being Catholic Now* as saying, "We're meant to be free, spiritually, emotionally, and physically; I don't think we can be talked out of this, once we're anchored in faith, once we see God present." Martin Sheen believes that the central mystery of Catholicism is as mysteriously empowering as it is ironically simple. He states, "God becomes human. Go figure."

Wednesday, September 29, 2010

Yesterday, an NBC network television news reporter interviewed President Obama. During discussion that lasted nearly thirty minutes, the president indicated that he hopes that America will progressively become identified as an "Education Nation." Promoting this perception of American education, Mr. Obama said that he supports extending school day hours or increasing the number of years that students attend schools. He also endorses training ten-thousand new math and science teachers. He has promised that states that develop model education programs and practices will be awarded government prize money, totaling four billion dollars.

During the interview, President Obama referenced political frustration that he continues to experience as the national unemployment rate currently remains near ten percent. Frankly, I am beginning to view economic recessions as resembling viral diseases. Recessions can be medicated, utilizing, for example, stimulus funds or work programs.

Political remedies may or may not assist economic recovery. Resembling human viruses, economic recessions as well as economic gold rushes generally continue until having run a course, so to speak. Once asked how long diagnosed cold symptoms generally last, if one is given medication, a physician replied, "Using medication, cold symptoms generally last about…seven days." When asked how long diagnosed cold symptoms generally last without using medication, the medical doctor commented, "Symptoms generally last about…seven days."

Thursday, September 30, 2010

Today found me reading *All Quiet on the Western Front*, which was first published in January of 1929, eleven years following the end of World War I. The late Erich Maria Remarque, novelist and WW I veteran, wrote the book. During the war, he served the German army on the Western Front—an over four hundred miles long stretch of land traversing though France and Belgium which included contested lands being controlled by Germany to the East and the Allies to the west. In *All Quiet on the Western Front,* Mr. Remarque depicted and relived situations and circumstances of World War I and the horrors of battle.

The setting of the conflict was Europe. Causes of the war included deep and unresolved political and economic divisions between then European Central Powers and the Allied countries. Countries then identified as European Central Powers were Austria-Hungary, Germany, Turkey, and Bulgaria. Allied countries then included the United Kingdom, the United States, Russia, France, Italy, Romania, Greece, Serbia, and Japan.

World War I lasted four years, from 1914 to 1918. Nine million military and seven million civilian casualties are reported to have occurred. WWI officially ended when the Treaty of Versailles was signed in France; the date of the signing was June 28, 1919. Signees included German leadership and political representatives of the Allied countries, including then U.S. President Woodrow Wilson.

A personal summary of a brief excerpt from *All Quiet on the Western Front* follows:

Nineteen-year-old Franz Kemmerick, who was gravely injured on the battlefield, is lying in a hospital bed. Paul Baumer, a comrade of Franz, was sitting beside him. Paul and Franz grew up together; Paul sometimes copied essays Franz wrote when the two friends were in school together.

Because it was severely damaged, one leg of Franz was amputated; Franz does not realize this when Mr. Baumer and two additional comrades of Franz arrived to visit him.

On page fourteen, Paul Baumer says, "He (Franz) looks ghastly, yellow, and wan. Under the skin, life no longer pulses; it has already pressed out the boundaries of the body. Death is working through from within." Denying the imminent death of Franz while he is conversing with him, Paul informs Franz that when he receives a new artificial limb he will hardly notice anything is missing.

Reality permeates Paul; he suddenly becomes somber. On page twenty-nine, he was quoted as saying, "That is Franz Kemmerick, nineteen-and-a-half years old and he doesn't want to die. Let him not die." Franz was not denying death. He said that when he dies, he wants Paul to give a comrade whose last name is Mueller, the lace-up combat boots Franz wore, when he was engaged in battle.

Lying in a hospital overflowing with wounded and dying soldiers, Franz is still. He is becoming increasingly pale. He asks comrade Paul to come closer to him. Beseeching Paul, Franz silently whispers, "If you find my watch, send this home." Mr. Baumer says, "I do not reply." Not one person can console Paul. "I am wretched with helplessness," he laments.

Having known Franz as a military comrade for over ten years, soldier Baumer suddenly leans toward Franz. Momentarily deluded, Paul proposes that perhaps Franz can soon enter a convalescent home; he imagines the recovery site as being a large villa, where Franz can play piano or venture outside, while he is returning to health. Meanwhile, Franz begins to breathe sparingly; he is also crying softly.

Reality again overcomes Paul. Surrendering he says, "What a fine mess I have made with my foolish talk. He (Franz) is entirely alone with his little life of nineteen years and he cries because it leaves him." The remark left me wondering whether Franz is crying essentially because he is passing away or because he is at peace with dying, which is allowing him to move beyond human limitation and horrendous effects of war.

Franz dies. The body of Franz is moved out of the hospital bed and enfolded into a waterproof sheet. Another seriously injured soldier lying on a hospital hallway is placed upon the hospital bed Franz occupied. Franz is the seventeenth hospitalized soldier who has died during the day, which is not yet over.

Stepping outside the hospital exit, Mr. Baumer experiences a spiritual presence in wind. Wind delivers him from internal darkness. Wind Spirit is steadying, invigorating and revitalizing—in mind, body, and soul. Deliverance is unmistakable, gentle, and mystifying.

Friday, October 1, 2010

Yesterday morning, Thursday, September 30, 2010, my niece Kristin Jenkins Sullivan delivered a healthy baby boy, who was named Clarkson Payden Sullivan. The time was approximately 3:30 a.m. Like his brother, Zachariah, Clarkson entered this world one week before he was scheduled to arrive. Though she began experiencing contractions several days before giving birth, Kristin continued to perform routine daily activities.

No epidural was used during the birth process. When Kristin and Payden, the husband of Kristin, arrived in a Boston hospital, baby Clark was good and near being born. When an infant is near being born, injecting anesthesia into the lower spine is unsafe. Recently asked whether she was experiencing pain when she entered the hospital, she selflessly stated Payden was "as white as a sheet." She said he was good and supportive, as baby Clarkson was entering this world.

Friday, October 8, 2010

Awkwardness permeated the atmosphere when a DanceSport Boston class I was attending started this evening. Tonight, substituting for the regular dance class instructor, Pace Lomacki, was dance instructor Jayson

Palmer. Comprising five students, the recently begun waltz class is made up of one couple and three single women, including me. Many students were absent, possibly because this is a long weekend which begins today and ends on Monday. The holiday on Monday is Columbus Day.

Somehow classroom anxiety evaporated, as Jayson proceeded with dance instruction. Later, in a small group, women without partners practiced waltz steps which were re-introduced tonight, while Jayson observed and then instructed a partnered couple. Sometimes we women held hands while we were practicing steps; doing so is a means of steadying one another, encouraging communication surrounding dance concepts, and building trust with dance partners.

Mr. Palmer alternated between watching and guiding the partnered couple with teaching and dancing with solo female students. Ballroom dancing skills and accompanying social confidence that have developed within me, while attending DanceSport Boston dance classes for a little over a year, although irregularly, were reaffirmed during the class, as Jayson and I danced together. Hoping to date again someday finds me grateful that Jayson has reassured me that dance partnerships, as all relationships, are developed through mutual demonstration of child-like kindness, respect, and cooperation, which is synonymous with accepting uncertainty.

Tuesday, October 26, 2010

I am not sure how this happened. While driving to Hanover, Massachusetts and at the same time using a newly purchased cell phone, I suddenly discovered that I was in the middle of a four-way intersection, directly below a glowing red traffic light. Almost instantly, car traffic began moving directly toward me, on both sides of the car. Putting extra pressure on the gas pedal, I drove beyond the middle of the intersection to the opposing street. Somehow, no accident happened. Deeply relieved and grateful, I immediately decided not to use a cell phone again while driving, unless I have pulled over to the side of a road.

Later, while returning to Cohasset, through Scituate, after window shopping in Hanover Mall, I unexpectedly saw a young man rollerblading. He was wearing shorts, a shirt, and a flapping unzipped jacket. Barreling down the street while enjoying sunny, warm weather, the young man was headed in a westerly direction. I was headed east. Increasingly curious, I squinted, leaned forward, and peered through the front windshield of the car, before I recognized that the young adult was nephew Rhett Jenkins.

When momentarily seeing Rhett, who was rollerblading down a street, I remembered watching him play hockey when he was around seven-years-old. Small-statured and able to skate fast while holding a hockey stick, he often darted around opposing players, while he was advancing a hockey puck. One winter weekend, when I was babysitting him for the weekend in Cohasset, we went to a skating club located in Hingham, Massachusetts. The rectangular shape clubhouse was painted dark red on the outside. The interior design of the clubhouse was rustic and the building contained a medium-size wood-burning furnace. I guessed that the capacity of the building was between thirty and forty people. The facility overlooked an open-air skating area. The outdoor rink abutted a large wooded area which served as natural fencing where fencing connected to the clubhouse ended.

College students playing intramural hockey here invited Rhett to join an ongoing hockey game. For over an hour, Rhett joined the college hockey players. Kneeling upon a bench and facing a clubhouse window permitted me to view the good-natured, feisty, and rapidly moving match. When Rhett returned inside the wood paneled clubhouse, and then sat upon a bench beside me, he was crying.

Initially, he was enthused when he actively joined the college players in a progressing hockey game. As he continued to participate in the vigorous match, he began to experience considerable foot pain. When he returned inside the clubhouse, Rhett admitted that he did not want fellow hockey players to be aware of the circumstance. When I removed each of the skates he had been wearing, reddened, cold, and swollen feet were clearly visible and sensitive to touch.

This afternoon, on a fall day, while he was rollerblading, Rhett was child-like, flying free, as birds do. The sight was thrilling. It was calming. It was reassuring.

Wednesday, October 27, 2010

Brother Jared, sister-in-law Elissa, and their children are vacationing in Cohasset for about a week. Jamus, Brynn, and Rylan are currently on school vacation. This Sunday, the Reagans will return to Geneva, Switzerland, where they are now residing during the school year. Elissa, seven-year-old Jamus, and I conversed briefly this morning, outside the Reagan family home in Cohasset. Wishing to speak with Jared, I had decided to drive to the house around mid-morning.

Elissa was seated in the driver seat of the family car and Jamus was sitting in the back seat of the vehicle; mother and son were ready to depart. She said that Jared is meeting with fellow employees who work in the New York office of the investment company that he owns and manages. Advising me that Jared will be returning home this evening, Elissa suggested that I revisit then.

Talking later today via telephone, Jared and I agreed to meet this evening. While we were conversing tonight, four-year-old Rylan entered the residential office, in which Jared and I were seated and conversing. Rylan was gleaming and at the same time, giggling.

He was wearing a long, flowing party dress whose owner is Brynn, a sister of Rylan. Rylan enjoys performing holy, healthy mischief. Rolling his eyes toward Heaven, Jared smiled. Then, turning toward me and grinning, he said, "If he wants to wear dresses when he is fifteen, I will be bewildered." Rylan probably enjoys occasionally wearing dresses, partially because during early years of life, all young boys and all young girls discover human androgyny. Throughout life, in varying circumstances, each and all humans become aware of demonstrating God-given male and female attributes.

This fact is biblically derived. In the English Revised Version of the *Bible*, a letter from Paul to the Galatians indicates that faith truly equalizes people, as when there is true faith, or true belief in God or Divinity, neither any individual nor any community is identified primarily in terms of worldly characteristics. The biblical passage cites "there can be neither Jew nor Greek, there can be neither bond nor free, there is no male and female." Therefore, the body of humanity, made in the image of God, reflects the spirit of God.

The human body is male or female; the human spirit is not. It is both. Experiencing feelings of being essentially masculine or feminine at some point or points in life is neither essentially normal nor abnormal. A male who is experiencing feeling dominantly feminine or a female who is experiencing feeling primarily masculine may be respectively rejecting male or female attributes, and therefore overemphasizing female or male traits.

The circumstance is usually a phase in a process in which a person is learning to understand or to reassess the nature of androgyny and while doing so, to equally embrace male and female attributes. Discussing and navigating feelings is useful and beneficial. Meanwhile, the truth is that it is likely that from time to time, four-year-old Rylan relishes wearing clothes that girls wear, simply because he realizes the activity unnerves Daddy.

Thursday, October 28, 2010

Condoleezza (Condi) Rice, former National Security Advisor (2001-2005) and former U.S. Secretary of State, (2005-2009), was sitting beside a forum moderator on a stage in the John F. Kennedy Library in Boston, where she was the featured speaker. Before attending the mid-morning forum, while driving the mini-SUV toward the JFK Library parking lot, I was not surprised to discover that the lot was filled. Additional nearby parking lots were also full. I continued to drive and at the same time surveyed the surrounding landscape, until I found a parking space located fifteen minutes walking distance from the library.

When entering the main auditorium of the library, I was advised that seats there and in the first library auditorium annex were filled. Standing in the back of the main auditorium was not possible; forum guests were standing behind the filled seats. Media crew and accompanying equipment filled any remaining standing space. Several minutes later, I found a seat, when I entered the second library auditorium annex. Being seated in an auditorium annex enables JFK library goers to view library programming on a film screen.

Ms. Rice and the forum moderator, R. Nicholas Burns, were sitting upon moderately sized upholstered chairs. A small round table was centered between them. A vase filled with arranged flowers and some water had been set upon the tabletop, between two glasses that were nearly filled with water.

Mr. Burns is now a Harvard University professor who teaches Diplomacy Practice and International Politics. He served in the two administrations of President George W. Bush, as U.S NATO Ambassador (2001-2005) and U.S State Department Political Affairs Secretary (2005-2008).

During the first administration of President Bill Clinton, he served as U.S. State Department Spokesperson (1995-1997). Former professional colleagues, Condi Rice and Nick Burns are also friends. Ms. Rice was employed at Stanford University as a Political Science professor in 1981. Entering public service for the first time in 1986, she served as Special Assistant to the Joint Chiefs of Staff in the Ronald Reagan Administration. President George H.W. Bush designated Ms. Rice as U.S National Security Foreign Affairs Special Assistant in 1989.

She resigned the position in 1991, when she returned to Stanford University, where she had previously been teaching. She continued in a professorship role until as the first female to do so, she assumed the position of Stanford University Provost, from 1993–1999.

Condi Rice resigned the provost position in 1999. Victorious in the November 1999 election, incoming President George W. Bush had named Ms. Rice the new Bush administration National Security Advisor, a position she held from 2001 until 2005.

In 2005, she was named U.S. Secretary of State, after President Bush was elected for a second term. Ms. Rice remained in the position until 2009. Condoleezza Rice has been employed as a Stanford University Graduate School Political Science Professor, since she returned there in 2009, when the second term of the George W. Bush administration ended.

Modestly and quickly Ms. Rice quelled thunderous applause that she received when she entered the main auditorium stage of the JFK library. I am not sure how she segued into talking about her childhood years. Having been distracted from time to time, I missed parts of the presentation Ms. Rice gave. I believe several comments she made, that I do remember, are worth sharing.

As Condi Rice recalled being a young girl growing up in Birmingham, Alabama, she recalled not being allowed to sit aside the Woolworth's department store lunch counter. She also reminisced not being allowed to enter Birmingham city pools. At some point, she realized that the reasons why the rules were established went beyond parental guidance.

Condoleezza Rice recalled the white supremacy ideology which motivated Ku Klux Klan (KKK) activities. She remembered four fellow young girls who were killed, while they were attending a Baptist Church in Birmingham. KKK members bombed the religious sanctuary, on Sunday, September 15, 1963. Condi was nine years old then. She lived near the church.

She was ten years old when The Civil Rights Act—banning segregation in public places and prohibiting discrimination based on race, color, religion, sex, or national origin—became law on June 2, 1964. Ms. Rice commented that although she attests to the occurrence of segregation and discrimination, she said that she has not ever believed that she is or was primarily a victim of either of these prejudicial practices. Wow. The statement figuratively grabbed me.

When one defines self solely in terms of being a victim, one views self essentially as being aggrieved or entitled, Ms. Rice testified. She also explained that when one views self as essentially being persecuted or ill-treated, one loses self-confidence. These statements are halting. These words are thought-provoking. These words are pure truth.

No human being is essentially a victim. Every human being has experienced being mistreated or victimized at one time or another. Condoleezza Rice exudes confidence, which one can summon only when he or she knows how to be generally joyful and patient, how to accept and to learn from suffering, and how to forgive and to move forward.

Sunday, November 7, 2010

Cohasset Cabaret opened and closed this weekend; St. Anthony Church parish hall stage was the show venue. Approximately one hundred and fifty people attended Cohasset Cabaret performances on Friday as well as Saturday evening. The show began at 8:00 p.m.

An estimated thirty cast members participated; twenty-nine acts filled the two-hour variety show, which was directed, rehearsed, and produced in less than six weeks. Acts included band-accompanied musical and rock and roll songs, guitar accompanied folk songs, comedic skits, and dancing.

Revenue from the show is donated to a local non-profit organization. In turn the non-profit organization donates the show proceeds to programs for Cohasset seniors, residents of the town who are sixty-five-years-old and over. Cohasset Cabaret performances generated approximately six thousand dollars this year.

Being a Cohasset Cabaret cast member was gratifying. Being chosen to be a vocal trio member and to sing a short solo, as did each trio member, was also good and contenting. As the event was ending, Jensen Baylor, show emcee as well as a cast member, addressed audience members. "Thank you, for coming tonight. We hope you enjoyed the show and want to come back next year. Remember, tonight is the night that we set the time back one hour on clocks; I usually set mine forward, but hey, this is me," said Jensen, as exiting audience and cast members guffawed.

Sunday, November 9, 2010

Late this afternoon, standing and applauding onlookers, including me, watched former First Lady Rosalynn Carter entering the John F. Kennedy Library auditorium stage. In January 2011, Rosalynn Carter will have been promoting programs that have served mentally ill Americans for at least forty years, since the early 1970s. She began the work before Jimmy Carter, the husband of Rosalynn, was President of the United States, from 1977-1981.

Today, Mrs. Carter again tackled mental health issues that Americans are facing. Intrigued, wanting to be increasingly educated about the issues, wishing to hear the former first lady speak publicly, and hoping to hear her present the recently published book she wrote, entitled, *Within Our Reach: Ending the Mental Health Crisis*, I decided to attend the hour-long forum. Brown University Professor of Clinical Psychology and book author Dr. Peter Kramer moderated the event.

As the program began, Rosalynn Carter recalled Jimmy Carter being a candidate for U.S. president, before he became president. After one campaign rally speech that Mr. Carter delivered, Rosalynn decided to stand among hundreds of people, who were waiting and wishing to greet and shake hands with the presidential candidate. The time was 4:30 a.m.

A woman employed at a cotton mill was standing beside Mrs. Carter. As the two ladies conversed, the mill employee said that she had recently finished working the late shift. Very early in the morning, she returns home and gives her mentally ill daughter care, while her husband, who gives the daughter overnight care, works during the day.

Surprised when he saw Rosalynn standing in line, Jimmy approached her, and then smiling, he said, "What are you doing here?"

Mrs. Carter responded directly and firmly, "As president, how will you serve mentally ill persons?"

Mr. Carter responded cheerfully, "When I am president, I will create an excellent nationwide program serving mentally ill persons, and you will be the head of the program."

Fulfilling the campaign promise, Jimmy Carter established a Presidential Commission on Mental Health, when he became President, in 1977. Although Rosalynn was not the head member, she was a board member. The board significantly influenced members of Congress to pass the Mental Health Systems Act of 1979 and prompted President Jimmy Carter to sign the bill, which converted it into law.

The act publicly acknowledged and disapproved of the overmedication of mentally ill patients, the exclusion of mentally ill patients in mental illness treatment plans and the housing of mentally ill persons in severely overcrowded state mental hospitals. Codified, the legislation improved services available to mentally and emotionally ill persons and initiated new freedoms and choices being given to mental health patients. The Mental Health Systems Act of 1979 fostered the opening of community mental health centers.

It promoted the construction of group homes for mentally ill persons, offering people who are mentally ill significantly increased chances of healing, through being able to live within deinstitutionalized settings and at the same time receiving mental health care services.

Dr. Kramer, sitting near Mrs. Carter upon the JFK Library auditorium stage observed, "You (Rosalynn) seem to have an affinity for families of people with mental illness. You also have an easy feeling for people with mental illness. I wonder why that is?"

Rosalynn commented that when Jimmy Carter was the governor of Georgia, (1971-1975), as the first lady of Georgia, she visited mental hospitals in the state. Georgia is the home state of Jimmy and Rosalynn Carter.

Mrs. Carter stated that while she toured these hospitals, she witnessed patients living in deplorable conditions. She viewed, for example, twelve-thousand mentally ill people crowded into a hospital with a patient capacity of three-thousand patients. She saw mentally ill persons who were wearing visible diapers. She viewed patients who were seated in chairs and aimlessly rocking back and forth.

She commented that during the 1970s, not long ago, the subject of mental illness was generally not discussed in public. This is true. Families who were unable to give a mentally ill family member(s) care, generally for a variety of reasons, sometimes including safety matters, often placed the mentally ill family member in state or private mental health hospitals, depending on family financial circumstances. Mentally ill patients often remained in the institutions until death, whether or not they were visited, former First Lady Rosalynn Carter stated. Mrs. Carter indicated that until the late 1970s, state hospitals were one of few options for mentally ill persons, outside being given care at home.

"But then an army base in Georgia that was not being used was made into a mental health care facility," Mrs. Carter stated. She said patients who lived in the building were allowed to choose daily attire, freely enter the cafeteria, and order personally desired foods. State mental hospitals generally did not permit these activities. Patients admitted or transferred to the mental health care facility in Georgia were given increased opportunities to interact with fellow patients in addition to health care staff.

The former first lady said, "It was wonderful to see what happens to people when they have a chance. This was not much of a chance. But it was a total difference."

Wondrously, Mrs. Carter commented that the night before Jimmy Carter was elected president, he was mopping the basement floor of the home in which he and Rosalynn had been living in Georgia. As president, Jimmy Carter facilitated the establishment of one hundred twenty-three community mental health centers nationwide. Solely offering general and contact information about mental health issues, some centers were basic. "At the same time, we were also trying to find new homes for mentally ill persons," Mrs. Carter said. She then segued into discussing and promoting *Within Our Reach: Ending the Mental Health Crisis.*

Writers Lizzie K. Golant and Kathryn E. Cade assisted Rosalynn Carter, in the writing of *Within Our Reach: Ending the Mental Health Crisis,* which illuminates surprising facts and myths surrounding mental illness. One of the facts is that significant research supports the theory that mental illness significantly influences twenty-five percent of productivity losses that occur in the workplace. Rosalynn Carter stunned JFK Library forum guests when she verbalized the truth, which is documented in the book she wrote.

Audience members, including me, gasped when hearing the mental health statistic, possibly because while illuminating this reality, she revealed a myth. Mental illness does not happen solely to persons that have been referenced as "those people." Persons who experience mental illness are not members of an isolated group.

Mrs. Carter commented that renowned now belated cultural anthropologist, author, and speaker, Margaret Mead, (1901-1978) significantly influenced endeavors that for decades, she (Rosalynn) has spearheaded, in order to raise awareness of mental health issues and to promote the development of new options for treating mentally ill persons. Rosalynn Carter and Margaret Mead met in 1971. Having studied human behavior and cultural patterns for many years, Ms. Mead advised Mrs. Carter, "When society embraces vulnerable human beings, civilization is humanized."

Asked why she wrote *Within Our Reach: Ending the Mental Health Crisis,* Rosalynn Carter said, "I want people to know that mentally ill persons can be diagnosed and treated." Mrs. Carter indicated many mentally ill persons do recover. "People don't know this," she said. "Back in 1978, when we were working on the Presidential Commission on Mental Health, we did not mention recovery. It (recovery) was not something that at the time we thought was possible."

The former First Lady is correct. Knowing two people who were diagnosed with serious mental health issues in the 1960's, I also recall that during these years, the general societal consensus about serious mental illness was that recovery from such illness was improbable.

"What are the changes you have seen in the way we have treated mentally ill diagnosed patients, since the 1970s?" Dr. Kramer asked Mrs. Carter.

Having for decades interacted with numerous mental health professionals as well as thousands of people whose lives have been affected by mental illness, Rosalynn Carter said, "We now know what to do. We've learned so much more about the brain and the power of individuals to recover, even from serious illnesses. We have more knowledge about effective treatment and effective models for treatment delivery. We have early intervention strategies to prevent serious mental health issues from developing in children and adults."

Mrs. Carter commented that not stigmatizing mentally ill persons and instead offering mentally unwell persons proper treatment, can transform individuals and communities. Rosalynn Carter may agree with me, regarding a personal belief that is being stated here. Major differences between mentally healthy individuals and mentally ill individuals are often not overtly noticeable. Mentally ill persons who become mentally healthy learn how to recognize triggers—circumstances or situations that evoke traumatic experiences and associated mental health matters—and while doing so, learn how to face, address, and move beyond the issues.

Wednesday, November 17, 2010

Last night, while walking with dog Jura upon a sidewalk across the street from St. Anthony Church Rectory in Cohasset and at the same time looking through a large-paned rectory living room window, I noticed lights glowing. While observing a vaguely identifiable image, I suddenly became increasingly curious, while wondering who or what was inside the rectory living room.

I thought that "someone" in the living room might not be human. What I was observing might be a life-like statue resembling a human being. I also mused that "someone" in the living room might indeed be a human being who was waiting to talk with the pastor of St. Anthony Church, who is Father Jerrard Malone.

As I continued to walk forward, strolling along South Main Street sidewalk, while also looking across the street and peering through the rectory living room window, I suddenly slammed into a telephone pole. The collision not only left me bruised on the nose and left cheek but also found me realizing, the hard way, that I had probably been viewing a statue, not a human being. Moments later, Jura and I continued walking forward on the sidewalk.

When attending an upcoming Sunday mass, and after the service, knocking upon the open church sacristy door, I viewed Father Malone, Deacon Pierce Toomey, church assistant Orton Lalley, and a parishioner, who were sharing conversation. They were standing inside the sacristy, where priests prepare for masses and where church vestments are stored. Fr. Malone addressed me, saying, "Rejoice and enter." These words psychologically and delightfully transported me into biblical times, for a few seconds.

After entering the church sacristy and greeting Fr. Malone, I confessed to having strolled on sidewalk of South Main Street that is across the street from the rectory and at the same time, having peered through the large rectory living room window, when I suddenly slammed face first into a nearby telephone pole. I admitted that at the time, I was wondering who or what was in the St. Anthony Church rectory living room. Respectfully amused, Reverend Malone confirmed that when I looked through the St. Anthony rectory living room window, what I observed was indeed not a human being. What I saw was a life-like bust of St. Anthony, set on a table.

Prevailing curiosity prompted me to question Fr. Malone again, as I commented, "Saint Anthony, isn't he the patron saint of lost causes, and if this is so, where the heck was he when he knew I was about to slam into a telephone pole?" Fr. Malone answered me, gleefully and good naturedly. Grinning and not using words, he was probably saying that St. Anthony *was* near me, asking me not to be overly curious, when walking by a church rectory.

P.S. St. Jude is referenced as the patron St. of lost causes. St. Anthony is referenced as the finder of lost articles.

CHAPTER FIFTEEN

TEMPORARY HOME, CHRISTMAS HALLELUJAH, CHARLES GIBSON, BLIZZARD

Thursday, November 25, 2010

For several hours this morning, Jura and I walked in woods. This Thanksgiving Day found me later sitting beside the Pembroke table in the apartment kitchen, while reading and writing and alternately watching television, as dog Jura laid near me upon a living room rug. Unexpectedly, I decided to attend an early afternoon church-sponsored Thanksgiving Day dinner celebration that I had seen advertised. After driving to and entering the church dining hall, which seats approximately fifty people, and seeing ten strangers, most being volunteer staff, I suddenly became frozen, momentarily unable to move or to talk.

Simultaneously, I recalled the first day of kindergarten class; Mom had accompanied me to school. Resisting entrance to a classroom through an open door, I did not yet want to be away from home without Mom or Dad. Moments later, I realized it was time for me to grow up. This experience resembled what happened at the church.

Initially, I wanted to exit the church as quickly as possible. Then someone suddenly approached me. Offering me assistance, a female volunteer staff member, who was standing near me, gingerly moved me toward a table where one dinner guest was sitting.

A fellow diner, Marion, who is nearly ninety-years-old, was wearing an elegant, A-line design and three-quarter length, powder blue dress. The pearl necklace and pearl earrings that she wore enhanced her appearance.

Though admiring clothing Marion was wearing, I was finding it difficult to remember what she was saying. Distracted, not being fully present, I was softly weeping and at the same time, quickly wiping falling facial tears. All at once, everything hurt.

Attending the church event caused me to remember being the director of an overnight homeless shelter for women; I oversaw operations and management of the shelter. I also recalled in later years, working alongside fellow volunteers in homeless shelters with kitchens and serving shelter residents cooked meals. Today, I was not the director of a homeless shelter. I was not a volunteer working at a homeless shelter. Like a homeless person, I was the guest of a charitable organization offering Thanksgiving dinner. The role reversal found me experiencing intense longing, vulnerability, and uncertainty.

A volunteer named Pam approached me. Observing me compassionately at first, she then viewed me quizzically. I was unresponsive. Then she kindly asked me whether or not I wanted a hot or cold beverage. When I answered, she slowly walked away. She returned moments later holding a glass of water that I had requested, which she properly set upon the dinner table.

Pam and I began conversing. Pain associated with personal losses that I am undergoing subsided, as did my flowing tears. When she and fellow volunteers finished serving dinner to about twenty-five guests, Pam sat down facing me. Pam, the husband of Pam, the two sons of the couple, Marion, and I, shared pleasant conversation and a delicious dinner and dessert, a meal that was begun and ended with a prayer of gratitude. When the gathering ended, renewed humility, hope and confidence entered me.

Leaving the Thanksgiving feast found me realizing that one cannot fully appreciate living, when one does not accept spiritual homelessness that all creation shares. Singer Carrie Underwood captured universal homelessness, when she wrote and later publicly performed a song called "Temporary Home," which topped the musical charts. The song was released in December 2009, nearly one year ago.

The beginning of the lyrics of "Temporary Home" depicts a young six-year-old boy who is being sent to "another new foster home, another new mom and dad, another new school, and another new house that will never be home." As Carrie continues singing the self-composed ballad she vocalizes, "When people ask him how he likes this place, he looks and says with a smile upon his face, This is my temporary home; it's not where I belong, (it's) windows and rooms, that I'm passing through. This is just a stop on the way to where I'm going; I'm not afraid because I know, this is my temporary home." The heartwarming and heart-wrenching song lyrics indicate that earthly living, including many paths of living, represents one stop leading toward where all creation is moving.

Friday, December 3, 2010

Mom and I went shopping for dresses today. Good and contenting was being with her outside home. We shared light as well as serious conversation and sufficient good humor.

In recent years, Mom has shrunk five inches. She was diagnosed with osteoporosis. Arthritis is the reason fingers on her hands are bent. Mom became eighty-one-years-old yesterday.

She awakens daily at 4:30 a.m. She reads newspapers and then makes breakfast foods that she shares with Dad, before she begins doing housework. Mom can drive locally when she decides to execute household errands. She also enjoys gardening, during spring, summer, and fall months.

Daily, Mom joins Dad when she and Dad want to read books, share meals, give dog Winston care, listen to music, or watch television programs. Mom and Dad also enjoy dining in a restaurant once a week as well as entertaining Reagan grandchildren on weekend days. Mom plays bridge. She forgets. I forget. All eventually forget. Where do days, weeks, and years go?

Waking early as does Mom, Dad also reads newspapers. He and Mom alternate breakfast-making duties. Mom makes lunch and dinner meals. Dad assists Mom with giving their dog Winston feeding and walking care before he starts making insurance business-related telephone calls. Now eighty-years-old, Dad continues to work. He is a part-time insurance business consultant, who works from home and in the office of an insurance company he co-founded with his nephew, Jeff Fannon.

Dad is currently ill, which may prevent him and Mom from vacationing in Florida–They go to Florida for several months every winter. The physician he sees has currently directed him to remain at home until the symptoms he is experiencing subside. For many years, Dad has repeatedly advised me that remaining faithful with single-life related principles, whether one ultimately marries, is admirable and noble. Dad has regularly encouraged me to reflect beyond life circumstances I am facing, whether the circumstances are generally enjoyable, challenging, or somewhere in between these two descriptions.

The ability to think deeply is a bittersweet God-given talent that was passed on to me through Dad, who is also a deep thinker. Deep thinkers have been defined as generally quiet persons, who process situations and circumstances primarily through observation rather than conversation. As deep thinkers are process-oriented, they can often readily see potential answers and stumbling blocks in matters being considered. Interestingly, deep thinkers have been discovered as often displaying good humor.

Deep thinkers can frustrate people who are worldly and therefore process circumstances and situations essentially through sharing conversation about material or external occurrences, rather than examining spiritual or internal teachings. It is true that excessive deep thinking delays progress. Meanwhile, being a deep thinker and being worldly are not mutually exclusive. Every human being demonstrates varying levels of both traits.

Saturday, December 4, 2010

Extended family member Janie Barnard Kaminsky sent me an email message which contained an attachment. The attachment contained a four minutes and fifty-seven seconds long, You Tube video titled, "Christmas Food Court Flash Mob Hallelujah." An online dictionary, Dictionary.com defines the words flash mob as a group of people who interact on social media, and while doing so agree to meet in a public place, to perform an unusual or entertaining activity of short duration.

Initially not knowing what the meaning of the words flash mob is, I thought that the video probably contained slapstick comedy. I decided to delete it. Seconds before pressing the delete key on a laptop computer, I experienced bewildering internal energy which mysteriously stopped me from doing removing the message. I clicked the play indicator on the video.

As the "Christmas Court Flash Mob Hallelujah" presentation began, someone holding a video camera was surveying a food court scene. Approximately one hundred people were situated in an indoor food court in a New York shopping mall. Many of the persons, accompanied or alone, who were sitting at tables, were alternately sharing conversation, eating, reading or viewing personal cell phones.

All of the people in the food court were exhibiting varied moods and expressions. A mature woman, possibly a sexagenarian, who was wearing pierced earrings and a Santa Claus hat, was playing Christmas music on a standing keyboard or moveable piano. Unexpectedly, another woman, who was initially filmed eating lunch while she was sitting beside a table, was pictured again, as she began rising from a chair and while doing so, was holding a cellphone near one ear. She was pretending to call someone. A professional vocalist, she was confidently, clearly, and concisely singing the Hallelujah chorus of *Messiah,* saying "Hallelujah, Hallelujah" as she elevated to a standing position.

Now two hundred-seventy-years-old, *Messiah* deserves explanation. German-born Composer George Frederic Handel (1685-1759), wrote the world-renowned operatic piece in twenty-four days. *Messiah* relates the Christian belief that Jesus was Anointed.

The Hallelujah chorus ends the classical music work. Having been residing in London, England for nearly thirty years, Mr. Handel was fifty-six years old when he composed the musical piece, in the summer of 1741. George Handel was then facing health problems as well as financial insolvency.

Publishing and performing the *Messiah* composition is reported to have overturned the serious health and financial circumstances Mr. Handel was experiencing. Name recognition of the classical composition steadily evolved from the time when it was first performed, on April 13, 1742, in Dublin, Ireland. It was presented nearly one year later, on March 23, 1743, in London, England. *Messiah* became universally beloved and acclaimed.

As the flash mob video continued, a male performer stood upon a chair and joined the female singer, vocalizing the Hallelujah chorus. The two performers resembled town criers; during Colonial years, town criers, who stood upon town and city sidewalks in strategic locations, were seen and heard shouting, "Hear Ye, Hear Ye, Hear Ye." The messengers announced current news and events.

Additional professional singers featured in the video, who were standing at the edge of the food court and on chairs, joined the performers who were singing the Hallelujah chorus. Some café guests began capturing the event on cell phone, hand-held or video cameras. Initial responses to the performers among café-goers ranged between apathy and wonder. As the number of singing professionals grows to about eight, food court guests steadily join the chorus.

As the singing of the Hallelujah chorus lyrics, "King of kings, and Lord of lords, and He shall reign forever and ever" crescendos, virtually all of the food court guests were standing and passionately singing along. Additional café-goers were photographing or videoing the occurrence. A young child standing upon a chair was expressing bewilderment mixed with delight, as he was grasping the hand of a family member or caregiver.

As the last Hallelujah chorus was being sung, nearly all the food court guests were participating; some raise their heads and both arms skyward. Some wiped away tears. As the performance ended, I also cried softly. Since it went public at 12:00 noon November 13, 2010, this performance of *Messiah* on You Tube video has captured beyond eleven million viewers.

Friday, December 10, 2010

Charles Gibson, former longtime ABC television network *Good Morning America* (GMA) program host and *World News Tonight* anchor, was the featured speaker at John F. Kennedy Library this evening. The forum moderator WGBH-Boston talk radio show host was Callie Crossley. Ms. Crossley and Mr. Gibson were seated in the center of the main auditorium in the library. Having enjoyed previous JFK Library forums, having viewed Mr. Gibson on air, and having continued to delight in witnessing the experiences of people I do not generally meet, I decided to attend the event.

Having become a Harvard University Shorenstein Center Fellow, Mr. Gibson is spending one college semester at Harvard University. He is researching and writing about political polarity, which he believes is increasing among members of Congress. He is investigating the political theory that partisan division in the U.S. Congress, now having been visible for more than thirty years, has markedly increased in recent times.

Before he began discussing the matter with Ms. Crossley, Mr. Gibson reflected upon the decades during which he was a broadcast journalist. He said that he adored the work. When he graduated from Princeton University in 1965, he began a career in broadcast journalism which lasted for forty-four years, until he retired. In the same year that he graduated from Princeton, he was offered and accepted a news director position at the student-run radio station of the university.

Tonight, Mr. Gibson again confessed to Ms. Crossley and forum audience members that he did not fully enjoy attending Princeton University. "There were no girls there," he said, exhibiting visible frustration, discomfort, and embarrassment as JFK forum guests howled with laugher. Mr. Gibson, who was seated near Ms. Crossley, was responding to questions she was posing. He admitted that Princeton University college policy, not allowing females to attend when he was a student there from 1961 to 1965, was not the sole reason he disliked the university. Located in Princeton, New Jersey, the college is about a fifteen-minute drive north of the city of Trenton, the capital of New Jersey or about an hour drive almost directly south of New York City.

While Ms. Crossley, an award-winning journalist, documentary film maker, and former ABC news producer, who is currently a Boston radio talk show host, continued to question Mr. Gibson, he commented that when he was a freshman at Princeton University and living on campus, he received a mysterious letter. The return address on the upper left side of the front of the envelope was The White House. The letter had originated from the office of President John F. Kennedy, in November of 1960.

The missive directly addressed unhappiness college freshman Charles Gibson was experiencing, being enrolled at an all-male university. Then an aspiring journalist, Mr. Gibson had actively followed the presidential campaigns of incumbent Vice-President Richard Nixon and John F. Kennedy. Mr. Kennedy was elected President on Tuesday, November 8th, 1960. While the 1960 presidential campaign was ongoing, Charles Gibson was a senior class student, attending Sidwell Friends school in Washington, D.C. The private co-ed school serves students who are enrolled in grades six through twelve.

Burdett and Georgianna Gibson, parents of Charles Gibson, were then residing in Washington, D.C. At the time, the Gibson family home was located two blocks from the home of Senator Kennedy. When he graduated from Sidwell Friends school, in the spring of 1961, Mr. Gibson had already been accepted as a Princeton University freshman and John F. Kennedy had become the 35th President of the United States.

In the fall of 1961, Charlie had written and sent a letter to his parents. In the letter, he bemoaned the absence of females at the university. In the missive, Charlie also admitted that he was failing a freshman economics class. This evening, while he was addressing JFK audience members, Mr. Gibson confessed, "This was the kind of letter no parent wants to receive from a child." JFK forum attendees responded in kind. Some smirked. Some chuckled. Some chortled.

For several years, when an occasion to write to Charlie arose, Georgianna and Burdett Gibson had regularly sent Charlie humorous letters. Envelopes containing the letters displayed comical return addresses; Charlie sent similar letters home. The letter young Mr. Gibson had sent to his parents from college was jokingly addressed to, "Mr. and Mrs. John F. Kennedy." The address written on the envelope containing the letter was then the home street address of Gibson family.

Somehow, the letter mysteriously wound up in the White House Oval Office. President John F. Kennedy, First Lady Jacqueline Kennedy and Letitia Baldridge, social secretary of First Lady Jacqueline Kennedy, subsequently read the letter that Charlie Gibson believed Burdett and Georgianna Gibson had received. Five or six days later, when he opened the student mailbox he was using, Charlie discovered a letter whose written return address was, "The White House." Mr. Gibson said that at first he thought, "Wow, Dad got his hands on a piece of White House stationery."

While he opened the envelope containing the letter, Charlie also saw the enclosed and folded letter that he had originally sent to his parents. White House secretary Letitia Baldridge had scribed and signed the response letter in the envelope. Initially experiencing parental admiration when he was opening the envelope containing the letters, Charlie quickly became overcome with remorse, when he began reading the response letter.

"Dear Mr. Gibson," Ms. Baldridge wrote, "The President, Mrs. Kennedy, and I have all read your letter and we are sorry you are having the difficulties you are now encountering at Princeton University. The President remembers the few weeks he spent on campus, when he was enrolled here (Princeton University) and he can share your unhappiness. We do hope things will get better there and that you will enjoy four years there, long term. The President says if you want to think about Harvard you might give this consideration."

The response letter represents the sole personal connection that Charles Gibson and former President Kennedy shared. Mr. Gibson declared, "I was so embarrassed and chagrined that I tore up the letter and threw it away. Can you imagine what this letter would be worth today?" Mr. Gibson then began grinned, which left the forum audience electrified, puzzled and yes, wondering.

Ironically, Charles Gibson attended Princeton University for four years. Today, Mr. Gibson remains a Princeton University benefactor. One year after being chosen to be the news director of the Princeton University radio station, WPRB-FM, when he graduated from Princeton in 1965, he was hired as an RKO General radio station producer in 1966.

Mr. Gibson segued into television broadcast journalism relatively quickly. Hired as a news reporter, he served local network television stations for nearly ten years.

In 1975, ABC News hired Charles Gibson as a general assignment reporter; later he became a Washington, D.C. correspondent for the news organization. Charlie Gibson was a co-anchor of *Good Morning America* morning news and feature program for eleven years, from 1987-1998. He worked alongside GMA co-anchor, Joan Lunden, until 1997.

When Joan left the network in 1977, ABC news journalists, Connie Chung and Diane Sawyer, successively worked with Mr. Gibson as co-anchors on *Good Morning America.* Initially leaving ABC in 1998, Mr. Gibson returned to the news organization in 1999. Again he co-anchored *Good Morning America* with co-anchor Diane Sawyer until 2006. In 2006, Mr. Gibson assumed a new position with ABC News as the anchor of *World News Tonight.* He remained in the position for three years. Mr. Gibson fully retired from the broadcast journalism profession in 2009.

Charles Gibson stated that when he began a career as a television broadcaster, there were three major television networks; now he says there are also 600 cable channels. He indicated that cable channels are essentially focused on food, medicine, education, law, and entertainment news. "Traditional means by which news is delivered is changing," he said.

"Eventually I think we will come to the point where computers and television sets will be linked and there will be no more cable," Mr. Gibson added. He commented that the New York Times is becoming a hybrid of printed paper and video. "I think we're going to find that computers will be linked with television sets and there will be an infinite number of channels," Charles Gibson commented.

Forum moderator Callie Crossley agreed with Charlie Gibson that the delivery system through which journalism has been operating is changing. Ms. Crossley queried Mr. Gibson, "Can the tenets of journalism be held up through whatever platform is able to distribute this information and, in doing so, can objectivity be carried forward?" "Objectivity is critically important in the news business," Charles Gibson said. He added that one of his former ABC news colleagues, the late David Brinkley, once said, "There is no objectivity; there are only lesser degrees of subjectivity." Respectfully, I disagree with the comment that Mr. Brinkley made. There is objectivity;

objectivity tolerates subjectivity, without encouraging subjectivity, just as earthly perfection tolerates imperfection, without encouraging imperfection.

Offering a few final comments on the subject of objectivity in reporting the news Charles Gibson said, "There are stories in which you may lean one way or the other. Generally, in a political context, you want to be as objective as you can. When I talk with young people, I encourage them to choose news sources that are objective; I still believe in the good slogan, 'We report, you decide,'" Mr. Gibson said.

Currently a Harvard University Shorenstein Fellow, Charles Gibson enjoys interacting with students, faculty, and additional university employees at the University in addition to conducting research surrounding political issues. Involving an application and acceptance process, Shorenstein fellowships last for one college semester. Based at the Kennedy School of Government at Harvard, the two-fold mission of the Joan Shorenstein Center involves first, advancing research in the fields of media, politics, and public policy and second, facilitating dialogue and reflection among recognized journalists, scholars, policy makers, and students who are currently attending Harvard University.

Joan Shorenstein (1947-1985) was a writer for the Washington Post. When she began working in this position, she was a journalist with no work experience. Later, she went on to be a producer for the CBS News television program, *Face the Nation.* She was thirty-eight years old when she died, some time after being diagnosed with cancer. Walter Shorenstein and Phyllis Finley, parents of Joan, donated money to Harvard University to establish what is now called The Shorenstein Center on Media, Politics and Public Policy.

Mr. Gibson stated that he has been examining increasing partisanship among members of Congress. He commented that for several years, he has observed that polarity has been increasing among federal lawmakers in Washington, D.C. "The degree of comity, socialization, and fraternization among Congressional members has changed," he said. He also asserted that since the late 1970s, fraternization occurring among U.S Congress members has been steadily decreasing.

Recently addressing a conference, including 15 freshmen U.S. Congress members, Mr. Gibson asked, "How many of you will be residing in Washington D.C.?" One freshman congressman out of fifteen, estimated being six percent, raised a hand. In the 1970s and 1980s, over sixty percent of congressional members working in Washington, D.C. lived there as well.

"Now the number of congressmen living and serving in Washington is a trace element," Charles Gibson stated.

"Congress now operates on an early Tuesday afternoon through Thursday night working schedule," he remarked, signaling that Congress members are generally not present in the legislative chambers beyond two work days, per work week. "Politicians spend more time on being re-elected once they are in office, than they do legislating." He said that the skyrocketing costs of re-election have precipitated the political reality.

Currently, there are congressional members who are considering legislation which supports the idea of congressmen and women remaining in Washington, D.C. while legislative matters are being addressed. The time period would last between two and three weeks per month. Congressional members would then return to respective home states, in order to continue fundraising efforts.

During the question-and-answer period, an audience member asked Mr. Gibson to recall any personal reporting experiences he wished to share about the tragedy that occurred on September 11, 2001. Charles Gibson stated that being a television reporter during this time was an extraordinary experience. He humbly recalled that on September 11, 2001, near mid-morning, *Good Morning America* was presenting a feature segment highlighting British royal family member Sarah Ferguson, Duchess of York.

Suddenly, GMA program co-anchors Charlie and Diane Sawyer received repeated reports from show producers which indicated that at the site of One World Trade Center, something tragic was happening. The Twin Towers skyscrapers, located side by side, were about a fifteen-minute drive from ABC studios. While they were momentarily off air, Charlie and Diane viewed video footage that was submitted to the news station.

Video footage showed smoke and flames emerging from a terrorist-manned airplane, as the airplane struck the former North Tower skyscraper at 8:46 a.m. Additional video camera recordings showed a second hijacked plane penetrating the South Tower edifice, at 9:03 a.m. *Good Morning America* show production staff had meanwhile grown near frantic, as they were feeding Charlie and Diane information surrounding devastating September 11, 2001 events. Suddenly, the head producer of GMA cued Charlie and Diane, "You are on air."

Charles Gibson said the tribulation of 9/11 deeply affected him as well as fellow media colleagues; he said that for weeks after the tragedy, he regularly became tearful, whether he was on or off air, when he recalled directly or indirectly interacting with people affected by the disaster. He said he remembers facial expressions he observed and spoken words he heard on September 11, 2001. Unexpectedly, he became visibly physically and emotionally shaken, as he was uttering, "They (September 11 terrorists) killed many people; they did not destroy the fabric and guts of this country."

Observing Ms. Crossley interview Mr. Gibson was gratifying. I am neither a longtime television or radio journalist nor a public figure. Professional competence that Charlie Gibson as well as Callie Crossley displayed is admirable. As an interviewee, Mr. Gibson motivated JFK Library forum guests to experience many emotions, including curiosity, intrigue, bewilderment, hilarity, and deep sadness. Although no person exactly resembles any fellow human, we are all very similar, no matter where we believe we come from or where we believe we are going.

Saturday, December 25, 2010

After rising, feeding Jura and eating breakfast, I continued to celebrate this Christmas day while playing music CDs, including *Messiah*, composed by George Handel, *These are Special Times* Christmas album by Celine Dion, and the "Joyful Noise" Christmas Concert presented by Atlantic Symphony Orchestra. Jura and I walked together for nearly two hours today, in the midst of silent, snow-covered, and empowering woods. When we returned home, I practiced foxtrot dance patterns on the hardwood floor of the apartment living room, while the CD player in the room played foxtrot ballroom dance music. For the second time this week, snow has fallen. This Christmas is white.

Monday, December 27, 2010

Last night, a snow blizzard, which swept over New England and included fifty miles per-hour wind gusts, dropped approximately eight inches of snow in Cohasset and surrounding towns. Coastal area residents witnessed one or two additional inches of snow falling today; flooding occurred. Boston received almost eighteen inches of snow; some parts of Massachusetts received nearly two feet of the white stuff.

High winds are continuing today. Weathermen and women are forecasting that daytime temperatures, now in the low twenties and descending throughout the day, will go into the teens tonight. Contrary to usual meteorological protocol, the storm has received no name. Therefore, some have referenced the blizzard as the No Name northeaster.

Cohasset, Scituate and Hull towns have organized temporary shelters; more than two thousand residents here lost electrical power and heat. Two Scituate homes caught fire and burned down completely during the storm. A short time ago, Dee Berens, a former fellow Hingham Cabaret and Cohasset Cabaret cast member, and Ron Berens, the husband of Dee, began residing in an oceanfront home in Scituate, which was recently constructed. I emailed Dee, and when doing so, inquired how the blizzard affected her and Ron.

Sending a response, Dee said the Berens home was significantly damaged. At high tide, waves tore through ceilings as well as one bedroom wall. The basement was considerably flooded. Surging tide waters had poured into the living room, through recessed lights. Two properties that Dee and Ron own which are located near shoreline are now uninhabitable. Aiding persons living in these apartments who are seeking temporary shelter, the couple has repeatedly been in contact with the American Red Cross.

Wednesday, December 29, 2010

One morning newspaper report indicates that the Northeaster blizzard began late last Sunday afternoon, ended late Monday evening, and resulted in home and property destruction in Scituate that will cost millions to repair. This past Monday, in the midst of freezing air temperatures, severe winds propelled a surging 3:30 a.m. high tide. Winds caused more damage than the snow. Although not as serious, the circumstances have also affected neighboring seaside towns of Cohasset, Hull, and Hingham.

Rescue personnel, utilizing specially designed boats, are continuing to assist people who are trapped in flooded homes. Flood victims are being offered temporary shelter and prepared meals. Last night, Cohasset police reported that power to eleven hundred Cohasset homes had been lost during the storm; utility service was restored in little more than twenty-four hours. Power has also been reinstated in the towns of Scituate and Hull.

Payden Sullivan, husband of niece Kristin, did not return home for nearly three days. An employee of a utility company subcontractor, he and fellow employees worked long and late hours in Boston and surrounding areas during the winter storm; for seventy-two hours, he alternated working long hours with sleeping for a few hours at a time in the work truck he uses, which was parked near the work site.

Miraculously, the December 27 snowstorm left the Scituate Harbor adjacent Mill Wharf restaurant unharmed. Last night, my sister Lizzie, nephew Jonas, Liane, the wife of Jonas, great-niece Alia, and nephew Rhett and I dined here. We received welcoming, prompt, and professional dinner service.

The waitress who served us explained that because of the snowstorm, the restaurant was short-staffed; she said that in addition to waiting on us, she was serving restaurant guests seated at twelve tables. I would last in the job for about five minutes. Service the waitress offered us in these circumstances was noticeably polite, cooperative, and efficient.

Jonas, Liane, and their two-year-old daughter Aliana, had departed from their New York City home and then traveled via car between five and six hours before they arrived in Scituate; they are now visiting Lizzie, the mother of Jonas, for three days, in her home. Tonight, while Jenkins family members and I were sharing ordered dinner meals, Jonas and I talked for a while about military service.

As I questioned him, he reflected upon serving in Iraq, from 2005 to 2006, with fellow National Guardsmen. The U.S. National Guard unit he served was stationed in the city of Ramadi, Anwar province; Jonas said he believes U.S. military presence in Iraq is warranted. Since 2003 U.S. military troops have been protecting Iraqi citizens against terrorist attacks. He indicated that there is high-level violence occurring here, daily. He admitted being relieved that former Iraqi president and renowned dictator Saddam Hussein was ousted. United States military troops assisted in the endeavor to remove the former president from office.

Nearly all of the National Guardsmen in the unit in which Jonas served returned home. For this, Jonas is deeply grateful. He is ready and willing to serve again, if called. Hopefully, he will not again be called.

This evening, Alia was generally quiet during dinner. While she was seated in a booster chair, she ate two French fries and two chicken nuggets. Then she drank a hand-held small bottle of milk, before falling asleep. Liane commented that Alia has recently begun forming sentences, using the third person tense. She is formulating sentences, such as, "Alia is playing with blocks now."

This afternoon, Jonas Liane, and Alia, accompanying niece Kristin, great nephew Zachariah, nephew Rhett, and sister Lizzie went snow tubing for two hours. As Alia and Zach were seated in a snow tube and racing down a snow-covered golf course hill, two-year-old Zach, who was sitting behind two years old Alia, wrapped both of his arms around her and was gleefully shouting, "Whee!"

2011

CHAPTER SIXTEEN

MISS SAIGON, WORLD NEWS, *THE FIGHTER,* FAMILY EXCHANGES

Tuesday, January 4, 2011

Realizing that nephew Rhett is now nearly thirty-years-old sometimes astounds me.

He resembles a teenager in appearance. While he is currently employed in a part-time construction job, Rhett is also seeking additional employment in this field. He has also been considering work in new areas. While we were traveling together via automobile today, he and I shared conversation about the play *Miss Saigon.* Rhett said he and Mariah Samos, the girlfriend of Rhett, and Mum, Lizzie Jenkins, recently went to see the theatrical production, which is now playing in Boston.

Set in Saigon, South Vietnam in 1974, during the last days of Vietnam War, *Miss Saigon* portrays a seventeen-year-old orphan named Kim. All of the family members of Kim, who were living in South Vietnam, were killed during the Vietnam War, which at the time, was ongoing. Sending U.S military forces into South Vietnam from 1959 to 1974 was intended to prevent military forces of the Communist North Vietnamese government from overrunning military forces of the quasi-democratic South Vietnamese government.

During Vietnam War years, South Vietnam was a Republic; the ruling system here resembled a Democracy. Communist government officials began governing South Vietnam in 1974 after communist North Vietnamese forces invaded Saigon. The action ended the fifteen-years-long Vietnam War.

Having been orphaned, Kim found a job at the Dreamland night club, which is truly a prostitution bar. U.S. Marines frequent the establishment. The manager of Dreamland wants to obtain a visa, which will allow him to escape Vietnam, when American G.I. soldiers leave the war-torn country in Far East Asia. Like additional girls working at Dreamland, Kim wants to meet American soldiers, one of whom might be able to help her go to America and thereby escape the war as well as working as a call girl.

The manager of Dreamland orchestrates a sham beauty contest. He asks club cocktail waitresses to enter the night club stage; American Marines observe the women and then select Miss Saigon. Moments before the contest starts, a U. S. Marine named Chris, has reluctantly walked into Dreamland. A fellow Marine named John accompanies him.

John has convinced Chris a night out will permit the two soldiers to temporarily escape the horrors of war. Chris meets Kim; John later sees that Chris and Kim are attracted to one another.

John and the Dreamland club manager converse; John pays the manager to allow Kim to accompany Chris this evening. When Chris offers Kim money as the evening is ending, Kim refuses payment. Innocent, she has not ever before been offered payment for sex.

Kim explains to Chris that she was betrothed when she was thirteen. Family members of Kim decided or arranged that she would marry a family cousin, named Thuy. Kim says she was not in love with Thuy. She explains that all the members of the family were killed when the village in which they were living was bombed and destroyed. She says there is no future for her, other than to continue being a prostitute. Chris is touched; he views Kim as dignified and decent. The two young people fall in love. Chris says he will bring Kim to America with him and that meanwhile, they can live together.

As time passes after the encounter, Chris telephones John, who is stationed at the U.S. Embassy in Vietnam. Chris says he is taking leave to be with Kim. John declares that the North Vietnamese army has entered Saigon. He urges Chris to come to the embassy soon. Meanwhile, Chris and Kim have begun living together. As Kim and fellow waitresses are enacting a mock wedding ceremony, Thuy, the estranged husband of Kim, arrives. He is angry and jealous. He wants to bring Kim home.

Thuy and Chris have each drawn guns and are facing one another. Kim vehemently informs Thuy that they are not married anymore because her parents, who arranged the marriage many years ago, are now deceased. Kim also says the marriage is null and void because Thuy betrayed her when he entered the communist North Vietnamese army.

Kim confesses that she is in love with Chris. Suddenly, pandemonium occurs; Communist forces have invaded Saigon. Thuy, Kim, and Chris become separated. When Chris departs Vietnam, Kim is not accompanying him.

Three years later, Kim and Thuy meet again; Thuy proposes marriage to Kim; Kim rebukes him again and repeats that she loves Chris. She introduces Thuy to three-year-old Tam, whose father is Chris. Thuy becomes enraged; he attempts to kill Tam. Furious, Kim draws out the holstered gun which is attached to the belt that Thuy is wearing. She shoots and kills him. Then while sobbing, Kim holds Thuy in her arms.

When three more years have passed, Kim has moved to Bangkok, Thailand with Tam; she continues to hope that Chris will eventually come to Thailand and bring her and Tam to America. Meanwhile, Chris is living in America. He works for an organization that connects children of war with their fathers. He has married a woman whose name is Ellen. He has also been experiencing nightmares about Kim for a long time; he fears she is dead. He is relieved when John informs him that Kim is still alive.

Chris finally talks with Ellen about Kim and Tam. John, Chris, and Ellen go to Bangkok in search of Kim. When John finds her, Kim is working as a dancer in a club.

She is overjoyed to hear that Chris has come to Thailand. John attempts to say that Chris has married, but Kim does not listen. She is devastated when she arrives at the hotel room where Chris is staying and she unexpectedly meets Ellen. John and Chris are not there. Kim says that she loves Chris, that he is the father of Tam and that she wants to talk directly with Chris.

Shortly after Kim leaves the hotel, John and Chris return. Ellen talks with Chris about what has happened. She asks him to choose what he wants to do. John, Chris and Ellen head toward the room in which Kim is living with Tam. Chris wants Kim to know that he loves and has married Ellen. He also wants to assure Kim that he admires and respects her and that he will financially support her and Tam. Meanwhile, having encountered Ellen, Kim becomes desperate. When she returns to the room in which she is living with Tam, she steps behind a curtain, retrieves a gun, points it inward and then fires the weapon. Gravely wounded, she falls to the floor.

Hearing a gunshot as he opens a door and enters the room with Ellen and John, Chris finds Kim. He holds her in his arms. Compassionately and sorrowfully, he asks her what she has done. Kim asks Chris to hold her closely, for one more time. Kim dies, as Chris is holding her close.

Rhett bought *Miss Saigon* show tickets, because Mariah and Lizzie said they wished to see the theatrical production. This morning, as he and I were seated in the station wagon I drive, he informed me that as the show was progressing, he suddenly discovered that Mariah and Lizzie, who were sitting beside him, were observing him with dismay. Mariah informed Rhett that while she and Lizzie were watching the play and becoming very emotional and even sobbing, he had fallen asleep.

Moreover, Mariah advised Rhett that while he was asleep, his head was tilted backwards and his mouth was wide open. Seated amongst hundreds of fellow show audience members, he had also been snoring. As he awoke, probably while being shaken awake, Mariah and Lizzie queried him, one by one, saying "How could you fall asleep during this dramatic, passionate and emotional performance?" Groggy, Rhett responded, "Um, gee, I don't know." He and I laughed out loud, as he was ending the story, while I was driving and he was sitting in the front passenger seat of the car.

Hearing about differing male and female responses rendered me wondering whether this scenario portrays differing male and female attitudes. Then again, minutes ago having today finished reading the *Miss Saigon* play synopsis found me experiencing deep compassion for Kim and having wished I was able to converse with her, well before the story ended. Viewing her with admiration and respect, I would have quietly said, "Kim, would you consider a simple reality check?"

Continuing, I would add, "You have bravely survived losing family members in the Vietnam War. You overcame being in an unhealthy marriage. You escaped working as a call girl and became a dancer. You love mothering Tam. Chris admires and respects you and has offered to support you financially. You can love again. Devoted love is not synonymous with being unable to live without a person. May I suggest you are looking at a life that is full as being empty?"

Thursday, January 6, 2011

Entering the home laundry room in the basement early this morning, Lizzie discovered a rooster standing here. Rooster had entered the laundry area through the basement bulkhead door, which had accidentally been left open. Rooster was facing Liz. The head of Rooster was bobbing backward and forward. Later, while talking with me via telephone and describing the scenario, Liz said that while his head was bobbing back and forth, Rooster was exclaiming, "Blaak, blaak, blaak, blaak, blaak, blaak, blaak."

She summoned her son, Rhett who is currently living with her. Near panic, she screamed, "Rhettie, there is a rooster in the basement." Hearing loud sounds, Rooster scurried behind a couch that was stored in the laundry room. Liz said she did not mind seeing Rooster; she simply did not expect an early morning rendezvous with him. Rhett escorted Rooster outside; following the bird, he escalated stairs below the open basement bulkhead, through which the male fowl had arrived.

Lately, four roosters have regularly been discovered wandering in the back yard outside the home of Lizzie. She said these mildly precocious roosters are generally harmless.

Two-year-old nephew Zachariah loves watching the attractive bold creatures roving about the backyard. When dogs Jura and Buddy recently entered the yard one afternoon, roosters crowing here were generally unruffled.

Friday, January 14, 2011

Today I was prompted to view a television news report indicating that shot and seriously injured Arizona Congresswoman Gabrielle Giffords has now awakened. She is now able to move fingers on her hands slightly. Six days ago, January 8, Ms. Giffords suffered a brain injury when a shooting rampage occurred outside a Tucson, Arizona grocery store, where she was conducting a "Congress on Your Corner" networking event. The observed shooter, Jared Lee Loughner, who has been incarcerated, is awaiting an upcoming jury trial.

News reports indicate eighteen people were wounded. Six people died. A federal judge and one nine-year-old girl are among the casualties. Recently having been elected an elementary school student council member, the nine-year-old girl was queued, waiting in line to meet Ms. Giffords, for the first time. After triumphantly declaring, "I'm next," she was slain. This news is shocking and devastating. Whether having been identified as mentally ill, how does a human being first, justify killing or critically injuring any fellow human being and then murder the person or persons? One does this not primarily because one is mentally ill; one does this because one has fully surrendered hope.

Sunday, January 16, 2011

This evening, I viewed an anchor person broadcasting a news story with related video, depicting a former radio personality who became addicted to drugs and alcohol, was for many years identified as homeless, has now been sober for two years, and has re-entered the public spotlight. Doral Chenoweth, a videographer for *The Columbus Dispatch* newspaper in Columbus, Ohio, and the wife of Doral, Robin Chenoweth, discovered fifty-three-year-old Ted Williams, as Doral was driving on the Ohio Interstate Highway. Doral and Robin viewed Mr. Williams panhandling. Ted was standing in the midst of a highway emergency lane holding a cardboard sign that read, "I have a God given gift of voice."

Stopping in the highway emergency lane, Doral asked Ted Williams to showcase the voice; Ted was given a one-dollar bill. Hearing the radio voice of Mr. Williams stunned the Chenoweth couple. The voice of Ted Williams is remarkable; it is rich, rolling, and baritone. Mr. Chenoweth, a Columbus Dispatch newspaper web producer, said that when he met and talked with Ted Williams, he did not suspect that the video he produced featuring Mr. Williams would receive skyrocketing public attention.

On a slow day in the news business in Columbus Ohio, a Columbus Dispatch editor urged Doral to submit some fresh video. Since being posted on the Columbus Dispatch website before being displayed on You Tube, the video featuring Ted Williams has garnered fans numbering in the millions. Ted Williams is reported to have been offered full-time work advertising nationally recognized foods. Mr. Williams was also offered an announcer position with the Cleveland Cavaliers basketball team, including an attractive salary and an expense account.

Ted Williams has recently been reunited with family members he had not seen during the past ten years. While a television reporter was recently interviewing him, Mr. Williams expressed gratitude. He said that massive public attention he has received since Doral and Robin Chenoweth discovered him has been overwhelming; Mr. Williams commented that he regularly converses with a psychologist who encourages utilizing meditation, not medication, when one is facing challenging circumstances. I wonder where rebirth Mr. Williams has experienced will lead him.

Monday, January 31, 2011

Seventeen inches of snow recently blanketed Cohasset as well as surrounding towns. Additional snow will begin falling tomorrow and continue falling, through Wednesday.

Outdoor air temperatures have been registering in the teens and twenties. Fortunately the atmosphere has been generally dry and cool, making walking in the woods relatively easy. Viewing snow-covered woods is spectacular experience.

Nephew Rhett visited me for several days this month. He arrived at the apartment on Tuesday, January 18 and departed on Saturday, January 22. During the respite, Rhett and I talked, laughed, watched movies, read, and shared meals. When the apartment became "tight quarters," he went walking outdoors or I left the apartment and drove to nearby Paul Pratt Library, where I wrote or read for a while. Rhett is a delightful and cooperative house guest. During the visit we shared, he carefully prepared several delicious dinner meals. One day he vacuumed the entire apartment. Rhett also purchased and later gave me a DVD player, as a parting gift.

One afternoon, as he gradually awoke, after having fallen asleep while lying on the living room couch, which was also serving as a very small guest bed, Rhett discovered Jura was directly facing him. He said Jura suddenly addressed him as though he was non-verbally saying, "Hey man, what's up? You wanna walk outside awhile?" Rhett responded non-verbally saying, "Sure man, you wanna walk outside; we'll walk outside together for a little while."

On Wednesday evening, January 19, Rhett and I viewed *The Fighter,* a film starring Mark Wahlberg and Christian Bale. We watched the acclaimed movie, which is currently being shown inside a theatre in the former Hingham Shipyard, which during the last several years has been undergoing major redevelopment. Based on a true story, *The Fighter* depicts two men who are half-brothers as well as professional boxers, Dicky Eklund (Christian Bale) and Micky Ward (Mark Wahlberg). The two siblings are facing professional sports, family, and addiction issues.

Dicky Eklund was a welterweight prize fighter. Following retiring from the boxing world, he became the boxing trainer of his half-brother, Micky. Alice Ward (Melissa Leo) is the mother of Dicky as well as Micky. Alice is also the mother of seven outspoken young women who also do not share the same father.

After earning prize fighter status, Dicky Eklund became a cocaine addict. While he was training Micky, he arranged a last-minute fight between Micky and a substitute fighter. Shortly after the two fighters entered the boxing ring, the substitute boxer clobbered Micky. Micky begins to consider loosening family ties and hiring a new trainer.

Charlene Fleming (Amy Adams), the new girlfriend of Micky, supports the idea of him hiring a new trainer. George Ward (Jack McGee), father of Micky, also condones the idea. Alice Ward reacts instantly; she insists that Micky immediately reinstate Dicky.

George Ward receives a *The Three Stooges*-style slap on the head with a frying pan which Alice delivers, when she and George are together again; Alice justifies the action by stating that George is not supporting her in re-establishing Dicky as the professional trainer of Micky. However, unlike The Three Stooges, a comedy act, Alice was not kidding, when she slapped George on the head with a frying pan. George was bruised. Fortunately, he was not seriously harmed.

By the way, *The Three Stooges* was a popular slapstick comedy show, which appeared in short films and on television. The production mainly involved the characters and actions of stooges named Larry, Moe, Curly and sometimes featured another stooge named Shemp. A stooge is a person who supports or serves others in a role that primarily involves performing unpleasant work. The Three Stooges, a vaudeville and comedy act, was popular for over forty years, from 1922 to 1970.

Near the end of the movie *The Fighter,* Micky enters an international welterweight boxing competition, shortly after having hired and begun working with a new trainer. Sitting ringside, family members of Micky as well as Charlene watch the fight. Dicky, recently convicted of drug charges and subsequently incarcerated, is also watching the televised intercontinental boxing match in a large prison meeting room, where prison security personnel are present. Enthusiastic, expressive prison inmates are with him.

Lowell, Massachusetts is the setting of the film. Today, the population of Lowell is approximately 103,000. In the early 1800s, Lowell was an industrial city, a reputed textile manufacturer. One hundred years later, beginning in the 1920s, Lowell manufacturing companies began relocating to southern parts of the United States. Low-cost textile businesses, which were initially established in the southern part of the United States, drove textile businesses in the northeast out of business. During recent years, manufacturing buildings in Lowell have been converted into residential units as well as space for commercial businesses.

Rhett and I enjoyed viewing *The Fighter*. We agreed that performances of headlining actors and actresses as well as actors and actresses who we did not recognize in the movie were comparable and equally believable. We also agreed that the emerging vulnerability, dignity, and resilience of characters in the true story-based movie, generally outstripped profanity-laced and agonizing family drama that occurs in the film.

Wednesday, February 2, 2011

Banks, schools, and the stock market in Cairo, Egypt have closed; trains are not running. Television news reports with accompanying video portray Egyptian citizens standing in long queues, waiting to buy food. Egyptians entering gas stations in automobiles and wanting to purchase gas are also waiting in long lines.

In the midst of an unsettled political and economic environment, Egypt is experiencing severe gas and food shortages. Simultaneously, Egyptian countrymen numbering in the hundreds of thousands continue to boisterously protest against the government of Egypt, as they enter the capital city of Cairo and move into Tahrir Square. Political protests began eight days ago, on January 25, 2011.

People are protesting the thirty-year-old government of ruling Egyptian President, Hosni Mubarak. The Mubarak administration has been charged with significantly influencing widespread inflation, poverty, and corruption. News reports indicate that protest organizers, who are advocating the ousting of Mr. Mubarak, are designating upcoming Friday, February 11, 2011, eight days from today, as the deadline President Mubarak is being given to resign.

Government military forces are present among rioters and both groups have been directed not to use force. News information also indicates that ninety-seven people have been killed during the protests. Thousands have been injured. Egyptians residing in the United States have been unable to reach loved ones in Egypt via telephone, since the protests began.

Thursday, February 10, 2011

Today I watched a morning television news program examining rising sugar dependency among Americans. Dr. Richard Besser, a medical correspondent for ABC News indicated that researchers are finding regularly ingesting sugar is as potentially addicting as crack or cocaine dependency. Whoa… Researchers have also discovered that during the 1700s, average sugar consumption worldwide was four pounds per year.

It is good and possible that during the 1700s, sweets and treats were foods which were consumed only on holidays and special occasions. By the 1800s, average sugar intake was eighteen pounds per annum and by the 1900s average sugar ingestion was sixty pounds annually. As of this year, 2011, average sugar intake has been recorded as having "ballooned," being one hundred fifty pounds per year.

Whoa. Whoa. Whoa… Who knows how many serious diseases have emerged from this radically increased level of sugar consumption?

Friday, February 11, 2011

Jura and I returned home, following walking in nearby woods early this morning. Entering the apartment living room and then powering the living room television remote at 11:15 a.m., Eastern Standard Time, (EST), 5:15 a.m. Cairo, Egypt time, I viewed a breaking news story. A news anchorman was stating that President, Hosni Mubarak, who ruled Egypt for thirty years, agreed to resign.

Seventeen days of Egyptian citizen protests are jubilantly and victoriously ending. Thousands of Egyptians who were stationed behind barricades and facing military personnel and tanks had in the last near three weeks been engaging in generally non-violent protests, which were intended to publicize public disapproval of the Mubarak government.

Millions of Egyptians are experiencing palpable joy as they revel in the capital city of Cairo, in Tahrir Square. Up until today, President Mubarak had publicly and defiantly resisted resigning. Fleeing Cairo, he was reported to have been observed being at a resort near the Red Sea in Sharma el-Sheikh, which is about five hundred miles southeast of Cairo. Today he capitulated. Hosni Mubarak is no longer the President of Egypt.

It is empowering to have witnessed reasonably dissatisfied country citizens who have organized generally non-violent political activities protesting grossly unfair government practices and activities. In doing so, protesters have effectuated the removal of a political leader who is widely believed to be unfit for office. Two weeks ago, wishing to pacify millions of protesters in Tahrir Square, now former President Mubarak publicly declared that he would not seek re-election. An upcoming election is set to happen in September of this year.

Until today, unmoved Egyptian citizens protested daily, in Tahrir Square. Today, fireworks are being widely displayed; automobile horns are blazing. Egyptian citizens standing about Tahrir Square are firing celebratory gunshots skyward. Witnessing recent political developments in Egypt, which American television networks have been broadcasting, has been remarkable experience.

The population of Egypt is currently about eighty million persons. According to a report by the U. S. State Department, average per capita income in Egypt is not beyond five thousand dollars annually. General Omar Suleiman, the unelected Vice-President serving the Mubarak administration, recently said that military personnel have been temporarily given political power. The Egyptian parliament has been dissolved. The Egyptian Constitution has been suspended; a new constitution is being drawn. New elections are required by law to occur within six months. Recent days are surely engendering heightened senses of hope and uncertainty which Egyptian citizens and Egyptian fellow citizens around the world are surely experiencing.

Thursday, March 3, 2011

I awoke this morning experiencing profound inner peace, not wishing to nostalgically replay any past circumstances, including childhood, high school, or college experiences and not wanting to revisit times when grown nieces and nephews were young. I do not want to return to any previously experienced personal or professional circumstances; frankly, this is impossible. The realization is contenting. Someone once said that when one dies, a U-Haul truck cannot be hitched to the Hearse. True. True.

My sister Valerie called me, via cell phone, at 10:00 p.m. this evening. We discussed three important criteria surrounding committed relationships. We agreed that readiness, profound love, and compatibility are basic components of permanent commitment.

Friday, March 4, 2011

This evening, a telephone conversation nephew Rhett and I shared left each and both of us upset, reeling, and disillusioned.

Saturday, March 5, 2011

This morning after entering Whitney Woods in Cohasset, Jura and I walked together for one-and-one-half hours. After we exited the woods and re-entered the car, I drove to a nearby large grocery store, where I bought a few items. After leaving the store, I completed some additional errands, before we returned home. When having opened a large door, ascended hallway stairs, and then entered the apartment, as Jura walked behind me, I rested a bag of groceries on the kitchen table. I had heard the land-line telephone on the secretary desk in the living room ringing.

Guessing that the caller might be Rhett, I hesitated to answer the phone. Suddenly, I envisioned a spiritual hand, resting above the telephone; Spiritual Hand suggested that I pick up the telephone receiver. Experiencing trust mingled with doubt, I also realized that the rings would stop soon. Wishing to honor Spiritual Hand, I lifted the receiver gently. Rhett and I greeted one another.

Several moments of silence followed before mutually healing words burst forth through Rhett as well as through me. We reconfirmed that when divisive matters arise between us we will admit the matters, respect differences between us, and then resolve issues in a mutually acceptable way. Before the conversation ended, we joked for a bit. We extended one another goodwill.

CHAPTER SEVENTEEN

MEMORIAL DAY, TORNADO, GRADUATION PARTY, STANLEY CUP, MACABRE SIGHT

Monday, May 30, 2011

Today, Memorial Day, while Jura and I were walking together this morning, we traversed Cohasset Village and environs, later passed Cohasset Harbor, and then re-entered Cohasset Village, before we returned home. The nearly five-mile marching route of the Cohasset Memorial Day parade commences on Cedar Street, in the north end of the town and continues on North Main Street before progressing onto South Main Street and then continuing on through Cohasset Village. Here the route bears left onto Elm Street before ending inside Cohasset Veterans Memorial Park, which is adjacent to Cohasset Harbor.

While walking with Jura on parts of the parade route, before the parade started, I viewed food, lemonade, and hot dog stands being erected and collapsible chairs being set upon sidewalks. Having missed the Cohasset Memorial Day Parade this year motivated me to attend the annual Cohasset Memorial Day ceremony. Following the parade hundreds of parade goers gather and then stand or sit in and outside Cohasset Veterans Memorial Park. The memorial ceremony is opened with a prayer said by a local clergyman. Military representatives as well as local officials offer speeches. Guns are fired into the air, honoring dead servicemen. The ceremony, lasting between thirty and sixty minutes, is ended with a prayer.

During spring and summer months, flowers adorn the memorial park. Medium-tall granite wall monuments displayed in the park identify hundreds of Cohasset servicemen who served in the World War I, World War II, Korean, and Vietnam wars. Near and across the street from the monuments is a Field of Honor or Healing Field, which exhibits numerous American flags, honoring U.S. veterans who died when serving as well as veterans who are living.

Former longtime Cohasset resident, Captain Stephen (Steve) Bowen, U. S. Navy Submarine Specialist and National Aeronautics and Space Administration program (NASA) astronaut, was the featured speaker at the memorial ceremony. Captain Bowen is the first United States Navy Submarine Specialist who was chosen by NASA to be an astronaut mission specialist. He has served on three missions to the International Space Station (ISS). Fifteen nations cooperated to build the massive structure which gathers, organizes, and displays scientific information. Weighing 460 tons, the inhabitable artificial space satellite, which has been described as being the size of a football field, is situated around two hundred fifty miles above Earth and has been orbiting the planet for twenty-three years, since 1998.

Space program crew members representing many nations have traveled to the ISS and have performed varied scientific experiments there. In November of 2008, May of 2010, and February of 2011, joining fellow astronauts, Steve Bowen entered a Space Shuttle stationed in Cape Canaveral, Florida. They rocketed toward the International Space Station, later exited the shuttle and boarded the ISS, bringing cargo and supplies to space station team members, before returning to Earth. Captain Bowen has currently logged forty days of space travel, including seven spacewalks.

This afternoon, US Navy Submariner and NASA astronaut Bowen talked about being inside the Space Shuttle Discovery during its third and final mission. While viewing the Earth from space, Mr. Bowen said he saw the world as "a big blue ball." For a moment, this caused me to remember being eight years old, sitting at home beside the kitchen table and while talking with Mom, viewing a black and white portable television screen and seeing astronaut John Glenn exit a NASA spaceship—that he named Friendship—after the ship splashed down into the Atlantic ocean eight hundred miles southeast of Bermuda and John Glenn became the first American to successfully circle the earth three times in space, on February 20, 1962.

Astronaut Bowen described the opportunity he was given to see the earth from over two hundred miles above the earth and enter the International Space Station as being rare and gratifying. He also said that experiences he underwent as an astronaut did not upstage what he learned about military service when he was growing up in Cohasset. For several years,

Steve walked beside fellow elementary school band members who participated in the annual Memorial Day Parade in Cohasset. As years passed and he entered Cohasset High School (CHS), he and fellow CHS attendees became acquainted with military families residing in Cohasset. "We started to make a connection," he said, indicating that the teenage boys began to experience new awareness that Memorial Day parades honor sacrifice as well as courage, resilience, and bravery that military life commitment entails.

When the Memorial Day ceremony in Cohasset ended, walking home with Jura found me suddenly spotting a Cohasset acquaintance. Also walking home with family was Chad Bradshaw, who was carrying his infant son Mark Bradshaw. The baby was sitting in an infant carrier which Chad had strapped around his back. Ella Bradshaw, the wife of Chad and additional Bradshaw family children, five-year-old Erica and three-year-old Richard, were walking beside him. Chad was wearing camouflage Army fatigues and a matching camouflage cap. "Didn't know you were an Army guy," I said. "Yeah, Desert Storm," he replied, smiling.

Conversation Chad and I shared following the Memorial Day parade was focused on military experiences that Clark underwent. Commissioned as an Army Lieutenant shortly after graduating from Norwich University in 1989, he joined one thousand fellow Seventh Military Battalion Marines who were deployed to Germany. One year later, on Christmas day in 1990, the battalion began participating in Operation Desert Storm. American military were being sent to Saudi Arabia, Kuwait, and Iraq.

Five hundred thousand American servicemen were sent there; thirty-four countries including the U.S. had deployed troops to the Middle East; Iraqi troops had attacked a neighbor—Persian Gulf country Kuwait—threatening Kuwait and one of its neighbors, Saudi Arabia. Kuwait and Saudi Arabia export large amounts of oil to the United States.

Asked what being engaged in active military service taught him, Chad replied, "There is genuine evil in the world; there are madmen who will not listen to reason." He said he believes that WWII life losses were considerably magnified because evil was not checked.

He stated that as a Desert Storm soldier, he became increasingly aware of mortality; he discovered that being engaged in war as a soldier heightens the desire to protect fellow soldiers, regardless of Army rank. While interviewing Chad, I suddenly recalled meeting a man who was a soldier during the Vietnam War. Since returning home, he has owned and managed a plumbing company in Quincy, Massachusetts for three to four decades. He and I met one night nearly twenty years ago, when I went to a karaoke bar to sing.

Dan Balducci was eighteen years old when he was deployed to Vietnam. He served with fellow U.S. Army soldiers aiding South Vietnamese military soldiers, who battled North Vietnamese Communist Rebels. As he and I were sitting beside one another at a bar in a Chinese restaurant and nightclub which offered karaoke entertainment, Dan briefly discussed being a soldier in Vietnam. Naively, I asked him, "Did you kill people?"

"Yes," he said softly, adding, "When you see friends going home in body bags, you realize that in war, it is kill or be killed." Hearing a surprisingly gentle, intelligent, and quiet former military guy relate the story unnerved me. Talking with him profoundly changed how I view military service. It deepened the admiration and respect within me for people who are service members. It clarified the reality that no person truly wants war, including people who serve in military forces. Talking with Dan helped me to understand that the issue of going to war, like any issue is not simply black and white.

This morning, Chad Bradshaw and I freely shared conversation while we ate muffins and drank beverages. As we sat outside a café and enjoyed glorious, sunny weather, I said that the idea of living amid an oppressive government is personally bewildering and honestly, almost incomprehensible. Chad said he empathizes with fellow Americans who struggle with understanding and accepting the concept of repressive regimes. He said that Americans are lucky that we have not ever lived amid generally oppressive governments.

Since 2006, Chad Bradshaw has been giving the Bradshaw children daytime and early evening child care, when Ella Bradshaw, the wife of Clark is working. Ella is a corporate attorney working with a company in Boston, Massachusetts. Five years ago, in August 2006, a Norwell, Massachusetts-based apparel retailer that was employing Chad as a sales representative, discontinued offering employees day care services. Ella was pregnant for the first time.

Chad and Ella had wanted their children to attend the day care center, as the circumstance would allow Chad to regularly interact with the children during lunch hours or work breaks. Meanwhile, Ella, who had formerly been employed in the financial services field, had obtained a law degree and passed the Massachusetts Bar exam, after having completed several years of part-time studies. Since then she has been employed as a corporate attorney representing a Boston-based firm.

In September of 2006, Erica Bradshaw was born. Chad and Ella had decided that Chad would provide Erica as well as any additional Bradshaw children with daytime childcare. Richard Bradshaw was born in 2008. Sixteen months ago, in 2010, Mark Bradshaw was born. Chad admits that leaving the business world and suddenly becoming a stay-at-home father providing morning, afternoon, and sometimes early evening child care, while Ella Bradshaw was nurturing Bradshaw family members with financial support, was life-changing.

Regularly performing such tasks as diapering babies and mixing baby milk formula was initially challenging, perplexing, and sometimes downright bewildering. "A guy isn't supposed to be doing this stuff," Chad said. "I was an army man; I used to jump out of planes. I rolled with some of the toughest guys on the planet, Seventh Infantry Battalion, one thousand men, serving Operation Desert Storm, who were deployed to Kuwait, Iraq, and Saudi Arabia. I love my children," he stated, indicating he genuinely enjoys being a stay-at-home dad. Caring about children is one legacy he hopes Bradshaw children will pass on when becoming adults, whether or not they become parents.

Chad has remained intermittently involved in the business world, since he became a stay-at-home Father. He meets monthly with former co-workers. They share a meal and conversation. He has noticed that mutual healthy jealousy surfaces among the former colleagues, from time to time. Chad has observed former male co-workers succeeding in climbing career ladders and earning steadily increasing incomes, while former colleagues of Chad have watched him flourishing as a dad who is giving Bradshaw children and the family dog, Ginger, daytime, afternoon, and early evening care. They have observed the role of a stay-at-home dad who has been able to watch his children and the family canine grow, and at the same time, has been content with earning no visible salary.

Saturday, June 4, 2011

Nephew Rhett and I greeted one another in a hospital recovery room, shortly after he awoke after he underwent day surgery in a Boston hospital. He appeared to be surprisingly refreshed and relaxed, as he and I were conversing. When we left the hospital, I drove for about one hour before arriving in Scituate, where he is living with sister Lizzie.

Lizzie was also released from a Boston hospital after having undergone a second hip replacement surgery a few days ago. She underwent the first hip replacement surgery three years ago. Liz realized the first hip replacement device she received was faulty, shortly after the first surgery. This evening she was radiant, while she was walking and holding a crutch, which gives the recuperating hip support. She was relieved that she had been able to return home relatively quickly after surgery. Seated in a den chair, she was holding one-year-old Clarkson Sullivan. Her three-year-old grandchild Zachariah Sullivan was near her; he was playing with toys strewn about the room. Lizzie is now a nursing profession retiree.

Sunday, June 5, 2011

Who knew partying could again be enjoyable? Looking through a window of the apartment in which I live, I saw two cars, which were parked in the driveway of the Payne and Feigel families, who reside next door. Several days ago, I received a graduation party invitation from the Payne family noting that a celebration honoring Laura Payne was scheduled to happen today, inside the Payne family home.

While anticipating the graduation party late this afternoon, I was nervous and hesitant about when to arrive at the party. I definitely did not want to show up too early. I did not see any cars in the Payne and Feigel driveways. The graduation gathering had begun over one half hour ago; the time was now 4:30 p.m.

Wearing dressy casual clothing and carrying a "Happy Graduation" flower bouquet, I stepped outside the apartment front door, walked down apartment hallway stairs, and then emerged outside the large hallway doors. I walked down three residence front steps and then across a driveway shared by the Payne, Feigel, and Callighan families. Gingerly opening the front door of the Payne home and crossing its threshold allowed me to view party guests, who were standing and also wandering about the kitchen, living room, dining room, and backyard. Invitees were alternately socializing, eating food, and drinking refreshing beverages. I realized there were no cars in the Payne and Feigel driveways because guests had parked on the street or in the nearby Cohasset Town Hall parking lot.

After greeting the party hosts, Jeremy Payne and Lila Payne, the wife of Jeremy Payne, and Gigi Feigel, mother of Lila and a grandmother of the Payne children, I presented Lila with the bouquet of wrapped flowers as well as an enclosed graduation card for Laura.

Nearby, Laura was engaged with fellow high school graduates in conversation. In the back yard, Hadley and Michaela Payne, junior sisters of Laura, had joined party invitees who were about the same age.

I breathed increasingly easily, as I observed approximately fifty guests, who were mingling casually and generally enthusiastically. Homemade food offerings included several dips, chips, salads, meatballs marinated in a red sauce and rice. Tasty beverages and savory desserts were also available. Seeking familiarity, I gravitated toward Mary Rita and Paul Callighan, respective landlady and landlord of the apartment in which I live. While Mary Rita, Paul, and I were talking, someone offered me a Margarita drink in tall slender glass. Containing alcohol, the beverage releases a strong lime aroma. The drink was politely and gently accepted.

Now drinking eight or nearly eight glasses of water daily and generally adding a lime wedge to the water drink, I am finding that drinking adequate amounts of water every day is relatively facile. This afternoon, while I intermittently observed the appearing Margarita slowly disappearing within a large glass, as I was sipping the green drink, I unexpectedly became unusually talkative, and well, "buzzed." Fortunately, no alcohol-related mishaps befell me today, beyond becoming overly enthusiastic and well, a bit loud.

When the drink was gone, I decided that when attending parties, from this day forward, I will imbibe only alcohol-free cocktails, also known as mocktails. Not wanting to remember uttering unreasonable statements or performing irrational actions while drinking alcohol and not wishing to be unable to recall having done so after drinking, are the primary reasons that I made the choice. People can hardly help behaving improperly or irrationally after excessively drinking alcohol, as alcohol becomes largely "in charge" of human behavior, shortly after one decides to swallow it.

As party moments passed, a former fellow Cohasset High School attendee, Deanne Alexander and Larry Alexander, the husband of Deanne, and the engaged daughter of Deanne and Larry, Kristie Alexander, greeted me. Kristie is about twenty five years old, is a college graduate, and is employed as a social worker. Another daughter of Deanne and Larry, named Brooke, was not able to be present here.

Deanne will soon retire; she has been teaching elementary school students in Norwell, Massachusetts for thirty-seven years. Mrs. Alexander says that although she occasionally becomes nervous when considering retirement, she is generally ready to retire. "Thursday, June thirtieth, will be the last time I'll be locking the homeroom class door and returning the door key," Deanne said.

Last year, Larry Alexander retired from teaching elementary school students in Pembroke, Massachusetts for twenty years. He had previously taught in Norwell Public Schools for seven years. Larry and Deanne met when both were Norwell Public Schools employees. Larry is now exploring personal retirement dreams, which include travel.

Deane, Larry, and Kristie are attending three graduation parties today. Deanne commented that it has been a while since she and Larry have partied. The admission instantly relieved social anxiety that I was experiencing. Previously I had been nervously thinking, *I'll bet Deanne and Larry are regular party goers.*

When she attended Cohasset High School, Deanne was popular. She was also the captain of the CHS varsity cheerleading team. Interacting with Deanne, Larry, and Kristie this afternoon enabled me to become calm, confident, and motivated and therefore, to continue peacefully socializing as the Alexanders exited the party and headed toward another celebration.

Moments later, seeing another party goer, I wandered over toward her, saying, "I think we've met before; do you work inside Cohasset Town Hall?"

"Yes, I do work inside Cohasset Town Hall and we have met before," the woman stated factually. Extending her right hand toward me, she said, "Seline Perry."

I extended my left hand toward her, and with it grasped and shook her right hand saying, "Merrie Reagan." Seline and I shared conversation surrounding employment as well as professional aspirations, a discussion which lasted nearly fifteen minutes.

As the exchange between Seline and I was ending, I remembered previously having been at home with Jura, looking outside the bedroom window facing the Payne family home, and at the same time, saying, "What do you wanna bet I'll be leaving the party no more than fifteen minutes after arriving there?" When viewing a large handsome clock, which was set on a living room wall, I realized that I had been attending the cheerful, festive, and flowing party for over two and a half hours. Suddenly, I thought, *"Leave now Merrie, before you wear out being welcome here."*

Near eight o'clock p.m., after thanking Lila and Jeremy Payne, I left the gathering, which continued, amid prevailing sun and desire-evoking weather. When I arrived home and opened the door leading into the apartment, Jura was standing near the entrance; he was facing me, directly. As I observed his loving bright eyes and vigorously wagging tail, I was filled with contentment, gratitude, and yes, guacamole dip.

Monday, June 6, 2011

Today, I spotted former fellow Cohasset High School graduate Hollyn Richardson. She was examining produce, inside a large grocery store in Cohasset. We exchanged greetings. Hollyn informed me that Noelle Winters, another CHS graduate who befriended Hollyn and me in high school, will be coming to see her soon in Cohasset.

Having resided in Florida for many years, Noelle has longtime been engaged in a career within the biology field. She is also the mother of two boys, who are by now, probably both adults, or near being adults. When we were seniors at Cohasset High School, Hollyn, Noelle, Brielle Morgan, Vicky Remick, Beverly Jennings and I often ate lunch together on school days. Some or all of us had previously dated; as seniors, none of us was dating, as far as I know. We were self-baptized as DWs or "Dateless Wonders" and we mutually acknowledged one another as such.

We had created nicknames such as Dufus, Gazooba, Wart, Fang, and "Raut". Who was "Fang? I can't remember. When seeing Hollyn this morning, I remarked, "I can't believe we wrote these nicknames in Tessahoc under our family names. Tessahoc is the name of the Cohasset High School yearbook. The name Tessahoc is Cohasset spelled backwards.

"No wonder we barely had social lives. What boy in high school would want to see or date a girl who has been publicly self-identified as Dufus, Wart, Fang, Raut or "Gazooba?

Whaat were we thinking?" I said aloud, as Hollyn Richardson, now named Babineau, and I, standing beside the juicy fruit section of the grocery store, gushed boisterous laughter, which was immediately circulated among nearby grocery store shoppers.

Thursday, June 9, 2011

Desiring change found me wanting a haircut; stylist Danielle and I met, at 2:30 p.m., this afternoon inside a Hingham salon. While Danielle was cutting my hair, she and I discussed book titles I proposed. *Remembering* is the initial title I suggested. "Good luck selling books with *this* title," Danielle said, non-verbally, while she yawned and indicated that she was clearly bored.

Chuckling, I suggested the second title, *Life Flashes* as she deftly continued cutting hair on my head which fell onto the salon floor. Suddenly, Danielle became intrigued. She said she wished to hear the third book title, *Flash Life*. As she and I ended deliberating about memoir titles, we chose the second title, *Life Flashes*. The haircut Danielle gave me was stylish, satisfactory, and appreciated.

Wednesday, June 15, 2011

Nephew Rhett agreed to meet two friends at a restaurant in Boston, Massachusetts. These three had initially decided to eat food and drink beverages here, while watching the final hockey game of the National Hockey League (NHL) Stanley Cup playoffs, which is happening this evening. The Boston Bruins team is playing the Vancouver Canucks team, of Vancouver, Canada. The game is in Vancouver.

Each of the two leading NHL teams has won three of the seven games played in the Stanley Cup Finals. To win the trophy, winning the majority of seven games is required. Thus far, both teams have won three games. The Canucks have won all the games played in Vancouver. Tonight, either the Bruins or the Canucks will become Stanley Cup victors. The first Stanley Cup game was played in 1894.

Before boarding a commuter train headed into Boston, Rhett, who was sitting beside me in the front passenger seat of the car that I was driving to the train station, leaned forward and dismounted the back pack he was transporting. After opening the pack, he checked and verbally noted some of the contents of the back pack aloud. "I brought a light jacket, in case it is cool outside when the game ends, and apple in case I am hungry." Chuckling, he added, "And, I brought a jackknife, in case anyone stabs me."

"You brought a *knife* in case anyone *stabs* you?" I said, shouting and nearly veering off the road.

"Merrie, I am *joking.*" Rhett chuckled. "I brought a jackknife to peel the apple," he uttered, as he giggled and demonstrated considerable satisfaction with having successfully riled me.

Boston Garden, an arena where professional games have been played since 1928, was renamed TD Garden in 2009. Tonight, shortly after departing a subway train that had arrived in Boston, Rhett entered the restaurant near TD Garden where he and two friends had chosen to meet and watch the game, which is being televised live. Friends who had agreed to meet him did not show up. Unworried, Rhett decided to watch the Stanley Cup Championship hockey game solo.

When he and I conversed after the game, when I picked him up at the train station where I had previously dropped him off, Rhett said that while he was sitting at the restaurant bar, eating and waiting for the game to start, he met a man who is about the same age as Ron Jenkins. Ron Jenkins is the father of Rhett, his sister Kristin, and his brother Jonas Jenkins. Two years ago, Ron, a retired social worker, moved to Colorado. Rhett and Ron have conversed regularly and have visited one another since Ron relocated. Tonight, Rhett and the restaurant goer that he met decided to order and share appetizers and beverages while watching the game.

Re-entering the home of sister Lizzie, after dropping Rhett off at the train station, I asked her if she wished to watch the game and if so, if she wanted company while watching the match. Nodding twice, she agreed. We each confessed to having previously experienced considerable uncertainty about watching the game. We do not want to be heartbroken if the Bruins lose the game.

Jimmy Trimmel, a Riggins Garage car mechanic, also admitted he experienced ambivalence when he considered watching the live game tonight. This afternoon, while the car I drive was undergoing an oil and filter change, Jimmy and I talked briefly outside the longtime well-reputed Cohasset garage. Jimmy also confessed that he did not want to see the Bruins lose the championship-determining game of the Stanley Cup competition. Having heard Jimmy also share the sentiment rendered me being stunned and relieved at the same time. I had wondered whether fears of loss I had been experiencing about watching the Bruins vs. Canucks hockey game were the kind of fears that only women vocalize.

This evening, seated in upholstered chairs and watching the Bruins vs. Canucks televised hockey game, sister Lizzie and I looked toward one another and simultaneously screamed delight, when the Bruins team scored goal number three during the third period.

This is the last period in the game. Having viewed the hat trick, which is the scoring of three successive goals, Liz and I both became confident that the Boston Bruins team was headed toward victory. We fully relaxed when the team scored goal number four, when one minute of game playing time remained. The final score of Stanley Cup game was Bruins 4, Canucks 0.

Game seven of the Boston Bruins vs. Vancouver Canucks in the Stanley Cup series is reported to have been the leading NHL game watched on television since 1972, when the Boston Bruins last won the Stanley Cup championship thirty-nine years ago. After the game, Bruins goalie, Tim Thomas, designated as being a highly valuable player in the Stanley Cup competition this year, spoke with media members. Newspaper reporters quoted Mr. Thomas, while he was addressing former Stanley Cup-starved Boston Bruins fans who had been at the game or had watched it on television. "You've been waiting a long time. You wanted it. You got it. We're bringing it home," he said.

Sunday June 19, 2011

Two weeks ago, nephew Rhett received hand surgery; a surgical pin was vertically pierced into the middle finger of his left hand; the pin is intended to hold fractured bones in the finger together. The finger was bandaged when the surgical process was completed.

Today, mysteriously using both hands, Rhett spent substantial time digging up grass, and while doing so, he created an open tunnel. It is thirty feet long, eight inches wide and several inches deep. The tunnel begins near the motor adjoined with a swimming pool, which is outside the home of sister Lizzie. After digging the underground tunnel, Rhett extended electrical wiring connected with the pool motor and then laid most of it in the vertical tunnel. He connected the plug on the end of the wiring with an electrical outlet in the basement, before he covered almost all of the wiring with grass and dirt.

Monday, June 20, 2011

Having received hip replacement surgery almost three weeks ago, Lizzie has been walking three miles nearly every day. The doctor who performed the surgery and the physical therapy professionals assisting Liz are stunned. In general, hip replacement patients restart regular exercising, three months following surgery. Remaining optimistic, Liz is healing.

Obliging me, Rhett removed the bandage a nurse had placed upon his left-hand middle finger after he underwent hand surgery two weeks ago. Viewing the surgical pin which was vertically placed inside the mid-section of his left-hand middle finger was startling, as the pin protrudes above the bandaged finger. The finger is noticeably bruised. Following surgery, Rhett utilized physician-prescribed antibiotics. Sadly, flesh on the surgically treated finger has become re-infected and turned red and purple in color.

Viewing the finger found me remembering a television show named "The Addams Family". The popular TV show was aired between 1964 and 1966. Members of the close-knit Addams family displayed eccentric personalities and highly unusual interests. When fellow human beings viewed Addams family members as being bizarre, Addams family members were unmoved.

"Blaagh," I responded, becoming nauseous when seeing the pin-punctured, multi-color bruised finger. Dumbfounded, I privately said, *How is it possible that Rhett dug a thirty foot long, several inches deep and eight inches wide underground tunnel for electrical wiring, using both hands?* Maybe he used only one.

CHAPTER EIGHTEEN

FEEDING FIVE THOUSAND, ECONOMIC CHALLENGES, WARREN BUFFETT, EDUCATION EXPERIENCES, NATIONAL NEWS

Sunday, July 31, 2011

Facing possible overdraft charges this morning, I called my sister Lizzie. Requesting to borrow fifty dollars, and I promised to repay her by Wednesday morning. She said lending me the money was not a problem; she stated that she is confident that the money will be returned. Then she invited me to attend the birthday party she is being given tonight. Her daughter Kristin, son-in-law Payden, and son Rhett are hosting the gathering.

When Jura and I entered the home of Lizzie late this afternoon, Rhett was cooking chicken, and fish on an outdoor grill. Kristin was in the kitchen, making salad and boiling corn on the cob, while Payden was watching his sons Zachariah and Clarkson. When we all were seated, facing a picnic table situated below a raised umbrella and sharing dinner, I addressed Kristin saying, "Kristin, you will become thirty-two years old, this October? Wow. Eight years from now, you will be forty years old."

"I don't mind being reminded about turning thirty-two, but I certainly do mind turning forty," Kristin retorted, politely. "Oh, no wonder I haven't been invited here for six months," I said, giggling and hearing agreeing family members laughing. After-dinner entertainment tonight was watching three-year-old Zachariah, who was wearing shorts, a shirt, and a cap turned backwards, as he drove a motorized toy tractor. In back yard, Zach maneuvered the vehicle forward, backward, and in half circles.

Later, Liz drove to a nearby bank where she does business. I accompanied her. The institution offers after-hours ATM services. After approaching the ATM machine, she withdrew cash and then re-entered the car. Handing me fifty dollars, she said, "I want you to have this." Stunned and surprised, I asked, "Are you sure?" Nodding, she indicated yes. The response found me being delighted, humbled, and suddenly remembering a Scripture reading a church lector read this morning.

Someone died. Thousands of mourners, including men, women, and children have walked many miles. They are seeking a remote area where they can rest, so that they can continue to pray and to comfort one another. Jesus has been leading the multitude. Suddenly, some mourners are worrying. The grieving persons have traveled a long distance and little nourishment is available. One person who wants the mourners to be able to eat, commands Jesus, "It is late. Dismiss these people; allow them to return home," he says.

Jesus says discharging the grieving praying people is not necessary. He says food present here is sufficient. "There isn't enough food," another mourner moans. "There are five bread loaves and two fish," another anxious person indicates, again rebuking Jesus.

In accordance with Scripture, Jesus requested available bread, loaves, and fish. He looked up toward Heaven, gave thanks, and then blessed the bread, and broke it. Followers of Jesus then distributed the bread. Jesus also divided the two fish among them all. All ate and were filled. Miraculously and mysteriously, five thousand people received and shared the food; uneaten food remained after the meal ended.

Today, while I considered the possibility of being overdrawn, I nervously sought a fifty-dollar loan this morning. I was not only gifted fifty dollars, but also invited to share dinner with family members, which was fully enjoyable. Thoughtfully prepared dinner food and stimulating conversation we shared was satisfying. When the meal ended, there was abundant leftover food. This story parallels the Biblical loaves and fishes account.

Tuesday, August 2, 2011

Following months of congressional debate preceding legislative approval, President Obama signed a bipartisan bill raising the U.S. national debt ceiling last night, as funds used for paying bills of the U.S government were two days shy of being depleted. The law allows the raising of the U.S.

national debt ceiling, which is currently slightly over fourteen trillion dollars. If the national debt ceiling is not raised when government funds are nearly depleted, a government defaults on borrowed money or loans and in turn, risks termination as a money borrower. Last night, facing the United States House of Representatives, President Obama delivered a nationally televised speech urging the legislative body to pass a proposed bill which will allow raising the national debt ceiling.

While being assisted, Arizona Congresswoman Gabrielle Giffords entered the House chambers last night, shortly before President Obama addressed the Congressional body. Stunned fellow Democratic and Republican Congress members showered Ms. Giffords with rousing applause. She accepted handshake offers and good wishes of fellow congressmen and congresswomen. She has courageously faced a continuing seven-months-long physical rehabilitation process, since she was shot and nearly fatally brain injured, on January 8, this year.

Congresswoman Giffords was standing outside a grocery store, greeting and conversing with constituents, when she was shot. A court recently judged the apprehended and incarcerated shooter, Jared Lee Loughner, as being legally mentally competent. Being judged legally mentally competent means one is able to understand and to withstand a lawful trial. Mr. Loughner is now facing an upcoming jury trial.

Congresswoman Giffords came to the House of Representatives intending to vote for raising the debt ceiling. Ms. Giffords as well as former colleagues of Ms. Giffords were tearful or near being so, as she entered the congressional chamber. She received thunderous applause, while many, including House Speaker John Boehner, greeted and embraced her. Observing the courage that Gabby Giffords has demonstrated while having undergone profoundly life-altering circumstances is mind boggling, humbling, and inspiring.

Thursday, August 4, 2011

Last night, while he was visiting his home state of Illinois, in Chicago, President Obama attended a televised birthday and campaign fundraising celebration honoring him. Addressing hundreds of supporters, Mr. President humbly confessed, "It is true I will turn fifty tomorrow. By the time I wake up tomorrow, I will receive an email from AARP (American Association for Retired Persons), asking me to call President Obama and remind him to protect Medicare." Rousing laughter and applause followed the witty remark.

White House News Correspondent Jake Tapper attended the event. Reporting on the story today, Mr. Tapper also commented that now fifty-year-old President Obama is strikingly physically fit. Video accompanying the report depicted Mr. Obama wearing only bathing shorts, evidencing flat abdomen muscles, and walking out of what appeared to be warm, wavy ocean waters. Heavenly background music emanated from the video clip, as sunlight gleamed through the commander-in-chief. Hilarious was viewing the tongue and cheek political commentary.

Saturday, August 6, 2011

I was invited to share dinner with Lizzie, Kristin, Rhett, Zachariah, and Clarkson. Kristin had ordered pick-up-style Mexican food over the telephone. No cooking was done this evening, as Liz had been briefly hospitalized twice this week, on two differing days, when the second surgically inserted hip replacement device she received in June this year suddenly malfunctioned for the first time.

Liz was seated at the dinner table with Kristin, Rhett, Zach, and Clark while they were eating frittatas for dinner, when the device suddenly broke down and was nearly protruding through skin on her left hip. Liz experienced intense pain. She began to cry, and then almost scream, as Kristin called the emergency telephone number 911. "Isn't Mimi (Gramma) lucky; she is going on an ambulance ride," Kristin said, turning toward Zach, who had also begun crying, while he was seeing Mimi in significant pain.

"Look, here comes an ambulance," Kristin said, wanting to distract Zach, as rescue vehicles arrived. After visiting a hospital emergency room and then returning home, Liz said, while laughing, "That will be the last time I eat frittatas." I do not know what happened or what she said when the second hip replacement device malfunctioned for a second time, again requiring a hospital emergency room visit. I would not be surprised if I heard that Liz said something such as, *what the heck was this about?*

Last night, after sharing dinner, Kristin Lizzie, and I conversed; Kristin related having last Thursday afternoon attended the weekly farmer's market. The event is held every Thursday afternoon on Cohasset Common, during spring, summer, and fall months, from the first week in June to the first week in October. Cohasset residents as well as Cohasset neighbors, residing in nearby towns, are offered locally grown fresh seasonal produce, prepared foods, and crafts. The market also features a single entertainer or small bands that perform music during the ongoing market. Sometimes another small band plays an additional free concert for a couple of hours, when the market closes.

Kristin remarked that while she was at the market, last Thursday afternoon, she met an accomplished female artist who paints rocks. This evening, as she was showing Liz several medium-size colored rocks that she had purchased, she reflected, "Mum, these painted rocks would make good Christmas presents, don't you think?" Unsolicited reaction from me was immediate.

"Don't give me one of those rocks as a Christmas present," I asserted, disapprovingly, while standing beside Kristin and Lizzie, as great nephews Zach and Clark, who had been placed upon a made-up guest bedroom double bed were being clothed, after having been given assistance with bathing in the bathroom tub.

"You're too late," Kate responded, grinning, sensing thanklessness having surfaced within me. "In fact, we're not giving you a painted rock this year; we're giving you a painted boulder," she added. Laughter burst forth through the humbled ingrate.

Monday, August 8, 2011

Facing media members during a televised press briefing, President Obama commented on a recent action of leading credit rating company Standard & Poor. The agency downgraded U.S. credit ratings and thereby partially restricted the ability of Americans to borrow money and at the same time, it increased interest rates which lending institutions will begin charging. Mr. Obama said that the downgraded American credit rating means that financial analysts are now questioning the economic stability of the United States.

He said that he believes that the credit crisis that America is now facing is resolvable and that the borrowing power of the U.S government is not in danger.

The president commented that current stock market activity indicates that American credit is considered generally safe worldwide. He also stated that world renowned investor, industrialist, and philanthropist Warren Buffett recently said that he would give America a quadruple-A credit rating if this was possible. President Obama stated that Congress is currently being challenged with increasing tax rates to bring down the multi-trillion-dollar U.S. national debt or continuing to borrow money to pay the charges.

"Last week we (Congress) reached an agreement making historic cuts in domestic and defense programs," Mr. Obama said. "We can't cut more, in either of these areas." He commented that restoring the American economy now requires combining cuts in domestic and defense programs with two additional steps: first, enacting tax reform that will ask Americans who can afford to do so to contribute increasing tax shares and second, making modest adjustments in programs such as Medicare.

Monday, August 15, 2011

Today found me reading a good and intriguing news report, indicating that billionaire Warren Buffett has requested Congress to increase taxes that wealthy Americans pay.

Mr. Buffett commented that such legislative action will not hurt American investors. News agency Reuters reported that in a published article that he recently submitted to the *New York Times*, eighty-year-old Mr. Buffett stated, "My friends and I have been coddled long enough by billionaire friendly Congress. It is time for our government to get serious about shared sacrifice."

In the newspaper article, Mr. Buffett indicated that he paid $6,938,744 in federal taxes last year. "That sounds like a lot of money. But what I paid was only 17.4 percent of my taxable income and that is actually a lower percentage than was paid by any of the other twenty people in our office. Their tax burdens ranged from thirty-three percent to forty-one percent and averaged thirty-six percent," Mr. Buffett said.

Warren Buffett said increased taxes will not discourage investment. "I have worked with investors for over sixty years and have yet to see anyone, even when capital gains tax rates were 39.9 percent in 1976-1977, shy away from a sensible investment because of the tax rate on the potential gain," Mr. Buffett stated. The U.S. capital gains tax rate is between ten and fifteen percent currently. "People invest money to make money; potential taxes have never scared them off," he remarked.

Tuesday, August 16, 2011

Curious is this. The last time America was debt free, in other words, not living largely on borrowed credit, was in 1835. Early this year, business writer Robert Smith, who is featured on the National Public Radio (NPR) website, "Planet Money-the Economy Explained" explained that in 1829, U.S President Andrew Jackson succeeded in paying back a U.S. national debt of fifty-eight million dollars in six years. Yes, six years. What did he do?

Mr. Smith indicated that Andrew Jackson consolidated U.S. government loans. As there was then an occurring real estate bubble, or rapidly increasing real estate prices, happening in the Western part of the United States, which was at the same time increasing land prices, President Jackson sold some government assets—expendable U.S government land. Robert Smith wrote that Mr. Jackson also vetoed numerous proposed government spending bills during the six years when the national debt of America was being eliminated.

Mr. Smith recounted that during this time, President Jackson also refused to re-charter the Second United States National Bank. The bank was dissolved. President Jackson believed that this private corporation, then controlling American government currency and at the same time being held accountable by Congress as well as the U.S. Treasury, was unethically conferring economic privileges.

Robert Smith depicted President Jackson as someone who intensely disliked debt. One time before he was elected president, Andrew Jackson incurred massive debt, when one land deal in which he was involved went awry. Mr. Smith wrote, "In Jackson's mind, debt was a moral failing and the idea that you could acquire stuff through debt seemed almost like black magic."

While considering the status of the current U.S. Government national debt, one might also wonder about the last time the government budget in America was balanced. It is written that in 1995, U.S. Congressman Newt Gingrich began rallying members of the Republican Caucus in the House of Representatives to promote the idea of eliminating the budget deficit, within seven years. The last time that the Unites States government budget displayed surpluses was in 1999, 2000, and 2001, when Democrat Bill Clinton was president of the U.S. Notably, Republican Congressmen and Congresswomen then represented the majority in the U.S. House of Representatives and Senate.

Is the national psyche of America not damaged or diseased, as the U.S. government continues to be largely dependent on borrowed credit?

Continually living on borrowed credit resembles living in a house with clutter, even if the clutter is solely in one room. Someone once wisely said, "Clutter is an outward demonstration of delayed decisions." Delayed decisions promote delayed clarity.

Experiencing mounting exponential national debt is not an American *fait accompli*. President Andrew Jackson exemplified this reality one hundred seventy-six years ago. Demonstrating reason, compassion, and cooperation as an economic guide, government leaders can successfully design a plan for gradually eliminating the national debt of the United States; the debt is currently over fifteen trillion dollars.

Political leaders can also devise a way to balance the budget of the U.S. government, as has been done in the past. The American credit rating can be fully restored. Americans can again experience numerous benefits associated with financially healthy government operations.

Tuesday, August 23, 2011

A magnitude 5.8 earthquake shook the United States east coast, today. Near 2:00 p.m. Washington, D.C., New York, and Boston residents experienced tremors that were centered in Virginia. ABC News *Good Morning America* show anchor, Robin Roberts, who reported on the weather-related development said she "didn't feel a thing," during the tremors, because she was in a yoga class. Humm…

No earthquake-related fatalities or injuries have been reported. Late this afternoon quake-affected, unsettled people abounded, including a Dorchester woman. She was sitting beside me on a Boston bound subway train. The work desk at which the woman had been sitting had begun shaking and moving, around 2:00 p.m.

Saturday, August 27, 2011

While walking past French Memories café in Cohasset, I viewed Barbara (Barbie) Carbone, who was a Deer Hill School secretary, when I attended this elementary school, from 1962-1965. Ms. Carbone remained employed here, in 1975 and 1976, after I had graduated from college and had been employed as a Deer Hill School Title I Tutor. This afternoon I ran into Barbara and Rosalie (Rosie), the sister of Barbara. The two ladies were sitting at a table outside French Memories café, underneath an awning protecting them from being overexposed to brilliant sunshine.

233

Ms. Carbone said she loved working at Deer Hill School as a secretary. She administratively assisted principals of Deer Hill School as well as teachers and students attending the elementary school. Barbie said she also genuinely enjoyed interacting with elementary school children, which she misses.

A Cohasset native, Ms. Carbone continues to live in Cohasset. Rosalie and Gerard (Gerry) Carbone, brother of Barbara and Rosie also continue living here. Joining Barbara and Rosalie found me recounting the years that I attended Cohasset public schools, including Joseph Osgood and Deer Hill School. Barbara and Rosalie figuratively walked with me, while I strolled down memory lane, recalling elementary school experiences. The two sisters listened, regularly commented and laughed, while they shared the nostalgic journey with me.

The sole recollection that comes to mind regarding attending kindergarten is walking toward a classroom on the first day of school at Joseph Osgood School in September 1957. Joseph Osgood School is made up of kindergarten through third grade classes. On the first day of school, I was holding the right hand of Mom, and while doing so, was resisting entering the classroom.

I did not yet want to be away from home for very long without Mom or Dad. I also recall a teacher whose name I do not remember, encouraging me to turn my left hand as well as writing paper I was using leftward and upward, while she was teaching me and fellow kindergarten class members to write. The suggestion was personally perplexing and truly unworkable. Unto this day, I write with the left hand and the writing paper turned rightward and nearly sideways.

In first grade, I was assigned to the class of Mrs. Lagourney, whom I loved. She was kind, enthusiastic, and compassionate and aided me considerably, as I regularly experienced difficulty with understanding reading and mathematics concepts. Meanwhile, sitting at a desk directly in front of classmate Tommy Chatterton found me regularly turning around, facing him, smiling, and clearly exhibiting appropriate girl-to-boy interest, for a-six-year-old. Tommy consistently responded, clearly indicating that he wanted nothing to do with me. He distinctly demonstrated this fact, while he performed simple, direct, and disapproving emoji style facial expressions.

When thinking of second grade, I draw a blank, so to speak. There is an aphorism, a saying stating, "No news is often good news." The late Mrs.

Rosemary McPherson, former longtime Joseph Osgood School third grade teacher, taught homeroom students, including me, academic subjects as well as morning prayers; class member recitations included Bible psalm twenty-three. In public schools, prayer was allowed for about five minutes, before classes began, until June, in 1962.

The Supreme Court of the United States deemed school prayer unconstitutional, on June 25, 1962. In the case of Engel vs. Vitale, a group of parents, including a man named Steven Engel, sued a school board president, William Vitale, on the grounds that a prayer that a Board of Regents created and authorized as being a prayer that students could voluntarily say before the start of each school day, contradicted the religious beliefs of the group of parents. The prayer states, "Almighty God, we acknowledge our dependence on thee and we ask for Thy blessings upon us, our parents, our teachers and our country."

The official summary of the decision of the U.S. Supreme Court judges states, "State officials may not compose an official state prayer and require that it be recited in the public schools in the state at the beginning of each school day, even if the prayer is denominationally neutral and pupils who wish to do so may remain silent or be excused to leave the room."

Reading the legal decision left me wondering how allowing voluntary prayer as well as discretionary silence is offensive. Isn't allowing students who do not wish to participate in optional prayer to be excused or leave the classroom respectful? Doesn't allowing public school students to participate in optional vocalized or silent prayer and at the same time allowing students who wish to be excused from prayer to be excused or to leave the classroom mean that the prayer is *not* required and that saying or not saying the prayer is therefore an expression of pure freedom?

Third-grade fellow class member, Eleanor (Ellie) Herendon, sat at a desk directly behind me; Ellie exuded a beautiful smile as well as a good sense of humor. Sadly, Ellie died before she finished high school. She had been afflicted with a serious illness.

Joseph Osgood School students moved up, or in other words, transferred to Deer Hill School, when they entered the fourth grade. When a student successfully completed the fourth, fifth and sixth grade curriculums at Deer Hill School, he or she graduated. If he or she desired, the student entered Cohasset High School, then starting in the seventh grade.

The 1962-1963 school year found me being seated aside fourth grade desk partner, Bonnie McGill, who a few times sternly warned me, that if I did not stop stealing ball point pens that homeroom teacher Mrs. White had given her, she (Bonnie) and I would not ever talk again. Every fourth grade student in the homeroom class of Mrs. White was given two translucent green ball point pens. After the first set of pens was given out at the beginning of the school year, students were required to ask Mrs. White for additional pens, unless Mrs. White had decided to give out new pens. I repeatedly stole pens from Bonnie because I was easily distracted in school, which caused me to routinely lose pens, and unlike Bonnie, I was fearful of asking Mrs. White for another pen. This does not mean that stealing was right.

Fourth-grade fellow homeroom class member, Beverly Jennings, hosted an all-girl weekend night sleepover party; this was probably the first sleepover party I attended. Beverly had invited seven fourth-grade girls, including me. After midnight, conducting a séance was proposed. Did we really levitate one girl? One girl was initially supine, lying down and facing upward, before we pajama-wearing girls gathered around her, placed the palms of our hands underneath her and at the same time, began mouthing words that I do not remember. I do remember communal screaming happened when the suspected levitation occurred.

Near the end of the 1963-1964 school year, fifth-grade fellow class member Richard Garrison and I won an annual spelling bee which was held in the fifth grade homeroom class of Mrs. Bainbridge. Another personal fifth-grade memory is lying while facing Mrs. Bainbridge, as well as nearly thirty fellow homeroom class students. One school day morning, I confessed to not being prepared to give a five to ten minutes long oral talk depicting the contents of a U.S. state research report we were asked to write and were given three weeks to compose. Seconds later, I invented and then tendered an excuse which Mrs. Bainbridge accepted, allowing me to instantly leave the classroom and to quickly enter a nearby lavatory. To this day, I can recall the feverish bodily discomfort I felt from head to toe, after lying in front of over twenty-five people.

One sixth-grade personal remembrance is having joined fellow students who were re-entering the homeroom class after recess and were quizzically viewing a large drawing on the classroom blackboard depicting the homeroom class teacher. Using white chalk, a fellow sixth-grader had artistically, exquisitely, and inaccurately illustrated the female homeroom teacher as a bodacious young woman, who was lying down with the right side of her body and facing forward. The teacher was depicted wearing an A-line, above the knee, cocktail party style dress as well as high heels. Her right leg was seductively bent over her left leg. Her left arm had been placed on her left hip; her right arm was raised, her right hand fingers were gently caressing a large, filled, and bubbling martini glass.

Settling into chairs beside classroom desks that were facing the blackboard that was in the front of the classroom, we fellow sixth-grade class members loquaciously anticipated the class homeroom teacher returning to the classroom and viewing the drawing. We were bewildered and stunned, as we considered an eleven-or twelve-year-old fellow class member demonstrating an adult level of awareness surrounding alcohol and sensuality. Although being not sure of what happened when the homeroom teacher returned, I am generally certain that shortly after being discovered as or having confessed to drawing the illustration, the young artist and fellow sixth-grader visited the reputed firm, gentle, and compassionate then Deer Hill School Principal, John Greamer.

Preparing to graduate from Deer Hill School in June 1965, before entering Cohasset High School is a final sixth grade personal recollection. Members of the Deer Hill School sixth-grade chorus, including me, practiced singing songs including "You'll Never Walk Alone," which became widely known and loved in 1963. I recall the chorus of the song, "walk on through the wind, walk on through the rain, though your dreams be tossed and blown; walk on, walk on with hope in your heart and you'll never walk alone; you'll never walk alone." It is not surprising when a person who sang these inspiring, calming, and encouraging lyrics fifty-eight years ago can readily remember all the words of the song.

Monday, August 29, 2011

Today finds me continuing to recall school experiences and reminiscing about attending Cohasset High School. Junior high and high school students attended the school. The first days of the seventh-grade 1965-1966 school year were personally overwhelming. The student body of Cohasset High School was three times the size of the student population of Deer Hill School. Changing classes for each subject and becoming acclimated with working with several teachers instead of one or two was also challenging.

On one of the first days that I attended Cohasset High School, after participating in a gym class I discovered that the bright red, pleated wool skirt with an elastic waist band that I had been wearing and had taken off and put in a gym locker before changing into gym clothes, was missing. Not finding the skirt, for the rest of the day I wore the designated one-piece blue denim gym suit with snaps for buttons. Before going home, I was emotionally overcome, confused, and weeping. I entered the CHS guidance office, where student counselor Mr. John Landry greeted me. He calmed, comforted, and motivated me.

Being a student in any of the English classes that then Cohasset High School seventh-and eighth-grade English teacher Miss Danton taught meant diagramming sentences in almost every class. We were asked to break sentences down into grammatical parts and to place each of the grammatical parts in a particular place within a schematic drawing.

On many days, this educational activity was assigned as partial classwork and homework. Having routinely performed the sometimes-tedious exercises for two school years has encouraged me—especially since I have begun to write again—to appreciate the mental organization skills that diagramming exercises develop.

I admired fellow junior high school classmates Alec Maguire and Timmy O'Donovan while we were students in the English class of Miss Danton. Tim and Alec were seated at desks in the front row of the English classroom, probably because they were class clowns who were regularly and generally delightfully mischievous. I sat at a desk situated diagonally across from them. Sadly, Alec transferred to another school and then died some years following high school graduation.

A final eighth-grade personal recollection is insisting that Mom allow me to attend an all-girl birthday party, which included a trip to a movie theatre to watch the 1963 widely popular teenage movie, *Bye, Bye Birdie.* The star of the motion picture was Jesse Pearson, whose heart throbbing, bodily gyrating singing style resembled that of another 1960s singer, Elvis Presley. The cinematic production of *Bye Bye Birdie* featured teenage girls wearing bikini bathing suits. After a full week of hearing me nagging her, Mom relented. She allowed me to join the birthday party girls in seeing a film that she then believed was far too graphic.

I remember that a physician diagnosed me with mononucleosis sometime in the winter or spring when I was in the ninth-grade. The illness was not serious. Mononucleosis is a blood disorder that is transmitted through saliva; therefore it can be contracted by kissing. This is why it is sometimes called "the kissing disease." One can also catch the viral disease by being exposed to a cough or a sneeze or sharing food or utensils with someone who has been diagnosed with the ailment.

Mom waited on me hand and foot while I was recuperating from the illness for a week; I admit that I fully enjoyed the kind attention she gave me. Contracting mononucleosis initially leaves one experiencing symptoms including a sore throat, swollen lymph nodes, fever, and considerable fatigue after being awake for a couple of hours. When I had fully recovered and resumed attending school classes, a biology class laboratory desk mate and partner informed me that while I was ill and at home, fellow class member Tim O'Donovan had said aloud in class, "Merrie probably caught mono from kissing her dog." Whether or not Reagan family owned a dog then, I do not wish to murder Timmy, anymore.

General enjoying school classes, academically excelling, and becoming interested in fellow Cohasset High School attendees Mitch Harrison and Brielle Morgan are what I also recall from attending ninth-grade. Gentle, knowledgeable, and stern Mr. James Farrell, then a ninth grade CHS biology class teacher, significantly influenced the academic success I experienced as a freshman high school student in the first semester of the 1967-1968 school year. This was clear. As a student, Mr. Farrell admired and respected me.

I remember working with Mr. Farrell while participating in a group performing an assigned biology class experiment. He was supervising me and fellow biology class students, during one of the regular science class experiments he assigned. When the class began, he performed a frog dissection procedure in front of the entire class, while he stood behind a large laboratory desk. Wondrously as well as bewilderingly, students observed the process, before Mr. Farrell organized us into small groups.

We were asked to follow the example of Mr. Farrell, which included wearing goggles, so that we would be protected, if frog blood or guts spurted during the dissection process, while it was being performed in small groups. We were advised that successful completion of the process would allow us to view several frog body parts. Frog dissection entails vertically inserting a surgical pin into the brain of a live frog, usually once or twice, until the frog dies, and then utilizing a scalpel and surgical scissors to cut open the underside of the frog, which allows one to view frog body parts.

When Mr. Farrell entered the small group into which he had assigned me, he reiterated the steps involved in the dissection procedure, which he had introduced in the beginning of the class. Then he instructed us to start the procedure. As he watched and advised students in the small group, nearly all of us were gagging or nearly gagging as someone was performing the first part of the process, killing the frog. I do remember assisting someone afterward, and in doing so, slitting the abdomen of the deceased frog all or part-way down, while utilizing a small knife-like instrument. All of the small group members we were intrigued, as we viewed frog anatomy parts, including the heart, lungs, stomach, and intestines, which resemble human body parts.

During the first term of ninth-grade, Mr. Farrell gave me an A- grade. The grade incorporated completed and accurate class homework, satisfactory interaction with the teacher and fellow class students and personal test scores which ranged from the low to high nineties percentiles. Being in the biology class represented the first and the last time that I experienced fulfillment in a science class.

Nearly failing chemistry and geometry classes and family grief is what I recall about being in the tenth-grade. Grampi (James) Reagan, the father of Dad and Aunt Anne (Reagan) Fannon, the sister of Dad, who had regularly lived with the Reagan and Fannon families, was suddenly diagnosed with terminal brain cancer in October of this school year. He died two months later, on December 10, 1968. He was sixty-three years old. I remember visiting him in a nursing home, shortly before he died. Emaciated and barely able to speak, he greeted me, smiling and softly calling me by name. He radiated love and inner peace.

Another bright spot that I recall from when I was a sophomore in high school was meeting Anthony (Tony) Damano and Kevin Thompson. Sister Lizzie and Kevin were fellow lifeguards, working at a pool inside a U.S. Naval Air Base in South Weymouth, Massachusetts. Tony and Kevin, who both lived in Weymouth, were friends. Liz, Kevin, Tony, and I went out together one night. I remember that we ate take-out food together. I do not remember anything else, except that we all enjoyed seeing one another.

A few days following the outing, Tony called me, wishing to see me again and after I sought and was given permission to do so from Mom and Dad, I agreed. Though he was experiencing health-related challenges, Tony rode a bicycle for twelve miles on a blisteringly hot and humid summer morning, before he entered the home in which Reagan family members were then living. Having experienced a relationship breakup eight months earlier, I did not want a new relationship.

Remaining interested, polite, and respectful, I was also not encouraging while Tony and I visited with one another on that late summer mid-morning. When Tony and I had decided to part, he and I exchanged smiles before he again rode his bicycle another twelve miles back to his home in Weymouth. Qualities that Tony quietly displayed—courage, humility, and compassion—have not been forgotten.

Haziness is what I experience when I remember being in the eleventh grade, except when I recall obtaining a driving license and then driving a family car for the first time. Fellow CHS class member Noelle Watson accompanied me. As I stepped on the gas pedal, the car almost immediately began speeding, traveling at eighty miles per hour southward, after we entered Route 3, a highway leading toward Plymouth, Massachusetts. Usually the round trip commute to Plymouth is about an hour long. Not so, this memorable day. Noelle and I returned to Cohasset forty minutes after departing here. Surprisingly and fortunately, I was not discovered speeding.

In 1970, Morgan family members, including Brielle Morgan, who befriended me when each of us entered the ninth-grade, had returned to Cohasset; they had previously relocated to Connecticut for two years. Brielle and I reconnected; we were both now car-driving Cohasset High School seniors. She and my brother Jared mutually developed fondness for one another during this year.

Brielle enjoyed joining me, on some school day afternoons when I drove to and from Cambridge, Massachusetts, so that I could give Jared a ride home from the private school he was attending. As senior school year progressed, the friendship relationship that Brielle and I shared continued to change. We again faced long-term separation. College years were approaching. Brielle had been accepted as a freshman at the University of Massachusetts in Amherst and I been accepted as an Emmanuel College freshman.

Although I was an intensely bashful adolescent, I had somehow enrolled in a public speaking class when I was a Cohasset High School senior. Mr. Kirk Rollins taught the elective course. The generally ebullient personality of Mr. Rollins moved me. He was an inspiring orator and enthusiastic teacher. He was a motivator. I am generally confident that I would not have passed the public speaking class without witnessing the example of confidence and good humor that he set.

The assigned final exam was a five minute long—no more, no less—timed speech on any personally chosen relevant topic, to be delivered while standing at a podium in front of the class, while facing standing Mr. Rollins and seated fellow students. Excited and shaking while performing the elocution, I was thrilled, as I steadily and successfully delivered and completed this first personal public speaking engagement. Ironically unto this day, I am humorously unable to remember either the topic of the speech or a single word that was spoken during the oration.

In the fall of 1971, I had been enrolled at Emmanuel College, a four year then all-female liberal arts institution. Lizzie and I commuted to the colleges we attended. Liz was a student at Boston University. Commuting to the schools on Mondays through Fridays involved between two-to-three-hour round trip travel, by car, subway train, and then for me, walking for about fifteen minutes, before arriving on campus.

Before attending Emmanuel College, I attended the EC Class of 1975 college orientation weekend, which occurred one weekend during the summer of 1971. Remaining at the college overnight during the two days and one night-long orientation weekend allowed me to join a group of adventurous fellow college freshman club goers on Saturday evening; we were seeking nighttime entertainment. At approximately 9:30 p.m., we entered one of several nightclubs then located in Kenmore Square. The club, which years later went out of business, was named "T.J.'s."

I left the girls I had accompanied to the club awhile after I was socializing and dancing with two gentlemen that I met there. Later, I left the club with the two boys. One of the boys offered to drive me back to the college campus; I accepted. We three then entered a dark green convertible MG evidencing two shiny leather seats. While one boy was driving and another boy was sitting in the passenger seat, I was seated between the two boys, atop the convertible open back end.

No funny business happened, except boisterous laughing that accompanied generally pleasant and good-humored conversation we were sharing. After arriving at the college, I thanked each of the boys for a pleasant evening, exited the car, and then re-entered a college dormitory at approximately 1:00 a.m. I was somberly greeted by a dismayed EC dormitory resident assistant as well as the girls whom I had abandoned.

All had been awaiting me. *Oh Oh...* I thought. Stunning me, no disciplinary action occurred, following the potentially dangerous escapade, beyond the very short lecture I received from the dormitory resident assistant after I apologized for being out late and leaving the girls with whom I had gone to the club.

Sustaining me through the years that I attended Emmanuel College was also meeting fellow class of 1975 member Clare Waitt. I also admired Rick Waitt, a brother of Clare. Endorsing Rick when he was a first-time candidate for the Boston City Council, I enthusiastically placed a bumper sticker supporting him on the rear bumper of the VW Beetle I was then driving. Rick ultimately won a seat on the council. Rick and Marilyn Waitt, now having been married for many years, are the parents of grown children. The last time that he and I talked, many years ago, Rick was continuing to practice law. Marilyn, a longtime educator, was continuing to work as an elementary school teacher.

Clare Waitt became Clare Waitt Grenham, the wife of Paul Grenham. Since then, she has also been a longtime elementary school teacher. Clare and Paul are the parents of five children, who are also adults or near being adults. Paul has been invested in the sale of computers and software sales for decades; I believe he now owns and manages a software related-business based in Boston.

Remembering Emmanuel College days also finds me recalling meeting William (Will) Powell during the summer of 1973, before I was about to enter the last year of college. I previously mentioned that we both worked at Paragon Park, an amusement park in Hull, Massachusetts. An additional person I remember meeting in the summer of '73 while working at Paragon Park was a boy named John Knoland; we shared two brief and memorable conversations.

Friendship between Brielle Morgan and I shared continued to evolve during that summer, while we were also fellow Paragon Park co-workers. Then attending the University of Massachusetts in Amherst, Brie was seriously dating and also demonstrating marital intentions. During the summer of '73, I considered dating and marriage as being intriguing, enigmatic, and bewildering...

An Emmanuel College professor influenced me, notably. In the third or fourth year that I was enrolled here, urban sociology class Professor Kirk Landon assigned students a final exam which involved writing a five pages-long paper. Mr. Landon requested that while writing the paper, students reflect not only upon life lessons learned in the class, but also about how the lessons were personally challenging and transforming. Referencing classroom lecture notes, classroom discussions, and assigned book readings was also encouraged.

Thinking that the final exam assignment would be "a cinch" or very easy, I clearly and neatly rewrote notes from class lectures and discussions and included a few references to assigned readings in the final exam. During one of the final urban sociology classes, Professor Landon was personally presented a neat and well-ordered exam paper which was written by me. When the exam was returned to me in the final class and I viewed C- grade, on the top of the first page of the paper, I was initially confused. Then I became upset.

Consulting Professor Landon, I queried why he gave me this near failing grade.

Mr. London said, "Merrie, performing well on this exam does not mean regurgitating class lecture notes, class discussion records, or the content of assigned book readings." Continuing, he stated, "Good performance on the final exam paper involves re-examining class lecture notes, recorded class discussions, and assigned readings notations, and then mentally identifying, deducing, and detailing the manner in which these combined educational experiences were challenging and life-changing, before writing about and therefore sharing the learned experiences in the exam." Are these words and words such as these not the words of a true professor?

"Whoa, this is deep," I responded. Professor Landon allowed me to re-submit the paper when it had been rewritten and he said that he would consider changing the initial grade, after he finished viewing it. While initially perusing the re-submitted final exam, Mr. Landon agreed that academic progress was made. When I viewed the B- final grade on the resubmitted exam which he had mailed back to me, I was generally satisfied, though I admit that I had hoped the revised exam would be given a different grade. An A- grade would also have been good and acceptable.

Barbara Walters, then a co-anchor of the *NBC Today Show,* was the guest speaker at the Emmanuel College 1975 commencement. Having been employed as a television journalist for over two decades, Ms. Walters entered the television broadcasting business after she graduated from Sarah Lawrence College, in Bronxville, New York, in 1953. She was hired to be an assistant to the publicity director of a television station. Before she assumed the assistant to the publicity director position, Ms. Walters had completed a temporary assignment as an administrative assistant at the television station.

In 1962, Ms. Walters joined the NBC *Today Show* as a show host, working with *Today Show* anchor, Hugh Downs, as the team reported news and feature stories. Barbara Walters became an official co-anchor of the show in 1974. Talking with Emmanuel College graduates in May of 1975, Barbara Walters said she was fortunate to have begun a successful career in the television business, shortly after graduating from college. Ms. Walters encouraged us to remain passionate about careers we had chosen. She advised us to be patient, while seeking and maintaining employment.

Barbara Walters reminded Emmanuel College graduates that career woman status is ennobling; she also said this status as any status, is no panacea.

Since graduating from Emmanuel College, I have many times remembered Ms. Walters encouraging Emmanuel College class of 1975 graduates. Now nearly forty years ago having graduated from college and not having been steadily employed for many years, I grin softly from time to time, while silently and sometimes heartbrokenly saying, "Yes, Barbara, I will continue to be passionate, patient, and persevering as I continue to seek a permanent job."

Truthfully, I have not ever wanted a career outside being a wife and homemaker. Though I am fifty-eight years old, as of this date, I remain interested in being a wife and a second mother. Shortly after I began attending Emmanuel College, I foresaw many years passing before I would be ready for a steady personal relationship. Fortunately, I did not then realize that the passing of many years signified several decades of waiting. As I was growing up, Mom repeatedly predicted that I would be a late bloomer. Late bloomer? I think she used inaccurate terminology. Frankly, I am on the verge of napping permanently, in dirt.

Attending Emmanuel College taught me that a woman can experience contentment whether not she is engaged in a relationship with a man, as a wife, friend, companion, sister, or soul sister. Emmanuel College enrollment also found me embracing solitude. Without regularly embracing solitude, one cannot fully appreciate human community.

2012

CHAPTER NINETEEN

RESTAURANT BUSINESS PASSION, FAMILY GATHERINGS, CHURCH EXPERIENCES, HURRICANE SANDY, SANDY HOOK ELEMENTARY SCHOOL

Friday, August 17, 2012

Today, around mid-morning, I encountered someone I met several years ago, when he interviewed me for an available restaurant position. He is Arthur Hartman, a seasoned former catering business owner as well as a former longtime restaurant owner, who is now semi-retired. An octogenarian, Mr. Hartman delighted me for nearly sixty minutes as we discussed Arthur Hartman Catering and The British Relief. Impassioned and devoted with both businesses, he oversaw management and operations of the two enterprises, including developing clientele, hiring employees, food and beverage operations, customer service, and financial matters. Mr. Hartman originated, managed, and maintained the two enterprises for forty-four years, before he sold The British Relief, in the early 2000s.

In 1968, Mr. Hartman, who had married, was a father, and was residing in Cohasset, started Arthur Hartman Catering business, which was based in Duxbury, Massachusetts. Food selections the business offered included tea sandwiches and hors d'oeuvres. Arthur prepared the food and hired six waitresses to assist him with serving at wedding receptions, funerals, and small dinner parties. Satisfied customers praised and recommended the congenial staff, food quality, and service of Hartman catering. As accolades recommending the business steadily grew throughout the years, Hartman Catering business increased.

In 1976, a United States senator called Arthur and asked him to cater to an event on July 4 which included celebrating the birth of America as an independent nation. Queen Elizabeth of England was intended to be recognized during the celebration. The location of the party was on a ship anchored in Boston, Massachusetts.

Mr. Hartman, who initially agreed to cater another event, later said that he could not be present at the party; he promised to send food and five exemplary Hartman Catering servers to manage food service at the gathering. As it turned out, Queen Elizabeth was unable to attend the party as well; she was ill. Meanwhile, the Independence Day buffet luncheon was successful. For a considerable amount of time after the event, Arthur received fifty telephone calls a day requesting Hartman Catering services.

Polly Logan, a former longtime politically active Cohasset resident, called Arthur one year after the July 4 luncheon. She asked Arthur to cater an event honoring President Gerald Ford (1974-1977). By 1977, Arthur Hartman Catering was employing almost twenty servers; as the times had changed and the company was expanding, male servers were also being added to the employee roster.

While attending the honorary event esteeming him, President Ford approached Mr. Hartman inside a large event tent set up outside Logan Airport in Boston, Massachusetts. Over two hundred guests were attending the reception.

While President Ford and Mr. Hartman were talking, for nearly five minutes, President Ford, suddenly seeing a multi-tiered cake resting on a table, nervously asked Arthur, "Am I cutting the cake?" The design of the cake honoring the president replicated the architecture of Old Faneuil Hall, a politically historic meeting venue and marketplace in downtown Boston. The edifice was built in 1742 and was re-converted into a marketplace and a meeting venue in the 1970s, after it had fallen into disuse and disrepair. As a dessert, the structure was nearly seven feet high. "Yes, Mr. President," replied grinning Mr. Hartman. He added, "Don't worry; two waitresses will assist you."

For over ten years, Arthur Hartman Catering expanded throughout and outside the South Shore cities and towns of Massachusetts. Growing the business required working late hours during all types of weather, during all four New England seasons. Twelve years after he began the enterprise, Arthur Hartman decided to localize it. He established The British Relief

restaurant in Hingham, Massachusetts. The combined restaurant and catering business kitchen was opened in 1980. Mr. Hartman continued part-time
catering operations and selected desired clients.

The British Relief breakfast offerings included muffins, scones, and additional bakery items as well as beverages; lunch fare consisted of soup, salads, and sandwiches. Breakfast service began at 7:30 a.m. Lunch service
began at 11:30 a.m. and ended at 2:00 p.m. Until 6:00 p.m., restaurant customers and walk-ins were able to purchase cooked dinners, molded salads,
and cookies. Refrigerated glass cases in the retail section of the restaurant
displayed daily choices of casseroles, stews, and pies which were freshly
prepared and cooked in The British Relief kitchen. Seating fifty-four people,
Open six days a week, the bistro was closed on Sundays.

On Wednesday evenings, The British Relief was the venue of Supper
in the Square. One dinner selection was offered for one price. Customers
were allowed to bring wine. No hard liquor was served.

Supper in the Square patrons were requested to arrive at 5:30 p.m. Most
Supper in the Square diners, who were regular British Relief customers, generally chose the same restaurant tables and seats each week. Reservations
for the semi- communal meal were not accepted. Dinner was served
promptly at 5:45 p.m. Arthur Hartman dinged a water goblet at 7:15 p.m.,
in order to signal that Supper in the Square was ending in fifteen minutes, as
punctually as it had begun.

Arthur Hartman grew up being what he termed, a "PK" aka a preacher's
kid, so he naturally enjoyed serving as well as and humoring local clergy
members. Mr. Hartman regularly posted an Episcopal Church flag next to
British and American flags that were hung one beside the other, outside The
British Relief restaurant. Facing one another, St. Paul Church of Hingham
and The British Relief were situated on opposite sides of North Street.

Mr. Hartman said that he hung an Episcopal flag outside The British
Relief solely to promote friendly competition between him and Fr. James
Raftery, the pastor of St. Paul Catholic Church. Having been a priest for
almost fifty years, including having served the parishioners of St. Paul
Church for eighteen years, Father Raftery who is now a senior priest, retired
this year, in June.

Fr. Raftery regularly entered The British Relief after celebrating 9:00
a.m. mass at St. Paul Church. He often joined St. Paul Church parishioners
who were seated in the bistro; he shared lively conversations and food with

the churchgoers. Mr. Hartman informed me that many St. Paul School going kids grew up eating British Relief casseroles. Before or after picking up their children at the school, after classes had ended, parents of St. Paul School students entered The British Relief once or twice a week, to purchase meals that could easily be re-heated in an oven and then served.

The late Father John Cullinan, former pastor of St. Anthony Catholic Church in Cohasset, often entered The British Relief carrying a bottle of wine that he had been given as a gift; Arthur Hartman allowed Fr. Cullinan to exchange one bottle of gifted wine for one casserole.

One day, the gentle, blue-eyed and good humored priest offered Arthur Hartman two bottles of wine and requested receiving two casseroles. Father Cullinan indicated that the bottled wines he was giving Mr. Hartman were indeed good spirits.

On the same day, for amusement purposes, Mr. Hartman sent a query letter and extracted samples of each of the two bottles of wine to a testing laboratory located in Norwell, Massachusetts. Response from the laboratory was swift. Some Supper in the Square customers knew that Arthur had sent samples of the wine that Fr. Cullinan had given him to a trusted testing laboratory.

During an upcoming Wednesday evening, after chatting with Supper in the Square patrons, including Father Cullinan, Arthur Hartman stood in the center of the restaurant. He was smiling and smirking. He gleefully informed Supper in the Square patrons that he decided to read aloud the response letter the test lab had sent him.

Removing the missive from an envelope, Arthur Hartman orally read, "Mr. Hartman, Thank you for your business; it is appreciated. Unfortunately, your horse is very sick."

Seated Fr. Cullinan, good and possibly not having heard the wine-testing rumors, arose immediately and defiantly from the chair in which he was sitting. Defensively, he remarked, "I don't have a horse." Then Father Cullinan giggled. He had realized that the letter was not about an ill horse. The good humored report clearly indicated that the wine that Fr. Cullinan gifted Mr. Hartman was feeble in quality.

The British Relief restaurant was sold eleven years ago. The establishment was re-opened, in the same year, 2001, after having been renovated and re-named Square Café.

Square Café owner Patty Landry calls the eating establishment, a "boutique style neighborhood restaurant serving Modern American and French-Asian influenced food." Patty and I recently discussed the opening as well as the operations of Square Café. She informed me that food concepts that the epicurean restaurant is introducing do contrast with the American style food formerly offered by The British Relief. Patty also said that she wants hospitality service at Square Café to emulate the reputable kitchen, food, and beverage service of the former restaurant.

Continuing to perform selected catering jobs, Arthur Hartman is these days also a volunteer van driver, serving the Cohasset Senior Center. From time to time, all four Hartman adult children have assisted Dad with the catering business. Mr. Hartman comes across as hoping that one or more of the Hartman children will someday continue the operations of the Arthur Hartman Catering business. Amid fondly mentioning former customers and employees of The British Relief restaurant and Hartman Catering, Mr. Hartman evidenced contentment. Delighting me for almost sixty minutes, Arthur humbly mentioned the well-known success of both enterprises once.

Friday, August 24, 2012

Utilizing terms such as Ice Cream Social Dance Party, Karaoke Dance Party, and Disco Dream Dance Party DanceSport Boston (DSB) business owners and lead instructors, Jayson and Alia Marie Palmer have decided to rename the weekly Friday evening practice dances that happen in the studio. The marketing strategy has been effective; attendance at the re-themed dances in the weekly re-decorated studio has increased. Enthusiasm surrounding the dance parties as well as enjoyment of the events has grown.

While making announcements during a break in the practice dance held tonight, Jayson said that he and Alia Marie recently returned from vacationing in Vermont. Asked whether she milked any cows while she was here, Alia Marie replied, "I am basically a city girl; you won't catch me milking any cows, unless I'm wearing high heels."

Before the practice dance tonight, fellow DanceSport Boston student Angelina Macari greeted and then addressed me, She commented that before she entered the dance studio tonight, she was home alone and practicing dance moves while she was prancing about the kitchen floor. Angelina confessed that she used the kitchen refrigerator double door handles as a substitute dance partner. She commented that utilizing the proper refrigerator door handle is important, because when a dancer is turning, if the wrong door handle of the double door refrigerator is used, the substitute male dance partner, aka a refrigerator door slams the face of the lady dancer.

Monday, September 10, 2012

Fall arrival has lately found me spending some weekly afternoons and early evenings visiting with sister Lizzie Jenkins, niece Kristin Sullivan and great nephews Zachariah and Clarkson Sullivan. Twice weekly, Jura, Buddy, the dog of sister Lizzie, and Shamrock or Sham, the Sullivan family dog, join me as we stroll about Conservation Park, in Scituate, Massachusetts. The park is situated beside Herring River, a salt water body which flows Atlantic into ocean waters.

Sometimes, when the dogs and I re-enter the home of sister Lizzie, Kate, Zachariah, Clarkson, Lizzie and I dine together. Toddler Clarkson has become very active. During the year and a half after he was born, Clark often sat contentedly, as he observed surroundings. Now two years old, Clark is talking, walking, running, and touching virtually anything that interests him.

The fourth birthday of Zachariah was celebrated on Saturday, July 28. The patio and backyard behind the home of sister Lizzie was the birthday event venue. Having been invited to join the birthday festivities, a new seven-year-old friend of Zach, named Johnny Savitolla, drove a mid-sized motorized toy Jeep out of the driveway outside the Savitolla home and across the street, before he entered the gravel driveway of next door neighbor Lizzie Reagan Jenkins. Johnny is the last of six siblings.

He admits that the toy Jeep he drives is a hand-me-down. Exiting a door of the sturdy vehicle, which is mainly composed of hard plastic, he viewed me, greeting him. Appearing good and uneasy, he suddenly uttered, "Ah, this is my Jeep. It is pink… I think I'm going to paint it camouflage."

When cake cutting time arrived, Zachariah was standing beside Mama Kristin, who was the designated birthday cake cutter. As the ceremony began, Zach suddenly became embarrassed and overwhelmed. Having become the center of attention, he began sobbing.

While Kristin was comforting him, she directed him toward the nearby large, inflated, and activated Bouncy Castle. Zach viewed his cousins and friend Johnny inside the Castle, bouncing up and down and all around the interior of the enclosed castle with transparent huge plastic windows.

Almost instantly recovering from being upset, he hastily entered the Castle, where he joined Johnny and similar-age family members.

Sunday, September 16, 2012

Ronald (Ron) Jenkins, the former husband of sister Lizzie and dad of nephews Rhett and Jonas and niece Kristin, who formerly resided in Colorado, died here on July 31, of this year, following a lengthy illness. Ron is loved and missed.

Friday, September 21, 2012

Eleven-year-old dog Jura is aging, slowing, as is the owner of Jura. Jura and I now stroll nearly three non-consecutive hours daily. Five years ago, when we began walking together, we were power walking, nearly five hours, every day. Becoming increasingly sentimental, Jura who will be twelve years old in January 2013 has in recent months begun whining, in order to awaken me at around 6:30 a.m., while he lies on the blanketed living room loveseat couch.

Jura no longer jumps upon the master bed, puts his right front paw on my back or right shoulder, thumps his tail, and urges me to move out of bed, as he did in the past. Now he enters the master bedroom, moves along the right side of the bed while I am sleeping and while doing so, he nuzzles any part of me that he can reach. When I awake, he greets me with bright eyes and a wagging tail.

Offering me affection, he nuzzles me again: he also wants breakfast. After eating breakfast, he sometimes receives and then licks a marrow bone, including the marrow inside the bone. Jura often remains beside me when I am lying down on the living room floor and performing stretching exercises, such as sit ups. He extends one front paw, which he rests upon my left shoulder or leg, depending upon where he is lying down.

Jura continues to join me when I am running errands, whether or not completing the errands involves walking or driving. When I am going to the library or anywhere where I can leave Jura outside, I attach one end of a long lead to the dog collar Jura wears. I extend the plastic coated wire before wrapping it around a nearby tree limb or tree trunk and then securing it. Generally, I remember to give him water after he has been outside for a while.

In the evenings, when Jura and I return home, Jura receives a massage treatment on the neck, back, hips, and legs and on all four paws. Massage offers animals considerable relief from joint and muscle pain. Initially considering dog massage as being unnatural or not representing an effective use of time, I have recently discovered that animal massage relieves arthritic pain that many animals experience as they age. The holistic practice also engenders relaxing, regenerating, and healing effects which also benefit the dog massager.

Remaining delightfully and mysteriously content, Jura continues to enjoy each and all daytime and evening activities. One day I will live without Jura. I can live without Jura. Profoundly uncertain is how I will someday do this.

Saturday, September 22, 2012

Newly single, sister Valerie and her children Grace, Myla, and Matthew continue to reside in Jacksonville, Florida. This past spring, Valerie resigned from a private elementary school teaching position in which she had been employed for several years. In a recent telephone conversation that she and I shared, she indicated that she enjoyed teaching, as she relishes working with children. She appreciated the flexible hours the position offered.

Valerie also admitted that during the past school year, she had found that working with growing numbers of classroom students, including increasing numbers of students with special-needs had become overwhelming. She was not trained to be a special-needs teacher. Little educational support in the classroom was available.

Having previously been employed as a public defense attorney, she decided to re-enter the legal profession. As federal laws can and do change and every state in America exhibits similar, yet not identical legal codes, an attorney who moves to a new state is required to repeat the bar exam for the state. Shortly after she completed a six-week long study program, which involved group study five-days-a week for eight-hours-a-day in addition to homework, Valerie entered a large room, where she joined five hundred Florida residing bar exam candidates who were sitting at exam desks.

Bar exams generally involve three days of tests. The first two are eight hours long. Examinees are tested on federal laws on the first day and state laws on the second day.On the third and final four-hours long test day, bar exam test takers are questioned about matters surrounding legal ethics.

Having passed the exam, Valerie has been employed as a corporate attorney, representing a Florida supermarket chain.

Grace Watson, who was twelve years old when I began writing *Life Flashes: A Memoir,* is now seventeen years old. A high school senior, she owns and drives a car. She also works part-time. Hoping to enter a college in Florida in the upcoming school year, she is currently considering a career in the public health field. Myla Watson, now fifteen years old, is a high school student. Matthew Watson, now thirteen years old, is enrolled in junior high school.

Grace, Myla, and Matt continue to study their respective academic curriculums. They also participate in after school sports. Before or after completing assigned homework, they attend church-related youth group activities. They spend time with family and friends.

Valerie, Grace, Myla. and Matthew Watson are now third-time dog owners. The first dog they adopted and named Sasha, is female. Their second dog, Lucky, unfortunately and unexpectedly passed away one weekend. The third dog that the Watson family members adopted was named George. The Watsons also own two cats. One cat is named Pinky.

In addition, the family adopted a number of small fish and a rabbit. When she was in college, Valerie seriously considered becoming a veterinarian.

Nephew Jonas Jenkins, who works with a New York City based financial services company, recently accepted a promotion and a workplace transfer. Having moved to Texas, Jonas, Liane, the wife of Jonas, and their children, four-years-old Alia and infant Savannah are living in a large condominium. They hope to eventually buy a home located near where Jonas works.

Nephew Rhett Jenkins remains in Florida. An air conditioning company based here has hired him. He also manages a frozen yogurt shop. Niece Kristin Jenkins Sullivan is continuing to savor and persevere through long, challenging workdays, while she is giving her young sons care. Zachariah is now four years old and Clarkson is now one year old. Kristin often works late while giving the boys care, as her husband, Payden, an employee of a subcontractor for a utility company, also often works late. Jim Sullivan, paternal grandfather of Zach and Clark, babysits the boys from time to time. Tomorrow, Zach will begin attending pre-school.

Someday wishing to work outside the home, Kristin is currently re-searching locally available jobs that offer part-time hours. Continuing to en-joy utility work, Payden is certainly a faithful utility company employee. During evening hours, while driving past the house which he and Kristin inhabit, which faces a street, one can see lights glowing in virtually every room, including the garage.

Brother Jared and sister-in-law Elissa and their children are now resid-ing in England almost year-round. They vacation in Cohasset during some school vacations and in summer months. During the 2011-2012 school year, touring Europe, Africa, and Asia, the Reagans traveled extensively. Two educational tutors whom Jared and Elissa hired accompanied the family. Ja-mus, Brynn, and Rylan enjoyed these out-of-the-box academic adventures. Recently the children began attending private schools again. This coming November, Jamus will be ten years old. Brynn will be eight years old in October. Rylan turned six years old in March.

Mom and Dad awaken daily around 5:00 a.m. and begin each day read-ing newspapers. Dad makes breakfast. From mid until late morning, Mom enjoys performing housecleaning activities as well as cooking and running errands. During spring, summer, and early fall, she also works outside, tend-ing gardens in the front and in the back of the home in which she and Dad live.

After reading several newspapers and eating breakfast, Dad commutes to the office of an insurance company in Quincy, Massachusetts, where he assists family member Jeff Fannon, as a business consultant. Dad has been successfully employed in the insurance business for over fifty years. He has repeatedly and wisely advised me that being successful in the business world requires only two things, which he summarizes, by simply saying, "Show up and do what you say you are going to do." Dad has also often said, "When the going gets tough, the tough get going."

Sunday, September 27, 2012

Not being fully sure how this happened, I began again attending St. Paul Church in Hingham, Massachusetts. Fr. Timothy Norton, the new St. Paul Church pastor, has been well received; he is witty, thought-provoking, and punctual. St. Paul Church pastoral associate Patricia Mincus has reassured me that the development of faith is not essentially an achievement. It is a process involving personal as well as communal commitment. Arising questions surrounding faith matters are often not instantly answered and sometimes not ever fully resolved, she counseled me.

I recently became a volunteer for the church. The director of religious education at St. Paul Church, Sister Terry Campos, initially interviewed me. Conversation we shared was candid, calming, and spiritually uplifting. When I confessed to not having attended church services regularly, for nearly thirty years, Sister Terry was quiet, attentive, and reassuring.

When I later admitted not knowing how the Rosary is prayed, Sister Terry, placed her right hand upon me in the mid-section of my forehead and then she began making the sign of the cross with her right hand forefinger. At the same time, she prayed—nearly aloud. Surprisingly, Sister Terry welcomed me as a new St. Paul Church fourth-grade religious education teacher, following a near sixty-minute-long interview.

Sunday, November 4, 2012

Today I viewed television newscasters reporting that a super storm, which initially developed in the Western Caribbean Sea and then became Hurricane Sandy, passed over the nations of Jamaica, Haiti, and the Dominic Republic. Considered to be a major storm, the category 3 hurricane brought heavy rain, flooding, and accompanying wind speeds of between fifty and one hundred ten miles per hour.

Having arrived in the United States and Canada yesterday, Sandy brought continuing torrential rain and high-speed winds. Twenty-four American states in Eastern, mid-Atlantic and Midwest parts of the country were impacted. Homes and businesses numbering millions have experienced losses of heat and electricity. Having lasted from October 22 to November 2, Hurricane Sandy is the tenth Atlantic gale that has developed thus far, during the 2012 hurricane season.

Hurricane Sandy has impacted seven countries: Jamaica, Cuba, Haiti, Puerto Rico, Bahamas, America, and Canada. Two hundred fifty-three storm-related deaths have been reported; hundreds of thousands of persons have suddenly become homeless. The losses do not include numbers of animals who have died or have become homeless. Hurricane Sandy traveled eleven hundred miles before it dissipated. The cost to repair the damage it has done in America is currently estimated to be sixty-five billion dollars.

One U.S. eastern seaboard state that hurricane Sandy devastated is New Jersey. The super storm ripped apart the famed, nearly one-hundred-fifty-years-old Atlantic City boardwalk; one fifty-foot-long section of the walkway was filmed drifting away, amid rising and hurling seawaters. Amusements, tourist attractions, businesses, and casinos which previously surrounded the Atlantic City boardwalk and had been newly rebuilt in 1962, were destroyed. The boardwalk had regularly attracted thousands of strollers, tourists, shoppers, and celebrities.

Hurricane Sandy flooded half of Hoboken, New Jersey. Hoboken is a small city located in northern New Jersey with a population of about forty-eight thousand. It is about sixty-four miles northeast of the capital of Trenton, a slightly larger city. Two million New Jersey residents have lost power. Currently, six thousand New Jersey inhabitants are estimated to be homeless.

Bordering New Jersey, the lower Manhattan area of New York City area was flooded. Seven subway tunnels, situated under the East River, a large waterway, became inundated with storm water and were inoperable. New York City schools were closed until November 2. News reports indicate that one hundred thousand homes have been damaged in Long Island, a densely populated isle in the southeastern part of New York.

Two thousand of the homes are estimated as being uninhabitable. Two and a half million homes and businesses in New York City have lost power. More than forty thousand people residing there are now homeless. New York City suburbs were also affected by Hurricane Sandy. I do not know what level of damage occurred there.

The New York City Marathon, an annual event attracting as many as fifty thousand U.S. and international athletes, which was formerly scheduled to happen today, has been cancelled. Representing America as well as fellow nations, hundreds of registered New York City Marathon runners arrived in the city today. Discovering that the race has been canceled this year, many runners decided to join city-wide Hurricane Sandy relief efforts. Television news cameras videoed marathoners running through various affected areas in New York, wearing backpacks and stopping to give out food and supplies that were donated by relief organizations. People are basically good, courageous, and persevering.

Tuesday, November 6, 2012

Facing a podium while standing on a large stage in a convention hall in Chicago, Illinois, re-elected President Barack Obama addressed hundreds of supporters at 1:30 a.m. Daughters of Mr. Obama and the First Lady, fourteen-year-old Malia Obama and eleven-year-old Sasha Obama, as well as campaign staffers stood by him. Now over, the long, spirited, and sometimes contentious Presidential race, between President Barack Obama and Mitt Romney, a businessman and former governor of Massachusetts was close; popular vote results indicate that the voting margins between the Presidential candidates were slim.

On Election Day, shortly after all of the polls closed, television news reports indicated that President Obama was capturing the majority of votes in key election states. The key election states include Ohio, Virginia, Iowa, New Hampshire, Wisconsin, Nevada, Colorado, and Pennsylvania. Later news reports signaled the voting count for Mr. Romney was surging ahead of the count for Mr. Obama. Final voting tallies showed that President Barack Obama won fifty percent of the popular vote and Mitt Romney won 49.1 percent of the vote. The margin of victory in the presidential race has been reported to have been slightly more than half a percent.

When the election was officially called, Mr. Romney had received two hundred six electoral college votes. Mr. Obama had received three hundred thirty-six such votes. The number of Electoral College votes required to win presidential election in the United States is two hundred seventy. A dignified former presidential candidate, Mr. Romney is also recognized as being an exemplary businessman, church minister, and family man. He exudes enthusiasm, humor, and wisdom.

Friday, December 14, 2012

This morning, between 9:35 a.m. and 9:45 am, a twenty-year-old Newtown, Connecticut resident, using two guns, forced a way into Sandy Hook Elementary School, and then murdered six school staff members and twenty children. Sandy Hook Elementary school administrators, teachers, and paraprofessionals were killed while they confronted the shooter and at the same time attempted to save students. The young victims were six and seven years old. The school principal, school psychologist, two teachers and two teacher aides, were among the shooting victims.

Newtown, Connecticut, is a town situated approximately sixty miles southeast of New York City. It was founded in 1705 and incorporated in 1711. It is now considered to be part of the greater metropolitan area of New York City. Current statistics show that the population of Newtown is about twenty-eight thousand people. The town is known for offering reputable educational and recreational programs and opportunities and displaying attractive landscapes and open spaces. Until today, the town had experienced one homicide in the past ten years.

Media accounts indicate that gunman Adam Lanza was a former honor student at Newtown High School. Mr. Lanza had not previously been observed or discovered as having committed any crime; no record of him displaying criminal behavior existed. He is reported to have been an exceedingly solitary young man who played violent video games.

Photographs of Mr. Lanza reveal him as having exhibited facial contortion which included widely dilated pupils. He had been prescribed and had been consuming an antidepressant named Lexapro. Adam Lanza had been medically diagnosed with psychiatric issues many years ago. News reports indicate that with the exception of medication, the psychological issues that twenty-year-old Mr. Lanza had been experiencing for over a decade were largely untreated.

When attending middle school, Mr. Lanza was diagnosed with Asperger's Syndrome. Significant communication and social interaction difficulties and abnormally repetitive and restrictive behavior patterns are some of the symptoms of the syndrome. Asperger's Syndrome and high functioning autism have been reported to be similar disorders.

Adam lived with Nancy Lanza, his mother. He shot and killed Nancy this morning, before he drove to Sandy Hook Elementary School. Forcing entry into the school, Mr. Lanza repeatedly shot one of four semi-automatic weapons through locked glass doors. Four hundred fifty-six students were attending Sandy Hook Elementary School. Shooting sounds were heard throughout the school, as a Sandy Hook Elementary School staff member was airing morning public announcements this morning. Firing one hundred fifty-four bullets from a gun in less than five minutes, Adam Lanza killed twenty-six fellow human beings, before he turned a firearm inward and committed suicide.

When the tragedy initially began to unfold, Sandy Hook Elementary School Principal Dawn Hochsprung and school psychologist Mary Sherlach, who heard gunfire while they were attending a professional meeting, rushed toward the location of the shooting. Seeing Mr. Lanza, the two women confronted him. Adam shot and killed Dawn Hochsprung as well as Mary Sherlach, almost instantly.

Subsequently entering the first-grade class of substitute teacher Lauren Rousseau, Adam Lanza murdered Ms. Rousseau as well as fourteen of the fifteen pupils in the class. Lauren had previously attempted to hide the students, whom she had ushered into the classroom bathroom. The surviving student in the class is reported to have pretended to be dead; miraculously, the student was neither discovered nor injured.

Having heard gunshots, first-grade teacher Valerie Leigh Soto quickly urged her students to hide in storage cupboards as well as the storage closet in the classroom. News reports state that when Mr. Lanza entered the classroom, Ms. Soto falsely informed him that students in the class were in the school auditorium. Suddenly, some of the students in the class emerged from the storage cupboards as well as the storage closet.

Adam Lanza then assassinated Valerie Soto as well as six of the students. Somehow six students survived, as they fled the classroom. Escaping the scene at the grammar school, the pupils ran toward and knocked on the doors of nearby residences. Here they found safety and comfort, as Newtown residents immediately rescued them.

Among the students and staff Mr. Lanza murdered was a special-needs student and a special-needs teacher aide, Anne Marie Murphy; Ms. Murphy was shielding a number of special-needs students. Teacher aide Rachel D'Avino was also killed while she was protecting pupils. Ms. D'Avino had been working at Sandy Hook Elementary School for little over one week. As the nearly five minutes long shocking, numbing, and devastating shooting rampage was ending, Mr. Lanza–seeing policemen entering the school– committed suicide using one of the firearms that he wielded to commit the murders of Sandy Hook elementary school students and staff.

An interfaith memorial service honoring slain Sandy Hook Elementary School children and staff will be held this Sunday, December 16. While holding a press briefing, President Obama characterized the massacre as a deeply sorrowful event. He stated that he and fellow congressional political colleagues will attend a Sunday morning church service honoring murdered Sandy Hook Elementary School staff and students. Individual funeral services will be held in upcoming days.

Whether Sandy Hook Elementary School will eventually be reopened is uncertain. Truthfully, surrendering faith, goodwill, or hope is what truly causes a person or persons to commit profoundly selfish, evil actions, whether a person or persons are considered to be generally mentally healthy or mentally ill.

2013

CHAPTER TWENTY

NEMO, NEW POPE,
FAMILY TRAGEDY AND JOY

Thursday, January 24, 2013

This morning, shortly after daybreak, amid cloudy skies and weather temperature registering seven degrees, sunlight appeared. Dogs Jura and Buddy remained outside the home of sister Lizzie for nearly an hour. Both dogs were lying on frozen backyard ground; each was contentedly licking the outside of a frosty marrow bone and then eating marrow inside the bone. Little over one week ago, outdoor temperatures had reached the mid-fifties, at one point during the day.

Today, one guest of the *CBS This Morning* television program was Jeff Kluger, a senior writer at *Time* magazine. Mr. Kluger stated that recent scientific studies suggest that America has sustained wild temperature fluctuations especially in the last ten years. Significant climatic fluctuation was occurring in America before the U.S. Industrial Revolution period, he indicated. The American Industrial Revolution occurred in the late eighteenth and early nineteenth centuries, from approximately 1760-1840, when products made in homes and small shops began to be mass produced, using large machines. This is how factories were born.

Mr. Kluger stated that during the Industrial Revolution years, scientists predicted that when carbons exceeding three hundred fifty parts per million (ppm) became incorporated into the atmosphere of the earth, significant climatic change would follow. He commented that there are currently carbons in the amount of three hundred ninety ppm circulating in the atmosphere of the United States. Carbon in the atmosphere, along with other gases, including nitrogen and oxygen, helps the atmosphere of the earth to retain warmth from the Sun during the day and night, so that the warmth is not released into space. Without carbon in the atmosphere, the temperature of the earth would drop dramatically and plant, animal, marine, and human life would experience disease that can result in death. Likewise, when there is too much carbon in the atmosphere, plants, animals, marine, and human life suffer disease that can result in death.

Jeff Kluger indicated that record-breaking heat, devastating droughts, wildfires, and super storms which occurred in America in 2012 suggest that climate change is occurring here, in other words that the earth is becoming excessively warm. A while ago, Dad and I talked briefly about climate change. He said that during the Middle Ages in Europe, or between the fifth and sixth centuries, climatic vacillations occurred regularly. Volcanic activity produced dark heavy clouds that covered the sky, allowing little daylight for prolonged periods.

Sunday, February 10, 2013

Many New England towns and cities received between two and three feet of snow and hurricane force winds which precipitated serious flooding, during the February 8 blizzard named Nemo. The snow event marked the first time in many years that large numbers of South Shore Massachusetts residents have faced prolonged power and heat losses. Niece Kristin Sullivan, and her sons, Zachariah and Clarkson and I remained in the home of sister Lizzie while she has been traveling. We experienced nearly two days of electrical power and heat losses, before we were offered and accepted refuge in a home equipped with a generator. We were lucky and grateful. Many South Shore residents were without power for more than a week.

Utility company employee Payden Sullivan worked three days straight, daily clocking in and clocking out hours numbering in the teens. He slept for short periods in the work truck he drives, somewhere near respective job sites. When he had worked for over sixty hours in three days, Payden was sent home. Many owners of seaside or near ocean side homes and businesses on the South Shore have been advised that some power and heat losses will not be recovered for one week, minimum.

Direct sunlight that shone through home windows was especially appreciated when Kristin, Zachariah, Clarkson and I were without heat and electrical power, especially during increasingly warm late morning and early afternoon hours. In the evenings, sharing cold food by candlelight and sitting together, while we talked and intermittently watched logs burning in a fireplace, sustained us, before we retired. Reading a book while sitting in bed, as dogs Jura and Buddy were sleeping on a bedspread covering the lower half of the bed offered me additional welcome relief from the storm Nemo.

Sunday, March 3, 2013

Almost five months have passed since fifteen fourth-grade students attending public schools in Hingham were enrolled in a weekly hour-long afterschool religious education class that I was requested to teach on Tuesday afternoons. St. Paul Church of Hingham offers pastoral programs, including religious instruction for public school students enrolled in kindergarten through twelfth grade. Religious education classes, which began here nearly four months ago, in the second week of October 2012, will end in the second week of April, this year. Having recently decided not to continue teaching the classes after this date has found me surrendering, accepting the choice, and while doing so experiencing gratitude and inner peace.

Students in the class that I teach are nine and ten years old. The pupils have regularly demonstrated spiritual curiosity, enthusiasm, compassion, good humor, and of course, on a few occasions, holy mischief. Together, we have discussed Bible passages, including the creation story in the Genesis book of the Bible, in which Adam and Eve, the first man and woman, the first representatives of human family, to whom God gave the breath of life as well as free will or freedom to choose. Adam and Eve succumb to sin when each and both deny truth and disobey God, on purpose.

Students learned that sin-intentional wrongdoing—differing from making a mistake, which is unintentional—offends God, fellow humanity, and self. We acknowledged that Adam and Eve, although being gifted with a God-given ability to be good, chose selfish behavior when they faced temptation and therefore, sinned. God mercifully held Adam and Eve responsible for their actions. Adam and Eve discovered the honest, disciplined, forgiving, and merciful nature of God, of true love, as they admitted and accepted responsibility for chosen sinful behavior and then they made amends, not only as individuals but also as a couple, or human community.

Another Old Testament story portrays God "calling" a man named Abraham, and asking him not only to leave ancient Mesopotamia—present day Iraq and parts of Turkey and Syria—with family and to walk thousands of miles before settling in the former Canaan—present day Lebanon, Syria, Jordan, and Israel. Both of the stories are also present in Judaic and Islamic religious works and traditions.

God and Abraham made a covenant. God asked Abraham to leave the home in which he and his wife Sarah had lived for a longtime. With Sarah, his nephew Lot, and some animals, Abraham was instructed to travel thousands of miles on foot before entering Canaan, the Promised Land, or new land and new life that God had promised him. Abraham was seventy-four years old when he made the agreement with God.

In return, God promised Abraham that there are rich rewards for one who accepts an invitation from God to travel to unfamiliar land and sacrifice that the journey entails. Abraham honored the agreement. In fact, Biblical accounts indicate septuagenarian Abraham answered the call without protest or hesitation. Abraham, Sarah, and Lot traveled to Canaan, bringing sheep as well as additional animals with them.

Conducting internet research, I discovered that the distance between Mesopotamia and Canaan was approximately 5,641 miles. In other words, the pilgrimage did not end after many days or months. In fact, the walking journey went on for years, before it was completed. The sojourn occurred during the time that all of civilization was basically nomadic, wandering from place to place. If this true story does not demonstrate that people can change at any age, at any time, I do not know what story does so.

While hearing the story of Abraham and family, one student in the class of Ms. Reagan humbly remarked, "Wow, I hardly ever walk anywhere." After arriving in Canaan and settling here, Abraham received land as well as inheritance money. Sarah bore Abraham seven sons in the years after they arrive in the Promised Land.

Students in the class of Ms. Reagan also discussed additional characters in the Old Testament of the Bible, including Cain and Abel, two sons of Adam and Eve. Jealousy between the brothers caused one to murder the other. Pupils were stunned and bewildered, while they considered murderous action occurring thousands of years ago and in present day scenarios. The massacre at Sandy Hook Elementary School on December 14, 2012, is a matter that students in the class and a visiting fourth-grade religious education class discussed one Tuesday afternoon.

Sitting in a chair and facing a desk, a visiting nine-year-old student said, "How did God let this happen? I struggle with this every day," he said, as he lowered his head and then, bending both elbows and leaning them on the desk, he clasped one hand with another, as one might do when one is praying.

"God did not want or allow this tragedy to happen. All human beings are gifted free will, in all life situations, from before birth, until death. Without being able to exercise free will at all times one cannot be fully human. All persons, whether being generally mentally healthy or mentally ill, make choices, each and every day," I assured him.

Persisting found me saying, "Adam Lanza was gravely mentally ill. He perceived the acts of people who injured him as being unforgivable. Amid being seriously mentally ill, he chose to kill his mother, Nancy Lanza. He chose to murder six Sandy Hook Elementary School staff members. He chose to assassinate twenty children attending the elementary school. He chose to commit suicide."

"Adam Lanza did not kill people primarily because he was mentally ill. He killed fellow human beings essentially because he surrendered hope. God mourns the Sandy Hook Elementary School tragedy. God has swiftly, compassionately, and justly handled evil involved in the tragic event. Be assured God has begun and will continue to heal and to strengthen each and every person affected by the tragedy of the shootings," I concluded.

During one class, using pencils, crayons, and drawing paper the students fashioned condolence cards for surviving students of the Sandy Hook school tragedy. While designing a card for Sandy Hook students who are continuing to grieve the event which happened three months ago, one pupil asked, "Can I write, how was the funeral?" Almost smiling, I softly replied, "No." As I walked around the classroom, I observed another student. The pupil was writing the words, "We hope you are now over this loss."

Then I realized that students in the class were not yet ready to make condolence cards. Discussion of grief and writing appropriate sympathy card language was warranted. When teacher-guided grief discussion and instruction surrounding proper sympathy card language was completed, students were re-invited to fashion condolence cards for Sandy Hook Elementary School students. The following day, I placed the completed cards in a large manila envelope, stamped it, drove to a nearby United States Post Office and inserted the envelope into a post office mailbox.

Conversation surrounding the Sandy Hook Elementary School shootings continued in the religious education class, when a fourth grade class that had previously visited us joined us again, two weeks after the first visit. Unexpectedly, students began discussing death. One fourth grade student said that discussing death, or specifically, talking about the murder of Jesus, is "morbid" behavior. She purported that the subject of death is not meant to be discussed publicly.

As conversation surrounding death and dying evolved, students mentioned seriously ill family members as well as the occurrence of healings, spiritual visions, afterlife experiences, and miracles.

No prompting from the teacher had happened. During the past four months, Ms. Reagan as well as students in the fourth grade religious education class of Ms. Reagan and sometimes visiting pupils, while sharing faith related matters, were spiritually informed, enlightened, and strengthened and as a result, we are experiencing renewed and continuing relationships with God, fellow humanity, and self.

Tuesday, March 26, 2013

Nephew Rhett has moved. A mortgage company hired him. For several months, he has been enjoying working and residing in Florida. Having sought and found new living accommodations, he loves living near the ocean again. Savoring Floridian life, Rhett says he is not sure when or if he will return to Massachusetts.

Formerly having worked in the landscaping and construction fields, Rhett is delighted that he succeeded in discovering a new career path. Having also performed electrical and HVAC (heating, ventilation and air-conditioning) work, he is grateful. He found all of the work experiences satisfying for various reasons. He also realizes that when he owns or shares a home, he will be able to forgo many charges related with home ownership, because he was previously employed in occupations related with home repair, maintenance, and improvement.

Thursday, March 28, 2013

On this day, three days before Easter, newly elected Catholic Church leader, Jorge Borgoglio, who will be called Pope Francis, has broken papal tradition. Emulating the example of Jesus, he recently knelt beneath the feet of twelve adolescent juveniles of differing nationalities and faiths during an evening mass at a detention facility for minors. Then he washed the feet of the young people.

Christian teachings uphold that Jesus lived selflessly, humbly, and sacrificially in a manner unlike any fellow human being, before he was crucified. He regularly performed miracles, or works which no natural or scientific laws can explain. Jesus also performed signs and wonders, or actions that exemplify the ever present mystifying, benevolent, humble, and forgiving nature of God. One among innumerable signs and wonders that Jesus performed was washing the feet of disciples.

Pope Francis also recently broke another centuries-old papal tradition, when he addressed one hundred fifty thousand supporters for the first time. Joining fellow clergy who were standing upon a balcony at the papal residence in Vatican City, located less than four miles from Rome, the capital of Italy, Pope Francis, facing supporters, asked them to pray for him as he was preparing to perform a papal blessing. Existing papal protocol stipulates that the Pope prays for and blesses supporters before addressing them. Pope Francis exemplifies humility. He is healing hearts. He is uplifting souls.

Though I am not a regular churchgoer, I am grateful every day for having received as well as taught religious education. As a Catholic I was taught that each and every member of humanity and fellow creation is precious and dignified. I learned that the bond between God and humanity is unbreakable under any circumstances and that the highly unconditional, humble, joyful, and sacrificial manner in which Jesus loved manifested this simple perpetual truth.

Having been exposed to Catholicism, I appreciate the value of prayer. I remember Dad teaching me the Our Father prayer in childhood years; he also taught brother John, sister Lizzie and sister Valerie the prayer. I remember Reagan family members saying grace nightly, in unison, for many years, before sharing meals at the dinner table. Inspiring, encouraging, and comforting is from time to time, reading the Our Father prayer, written in calligraphy, in addition with a number of deeply inspiring Bible passages that I re-scripted on writing paper and then matted, framed, and mounted on walls in nearly every room of the condominium in which I live.

Catholic teachings uphold human relationships. These interrelated relationships include family, friendship, girl friendship, guy friendship, companionship, and soul family patterns. Being truly connected with another human being is not fully dependent upon compatibility. Compatibility does influence but does not control the development of any bond. Catholic teachings support the truth that no relationship can grow without discipline and that God lovingly disciplines or punishes each and all persons, not only through displaying just and holy anger but also through mercifully revealing truth that is intended to instruct us about how to be holy or how to be at peace with God, neighbor, and self. Throughout each and every day and night, the sole desire of God is to love all creation.

Earthly satisfaction is intended to be found in activities such as buying a new car or home, beginning a new relationship or publishing a book. Happiness that earthly actions such as these bring is temporary or fleeting. Faith alone teaches people how to be at peace amid each and all life circumstances, whether one is facing a situation that is primarily triumphant or tragic. Truthfully, all situations are some combination of both.

Personal experiences with Catholicism taught me about the importance of welcoming fellow Christians, members of different faiths, and people who are not religious. All people are children of God. No exceptions. None.

Amid evolving and emerging beyond tragedy, a renewed Catholic Church is emerging. and as this is happening, the church is continuing to disseminate the wisdom of hundreds of years of spiritual teachings. These include acknowledging the value and dignity of every person, the unbreakable connection between God and all creation, the fulfillment that is found in living and loving as Jesus did, the importance of employing discipline in every relationship as a means of understanding and growth, the value of prayer as a measure of connecting with God and fellow creation, the benefit of embracing spiritual contentment versus being consumed with earthly desires for happiness, and the recognition of all humanity as being children of God.

Many hope that the Catholic Church will continue to be reinvigorated by allowing priests to choose or not to choose marital life. Interestingly, longtime Catholic Church policy, requiring priests to be and remain unmarried, not only adversely affects priests who desire marriage, but also negatively impacts priests who are content with single life. Why?

Not allowing priests or priesthood candidates to marry creates an emotional environment that induces shame, secrecy, and guilt that not only affects priests and priesthood candidates who experience single life as fulfilling but also priests and priesthood candidates who are interested in marriage.

Many people, including priests, genuinely do not realize wanting to be permanently single, married, or some combination of both, until reaching mid or even late-life years. Being unmarried or married does not essentially determine whether one can adequately love or serve God. Being unmarried or married does influence how one expresses loving and serving God. Catholic priests who are converts from another faith and are married have been allowed to perform priestly functions in remote living areas, where shortages of priests exist. Freely chosen marital or single status is individually and communally valid. It is valuable and uplifting.

It is justifiable for Catholic Church leadership to seriously consider permitting women to become deacons, until the church is ready to re-evaluate female priesthood. A number of Ecclesiastical studies support the assertion that in early Christian church, there were women priests. Catholic Church policy, not permitting female priesthood, citing that the apostles of Jesus were solely male, has been widely challenged. Many modern New Testament scholars generally agree there were female apostles.

For example, Theologian Eldon Jay Epp, author of *Junia* wrote that ecclesiastical studies show that the first female apostle, Junia, is cited in an early version of the the New Testament of the Bible, which was written several decades after Jesus died. Mr. Epp referenced lines of scripture in the book of Romans, which the apostle Paul wrote. Jay Epp commented that in chapter sixteen, verse seven Paul identifies Junia and a man named Andronicus as being well-respected among apostles and as having known Jesus, before Paul knew Jesus.

Mr. Epp stipulates that Church fathers did not agree that the identity of Junia was male. He and additional Biblical scholars have proposed that when the Latin version of the New Testament of the Bible was written, the female name Junia was changed to the male form of Junias—the male form of Junia—in order to suppress the identity of Junia.

Two thousand years of societal evolvement has regularly inspired and motivated men and women to continue embracing leadership roles in virtually every profession considered to be essentially male as well as female-oriented. Readdressing the entry of women into leadership roles in the Catholic Church as deacons and eventually as priests is at hand.

Also warranting Vatican re-examination is allowing Catholics who wish to remarry and whose marriage has not been annulled by Catholic Church officials, to be allowed to be included in the Eucharistic or

Communion celebration. Permitting this will end the enforcement of a Catholic Church mandate indicating that when a marriage ceremony has been performed in the Catholic Church and the marriage subsequently ends, the marriage is required to be annulled by leadership of the church, before divorced persons who wish to remarry can participate in the sacrament of Communion. Legal divorce is widely available. Pastoral counseling that Catholic churches have offered for decades surrounding marriage, divorce, and additional issues has been and will continue to be genuine pastoral aid.

Thursday, May 2, 2013

Today I viewed a television news report depicting ironworkers cheering while they were standing on a platform connected with a crane which had been raised above the roof of the newly constructed One World Trade Center, which is located in the Lower Manhattan part of New York City. They were observing fellow safely supported ironworkers, standing on an unenclosed platform at the peak of the skyscraper, while the workers secured the last two of eighteen four-hundred-foot-high steel spires. Each spire weighs seventy tons.

The re-created One World Trade Center is located slightly north of the former One World Trade Center. The steeple or spire makes the 1,776 foot high structure, containing one hundred and four stories, one of the leading tall buildings in the Western Hemisphere. Able to be utilized as a broadcast antenna, the spire will also emit beacons of light that can be seen from as far away as seventy miles. Serving as a fellow symbol of freedom, the new One World Trade Center overlooks Ellis Island and the Statue of Liberty.

Four additional World Trade Center (WTC) buildings will eventually be built in lower Manhattan. The initial seven WTC buildings were located here. The edifices were opened in the early 1970s. The original WTC Twin Tower buildings, imploded September 11, 2001, when terrorist-manned passenger planes struck and penetrated the skyscrapers. The five additional original World Trade Center skyscrapers, which were seriously damaged on that day, were later demolished.

Construction of the new One World Trade Center skyscraper preceded the development of four additional World Trade Center (WTC) projects, which are underway. Another new World Trade Center building will be completed sometime in August. The building of two additional WTC skyscrapers is near completion. The fifth and final World Trade Center building is slated to open in 2020. Wondrous, inspiring, and contenting is not only hearing and seeing stories of persons affected by the September 11 tragedy who are persevering, but also being informed about the steady construction of the new World Trade Center buildings, 9/11 monuments and 9/11 museum.

Sunday, May 12, 2013

Former high school boyfriend Mitch Harrison and I accidentally met today.

"Mitch?" I said, smiling, when I observed an interesting man walking past French Memories café in Cohasset. Mitch and I recognized one another; at the same time, each of us observed mutually developing gray hairs and squinting eyes. More than forty years have passed since Mitch and I met. Content, uncertain, and uncomfortable, we acknowledged and hugged one another.

Mitch said that since Friday, he had been visiting his in-laws, family members of Ellen (Edwards) Harrison, the wife of Mitch. "I bought Mum breakfast; I am visiting her and then flying home." During two weekends a month, Mitch travels hundreds of miles from home via airplane to Boston, Massachusetts, before taxiing to the South Shore. When arriving there, he visits with Edwards and Harrison family members. A couple of days later he is on a plane again, traveling hundreds of miles, and going home.

Mitch remains enthusiastic, gentle, and good-humored. He taught me an important relationship lesson, which I have grown to fully appreciate through the years. He helped me to realize that honesty in each and all relationships is important, because representing self as being someone who one is not, due to fear of losing someone one loves, actually harms the relationship that one wants to protect. Whether honesty influences a relationship to end, honesty also leaves individual as well as mutual trust intact. Love abides.

Wednesday, June 5, 2013

Joseph Westford, who lives in a house which is near the home in which I rent an apartment, talked with me today. Joseph said that he will be entering the eighth grade, this coming September. He and I have been acquainted for six years, since I moved into the Cohasset apartment. He resides with his mother, Trina, father Ethan, and brothers Vance and Rex.

This afternoon, I observed Joseph, another boy and two girls resting on the upper trunk and branches of a large tree on Cohasset Common, As Jura and I momentarily paused, while passing the tree, Joe answered a question I had asked him, from a distance, saying, "Oh yeah, most eighth grade boys are now into girls."

Asked how he views girls, Joe offered a response that probably typifies how eighth-grade boys generally feel about eighth grade girls, "Girls are good; they *sure do talk a lot*," he responded. Socially healthy, Joe says he enjoys "guy time" as well as "girl time."

Wednesday, June 19, 2013

Late this afternoon, while Jura and I were ambling beyond Cohasset Village, near Cohasset Harbor, a young boy, named James, approached me on a bicycle. He indicated that he and two friends were selling root beer, cherry, and berry-flavored snow cones. He directed me toward a snow cone stand where fellow snow cone sellers were standing.

Having arrived at the stand one or two moments before me, James, a good amateur salesman, introduced me to Kyle Oliver and Scott Whitman, two snow cone stand operators and managers working with him. All are eleven years old and will be entering sixth grade. With a small metal shovel, James removed a portion of ice stored in a cooler, after I had given him an order. Then he inserted the ice into a cone-shaped paper cup and covered the ice with one of several available syrups, before he served me the created snow cone.

While conversing with the three boys and licking flavored ice, I asked, "How are snow cones sales going?" James, displaying disappointment, said the boys had made ten dollars in one hour. "Ten dollars, isn't that good?" I queried. Scott replied, "No, on a sixty-five- degree day in December when I was selling hot chocolate, I earned thirty-five dollars in forty-five minutes."

"Wow," I exclaimed, thinking homemade snow cone, lemonade, and hot chocolate stand operations sure have changed, since I was a kid in the late 1950s and early 1960s. Kids operating homemade lemonade as well as snow cone stands then charged between ten and twenty-five cents per cup. As I do not generally carry cash when I am walking, with or without Jura, I offered to return later with payment. Handing me a free snow cone, James said he did not care about the cost. Tomorrow, I will drive to the home where James lives and bring him payment.

Sunday, June 23, 2013

Brother Jared is again visiting Cohasset, with his children, Rylan Brynn, and Jamus. Jared, Elissa, the wife of Jared, Jamus, Brynn, and Rylan are beginning a near three months-long summer vacation here. Elissa will arrive this coming Saturday. Currently in England, she is tending to personal matters. Yesterday, when entering the Reagan family Cohasset home, Jura and I were cheerfully greeted, as Jared, Jamus, Rylan and Brynn, stationed in the kitchen, were cooperatively preparing lunch: Caesar salad, tuna fish salad, sliced breads, and various cut cheeses.

This sunny, warm, and humid day, we shared lunch as we sat in a screened porch attached to the house. Relaxing here brought us satisfying ocean breezes, as we ate and discussed the international school Jamus, Brynn, and Rylan are now attending. During the past school year, the children especially enjoyed re-entering formal education classes, as during the previous school year, accompanying their father and mother, Jared and Elissa, they were touring Europe, Australia, and Africa.

Two hired tutors, who also accompanied the traveling family, home-schooled the children in various subjects and continued to instruct them in additional world languages.

Jamus will be eleven years old in November. Brynn will be nine years old in October. Rylan turned seven years old in March.

When all finished eating lunch, the children entered the playroom. Jared and I moved outdoors and sat upon veranda chairs. Comfortable, light-hearted, and amusing defines conversation Jared and I shared today. Following the exchange, we rejoined Rylan, Jamus, and Brynn. All decided to put on bathing suits and clothing covering the bathing suits, before we departed the house and then stepped into a motorized dinghy that in summer months, is docked nearby. Commuting a short distance, we arrived at the family yacht, which in summer months, is moored in ocean waters outside Cohasset Harbor, slightly beyond the Reagan home.

As we entered the yacht, Jamus and Brynn immediately climbed a ladder leading to the second story. Preparing to jump off the port side of the boat, one after another, Jamus and Brynn entreated me to join them in the activity. Standing on the first-floor deck, I said, "Sure," before climbing a ladder and entering the second story of the boat. Suddenly I became very nervous. Then calmly and firmly, I requested silence.

Seconds later, I leaped beyond the boat and plunged into ocean waters, feet first, descending an estimated twenty to thirty feet below the surface of the sea. Having reached the limit of the plunge allowed me to immediately change direction and to begin rising above intensely dark waters. Engaging both arms and legs in a mermaid-like manner, I successfully rose above the surface and then gasped for air, for a few profoundly gratifying moments. Having experienced deep darkness and then having emerged into brilliant sunlight found me being profoundly grateful, humbled, and peaceful, and reverently uttering, "Jesus Christ Almighty."

Moments later, Jamus and Brynn jumped off the roof of the boat, one by one, demonstrating no fear. When we finished the jumping activity, we joined Jared and Rylan, who were sitting in the stern. We decided to dive off the back side of the boat, in turn, as the water temperature was about sixty degrees. Repeatedly jumping into the ocean rendered each and all of us experiencing the water as being increasingly warm. While waiting to jump, Rylan was shivering. His tiny lips were turning blue. When I said, "Rylan, are you cold?" he remained unfazed. "No, I don't weigh very much," he remarked. When all of us had returned to dry land and had showered and changed into dry clothing, Brynn drew and then presented me a shockingly good Jura drawing, which she dated and signed.

Thursday, June 27, 2013

Having experienced a seizure, Mom was hospitalized last Saturday. She returned home yesterday afternoon. Until Tuesday, she was unable to talk; she remained asleep.

Doctors and nurses treating Mom have said her recovery is remarkable. They hope that Mom will be able to be fully mobile within two to four weeks. Dad has been with Mom while she has been hospitalized; he has been sleeping beside her in a hospital bed which resembles a recliner chair.

Mom returned home with Dad today. Lizzie, Jared, and Kristin and I will now be able to visit Mom regularly, as we are living nearby. Valerie, who visited Mom last weekend, when Mom was hospitalized, has returned to Florida. Mom has received telephone calls from several grandsons.

This afternoon, while we were sitting in the living room of the North Main Street home in which we all lived many years ago, Mom, Dad, Lizzie, John, and I were reminiscing about family experiences from decades ago. When Lizzie, Jared, Valerie and I attended elementary school and school friends requested to know where we lived,fellow students did not understand us when we said that we lived near Cedar Street, on North Main Street.

When we explained that North Main Street is near "The Dump Road," friends would immediately say, "Oh yeah, now I know where the house is." Liz said that if Mom and Dad decide to sell the house, it can be advertised as being located "one hop, skip and a jump to the Dump." Golly gee, I forgot, "The Dump" has been renamed the Recycling Transfer Center. Advertising a house for sale as being "one hop, skip and a jump to the Recycling Transfer Center might be, well…, awkward. Agreed?

CHAPTER TWENTY-ONE

ONE NIGHT STAND, MIRACLE AFTER MIRACLE, POLITICAL FAILURE AND REDEMPTION, THE DEATH OF A PRESIDENT

Friday, August 23, 2013

Unaccompanied and wanting to see Frankie Valli and the Four Seasons, who are performing this evening inside South Shore Music Circus (SSMC) in Cohasset, found me entering the car I drive, driving half a mile, and moments later, accessing the almost full, Paul Pratt Library parking lot. This is one spot where show goers can park when the SSMC parking lot is full. The large, round South Shore Music Circus tent is visible from here.

Tonight was a glorious, warm, and tranquil August evening; there were some white, puffy cumulus clouds in the sky. As the sun was about to set, the time was nearly 8:15 p.m. The concert had begun at 8:00 p.m. The enthusiasm, musical lyrics, and rock and doo wop sound of Frankie Valli and the Four Seasons was palpable, whether or not one could see the band or fully hear the music. I had heard and read that the show was sold out.

Two thousand three hundred audience members went wild, as seventy-nine-year old vocalist Frankie Valli and the Four Seasons rocked the night away, singing selections such as, "I've Got You Under My Skin," "Let's Hang On To What We've Got," "Bye Bye Baby (Baby Good bye)," "My Eyes Adored You," "I'm Working My Way Back to You," and "Oh What a Night." Frankie Valli has been performing for over fifty years, since 1960. The sound of seventy-nine-year-old Frankie Valli and the Four Seasons

282

continues to resemble young adult professional singers whose voices are clear, innocent and sweet.

Although I was unable to hear all of the song lyrics, I sensed love rekindling quickly between Frankie Valli and the Four Seasons rock band and the Music Circus audience, during the one-night stand of the group at the South Shore Music Circus. Prolonged nostalgia permeated the atmosphere inside and outside the tent. Song lyrics may have prompted concert guests to remember being youthful and to recall the starting, changing, and possibly the ending of relationships, whether the relationships began during high school, college, or even in later years.

Radio stations played hit records the band made, when the group initially became popular during the 1960s. The group struggled for over ten years before they made their first hit song, "Sherry." Beloved songs of the Frankie Valli and the Four Seasons were played on CD's, in the 1980's. Frankie Valli is recognized worldwide for being able to create falsetto. Falsetto is a method of singing that vocalists, especially male tenors, use to sing notes which reach significantly beyond the normal range in which they sing. When Frankie produces falsetto, he is especially captivating, mystifying, and empowering.

In days following this SSMC show, a lady who lives next door to me and has been a longtime South Shore Music Circus employee, informed me that Mr. Valli demonstrates high entertainment standards. She said that during the show, he wore several show outfits, which had previously been placed in his dressing room. Before the show began, Mr. Valli asked an usherette to iron show outfits he intended to wear—three times—before he indicated that he was satisfied with the appearance of the show outfits. Only after this task was completed were he and the Four Seasons nearly ready and willing to descend one of several aisles in the South Shore Music Circus tent, enter the SSMC circular rotating stage set above the orchestra pit and begin performing.

Sunday, September 8, 2013

Tonight I attended a Hingham, Massachusetts meeting; the weekly gathering begins at 7:00 p.m. and ends at 8:00 p.m. After the meeting was over, I unleashed Jura, who had been sitting outside; we began a final evening walk. As moments passed, I realized that I had become distracted. Jura was missing. He had entered a wooded area outside the building where the meeting was held. The weekly meeting happens in a combined residential and commercial location. After walking and seeking Jura for almost ninety minutes, I did not find him.

Suddenly, I remembered that I had left the oven on at home. Sliced vegetables that I had put in an olive oil lined roasting pan which had been placed in the oven on low heat had been unattended for nearly four hours. Initially hesitating to leave the meeting site, I decided to return to the apartment. I realized that not doing so could result in an apartment fire; I also accepted that returning home would considerably complicate the matter of finding Jura. Moments later, understanding that when I returned to the meeting place after going home, I might not be able to find Jura or I might discover that he had been hit and killed by a car, I drove home.

When returning to the apartment, I opened the door of the main entrance, quickly ascended the hallway stairs, opened the apartment front door, walked into the kitchen area, and then opened the oven door. Nearly blackened, overcooked, and fortunately still-edible vegetables were visible. The roasting pan containing the vegetables was hastily removed, covered with aluminum foil, and placed vertically atop two stovetop burners.

After re-entering the car around 10:00 p.m. and returning to the parking lot of the meeting place ten minutes later, I discovered Jura standing in the driveway. He was commanding a spot close to where we had begun walking together. Jura observed me and addressed me non-verbally, as though he was saying, "It is good to see you; I missed you." The experience left me speechless, profoundly grateful, and utterly bewildered.

Wednesday, September 11, 2013

Currently being constructed, the National World Trade Center Museum is scheduled to open in the spring of 2014. It is adjacent to the World Trade Center Memorial, which was opened three years ago tomorrow. Names of victims of the 9/11 tragedy are inscribed on bronze panels. The memorial panels surround two waterfall pools. Each pool is nearly one acre in size.

Retrieved 9/11 artifacts are currently being stored inside the National World Trade Center Museum, which is situated underneath the site of the destroyed One Word Trade Center and the Twin Towers buildings. The memorabilia will be displayed inside the fully constructed museum. Some artifacts are personal items; others are for example, mangled steel recovered from the site where the Twin Towers were struck by hijacked planes and then imploded. Another remnant is a battered staircase which survivors of the bombed Twin Towers used to escape. Museum goers will descend the staircase.

Kathy Sussex Manard, a Hingham, Massachusetts resident, was previously employed with a worldwide professional services company with headquarters in New York City and an office in Boston, Massachusetts. Based in Dublin, Ireland, the international company sells financial risk mitigation products, including insurance, health insurance and pension administration plans. Kathy intended to attend a training meeting in the New York office on September 11, 2001. The meeting was being held in the South Twin Tower building in a conference room, on the 92nd floor. The scheduled meeting time was 8:30 a.m. Two days a week, Kathy and fellow company risk managers conferred there. Traveling there via plane, she departed from Boston and arrived in New York City, approximately one hour later.

In August of 2011, Kathy and Peter Manard, the husband of Kathy, sought and found travel agent assistance and were planning a two-week vacation, comprised of touring France and Italy. The return flight was scheduled to depart De Gaulle Airport in Paris, France on Monday September 10, 2001 and arrive at Logan Airport in Boston, seven to eight hours later. Kathy intended to commute to New York City the following day in order to attend the Tuesday 9/11 training meeting.

While Peter and Kathy were in a travel agency office and confirming travel arrangements with an agent, the agent was about to hand them airline tickets that they had purchased and an itinerary plan, when Kathy suddenly exclaimed, "I don't want to come home on the tenth; I want to be in Paris one more day." Although he was unenthused with changing the travel plan, Peter consented to the rearrangement. Peter and Kathy were reassigned to depart France on September 11, 2001. Unto this day, Kathy says she does not recall what or who motivated her to initiate the itinerary change.

After they had ended vacationing in France, Peter and Kathy were seated inside an Air France air plane, which was ascending, beyond Charles De Gaulle Airport runway, on Tuesday morning, September 11, when the pilot suddenly informed the passengers that Americans were facing a national emergency. International air space was being closed. Airline officials were requesting all pilots to land immediately or as soon as possible.

Moments later, the pilot further advised passengers in the aircraft that two terrorist-hijacked planes had struck the North as well as the South

Tower buildings at One World Trade Center and a third terrorist-manned plane had hit the Pentagon building in Washington, D.C. The pilot also stated that a fourth hijacked plane had crashed into a field in Shanksville, Pennsylvania and that there were no survivors from any of the crashes.

Not counting time involved in landing solely to refuel, the Air France aircraft in which Kathy and Peter were traveling was airborne for ten hours, before the pilot was able to safely land the plane at De Gaulle airport. Upon arrival, shocked and grieving passengers were unable to re-book return flights to America, until days following the events of September 11. Closed air space influenced the delay.

Kathy commented that Parisian hospitality that airplane passengers were offered while being temporarily confined in Paris was remarkable. "People opened their hotels, restaurants and hearts to us," she said. She also pointed out that Americans who had traveled to France via air travel on 9/11 were not charged any hotel or meal expenses for several days after the American tragedy occurred. She stated that French hotel and restaurant personnel regularly became tearful during this time, as did travelers from the United States, while they were interacting with one another.

In August 2002, Kathy was chosen to run in the 2002 New York Marathon. Having submitted an application to run in the 26.2 mile-event, she had been selected to run the race through a lottery system. This method is often used to select marathon runners, as marathons can attract tens of thousands of runners. While Kathy was running the race in November of 2002 she was wearing running pants and a tee shirt: the front side of the tee shirt pictured Eleanore Sussex, the mother of Kathy, and the seven siblings of Kathy. Eleanore Sussex died in August 2000, after battling cancer for three months.

The backside of the tee shirt Kathy wore while she was running the marathon displayed the names of co-workers with whom she had worked, who were killed during the deadly violence that occurred on the morning of 9/11. When she finished the race, six hours after starting the course, Kathy had raised four thousand dollars, which supporters sponsoring her had pledged. The donations were placed in an education fund which is being used to support surviving children of 9/11 victims who had been employed at the company at which Kathy was then working. Currently, Kathy and I walk several days a week with Jura as well as Heather and Daisy, dogs that Kathy and Peter own.

Wednesday, September 12, 2013

Emma Alexandra Reagan was born today at 11:00 p.m. A doctor and nurses assisting the doctor aided the delivery. Mother and daughter are well. Talking with me via telephone, brother Jared said he is with Elissa and their newborn daughter. She will be called Emma.

Friday, September 27, 2013

American and Iranian leaders have not talked for thirty-four years, since the 1978-1979 Iranian Revolution. During the revolt, thirty-eight-year Iranian leader, Mohammad Reza Shah Pahlavi was overthrown and the new religious leader, the Grand Ayatollah Ruhollah Khomeini, replaced the shah. Ruhollah Khomeini then ordered the holding of fifty-two Americans hostage inside the American Embassy in Tehran, the capital city of Iran. The captivity lasted for four hundred and forty-four days: supporters of the Iranian Revolution supporters had seized the consulate.

A stalemate relationship of nearly forty years between the two countries began to break down today, as goodwill-based telephone conversation between President Obama and Iranian President Hassan Rouhani evolved. Media reports indicate that Mr. Rouhani has been involved in United Nations General Assembly meetings for several days.

Located in New York City, the United Nations is an international organization that was initially formed in 1945 to promote international peace, security, and cooperation. Having delivered several speeches here in recent days, President Rouhani has commented that Iran welcomes deepening American and Western ties. Mr. Rouhani also indicated that Iran wishes to address and to resolve issues that have been raised regarding Iranian nuclear power programs.

Amid telephone conversation, presidents Obama and Rouhani discussed political issues that America and Iran share. Mr. Obama indicated that the exchange between the two men generated optimism about settling political conflicts between the two countries. The two leaders have agreed to confirm political agreements made among Iran, America, and cooperating nations in writing. Generally, the overriding foreign policy management strategy that President Obama employs is building and also rebuilding international political relationships through the development of mutual trust, respect, and cooperation.

Monday, September 30, 2013

Shutting down of the United States federal government began today. Starting tomorrow, eight hundred thousand federal workers will be indefinitely furloughed. National parks, museums, and monuments are now closed. Virtually all federal offices are also closed. One *Washington Post* newspaper story reports that thousands of United States air traffic controllers, border patrol agents, and prison guards will continue to work. However, paychecks for these government employees may be delayed.

Why? Bitter dispute has arisen among congressional leaders around the passage of government spending bills—legislation which approves or defunds the operation and management of federal government programs. The current battle includes funding for the Patient Affordable Care Act, which Congress approved and the president signed into law two years ago. Nicknamed "Obamacare," the statute will be effective beginning tomorrow, October 1, 2013.

For the U.S. government, the fiscal year runs from October 1 through September 30. If congressional upheaval continues beyond October 17, the current national debt ceiling will not be raised and therefore loans to the federal government will not be paid. America will default on the loans for the first time in U.S. history.

Allowing the budget of the U.S. government to indefinitely remain imbalanced, concordantly permitting the national debt of America to increase exponentially, and at the same, time not developing a substantial plan for significant reduction of the national debt leading to its elimination is highly questionable fiscal policy. Meanwhile, temporarily raising the national debt ceiling, while consolidating government loans, selling or possibly leasing unused or underutilized government assets—i.e., land and real estate—and reasonably and compassionately streamlining government programs and government-related organizations is advisable. Such action allows government loans to be repaid, thereby lowering the national debt ceiling, promoting the balancing of the U.S. government budget, and motivating the fiscal well-being of all Americans.

Thursday, October 17, 2013

Eleventh-hour congressional action has occurred. An interim 2014 government appropriations bill that allowed the U.S. debt ceiling to be raised was approved. President Obama has now made the legislation law; he signed the bill, shortly after midnight-last night.

The action ended a sixteen-day shutdown of virtually all United States government operations. U.S. government programs will be funded for three months, until January 15, 2014. The United States debt ceiling was lifted until February 7, 2014. Congressional action in January 2014 will or will not move this budget matter forward.

Thursday, October 31, 12013

This evening was glorious. While sitting on a chair below a lighted chandelier in the hallway entrance to the apartment in which I live with Jura, I offered a number of elementary and middle school children wearing varied Halloween costumes some candy, an apple, and baked banana bread that I had placed in plastic sandwich bags. A parent or parents accompanied some but not all arriving trick-or-treaters.

Many Halloween outfits were unfamiliar to me. A number of television, computer, and video game characters represented on the apparel were un-recognizable to me. No worries. Observing elementary and middle school age-children wearing recognizable as well as unidentifiable Halloween en-sembles was a welcome Halloween Eve distraction.

Most of the trick-or-treaters were carrying pillow cases; they were using these as Halloween candy holders. Viewing the partially filled Halloween candy bags found me fondly remembering celebrating Halloween with brother Jared, sister Valerie, and sister Liz during childhood years. Being good and ambitious trick-or-treaters, we also used pillow cases as candy-holding sacks.

Monday, November 4, 2013

Enactment of The Patient Affordable Care Act, (PAC), which went into effect on October 1, is faltering. Because it was deluged with consumers who wanted to view patient affordable care act-compatible healthcare insur-ance plans, the Obamacare website shutdown on October 1, the same day that it went live. President Obama as well as United States Government Health and Human Services Secretary, Kathleen Sibelius have acknowl-edged and accepted responsibility for the failure. Mr. Obama has promised Americans that the malfunctioning Obamacare website will be rebooted and working properly by late November.

Another surfacing glitch in the Patient Affordable Care Act is that although all health insurance policy holders have been repeatedly promised that changing health plans will not be required, if their current health plan is PAC-compatible, some policy holders are finding that their policies have been unexpectedly cancelled. When purchasing new healthcare plans, some consumers whose policies have been cancelled are being charged notably increased premiums.

Today, Bloomberg News, which is headquartered in New York City and reporting business and financial news, revealed a third PAC problem. Another provision of the new law states that insurance policies not offering Patient Affordable Care related benefits cannot be sold beyond this year, even if these reduce the cost of insurance policies. Opposition to this aspect of the Patient Affordable Care Act has also arisen.

Friday, November 15, 2013

The previously malfunctioning "Obama care" or Patient Affordable Care Act website is again up and running. President Barack Obama has also signed legislation that Congress approved, allowing insurance companies to reinstate healthcare insurance policies which were previously cancelled, due to not meeting PAC law provisions. Newly approved PAC-related legislation mandates that reinstated health insurance policies will remain in effect for one year. Until then, healthcare insurance companies may continue offering insurance plans that do not directly meet PAC standards.

These political actions come across as being fair and equitable. Heartening is witnessing leaders humbly acknowledging and accepting responsibility for failure. Heartwarming is observing leaders clearly vocalizing a desire to resolve conflicts. Galvanizing is witnessing officials utilizing problem solving skills to address political issues, while welcoming cooperation on the matters.

Monday, November 17, 2013

As he talked during a large meeting held this evening, a man was discussing recovery from the disease of alcoholism. Standing, facing a podium and using a microphone, he was one of a number of meeting goers who shared inspiring, vivid, and personal stories of recovery, during the hour-long gathering. Words he used were neither self-aggrandizing nor self-pitying. He displayed humility as well as good humor.

Approaching the man after the meeting, I thanked and commended him. I also suggested that he might enjoy reading *An Invisible Thread*. The memoir portrays a young boy living in a New York City housing project. Daily, standing on city sidewalks, the pre-adolescent boy panhandles for food money. He has not eaten for two days, as *An Invisible Thread* begins.

On September 1, 1986, a thirty-five-year-old woman, who walked past the boy, heard him say, "Excuse me lady, do you have any spare change?" The woman, an advertising executive, stepped off a sidewalk onto a street and continued walking. Suddenly she stopped moving, turned around, viewed the boy quizzically, walked toward him, and began a conversation with him. Refusing to give him money, she offered to buy him breakfast. The fateful moment began a now continuing twenty-seven-year-long mentoring relationship between Laura Schroff, who is now sixty-two-years old and Maurice Mazyck, who is now thirty-nine-years old.

Co-authors Laura Schroff and Alex Tresniowski wrote *An Invisible Thread*, which depicts the developing relationship between Mr. Mazyck and Ms. Schroff. One of the pages of the memoir highlights a mystical Chinese proverb, which states that invisible red thread connects people who are destined to meet and that life circumstances can delay, but not deter the occurrence of the meeting.

The written proverb states that invisible thread may stretch. It may tangle. It will not break. Reading about the developing relationship between Maurice and Laura was intriguing and inspiring experience. The Chinese proverb surrounding invisible thread is wondrous and puzzling. I wonder what the significance of red thread is.

Friday, November 22, 2013

Today, for the first time, Dallas, Texas citizens hosted a memorial ceremony honoring John F. Kennedy, the 35th President of the United States. The commemoration location was Dealey Plaza, where President Kennedy was assassinated fifty-five years ago today. The weather in Dallas was sunny, crisp, and near cloudless. The temperature was approximately fifty-five degrees.

Paradoxically, as the memorial ceremony began this morning, the weather temperature in Dallas was slightly above freezing, at thirty-nine degrees. Light rain accompanied the winter-like chill in the air. A *Dallas Morning News* reporter quoted Mayor Michael Rawlings as saying, "The weather was perfect. It was poetically perfect. It seemed like the skies were weeping."

On November 22, 1963, while he was standing and facing an open window near a corner of the sixth floor of the School Depository building diagonally facing Dealey Plaza, twenty four-year-old Lee Harvey Oswald, a Texas resident, shot President Kennedy and Texas Governor John Connolly, as the limousine in which the President, First Lady Jacqueline Bouvier Kennedy and Governor Connolly were traveling turned onto Elm Street in Dealey Plaza.

Lee Oswald fired a mail-ordered 6.5 mm Carcano carbine at President Kennedy. Numerous reports indicated that he fired three shots at the president before he turned the gun on Governor Connolly. The time was 12:35 p.m., Central Standard Time (CST).

President Kennedy had traveled to Dallas, while he was campaigning to be re-elected in the upcoming 1964 presidential election. Twenty thousand spectators had been standing or sitting upon Dallas sidewalks, while observing, waiting to view, or having seen the passing presidential motorcade, when the president and governor were shot. First Lady Jacqueline Kennedy was physically unharmed.

Speeding ambulances rushed Governor Connolly and President Kennedy to Parkland Memorial Hospital, an eight minutes-long drive north from Dealey Plaza. President John F. Kennedy was declared dead at 1:35 p.m., Central Standard Time. I remember watching an unsettling newscast during which news anchor Walter Cronkite struggled to maintain composure, as he delivered the tragic news. Critically wounded Governor John Connolly survived the tragic incident.

Dealey Plaza became dilapidated in years following the assassination of the president. For decades, many people residing in Dallas harbored intense grief and humiliation surrounding the murder of JFK, as the assassination happened there. In the last ten years, the metropolis has been resurrected, revitalized, and renewed.

Today, the late President John F. Kennedy was observed as having confronted major political challenges. Many view him as having demonstrated inspirational, courageous, and visionary leadership while he faced considerable professional as well as personal obstacles. Selected by a lottery system, five thousand guests attended the memorial ceremony, which began this morning at 10:00 a.m. Bishop, Kevin J. Farrell, representing the Catholic

Archdiocese of Dallas, Dallas Mayor Michael Rawlings, and historian, author, narrator and lecturer, David McCullough, were guest speakers selected for the memorial event.

Booker T. Washington High School for the Performing Arts 2012 graduate, Monica Saldivar, sang the national anthem of America, "The Star Spangled Banner." While addressing memorial guests, Bishop Farrell recalled decades during which Dallas citizens suffered considerably, knowing that Lee Harvey Oswald was living and working in Dallas during the week when he murdered President Kennedy. "Lord, you have lifted us up from a terrible tragedy enacted in this place," he said.

Dallas Mayor Michael (Mike) Rawlings, addressing invitees and recalling the assassination of the president said, "We all grew up that day." Mr. Rawlings described the day as one in which "hope and hatred collided" in Dallas. "These five decades have seen us turn civic heartache into hard work," he commented. Mr. Rawlings added, "Today, we pay tribute to an idealist without illusions, who helped build a more just and equal world."

Continuing, Mayor Rawlings observed, "Dallas citizens honor the life, legacy, and leadership of President Kennedy, who said, "Ask not what your country can do for you; ask what you can do for your country." The mayor unveiled a stone monument which exhibits inscribed prophetic words from the first verse of the biblical Psalm 127. President Kennedy had intended to quote the scriptural words during a speech that he had hoped to deliver on the day he was murdered. The words read, "Except the Lord, keep the city; the watchman waketh, but in vain."

Author, biographer, and historian David McCullough honored the late president, as he quoted words John F. Kennedy stated; "We will not be remembered for our victories or our defeats, but for our contributions to the human spirit." Mr. McCullough observed "Rarely has a United States Commander-in-Chief addressed this nation with such a command of language; he (President Kennedy) spoke with confidence and to the point. He knew that words matter. His words changed lives. His words changed history. He was ambitious to make this a better world and so were we. He had high hopes and so do we. On we go!" Mr. McCullough resolutely cheered.

In 1963, American television was a relatively new medium; it was little beyond thirty years old. There were no television cameras present when President Kennedy and Governor Connolly were shot. The sole reason that the murder scene became widely publicized is that an admirer of the president, a Russia-born, Dallas-based manufacturer of clothing for women, Abraham Zapruder, unwittingly filmed the assassination while he was observing the passing presidential motorcade. He was using an 8mm camera. Ms. Marilyn Sitzman, an assistant to Mr. Zapruder, was standing behind him. She was steadying him.

Following the murder of President Kennedy, grief stricken Mr. Zapruder gave Forest Sorells—who was then a Secret Service Agent—a roll of camera film that he was shooting when he unexpectedly recorded the assassination. Mr. Zapruder asked Mr. Sorrels not to use the film for purposes other than investigation. He also advised a *Life* magazine editor as well as additional media outlets seeking film copies that he did not want the home movie to be publicly seen at a close range. Abraham Zapruder died in 1970, seven years after the president was killed.

One guest attending the memorial service was Mrs. Marie Tippit, whose late husband, J.D. Tippit, was also murdered on the same day as President Kennedy. Officer Tippit was shot and killed by Lee Oswald while he was pursuing Mr. Oswald. Shortly after the November 22, 1963 tragedies, Jacqueline Kennedy sent Mrs. Tippit a condolence letter.

Mrs. Tippit recently made the correspondence public information. Demonstrating profound grace, Jackie Kennedy wrote that she believes the eternal flame that continues to burn at the head of the gravestone of President John F. Kennedy also memorializes the late Dallas police officer J.D. Tippit. The grave site of the former president is in Arlington National Cemetery in Arlington, Virginia.

The assassination, which one newspaper reporter described as "the shot heard around the world" marked the first time many children living in the 1960s era, including me, saw one or both parents cry. It was reported that when an eight-year-old Nigerian girl, heard news of the death of President Kennedy, she began reciting the inaugural address that he had delivered in 1961,when he became President, The father of the young girl, who was standing beside her, quietly began weeping. It has also been written on the day JFK died, people residing in Germany, inhabiting both sides of the former Berlin Wall, which divided Communist East Germany and Socialist West Germany, set candles atop the wall. The Berlin Wall was deconstructed in 1989.

While profoundly grieving the loss of John F. Kennedy, not only as a president but also a fellow human being, Americans exuded deep unity and strength. Exemplifying nationwide community, hundreds of thousands of Americans observed the casket of the president, which on the day before the funeral, was placed on a covered platform inside the rotunda of the U.S. Capitol building. An American flag was draped over the casket.

Approximately eight hundred thousand people stood on Washington, D.C. streets, while they viewed the televised funeral procession which ended at Arlington National Cemetery, in Arlington Virginia. On June 6, 1968, nearly five years after the murder of President Kennedy, Senator Robert F. Kennedy, a brother of JFK, was killed by one of thirteen bullets that an assassin fired at him, while he was campaigning for the presidency of the United States.He was buried near President Kennedy.

Fifty television cameras were summoned to be used in the recording of the funeral of President Kennedy, which at the time, was the most widely watched television event. Now recalling sitting near family members seated at the kitchen table, while watching the funeral proceedings for several hours, finds me remembering that barely a word was spoken among us. This morning in Dallas, the outdoor memorial service held for the late president lasted thirty-seven minutes; the event was prematurely ended as light rain suddenly became steady precipitation, including sleet.

Tuesday, December 31, 2013

The time is 11:50 p.m., ten minutes until a new year begins. Jura is sitting near me. Sitting on the living room floor and employing scissors, I am shredding the second draft of *Life Flashes: A Memoir* and three copies of the number two draft of the book, as I am now working on a third draft and do not want previous drafts or copies of drafts to be lying around anywhere. Watching television at the same time has found me observing several million cheering revelers, who are standing in Times Square, New York, below the One Times Square building. The edifice is three hundred sixty-three feet high.

Partying there, New Year eve celebrators are also observing the New Year Ball. It is a geosphere of Waterford crystal LED (light emitting diode). Twelve feet in diameter, the ball weighs eleven thousand, eight hundred seventy-five pounds. Containing an opening, running through it from the top to the bottom of the sphere, the ball was inserted into the top of a flagpole.

The decorative ball remains above the Times Square building until shortly before midnight, when as many as a million people–standing in

Times Square, in New York City, –and anticipating the dawn of a new year, witness as well as count down the lowering of the ball. Beginning sixty seconds before midnight, the ball slowly drops one hundred forty-four feet, until at the stroke of midnight it rests where it is on the flagpole. A new year has begun.

In 1904, two hundred thousand revelers gathered in Times Square for the first time on New Year Eve to watch fireworks while they were celebrating the coming of a new year. The tradition of lowering a ball that had been inserted into a pole began in 1907, three years later. The first ball, which was largely composed of iron and wood, contained one hundred light bulbs. The ball weighed seven hundred pounds.

A decorative ball designed with iron was utilized in 1920. A computer-controlled ball made of aluminum skin and rhinestone, which came into use in 1995, was followed by the employment of a crystal ball in 1999. The employment of an enormous LED bulb began in 2007 and one year later, in 2008, the utilization of an LED crystal ball began and is currently continuing. Happy one hundred years-old birthday, Ball Drop. Happy New Year with All, and as Tiny Tim Cratchit memorably said during one Christmas Day Dinner, "God Bless us everyone."

Timothy "Tiny Tim" Cratchit is fictional character in *A Christmas Carol,* a short novel by Charles Dickens The work portrays characters including a young boy who is steadily cheerful, respectful, and cooperative, though he is seriously ill and is unable to walk without using a cane.

2014

CHAPTER TWENTY-TWO

BACK TO THE FUTURE, HOLISTIC HEALING, NEW HOME, DEATH IN THE FAMILY, RAIN, REIGN

Friday, January 31, 2014

Late this afternoon, I was walking near two boys, ages four and eight, who were standing beside their mother, while she was grocery shopping inside Roxies supermarket in Quincy, Massachusetts. I addressed the children, saying, "A big snowstorm is coming this week; at least one day this week there will be no school."

"No school? We'll have to charge our Dells," one of the brothers said. The similar aged sibling agreed. The young boy referencing "Dells" meant the Dell computers that both of these boys use. Using the technological devices allows them to play computer games.

"Whoa," I silently uttered, while overhearing the two boys conversing, while I wondered how many children have regularly discussed snow day activities for over a decade, without mentioning sledding, runner sleds, metal snow saucers, or cafeteria trays, which can be used as makeshift sleds. Does the Dell computer remark not clearly indicate that the 21st century has undeniably arrived?

Saturday, April 19, 2014

Unto nephew Jonas Jenkins and Liane Jenkins, the wife of Jonas, a son named Luke, who will be called Lukie, was born one month ago today. Aliana, six-year-old sister of Lukie, likes dropping him, gently upon bedding.

Monday, May 19, 2014

Jura suddenly sat down and nearly became immobile while we were walking. We were returning home, one day late last week. A veterinarian specialist that Dr. Charles (Chuck) Wilford of Hingham Animal Clinic recommended, Dr. Bob Hindon, recently examined Jura; Dr. Hindon diagnosed Jura with severe spinal stenosis, arthritis, and possible bone cancer. Jura will not receive a bone cancer biopsy. A positive biopsy result would mean deciding whether to allow amputation of the left hind leg of Jura. Jura is now thirteen-years-old.

This past weekend Jura was hospitalized; he is unable to walk without wearing a dog harness with an attached handle. A harness is a piece of equipment with or without a handle that can be used in lieu of a dog collar or in addition to a collar, with or without a leash attachment. A harness gives a dog walking support and relieves pressure and discomfort that a dog experiences when a dog collar is being pulled by a leash. The type of harness that I bought Jura is looped around the neck, and as the dog steps into the lower part of the harness with the left front foot, the lower part of the harness is extended to and beyond the right front foot and around the torso of the dog, before it is then buckled or snapped.

Holding the handle on the top of a harness secured around Jura allows me to give him additional support when he is walking independently. In addition to the harness, I employ a sling with two hand-held handles.

The sling is wrapped around the underbelly of Jura, in front of his hind legs, allowing me to hold the sling handles with one hand, leaving the other hand free to grasp the handle of the fitted and buckled harness. Another veterinarian who examined Jura said Jura will probably not live for more than another four weeks.

Thursday, July 4, 2014

Yesterday, nephew Jamus emailed me an accurate July 4, 2014 weather forecast, projecting pouring rain all day. The first and probably the last poem I will write follows.

Rain, Reign

Rain, rain, is coming, coming down, Falling, falling, gently on Ground.
Heat relief instills Belief; Hearts Soften, as hearts do often,
Love reigns Supreme.

Monday, July 15, 2014

Another miracle has occurred. Eight weeks ago having been given a prognosis of one month to live, Jura is walking again, fully independently. Securing a harness with a handle around Jura and wrapping a sling with two handles around him while I am walking with him, which was vital two months ago, is now unnecessary. What happened? Jura received four weekly acupuncture treatments. Having practiced acupuncture for thirty years, Dr. Maria Cogill, an acupuncturist who treats animals as well as people and is affiliated with Boston Medical Center, administered the first acupuncture treatment that Jura received.

Following the first treatment, Jura began putting noticeable weight upon a former barely movable left hind hip, leg, and foot. The healing astounded me. At first I thought I might be seeing things, when I viewed the expanding range of motion that Jura was showing with the left hind hip, leg, and foot. Moments later, I realized that I was not imagining anything; Jura had legitimately begun to move the hip, leg, and foot with an increasing range of motion. Since then, Jura has re-visited Hingham Animal Clinic, where he received two additional acupuncture treatments, which enabled him to walk freely.

Dr. Harriet Lakus, a veterinarian and an animal acupuncture specialist, performed the final three additional acupuncture treatments that Jura received. Support staff members at the clinic—Amy Wilson, Patty McLaughlin, Shelley Zolun, Rita Allen, and Emily Mollen—have been consistently professional, efficient, and compassionate throughout the six years that Jura has received intermittent treatment at the clinic. The practice recently became incorporated. Thankfully, thus far, the atmosphere and operations of the clinic atmosphere continues to resemble a long-time operating and trusted small country veterinary office with one or two examining rooms.

Since the acupuncture treatments were completed, Jura has been able to walk three times daily, each time for up to thirty minutes. He is swimming at nearby beaches nearly every day. Jura continues to enjoy walking, wandering about beaches, swimming, riding in cars, meeting new dogs and people, and well, yes eating virtually anything.

Sunday, July 20, 2014

On this day, one year ago Mom was able to walk, read, cook or clean. Having experienced two seizures since then, she is now experiencing difficulty with talking as well as performing daily activities. She is being given nursing home care. Mom smiles softly and regularly. She recognizes visitors. From time to time, she suddenly, surprisingly, and quietly sings the first stanzas of old songs, including "Somewhere over the Rainbow," "Amazing Grace," "When You Wish upon a Star," "When Irish eyes are Smiling, "A Bicycle Built for Two," and "Danny Boy."

A year ago, Mom and I shared lunch for the last time, inside a relatively new restaurant in Hingham Shipyard. She was physically frail. She exhibited a pasty complexion. She moved slowly and unsteadily. While we were eating, heavy rain began falling. Meanwhile, we fully enjoyed being together.

After lunch, Mom and I decided to go shopping at a nearby clothing store. As she and I walked across Shipyard Drive, arm in arm, while we were headed toward the clothing store, I opened and raised a large umbrella, which sheltered us from steadily falling rain. These moments found me alternately looking directly and fondly at Mom, smiling and then looking straight ahead, while vocalizing "Singing in the Rain" lyrics and at the same time imagining Fred Astaire and Ginger Rogers dancing delightfully in front of us.

Thursday, October 30, 2014

Beloved Boston Mayor, Thomas Menino, who served an unprecedented five terms, has died, after battling cancer for six months. Good and saddening was hearing the news, which came through my car radio. Mayor Menino was observed by many as being professionally and personally kind, cooperative, and respectful.

Tuesday, December 2, 2014

Today Mom turned eighty-five-years old. Mom is dying. Having been seriously ill for over twelve months, Mom has been steadily declining. One moment finds me embracing acceptance. Another moment renders me experiencing disbelief.

Mom was hospitalized last year after experiencing a seizure. Serious health complications ensued. She was admitted to an assisted living facility. She was later re-hospitalized, before being admitted to a nearby nursing home. She has been given care here since May of this year.

Family members have regularly visited Mom since she became ill. This afternoon, I brought a formal, over-the-knee, black dress to trusted longtime Cohasset Plaza Cleaners business owners, Daniel and Barbara Thoi. After the garment is cleaned, it will probably be worn soon, at the funeral mass for Mom.

A beloved dog of Mom and Dad, named Winston, died yesterday morning, shortly after he experienced a second stroke. Dad was giving him care while Mom was ill. While he and I were walking together, last Friday morning, fifteen-year-old Winston, who was blind and deaf and hobbled on a crippled left hind leg, intermittently stopped and smelled snowy tree leaves and bushes. Strong wind gusts accompanied temperatures in the high thirties. Winston demonstrated no concern. When he was back at home, he was discovered licking the faces of family members.

Today rendered me tenderly remembering being eleven years old and sharing dinner nightly with sister Lizzie, then twelve years old, brother Jared, then eight years old, and sister Valerie, then five years old. One evening, while we were eating dinner, we were teasing Mom, who was in the kitchen and had spent nearly two hours making spaghetti sauce covering cooked and plated pasta we were eating. Disciplinarian Dad was not home that evening; he was working. Desiring to climb the insurance career ladder, he regularly worked long and late hours.

"You'll miss me when I'm gone," Mom said then. Visibly frustrated she had become tearful, while tolerating the antics of four juveniles. One child, probably me, sarcastically responded to Mom, saying, "You're not going to die." Jared, Lizzie, and Valerie agreed with me as we continued to good naturedly make fun of Mom. While we were laughing heartily, milk we were drinking from glasses began spurting through mouths as well as noses.

Remembering the incident now finds me suddenly and soberly envisioning some, not all, of the lyrics from the last stanza of "Both Sides Now," a song written in 1967 by singer and songwriter Joni Mitchell. In 1969, long-time vocalist Judy Collins recorded the first released version of the song. Partial lyrics in the last lines of the song read, "I've looked at life from both sides now, from win and lose, and still somehow, I really don't know life… at all."

Wednesday, December 24, 2014

Goodwill enabled me to attend two Christmas Eve open houses tonight. Mid-evening time found me joining condominium neighbors Janine

Hartwell as well as the children of Janine; Jeralyn is eighteen years old and Darren is twenty three years old. I also visited with condominium neighbor Sally Scott and her children; Gerry is twenty three years old, Donna is twenty six years old, Roy is twenty eight years old and the fiancée of Roy, Jane Marcus, is thirty three years old. While interacting with new people and eating thoughtfully prepared homemade food during each of the Open House parties that Janine and Sally were hosting, I experienced serenity, comfort and acceptance.

Brother Jared as well as a new property manager whom Jared employed, Bill St. George, discovered that the condo beside the units in which Janine and Sally live—two of four condominiums located near Cohasset Village—was for sale in late 2013. Jared and Bill encouraged me to live here. Last March, Jura and I moved into the condominium. Residing in the two story residence allows Jura to sleep in the living room on the first floor. Living here substantially minimizes the amount of stairs Jura climbs every day. The entrance to the condominium is comprised of three steps.

When we were living in an apartment, Jura negotiated three apartment entrance steps and eighteen apartment hallway stairs, six to eight times daily. In addition, he walked with me, for several hours a day. Two months after Jura and I began living in the condo, Jura was diagnosed with severe spinal stenosis, severe arthritis, and possible bone cancer. Heartwarming is seeing him being nearly fully recovered from the maladies and being able to easily walk outdoors.

The spinal stenosis and arthritis symptoms Jura was experiencing have almost completely disappeared. He remains able to walk four times daily, for about thirty minutes each time. He receives daily massage treatments from me as well as intermittent acupuncture treatments; both relieve back, hip, and joint pains he experiences.

Living in a condominium offering increased living and storage space has been stabilizing and gratifying. Feisty, good-humored condo neighbor Marjorie Kent, who lives in another unit, has several times offered me counsel, compassion, good humor, and lunch. Talking with Marjorie has found me realizing that Marjorie and Mom, of similar ages and previously having been acquainted, as fellow bridge players, demonstrate similar refined, feisty, and comical temperaments.

2015

CHAPTER TWENTY-THREE

ON A CLEAR DAY, NEW LEADERSHIP, PLACEBOS VS. DRUGS, KID STUFF, MORE SIGNS AND MIRACLES

January 1, 2015

Happy New Year. While watching Hingham Cabaret auditions this afternoon, I suddenly became impassioned. Standing in the entrance of the audition room and having previously decided not to tryout, I suddenly began silently singing, "On a Clear Day."

The tune, written by Burton Lane and Alan Jay Lerner, was featured in the 1965 Grammy Award-winning musical bearing the name of the song. Five years later, the musical "On a Clear Day" had been transformed into a movie, also bearing the same name; the film starred renowned singer, Barbara Streisand and legendary late actor, Omar Sharif. Stunning and bewildering me this afternoon was being able to recall all of the lyrics of the song, considering that I had not sung the tune for decades. Seconds later, I heard a voice saying, "Merrie, sing this song." The wise instruction came from Mom, no doubt. "On A Clear Day" lyrics are as follows:

On a clear day, Rise and look around you, and you'll see who you are,
On a clear day, how it will astound you,
That the glow of your being out shines every star.
You'll be part of, every mountain, sea, and shore,
You will hear from far and near, a world you've never heard before
On a clear day, on a clear day, you can see forever and ever and ever more.

Mom died on Friday, December 5th, 2014, at 1:05 a.m. I remember the spine-chilling disbelief that permeated me when Lizzie awakened Valerie

307

and me and solemnly delivered the grim news. Having a little over an hour ago left the nursing home where Mom was being given hospice care, Valerie and I had fallen asleep in the master bed in the bedroom in which Liz sleeps. Jura and Buddy were asleep at the foot of the bed.

Attempting to process what Liz had said, I was silently and mournfully wondering, *Are we really not ever going to see Mom again?* I do admit having also felt profound relief, trusting that Mom is not suffering anymore. Then, bewilderment returned.

Mom had become unconscious, a couple of days before she died. At one point, I was kneeling beside the hospital bed in which she lay and was for the first time, acknowledging that Mom was not going to recover from being ill. Holding the right hand of Mom, I said, "Mom, don't leave us. We love you," and then I began to weep. Mom strengthened the grasp of her right hand on my left hand, for a few precious and timeless moments.

On the following evening, the night that she died, I held her hand again, as she remained unconscious. I heard Mom say, "I love you, I cannot hold on any more; it is time for me to go Home."

I remember the reception that was held at the home of Jared following the funeral mass that was celebrated for Mom, several days after she died. One hundred people came to the church service and the funeral reception. I recall the peace and comfort that I experienced being amid community of people who were expressing faith and who also loved Mom. I remember non-verbally saying, *I believe this is the reason why churches were born.* The communal experience steadied me emotionally in the first months after Mom died.

While personal moments of disbelief that Mom has passed away have not ended, realizing that Mom is now free from any suffering brings me inner calm. The relationship that Mom and I shared now continues to evolve and has deepened. Death is clarifying. Death is rebirth. When she was near death, before she became unconscious, Mom miraculously continued to remember partial song lyrics that she had learned decades ago, including "Danny Boy," "Smile," "When You Wish Upon a Star," and "When Irish Eyes are Smiling." Mom is smiling; she can now see forever and ever and evermore.

Tuesday, April 21, 2015

Considering the subject of government business as well as driving into Boston, I initially resisted leaving home this evening. Later, I decided to attend a forum at the John F. Kennedy Library in Boston, featuring Massachusetts Governor Charlie Baker, who was recently elected, on Tuesday, November 4, 2014. An estimated six hundred people attended the full house JFK Library event. Brian McGrory, novel writer, longtime *Boston Globe* newspaper reporter and columnist and *Globe* Editor since 2012, moderated the living-room style-forum. Leaving the early evening event after it ended and walking outside into windy spring air found me experiencing heightened senses of renewal, contentment, and uncertainty.

Attending the late afternoon forum also rendered me experiencing resurging confidence, surrounding the legislative leadership of Massachusetts. Gladdened that Governor Baker is the new leader of the Massachusetts legislature I am one of many who do not wish to lose him as such. Hearing him speak for a few minutes rendered me sensing Charlie Baker demonstrates presidential qualifications, although when I admit this, I also confess that I do not fully realize what demonstrating presidential qualifications means.

Brian McGrory and Governor Baker were seated near one another in the center of the JFK Library main auditorium stage. Two deep-blue color water-filled goblets rested atop a small round coffee table set between them. Direct and insightful were questions that Mr. McGrory asked the governor, including inquiring about what he learned during the first one hundred days since he assumed the new role.

Grinning, Governor Baker quipped, "I learned a lot about snow," which stunned and charmed the audience. Massachusetts received 110.8 inches of snow this winter, which fell in little more than six weeks, beginning in late January. The state of Alaska usually leads America in snowfall totals. This past winter, snowfall accumulation in Massachusetts surpassed the amount of snow that the state of Alaska received.

Governor Baker said that as a result of recent major snowstorms affecting much of the state of Massachusetts, overseeing many snow removal projects and resolving public safety issues related to significant snow accumulation and removal was required. The weather prompted nearly continual conversation among officials representing one hundred fifty Massachusetts communities. State, local, and interstate officials shared lively discussions surrounding blizzard weather conditions, public safety matters and snow removal.

"This gave us a chance to work positively with people with whom we will be working in the next four years," the governor said. He indicated that generally cooperative interactions and resulting plans and actions initiated the building of a solid Baker administration foundation. As did many of their fellow Massachusetts residents, Charlie Baker and Lauren Baker, the wife of Charlie and the First Lady of the Commonwealth, learned for the first time how to rake snow off the roof of the home in which they reside.

Unusually high snowfall amounts can and do collapse roofs. In the Boston region 128 roofs had collapsed as of late February 2015, and news reports indicated most collapses have occurred in flat-roofed storage buildings.

Asked why he has appointed numerous Democrats to serve in the new administration, the governor having formerly served as Health and Human Services Secretary during the administration of former Governor Bill Weld (1991-1997) and as Administration and Finance Secretary in the administration of now deceased Governor Paul Cellucci (1997-2001) said one thing he learned while serving the two political Administrations is that "thinking Democrats are going to have all the right answers is likely going to be wrong."

"Thinking Republicans are going to have all the right answers is likely going to be wrong as well." Mr. Baker said, completing a train of thought. He indicated that while he was serving the administrations of Governors Weld and Cellucci he could not identify the party affiliations of many fellow legislators. "I could easily identify what fellow legislators serving these administrations were good at and why you would go to them for counsel," he stated.

Surprising the audience, Mr. Baker commented that ridership on the Massachusetts Bay Transportation Authority (MBTA) commuter rail is increasing, despite continuing management and operations challenges the subway and bus transportation system is facing. The issues were highlighted during the recent severe 2014-2015 New England winter, as passengers waiting for trains and buses experienced serious delays in service. Transit system users were also frustrated with prolonged shutdowns of service.

Despite current obstacles to utilizing public transportation, Governor Baker said that he believes MBTA services are critical. He said that he and fellow legislative colleagues are addressing MBTA issues, including employee absenteeism, re-purposing currently unused or underused large MBTA land tracts, and the under spending of MBTA capital, in view of the failing infrastructure of the transit system.

Mr. Baker said that when he was driving home, at around 10:00 p.m. on Thursday, January 8, following the gubernatorial inauguration festivities held at Boston Convention Center, he received a call from Boston Mayor Martin (Marty) Walsh. Mayor Walsh requested Governor Baker to be present at a 7:00 a.m. press conference that United States Olympic Committee officials were holding outside the State House, the next morning. The primary intention of the media event was to officially announce the Commonwealth of Massachusetts as among international bidders who wish to host the 2024 Olympic Games. Newly elected Charlie Baker suddenly exuded sensitivity and boyishness, as he admitted out loud, "I thought, no one is going to care about me being inaugurated." *Boston Globe* editor Brian McGrory responded immediately. He informed Governor Baker and audience members that when he was considering the layout of the front page of the newspaper for the day after the inauguration, another member of the editorial team tentatively advised him, "We usually lead with the inauguration." Brian McGrory quipped, "Nobody cares about the inauguration." Governor Baker and the forum audience burst into self-deprecating laughter and applause.

Sunday, May 17, 2015

Niece Myla Watson will graduate from high school today. She will be a freshman at a Florida university this fall. Her sister Grace, who has been attending a Florida university, is now a junior. Matthew, the brother of Grace and Myla, is hoping to attend a private school in New England this fall. Grace and Myla have expressed desires to eventually attend graduate schools in Boston. Will the re-location of Watson family members follow?

A recruiting company has been employing nephew Rhett Jenkins for nearly two years. He had previously worked at a mortgage company whose operations were moved to a new location which meant Rhett would be required to drive an unreasonable distance to work, every work day. He is enjoying a new career, which involves helping people find positions in health field related jobs. He enjoys work requiring solid communications skills, organizational abilities, and direct people contact.

Monday, May 25, 2015

This day mysteriously found me attending a Hingham Memorial Day event. One hour long, the commemorative ceremony named and honored

Hingham veterans who died during the last twelve months. One of the servicemen was eighty-five-year-old William Edward Hadley. William Hadley was a former U.S. Marine Corps lieutenant who served during the Korean War. Seriously injured twice, Mr. Hadley received a military commendation and the Purple Heart with a Star award.

William and Barbie Hadley were married sixty-one years and reared five children. They were also grandparents of five children and were great-grandparents of one child. A former attorney, Mr. Hadley had practiced law for over fifty years. He worked in a law office based in Quincy, Massachusetts, near a district courthouse.

William Hadley died on October 21, 2014, following a longtime illness. Having been friends for many years, Dad, William, and Mom met when William and Dad were enrolled in Boston College Law School, in the 1950s. William, Barbie and Mom and Dad socialized for a number of years and they continued to exchange Christmas cards when they curiously stopped socializing. Somehow, they lost touch.

Tuesday, May 26, 2015

Today found me making and delivering submarine sandwiches to the mechanics of Wilder Brothers, who currently service the car I drive. The vehicle is not American made. Wilder Brothers is located in Scituate, Massachusetts.

Half of the men working here ordered egg salad subs; the remaining men and one woman employed here ordered vegetarian meatball subs. Real men do eat vegetarian food. Not all vegetarians live in the woods and wear bandanas. Who knew? Ha ha.

Monday, June 1, 2015

This morning I watched a video of a *60 Minutes* television program that CBS initially aired on February 19, 2012. One segment of the program featured Dr. Irving Kirsch, who is the director of Placebo Studies and a lecturer in medicine at Harvard University Medical School as well as Beth Israel Deaconess Medical Center. Dr. Kirsch, who is a psychologist, stunned CBS news correspondent Leslie Stahl as well as *60 Minutes* viewers when he said numerous studies of placebos and anti-depressants which he has lead for thirty-six years, have clearly indicated that people who have been diagnosed with mild and moderate depression symptoms and who are being prescribed antidepressant medication, are becoming well essentially through experiencing empowering placebo-resembling effects of the medications, not chemicals present in the antidepressants.

Probing Dr. Kirsch, Ms. Stahl asked whether people who are consuming anti-depressant medication would see the same effects if they ingested placebos or sugar pills. Dr. Kirsch replied, "They'd have almost as large an effect and whatever the difference, it would be clinically insignificant." Disputing Dr. Kirsch, Ms. Stahl instantly rebutted, firmly saying, "But people are getting better, taking anti-depressants. I know them; we all know them."

Dr. Kirsch responded, "People do get better when they ingest the drug, but it's not the chemical ingredients in the drug making them better; it's the placebo effect." Dr. Kirsch reiterated that when one swallows a pill containing an antidepressant medication or a pill containing a placebo—a substance containing starch or sugar which is designed to have no therapeutic value—this creates a placebo effect, also known as a powerful belief in healing, which temporarily alleviates depression symptoms.

Observing Dr. Kirsch speak confirmed a long-held belief within me that utilizing anti-depressant medication, unless the medication is prescribed for a short term in a serious mental health matter, is generally ineffective. In general, side effects of all anti-depression medications, which include possibly experiencing suicidal thoughts, far outweigh the benefits of the drugs. Seventeen million Americans, including children as young as age six, are now being prescribed antidepressants, the *60 Minutes* segment revealed. The feature story revealed that in 2012, the annual revenue of pharmacology companies producing antidepressants was approximately $11.3 billion. Since the 1980s, when the depression medication Prozac was introduced, prescriptions for antidepressants in the U.S have soared four hundred percent.

Thursday, June 11, 2015

Niece Kristin called me today and informed me that Buddy, a dog that sister Lizzie owned, has died. Buddy was fourteen years old. For the past several years, he struggled bravely with severe arthritis. He experienced difficulty with rising, walking, climbing stairs, and entering and exiting cars. Having demonstrated continual kindness, loyalty, enthusiasm, and obedience, Buddy is loved, fondly remembered and tenderly missed.

Sunday, June 28, 2015

Convicted felon James "Whitey" Bulger answered a letter that three seventeen-year-old girls attending Apponequet High School in Lakeville, Massachusetts sent him. For sixteen years, he had successfully evaded world-wide pursuit by law enforcement agencies, until he was discovered and arrested four years ago in June of 2011. He was charged with and later convicted of complicity in nineteen murders and thirty-one counts of extortion, money laundering, racketeering, and weapons charges. Mr. Bulger was sentenced to a lifetime plus five years in a federal penitentiary.

Three students, named Brittany, Molly, and Michaela worked together to compose the letter Mr. Bulger received. The girls had been assigned a research and writing project focused on leadership and they believed that contacting and interviewing Mr. Bulger through written communication would make the finished report exemplary. The contents of the letter they wrote included a request for help from Mr. Bulger.

Recently made public on February 24, 2015, the response that James Bulger sent to the girls was composed on a single sheet of loose-leaf notebook paper. The dated missive displayed perfect penmanship, from start to finish. Mr. Bulger signed the letter and sent it to Brittany, Molly, and Michaela. Indicating that he cannot assist the students with the project; eighty-five-year-old Mr. Bulger wrote, "I took the wrong road. My life was foolishly wasted." He acknowledged having shamed the Bulger family.

He suggested that Brittany, Molly, and Michaela create a website honoring heroic Massachusetts servicemen, "who are patients, in for instance, in Walter Reed Hospital, good men isolated from society, due to war wounds." Near the end of the letter Mr. Bulger wrote, "I know only one thing for sure; if you want to make crime pay, go to law school." When closing the letter, he penned, "Sincerely, James Bulger."

Although there is some truth in the statement Mr. Bulger wrote indicating that he cannot assist the high school students, the assertion is not fully true. Honestly, Mr. Bulger has assisted the leadership project; it is good and probable that the letter he wrote has positively and permanently impacted many people, including the high school students who wrote to him.

Tuesday, July 28, 2015

Co-owners Mike and Jill Kushner operate South Shore Athletic Club in Cohasset. Jill suggested that I enter one or more of the Pilates and Bar (ballet bar) classes that are offered here, as instructors of the classes teach students stretching and weight-bearing exercises. Having been enrolled in a Pilates and a Bar (ballet bar) class for two months, I am finding torso and particularly core strengthening exercises significantly relieve arthritic stiffness and strengthen posture.

An SSAC Pilates class teacher, sexagenarian, Dina Zesta, said that since she enrolled in and then later began teaching Pilates and Bar classes, her spine has grown one-and one-half inches. "Wow," I said, when hearing this, having previously believed that deterioration of the spine which occurs after one enters mid-life years, is irreversible.

Monday, August 17, 2015

Bailey St. James, the owner and manager of St. James Masonry, brother Jared, and I crossed paths this morning, as Jared, who is vacationing in Cohasset with family, was exiting a convenience store in Cohasset Village, Bailey was entering the store and Jura and I were walking past the shop. Several years ago, employees of St. James Masonry skillfully and solidly replaced a formerly destabilized nearly one-hundred-year-old bridge which led to the summer home of Jared and Elissa and family.

This morning, Bailey informed Jared and me that he bought all six St. James children, all under the age of twelve, a new trampoline. He assembled the play equipment in the backyard of the family home, several feet away from the above-ground pool. Arriving home one day after work, Bailey looked through a window in the kitchen facing the backyard and then remarked, "What the heck?"

St. James children had moved the new trampoline; it was beside the above ground pool. Bailey viewed the children as one after another, they were jumping up and down and then jumping up again and sometimes performing somersaults and additional body moves, before each of them catapulted off the trampoline and then dropped into the pool waters. Bewildered, Bailey turned toward Aggie St. James, the wife of Bailey, who was standing near him. "I know; don't look anymore," Aggie said.

This morning, joking and politely goading Bailey, Jared asked him what he would have done when he was a kid, if his father had bought him and his siblings a trampoline and placed it in the backyard, several feet away from an already set-up outdoor pool. "Same thing," said Bailey We three burst into mirth.

Monday, August 31, 2015

Late this morning, Jura and I were walking inside Norris Reservation. The woodsy habitat in Norwell, Massachusetts is approximately six miles from Cohasset and five miles from neighboring Scituate. Today, the atmosphere was hot and humid; the temperature was nearly ninety degrees. Foot traffic here was minimal.

Jura and I entered a section of Norris Reservation woods abutting the North River, which is located approximately one mile from the entrance of the reservation. This morning, North River was showing noticeable current. Observing this was not alarming, as Jura, having on previous occasions entered the water body, had negotiated the river current with relative ease. Today, when he entered the river, rapidly flowing waters quickly and firmly grasped him, as I was watched and became stupefied.

Unable to fight the quickly moving current, Jura was steadily moving away from me. For a moment or two, I believed I could save him. Seconds later, I realized that I did not harbor sufficient swimming strength to enable me to rescue him. Standing upon the river bank, experiencing emotional paralysis, and intensely grieving being unable to aid Jura, I called out to him, expressing love and sorrow.

Suddenly, a voice, bursting through clouds, addressed me. The Voice, evidencing unexplainable, massive physical and spiritual energy, said, "Merrie, do not be afraid; I am here." Almost instantly, a small motorboat navigating around a river bend miraculously appeared. Two people were seated inside the craft. A man seated in the bow section was guiding the boat, using the handle of an outboard motor secured to the boat.

A woman seated in the mid-section of the boat was talking with him; she was probably giving him additional direction about possible ways to continue moving the boat through the restless waters. Seeing me, the woman hollered, "Do you want help?"

"Yes," I urgently responded. The boat then continued moving down the river, past Jura, leaving me with resurging feelings of confusion and abandonment. Seconds later, the woman called out to me again, saying, "Do you want help?"

"Yes," I replied again, beseechingly.

At the time, I did not realize the boaters had probably been strategizing a rescue method and had surmised that pulling a water-soaked dog weighing over seventy pounds into a small craft would probably have caused the boat to capsize. It is good and possible that they also wanted to avoid running into Jura.

Steering the motorboat toward Jura, the male guardian angel sidled the small craft beside Jura and then headed the motorboat toward shore. Moments later, water logged and exhausted Jura walked unsteadily onto land. The female guardian angel in the boat threw a filled plastic water bottle toward me; she indicated that drenched and fatigued Jura might be thirsty.

Hugging Jura and kissing him on the nose found me being grateful that cool water had soaked the body of Jura on this hot and humid day. As Jura and I slowly returned to the reservation parking lot, I momentarily became distracted. Regaining focus found me realizing Jura was again missing. While searching for him, I discovered a mother with her three young children; all were strolling near me in the Norris Reservation. Advised that Jura was missing, the kind, cooperative, and respectful people insisted upon helping me look for Jura. Fifteen minutes later, we found him. He was standing in the reservation parking lot, beside the SUV in which we had arrived there.

Sunday, September 13, 2015

Nephew Jonas Jenkins, and Liane Jenkins, the wife of Jonas, have welcomed a fourth child into the world. Ella Jenkins was born today.

Tuesday, October 21, 2015

Twelve-year-old dog Shamrock (Sham) died this evening. Niece Kristin Sullivan and Payden Sullivan, husband of Kristin, and their sons, Zachariah and Clarkson were the human family of Shamrock. Payden had informed me that Shamrock had experienced an increasing number of nosebleeds.

Later, Sham was diagnosed with brain cancer. Sham, Jura, and Buddy had played together on many occasions. Demonstrating soulful eyes, Shamrock was kind, playful, and enthusiastic. He is lovingly as well as longingly remembered.

Thursday, November 26, 2015

Having accepted a Thanksgiving dinner invitation, I was thirty minutes late, when arriving at the home of sister Lizzie Jenkins. After entering the house and apologizing, I viewed seven-year-old great nephew, Zachariah.

He ran toward me, offering me hugs and kisses. He asked if he could put food upon the dinner plate I was assigned. Later, Clarkson, the five-year old brother of Zachariah approached me, saying, "I go with God. Do you go with God?"

"Yes," I quietly replied. No matter how miserably was implied. During dinner, Clark nonchalantly informed us that he found a couple of girlfriends at school. Then appearing to be frustrated, he said that he is "still looking."

2016

CHAPTER TWENTY-FOUR

FINALE

Monday, January 4, 2016

New year. New life. New hope. Dog Jura is now fifteen years old. He is unable to jump into the back or front seat of a car anymore. In fact, he cannot enter a car without being physically assisted. He is able to walk three or four times daily, cumulatively for one-and one-half hours. He eats well. The amount of time that Jura sleeps is noticeably increasing. Nearly two years have passed since a veterinarian who diagnosed him with severe spinal stenosis said Jura would probably be deceased within one month. Jura continues to be enthusiastic, accepting, and humble amid each and all life circumstances.

Monday, March 21, 2016

Seth Moulton, a U.S Congressman from Massachusetts, recently visited Cuba. He accompanied President Obama and U.S. Congressman Jim McGovern. The trip marked the first time a sitting President has visited Cuba in ninety-one years. Mr. Moulton indicated that he is grateful for having embraced the opportunity to travel there. One year ago, President Obama announced the intention of the U.S. government to gradually and peacefully restore full diplomatic ties with Cuba. The intention of the diplomatic tour was not only to renew goodwill between America and Cuba but also to increase physical interaction between the two countries.

Government and business officials in American and Cuba have begun to exchange trade, travel, and diplomacy-based ideas. Commercial flights to and from neighboring Cuba will re-commence in August this year, for the first time in over fifty years. American citizens have reportedly been supporting the developments. Congressman Moulton said Cuban people are expressing a yearning for increased freedoms; these include increased business interactions with U.S. counterparts.

Seth Moulton stated that the Cubans he met welcome American tourists and want to learn about American culture. He remarked that the socialist government of Cuba is becoming increasingly open. He said that there are now more private Cuban restaurants in the country than in the past and that there is currently considerably more cell phone usage there than there was ten years ago.

Thirty-six-year-old Seth Moulton grew up on the North Shore of Massachusetts, where he currently continues to intermittently reside. He comes across as being internally grounded and content. He demonstrates support for thoughtful, action-based, steady government, grounded upon bi-partisan kindness, cooperation, and respect.

Sunday, March 27, 2016

Easter Sunday. Entering Resurrection Church in Hingham at 11:30 a.m. this morning found me surrounded by an overflowing crowd. Churchgoers filled pews, side and rear aisles, and the foyer. Hearing melodious religious music and the thoughtful sermon Fr. Quinn offered and receiving Communion motivated me to suddenly imagine love developing here and in worldwide church services occurring today naturally streaming into and throughout the universe.

Saturday, June 4, 2016

Enchanting was being an audience member who was watching the DanceSport Boston (DSB) Spring Showcase of ballroom dancing tonight. Over one hundred guests were seated at round tables that were covered with formal tablecloths and decorated with centered vases filled water and brightly colored flowers. Guest tables surrounded the perimeter of the ballroom. The atmosphere was inviting. It was lively. It was daring.

DSB students and teachers performed pro-am (professional and amateur) dance presentations with accompanying storylines and live band music. The well-received pro-am showcase presentations were followed by a magical professional showcase given by DSB dance instructors. Guests as well as DSB students were then challenged to learn a new dance and then perform the dance to live music, after five to seven minutes of instruction.

Showcase attendees were able to dance before and after the showcase presentations. Delicious hors d'oeuvres, desserts, and mocktails, in addition to bottled water, were available for guests when they wanted to eat or drink.

The showcase part of the evening lasted nearly an hour. Some dances were partnered dances; others were group presentations. DanceSport Boston lead dance instructors, Jayson and Alia Marie Palmer, Noor Lerry Trin, and Fabio Solinga, and adjunct instructor, Aubrey Jane Humira trained the participating students, whether the students performed with a dance partner, danced in a group with an instructor or were individually partnered with a DSB instructor. The 1930s to late 1940s style Swing Era big band, "White Heat," played during the large, bubbly, and sold out event. Watching dignified, elegant, and refined costumed ballroom dancers moving to the unique, festive and uplifting sound of "White Heat" musicians and the lead singer of the band was "out of the box" experience.

I was surprised to see me my niece Kristin and a friend of Kristin, named Jeannie, who were also guests here. Also unexpected was hearing the name of my sister, Lizzie Jenkins, being announced; she was one of a number of dancers performing in a showcase Latin dance group number. The "ladies only" festive dance presentation included women wearing brightly colored, tea-length, and flouncy dance dresses, while dancing expressively, uniformly, and sensually, generally in a circle formation.

Kristin informed me that Lizzie has been enrolled in DanceSport Boston ballroom private and group dance classes for over one year. Although I have been a DSB dance school student since 2009 and have enjoyed participating in group classes that the school offers, I hereby confess to being a frequent and current school dropout; I have not attended classes for a long time.

The entire cast of the DanceSport Boston Spring Showcase cast received rousing applause, as the forty-five-minutes-long performance ended. While Kristin, Jeannie, and I were suddenly sitting beside one another, Kristin admitted that the ballroom dance event is the first ballroom dance event that she has attended. Astonishing me, Kristin, who is now over thirty-years-old said she enjoyed hearing the swing era sound of "White Heat."

Kristin, Jeannie, and I mutually savored watching DSB showcases, featuring fluid, precise, and timely partnered as well as group performances. Accessible tasty hors d'oeuvres and savory desserts enhanced the dance celebration.

Reconnecting with Kristin and Lizzie was contenting. Invigorating was joining DanceSport Boston Spring dance attendees and performers after the pro-am and pro-show presentations, when DSB adjunct instructor Gavin Walker requested that guests who wished to do so to enter the dance floor regardless of dance experience. Fifty dance guests were then organized in several horizontal lines, with ten people in each line. Gavin then taught us The Electric Slide dance. First he taught us individual dance patterns of the line dance, utilizing simple walking and turning ballroom dance steps. He asked us to repeat each dance pattern.

Afterwards, he put the patterns together into a finished combination. As he did with individual patterns, he asked us to repeat the finished dance combination. When performing individual patterns and the finished combination, students were able to follow Gavin and DSB instructors, who aided the teach-in. After seven to ten minutes of instruction, Gavin challenged us again, this time asking us to perform the Electric Slide to the live music of the "White Heat" band.

Excitement and nervous giggling circulated throughout the dance floor moments before the band began playing. Band music does not stop when dance mistakes are made. Audience members who remained seated watch as the impromptu performance of the dance played out. Pure joy, relief, and laughter burst into the ballroom atmosphere, as guest dancers and DSB students executed the line dance with musical accompaniment, with or without mistakes. DanceSport Boston staff members remained with us; each instructor performed the dance on varied parts of the dance floor; all of the dancers were encouraged. Before the Showcase performances and following the line dance presentation, ballroom dance attendees and dance partners could be seen chasseing (sha-say-ing), or gliding about the ballroom dance floor.

Wednesday, June 8, 2016

Americans will choose the 45th president of the United States in November this year.

The nominees for the position are New York Senator and former First Lady Hillary Rodham Clinton and longtime businessman and media personality Donald Trump.

Viewing ongoing campaign activities has found me newly believing the electoral process is intended to resemble an entertaining sports competition.

The Presidential election process is intended to include informative, inspiring, and entertaining debates. Political debate, resembling game play activity, is meant to highlight political personas and positions of respective party candidates, to promote understanding and respect for differences between the candidates, to generate timely humor, and to foster and maintain goodwill between or among the candidates, depending upon the number of candidates who are involved in the debate. The candidate who wins the competition or the debate is an individual who displays notable ability to inspire, inform, and entertain the electorate through effectively communicating relevant political ideas, policies, and programs and at the same time, the victorious candidate maintains goodwill toward fellow candidates and the electorate. Other than these winning qualifications, determining the winner of the debate resembles a crapshoot, or the throwing of dice.

Campaign debates and speeches are meant to bolster voter support and respect for each and all of the candidates and political parties represented. At the same time, political candidates are intended to participate in lively political discussions, which include friendly competition and good humor. This type of debate invariably draws large numbers of enthusiastic viewers, whether the viewers are watching the debate in person, hearing it on the radio, or seeing it on television. What has happened to political debates, to the campaign process during the current presidential election cycle?

Sunday, August 7, 2016

As he promised, this past May, Pope Francis has created a commission comprising six men and six women, who will consider whether to allow Catholic women to serve as church deacons. Currently, male deacons can preach and perform baptisms, weddings, and funerals and sometimes serve Communion. When assisting a parish pastor, a deacon can handle activities surrounding parish management. Deacons cannot perform the primary duties of a priest. The duration of the papal commission has not yet been established.

This is an interesting ecclesiastical development. Many people hope that Catholic Church leadership, while partnering with lay staff and parishioners, will carefully consider the matter in a timely manner. The outcome of the conversations will notably influence not only how the Catholic Church will evolve long term, if women are allowed to become deacons and eventually priests and senior leaders, but also how the church will develop if women are prohibited from serving increasingly in the church.

Tuesday, August 9, 2016

Late last summer, I began giving Jura canine natural supplements which relieve back, hip, and joint pain he experiences. Jura is also being given a natural supplement for dogs that boosts the canine immune system and therefore fights cancer. There are fatty tumors as well as benign growths on Jura. Miraculously, consuming an all-natural cancer-fighting herbal supplement, which contains high levels of anti-oxidants, has influenced the growths either to shrink considerably or not to become noticeably enlarged.

Jura has also been consuming small amounts of a bee pollen supplement which is inserted daily into the food he eats. Witnessing the relief from allergic inflammation that he has experienced through ingesting the supplements is gratifying. Observing the healing Jura demonstrates eases the sadness that I feel about having resisted giving him bee pollen for many years, due to having not trusted natural medicine in the past.

Since I began giving Jura care, this is the first summer he has not been regularly scratching himself, sometimes to the point of bleeding, due to allergies. No over the counter or herbal remedies that I used to aid him in the past were consistently successful. He did receive two cortisone shots. However, cortisone, although being an anti-inflammatory drug, also destroys bone.

A small American company located in Maryland, develops the natural supplements that Jura is given. For four decades, the company has produced herbal supplements for dogs, horses, and yes, people. All of the remedies that I have been giving Jura are working remarkably well. In the past, Jura consistently resisted consuming prescription medication, sadly prompting me to pull his jaws open, before inserting the medicine.

Notably, Jura accepts herbal remedies without complaint; he views the health aids as food treats. Natural supplements do not produce harmful side effects. Watching fifteen-year-old Jura continue to enjoy a high level of enthusiasm and life quality is irreplaceably heartwarming and uplifting.

Tuesday, September 12, 2016

Quietly, confidently, and respectfully, rebuilt Sandy Hook Elementary school, in Newtown, Connecticut has been re-opened. Media members, including journalists and photographers who were invited to tour the school, in late July, honored the continuing request of the Sandy Hook Elementary School community for privacy. Intriguingly, increased technological devices present within the newly built Sandy Hook Elementary School are not plainly observable.

Diana Budds, the website developer for the architectural company Co. Design, critiqued the new school structure. She wrote "security measures are subtly embedded within the (school) design." Ms. Budds added that the new architectural scheme features "a wavy roofline, wood and fieldstone cladding, large expanses of glass, and plenty of art."

She indicated that the artistic pattern is intended to provide a "safe and welcoming educational space." Ms. Budds commented that the new look of the school is meant to highlight the natural beauty of Newtown, Connecticut rather than to evoke the memory of an isolated catastrophic event from the overall commendable three-hundred-and eleven- year history of the town.

Tuesday November 1, 2016

Having lived in Cohasset for fifty-eight years, I have been considering a move to Hingham, for several years. I lived in Hingham for about five years, when I was between forty and forty-five-years-old. I remember friendly, kind and compassionate former Hingham neighbors, Sherrie and Lee Sherwin; we shared pleasant conversations. When living in Hingham, I was not and am now not yet ready to be permanently committed to living anywhere. Frankly, I am not sure what readiness for permanent physical commitment involves.

Considering a move to Hingham, a citified, seaside ocean town neighboring Cohasset, with a population of twenty-two thousand people and located about twenty-three miles south of Boston, enables me to re-examine and appreciate life in Cohasset, whether or not I ultimately become a Hingham resident. As poet T.S. Eliot wrote, "We shall not cease from exploration, and the end of our exploring will be to arrive where we started, and to know the place for the first time."

Having recently completed two interviews with restaurant managers has found me appreciating being retired. Masso Shoua, an acquaintance and manager of Crow Point Pizzeria in Hingham once informed me that she went into the restaurant business because when she was a little girl. growing up in Greece, her family lived above a coffee shop that they owned. She loved hearing the sound of conversations going on in the coffee shop as well as the moderate din of restaurant machinery.

Having quietly and contentedly been a homemaker as well as a freelance writer for nine years and having given dog Jura full-time care for eight years, I now realize why I was not meant to be employed in the restaurant business. While considering moving to Hingham, I have been steadied, when recalling lyrics in the 2004 hit song "Que Sera Sera," sung by longtime actress Doris Day. Que sera, sera means what will be, will be.

Wednesday, November 9, 2016

In a stunning turn of events, Donald Trump, who is not a politician and did not win the popular vote in the recent presidential election, has defeated political opponent Hillary Clinton, a former U.S. Secretary of State (2009-2013) and former U.S. Senator of New York (2001-2009). Since 1971, Mr. Trump, a longtime businessman, has been the sole proprietor, president, and chief executive officer of the Trump Organization. The group comprises approximately five hundred business entities, in which nearly twenty-three thousand people are employed. Donald Trump formerly hosted the television show series, *Celebrity Apprentice,* during which he interviewed, tested, hired, and fired candidates who sought and sometimes gained employment in the Trump Organization.

Donald John Trump will be inaugurated President of the United States on Friday, January 20, 2017. Vice President- elect, Michael (Mike) Pence, the running mate of President-elect Trump and the former governor of Indiana will also be sworn-in on inauguration day. Voting results indicate that popular political support Hillary Clinton and Donald Trump received was comparable; Hillary Clinton received 48 percent of the vote; Mr. Trump received 45.9 percent.

The Trump-Pence presidential ticket won the election because the Trump-Pence political team received three hundred and six votes from the Electoral College. The running mate of Hillary Clinton was Tim Kaine, a U.S. senator from Virginia. The Clinton-Kaine ticket lost the election because the Clinton-Kaine team received two hundred thirty-two votes from the Electoral College. The number of electoral college votes required to win the presidential election is two hundred and seventy. Every four years, five hundred thirty-eight officially chosen electors, called the Electoral College, who are in general, chosen at state party conventions, come together to vote for a president and vice-president. When establishing an electoral system, the framers of the United States Constitution wanted to provide a balance between the election of a President in Congress and the election of a president by popular vote.

President-elect Trump, who recently appeared on the CBS television network program *60 minutes*, in an interview with correspondent Leslie Stahl, pledged that the Trump presidency is "going to be a beautiful thing." Donald Trump promised to be a "president for all people" who will support the rebuilding of the United States and the renewal of the American dream. "We will seek common ground, not hostility, we will seek partnership, not conflict," Mr. Trump vowed.

Friday, November 11, 2016

Formerly homeless and addicted to drugs for twenty-two years, Ted Williams, an Ohio resident who has been referenced as displaying a "golden voice" is now employed at the radio station in Columbus, Ohio where he was employed for the first time after he originally entered the radio broadcasting profession, sometime in the 1980s. Mr. Williams was re-discovered five years ago, in January 2011.

Columbus Dispatch videographer, Doral Chenoweth and Robin Chenoweth, the wife of Doral, spotted him standing in the midst of an Ohio interstate highway breakdown lane. Ted Williams was panhandling.

He was also displaying a cardboard sign that he made, which read, "I have a God given gift of voice. I am an ex-radio announcer who has fallen on hard times." When Doral and Robin heard the radio voice of Mr. Williams, they were delightfully shocked.

Mr. Williams recently began hosting a biblically based radio show on WKVO radio station in Columbus, Ohio. The name of the show is "The Praise." This is the first steady job that Mr. Williams has held in over two decades. The general manager of WKVO radio station said that he did not deliberate for long about re-hiring Ted Williams. He said the WKVO management team embraces "giving people second chances."

Saturday, December 2, 2016

Tonight found me hearing as well as sharing memorable conversation during a dinner celebration, including brother Jared, sister-in-law Elissa, fourteen-year-old nephew Jamus, twelve-year-old niece Brynn, ten-year-old nephew Rylan three-year-old niece Emma, sister Lizzie Jenkins, niece Kristin Jenkins Sullivan, eight-year-old Zachariah Sullivan, and six-year-old Clarkson Sullivan. Jared and Elissa invited us to share a pre-Christmas dinner with them and family in their new home in Boston, Massachusetts. They have lived here for several months. The new puppy of the Reagans, named Lulu, was also with us, but not during dinner.

Sister Valerie, her seventeen-year-old-son Matt Watson and Gerry Malloy, husband of Valerie, also joined us. Now living in Pennsylvania, Valerie and Gerry married one year ago, after dating for about one year. Both are employed as attorneys.

This evening, we enjoyed socializing, sharing dinner and a wondrous panoramic view of Boston, including Boston Common, on which there are now numerous large, lighted single and multi-colored Christmas trees. Before dinner, three-year-old Emma acquainted me with toys with which she plays. Remaining relatively quiet during dinner, twelve-year-old Brynn came across as being homesick for life in England. Contentedly anticipating a visit to England during the upcoming school Christmas break is comforting her.

Now attending a private middle school, Brynn is finding that commuting to and from school for two or more hours a day in addition with participating in rigorous classes in academics followed with scheduled after-school activities, for five days a week and half a day on Saturday is quite challenging. Fortunately, at the end of each school day before commuting home, Brynn is able to ride her horse named Hamilton, who is stabled and given care at a location near the school. The school offers a riding program.

Fourteen-year-old Jamus is also attending a private high school and becoming a masterful tennis player. He enjoys academic life. He relishes playing polo. Little more than one year from now, Jamus will be eligible for driving lessons. Ten-year-old Rylan is hoping to enter a new private school this coming January. He has successfully completed testing requirements for the school and will be interviewed for admission soon.

Two years away from being twelve years old, Rylan shocked me, when during dinner he commented that he read the novel *The Boy in the Striped Pajamas*. Author John Boyne has said that he wrote the first draft of the book—over two hundred pages—in two and a half days, without sleeping much. The empowering and intense novel is rated as fitting for children who are twelve years old and over. The book primarily depicts an unlikely relationship between two young boys.

Bruno is a nine-year-old boy whose father is a German army officer during WWII. Shmuel is a boy who is the same age as Bruno. The Jewish family of Shmuel has been imprisoned in a concentration camp in Germany. I have also read *The Boy in the Striped Pajamas* and watched the movie of the same name. After having watched the film at nearby retreat center conference room, during a dinner and a movie event held there,I was barely able to drive home. Although it is not based on a true story, the film clearly portrays realities of WWII circumstances and situations. Besides being deeply moving, the slightly beyond ninety minutes long poignant film is highly disturbing.

Accompanied by Elissa, Jamus, Brynn, and Rylan—when desiring school work relief on virtually every Saturday—go horseback riding. Regularly commuting to and from England, from Boston, Elissa produced a play which was well received in London. She is now considering producing two additional plays. She was recently named a board member of a Boston theatre company. Jared continues to work long hours in the investment business he owns and manages. He is increasingly working at home, which allows him to spend additional time with Jamus, Brynn, Rylan, and Emma.

Matthew Watson is now six feet, five inches tall and a junior at a co-ed private high school; he lives at the school. Matt said that he has enjoyed meeting new people; he added that there is little time to socialize at school, due to academic challenges. Enthused, he commented that he recently completed a driving course and a subsequent driving test and was later issued a Massachusetts driving permit.

Grace and Myla Watson, sisters of Matt, were unable to attend the family gathering held this evening. Grace, now twenty one years old, is currently a senior student at a university in Florida. Initially interested in becoming a physician assistant or establishing a career in the public health field, she is now considering becoming an attorney. She has recently completed LSAT testing and hopes to enter law school in the fall. Nineteen-year-old Myla, a sophomore at a university in North Carolina is currently majoring in biology and wishes someday to be a physician assistant.

Six-year old Clarkson Sulllivan and eight-year old Zachariah Sullivan are enrolled in public school classes in Cohasset. Clark is currently a kindergarten student. Zach is now in second grade. This evening, Zach and Clark enjoyed playing with cousin Rylan for nearly one hour after dinner was over. When Kristin, Lizzie, Zachariah, Clarkson and I were departing the home of Jared and Elissa and family, Zach indicated he enjoyed the evening. Nostalgically he said, "I didn't want to leave."

2018

CHAPTER TWENTY-FIVE

EPILOGUE

January 1, 2018

Writing *Life Flashes: A Memoir* has nearly come to an end. The now eleven-years-long writing journey has been irreplaceable, character building, and satisfying. The past year also allowed me to continue to write, perform in-home and yard-related tasks, give dog Jura care, read from time to time, and re-enter private and group ballroom dance classes.

Practicing dance between two-and two-and-a-half hours daily and attending weekly individual and group dance lessons enabled me to perform with DanceSport Boston (DSB) dance teacher, choreographer, and performer Fabio Solinga in one of five professional and amateur (pro-am) showcases presented at the DSB Winter Showcase and Dance in December 2017. As Fabio and I danced to Foxtrot music, we expressed choreography and an accompanying storyline which complemented music and lyrics of the song "The Sunny Side of the Street."

Participating in a dance showcase performance requires several months of rigorous training, including learning additional dance steps and combinations, developing technique and arm styling, and performing the choreographed showcase routine to music. Creating a storyline that is connected with the dance choreography and will appeal to an audience is also important. Without a definitive storyline, there is dancing. There is no showcase.

Working with Fabio, who is free-spirited, humorous, disciplined, and challenging is in general, pure joy. He is trustworthy, competent, funny, and strict. A little over a year ago, when we began working together, I was clumsy, shy, and not confident. There were times that I could not understand what he was saying. After a very brief period, I quit working with him and then reconsidered, several months later. Almost immediately after he and I began working together again, I wondered, *what on earth I was I thinking when I quit?*

Since then, we have worked together once or twice weekly. Fabio regularly raises a hand and offers me a "high five" which is reciprocated, expressing mutual good work during or at the end of a dance lesson. When I am frustrated with being unable to learn a dance pattern, one way in which he re-assures me is by saying, "This is not difficult: it is practically impossible."

I laugh out loud. And then I don't feel so bad. Yes, I borrowed the last sentence from the song "My Favorite Things" which is a song from the 1965 musical drama film produced by Robert Wise called, *The Sound of Music*. Refocusing, I admit that at other times when I am struggling, Fabio again assures me, as he supportively says, "No worries, this is an easy fix." As teacher and student and as a dance couple, he and I savor the out of body experience that performing offers us, whether we are sharing a private lesson, participating in a weekly practice dance, or entertaining an audience during a spring or winter showcase.

Opening a Thank You card Fabio sent me after the 2017 DanceSport Boston Winter Showcase found me becoming tearful, as I recalled abruptly quitting dance lessons shortly after beginning to work with him, reconsidering several months later, and then re-entering private dance lessons with him. Within the note, Fabio had written, "Thank you for not giving up on me." Tearful, *I thought, are you kidding? -Thank you, for not giving up on me.*

DanceSport Boston teacher, choreographer, and performer, Noor Lerry Trin also assisted me with refining dance technique I utilized in the December showcase. Although Noor resigned from teaching at DanceSport Boston in order to pursue a desire to re-commence competing as a professional dancer, I continue to utilize superb instruction she gave me involving steps and technique associated with rhythm ballroom dances, including rumba, cha-cha, bolero, and east coast swing. Ms. Trin provided me with tailored posture, balance, and stretching exercises which I perform five days a week, before practicing dance combinations and technique. In addition, she offered me professional coaching.

Noor repeatedly and gently impressed upon me the importance of putting dance passion first, not excessive hours of dance practice or performance or what others think of me. When one is focused on proving self-worth rather than expressing passion for living one is not truly dancing or living anymore. Abandoning focus on achievement has enabled me to experience previously unimaginable joy and to mature rather than regress as a dancer. I do not practice dance for as many hours or as many days as I used to do. Now not often negatively considering what others are thinking about me, I have realized that in general, all living persons wake up each and every day, put one foot in front of the other, and go about doing what each and all believe is willed, or genuinely important.

Maturing as a dance student has given me an opportunity to appreciate the values of devotion, determination, and discipline, not only in dance studies and practice but also in every aspect of life. While I was working with Noor, I began to increasingly embrace the female as well as the male attributes I was gifted and while doing so, I started to experience increased enthusiasm for living, including a heightened sense of gratitude. Dance training that Noor gave me has continued to inspire, invigorate, and renew me, for far beyond the fifteen or sixteen months that she and I worked together.

DanceSport Boston proprietors, managers, teachers, choreographers, and performers, Jayson and Alia Marie Palmer hosted the DSB Winter showcase, performed with amateur students they had trained, and in addition, choreographed and performed a professional showcase in which they included Fabio and Noor. The welcoming, competent, and good humored dance instruction of DanceSport Boston dance school has not only enabled me to continue developing and refining personal ballroom dance skills, but also has allowed me to develop astoundingly improved posture and balance, mental organization abilities, communication capabilities, and eating habits.

Personally amusing is recalling many years ago, before enrolling in ballroom dance classes, having viewed people performing ballroom dancing during summer months inside an outdoor pavilion overlooking ocean. I remember then thinking, *ballroom dancing is so corny; ballroom dancing is for old people. I would never do that!* Ironically, being a ballroom dance student has allowed me to discover a fountain of youth as well as joy that I did not know existed.

2017 found me experiencing new losses. Due to a longtime heart condition as well as natural causes, Dad died at home, on Sunday evening June 18, 2017, at approximately 7:00 p.m. He was eighty-five-years-old. As at this time sister Valerie and I were driving from Logan Airport in Boston to the Cohasset home in which we grew up, we were unable to be with Dad before he passed away. Sister Lizzie as well as brother Jared and niece Kristin were at the house when Valerie and I arrived here.

For a few moments, I was hesitant about walking into the bedroom where Dad lay. When I observed him, I experienced no fear. Dad was profoundly peaceful; he resembled a sleeping young teenage boy in appearance. I leaned over and kissed him on the forehead. It was gratifying to be reassured that Dad is at peace; there was no strain or anxiety visible on the face of Dad. Earthly cares that he encountered had been washed away. As it did when Mom died, disbelief initially overcame me. When undertakers came to the house, they covered the body of Dad, placed him on a stretcher, wheeled the stretcher outside, put the stretcher in a hearse, and then drove to a nearby funeral home.

Dad was memorialized in a private service which was held at the home of Jared, several months after Dad died. Dad was brilliant, He was witty. He was a deep thinker. He taught me invaluable life lessons, some of which have been mentioned in the memoir. As an adult, for a number of reasons, I did not spend a good deal of time with Mom or Dad, even when we lived together. Fortunately, the quality of a relationship, although being influenced by the frequency of time physically spent together, is not essentially defined by the amount of time people are physically together. I am grateful for having loved Mom and Dad, for the sacrifices they made for people, including family members, and for the heartwarming, heartbreaking, and irreplaceable lessons that they taught me as individuals and as a couple.

Humbling and gratifying was being willed the two-year-old car Dad drove. A few weeks after Jura and I were involved in a hit-and-run car accident, the vehicle mysteriously became available. On Monday evening, November 14, 2017, at around 7:00 p.m., someone driving a compact car without working headlights emerged from a side street, crashed into the right front end of the station wagon I was driving, backed away, crashed into the front end of the car again, backed up again, drove away from the accident scene toward a nearby rotary, and then drove back toward and sped past the accident scene. Jura, who had been lying in the car back seat, was thrown head first onto car flooring behind the front passenger seat.

A policeman arrived at the accident scene within minutes. He inquired about how I was feeling and suggested that I go to a nearby hospital to be checked out. Refusing to leave Jura, I respectfully declined. The policeman assisted me with contacting a car towing business that was able to transport the totaled station wagon to a junk yard.

Fortunately, a witness to the unfortunate incident advised me that as the offending car driver returned to and then passed the accident scene, the rear license plate on the back of the car being driven suddenly and mysteriously dropped onto the street. Without obtaining information contained on the license plate, I would not have been able to file an insurance claim or police report. A kind taxi cab driver transported Jura and me home, shortly after the policeman with whom I had been conferring at the accident scene ended talking.

Jura passed away on Tuesday, November 21, 2017, at approximately 1:40 p.m., when internal organs within him had fully failed. For over a year, he had been steadily slowing down metabolically. A Cohasset neighbor, Elise Mangano, accompanied me as I entered Hingham Animal Clinic, while carrying Jura. He suddenly hemorrhaged, as he was laid on the Hingham Animal Hospital entrance hallway floor.

For several years, I had hoped and prayed that when Jura died, I would be holding him. As Jura lay dying, he was almost fully resting in my lap and in both arms. Hingham Animal Clinic veterinarian, Dr. Harriet Lakus and additional clinic staff, who had given Jura high-level care for nearly ten years, lovingly surrounded Jura, while he was near death and then passed away. During previous veterinary visits, when she had viewed me becoming emotional and sometimes tearful when we discussed the continuing decline of Jura, Dr. Lakus asked me, "Are you going to be able handle losing Jura, when the time comes?"

No response followed. On the afternoon of November 21, 2017, as Dr. Lakus viewed Jura suddenly hemorrhaging, she gasped, and then she looked toward me, saying, "He's almost gone." She administered a euthanizing shot; then she suddenly surprised me.

She had become good and tearful. Love in the form of care she gave Jura pierced me then, as love now does. Jura clearly trusted and respected

Dr. Lakus as well as additional Hingham Animal Clinic staff. During almost ten years of intermittently being treated there, not once did he resist entering the clinic, which to this day, continues to exemplify the home-like atmosphere of the office and examining rooms of a veterinarian practicing in a rural area.

I remember Jura as resembling a beloved, humble, and wise King. In the years that we were together, I did not at any time observe Jura treating anyone or anything without kindness, respect, and cooperation. The night before he died, he was missing, at around 5:30 p.m., ten minutes after having been brought outside. For over one week, Jura had not strayed from the condominium environs when we were walking around it. He had become near fully blind and deaf and could walk only short distances.

Running late for a scheduled private dance lesson, I decided to let Jura out alone in the backyard for a few minutes, make him dinner in the meantime, and then escort him back into the condominium before driving to the dance school. When I sought Jura, five minutes after letting him out, he was gone; I called the studio and cancelled the lesson.

A few moments later, I spoke with neighbor Elise Mangano and Riggins Garage owner Warren Riggins, who was conferring with Jean about a car repair matter. Warren offered to drive about Cohasset looking for Jura. While we walked about neighborhood areas, Elise and I methodically searched the whereabouts of Jura, using large flashlights, allowing us to diligently observe nearby spots where Jura might be found.

Nearly sixty minutes later, believing Jura did not want to be discovered found me thanking Jean for assisting me and expressing a desire to return home. Heartbroken, I did not want to lose Jura amid these circumstances. When I returned home, I re-entered the living room. Shortly thereafter, Warren telephoned me and said that he had not found Jura. Thirty minutes later, while sitting on an oversized living room chair and continuing to experience profound grief, I decided to leave the condominium, enter the station wagon I drive, and travel about Cohasset, looking for Jura.

Doing so, unsurprisingly not finding Jura, and therefore returning home at 8:15 p.m., I parked the car in the driveway and sat numbly on the seat of a rental car I was then driving until 8:45 p.m. After leaving the car and walking very slowly toward the condominium front door, I viewed seriously ill Jura, quietly and soulfully standing near the door, facing me. He was patiently waiting to re-enter the earthly home in which he had lived for a little over three years, for almost the last time. Jura had been missing for three-and-a-half hours. I will not again experience unconditional love in the same manner that I did when loving and giving Jura care.

A few weeks after Jura died, he came back to life. He was at home with me, standing in the kitchen. He was radiant. I was overjoyed. I asked him if he had really come back to life.

He said, "Yes. I can be here for a few moments." I hugged him and kissed him on the nose several times. I felt fur on Jura and warmth of the body of Jura. As we bonded again, I recalled pure joy, humility, and profound acceptance of uncertainty that Jura continually and faithfully displayed. Then he was gone and I woke up. I had been dreaming.

Bereft, I asked Jura in prayer why he came back to me only to leave me again.

Moments later, I recalled the biblical story entitled the "Road to Emmaus". In the passage, two people who were devastated when Jesus was crucified were walking together, shortly after he died. Adding to the circumstance, the body of Jesus which had been laid in a tomb was missing.

Suddenly Jesus spiritually appeared to the two men, who were at first profoundly bewildered by the vision; neither of the men recognizes him as being risen. Jesus comforted the deeply grieving fellow humans, while they talked with him about the prophecies, miracles, and signs that Jesus performed while he was living, before he was persecuted and then crucified.

In spirit, Jesus remained with the men and later he broke bread with them, as he did during a meal that he shared with followers, on the night before he died. The two men suddenly realized that it is Jesus who is truly with them and that the spirit of Jesus is not a ghost. As fellow human beings, the two men experienced the real physical presence of Jesus, embodied in the Holy Spirit.

I experienced the physical presence of Jura in a similar manner after he died when I dreamed about him. I touched fur on Jura. I felt the warmth of the body of Jura. Intermittently, I recall and cherish the occurrence. Recalling the Road to Emmaus story prompted me to recall what I believe God said to me on the night that I dreamed about Jura after he died. Through the love of God, Jura said, "I am here. I love you. I did not leave you; I will not ever leave you. We are expressing love for one another in a new way."

The dream has considerably helped to me accept the loss of Mom and Dad as well as Jura and to generally accept loss and death as a natural part of life. The dream encouraged me not to deceptively depend upon the physical aspect of any relationship.

Recent days have found me longing to mentally, physically, and spiritually surrender *Life Flashes: A Memoir* manuscript. When the mind, body, and soul are wishing to release a written manuscript, the literary work is finished, or nearly complete. Writers have been given an opportunity to re-examine life experiences and to varying degrees, intertwine recording the experiences with communicating underlying personal thoughts, feelings, and beliefs surrounding the occurrences. Writing is Redemption. Writing is Resurrection. Writing is Renewal.

Many personal and professional relationships in which I have been engaged have been remarkably sustained and healed during the past eleven years. These years have found me realizing that the foundation of all relationships is goodwill, not depth of love, physicality, compatibility, or readiness. Depth of love, physicality, compatibility, and readiness do influence the way in which a relationship is expressed; none of these attributes control any relationship. Goodwill holds each and all relationships together.

No human being knows another fellow human completely. Children innately understand and demonstrate this reality and are unmoved by it. Accepting this truth allows each and all persons who are no longer children to be childlike. No human being knows self fully. Ironically, colloquially speaking, we are all a little bit of everything we see in fellow humanity. All relationships exude passion, which is expressed in innumerable ways.

What remains between two or more people when passion in a relationship ceases, displays the true nature of the relationship or relationships. Division is a natural and regularly occurring element of each and every relationship. What is not natural is the belief that division is essentially an immovable barrier, rather than what it truly is, an opportunity for reflection and renewed growth. Embracing these truths allows each and all to be free, enjoying living and loving or in other words, being as happy as a seagull grasping a French fry or a toddler sitting in a stroller, looking upward, expressing wonder, and having raised both arms toward sky. This is also known as being as content as a person who is smiling while demonstrating a song filled heart and dance-ready feet.

2020-2021

CHAPTER TWENTY-SIX

LAST GASP

Wednesday, January 1, 2020

Something's coming. Something good. If I can wait… 2018 and 2019 found me sending hundreds query letters to book publishers via postal mail or email service, attending author talks, and continuing to write and edit *Life Flashes: A Memoir*.

No publishing contract is in sight. Am I unrealistic? Hope not.

Friday, October 29, 2021

As it turns out, when I wrote something's coming, if I can wait, something coming was not a publishing deal; it was a worldwide Coronavirus pandemic. Also referenced as the Covid-19 epidemic, it has been reported to have begun in Wuhan, China in December of 2019, spread world-wide and is to date the cause of the deaths of over 2.56 million people around the world. Highly contagious, the disease affects the respiratory system, generating flu-like or pneumonia-similar viral symptoms, including headache, fever, chills, cough, and sore throat, which often accompany symptoms of shortness of breath, difficulty breathing, and fatigue.

By February of 2020, the viral symptoms were being observed in devastatingly large numbers in Italy and then in March as well as Spain. A Seattle, Washington resident who had recently traveled to Wuhan, China, contracted the first recorded case of Coronavirus in the United States, in late January. Shortly thereafter, Covid-19 cases began surging across the country. Following the leadership of fellow world nations, nearly all of America went into lockdown in the middle of March 2020.

Near the end of March of 2020, one hundred thousand cases of Covid-19 in the United States outnumbered cases worldwide. Except for businesses involving essential services, all commerce was shut down.

People were requested not to leave home unless they were going grocery shopping or attending a medical appointment. Schools and universities were closed. Respective elementary, high school, and college administrators, teachers, and professors began developing and implementing plans for online leaning. People employed in virtually every profession began working from home.

Although large numbers of people were working at home, unemployment skyrocketed in countries around the world. Some nations ticketed or fined people who had been discovered leaving home without governmental permission. People were requested to wear face masks, to remain six feet apart when in contact with one another, to wash their hands frequently and to utilize hand sanitizer often. Grocery stores, discount stores, and hardware stores were allowed to remain open for limited hours.

Restaurants were able to remain open for take-out only, largely as a means of servicing thousands of doctors, physician assistants, nurses, and fellow hospital employees, as many people employed in essential services were working numerous overtime shifts. At the end of March 2020, New York City hospital records indicated that 44,635 residents had been diagnosed with the Coronavirus and five hundred nineteen people had died, rendering the city then being the epicenter of the disease in the United States.

Because the virus is highly contagious and hospitals were filled to capacity, family members could not visit loved ones ill with Covid-19, even when a loved one was dying. New epicenters emerged in Texas, California, and Florida. Meanwhile, hospital administrators in many American states were experiencing considerable difficulty with procuring Personal Protective Equipment (PPE), including medical face masks. Hospitals were overcrowded and many personnel working together were working without wearing a mask; doing so influences chances of contracting viral disease. As the response of the federal government was considerably delayed, state government officials began bidding for contracts with medical mask suppliers.

Aiding requests from first responders for additional proper medical protection, Americans began making face masks and hospital smocks at home and in small companies and then donating or selling them to hospitals, as available supplies had sold out. As the Covid-19 pandemic continued, some American companies such as auto manufacturers whose businesses had significantly slowed down temporarily converted the businesses into ventilator manufacturing plants. Thirty to thirty five percent of gravely ill Covid-19 patients who have received ventilator assistance have survived. The use of a ventilator supports the functioning of the lungs, while a patient is fighting the respiratory disease.

By the end of May 2020, National Public Radio reported that 40.8 million Americans had filed for unemployment. Though not matching the 24.9 percent unemployment rate that happened during the Great Depression, the unemployment rate in America May 2020 was a staggering fifteen percent. By June of the same year, lockdown restrictions had been lightened; they were not fully lifted in a number of states, including Massachusetts. Lockdown restrictions and the terms of lifting lockdown restrictions varied from state to state, and sometimes widely. In the month of June, Covid-19 cases had begun to decrease notably, allowing some people to return to working outside home. The U.S. Bureau of Labor and Statistics then reported unemployment as having fallen to 8.4%. Generally, the unemployment rate hovers between 3.5% and 4.5%.

During the spring, summer, and fall months of 2020 there was considerable civil unrest. Numerous protests surrounding social injustice matters and political ideologies and programs occurred. Thankfully, organized marches and protests were relatively peaceful. The 2020 Presidential election results were officially called four days after Election Day, which was Tuesday, November 3. On Saturday, November 7, shortly before twelve o'clock in the afternoon, media outlets announced that Senator Joe Biden and Kamala Harris, the running mate of Mr. Biden had defeated President Donald Trump and Vice-President Mike Pence in the election.

The Joe Biden-Kamala Harris ticket had received eighty-one million popular votes and three hundred six Electoral College votes. The President Trump and Vice President Pence presidential ticket had received seventy-four million popular votes and two-hundred thirty-two electoral college votes. Two hundred seventy Electoral College votes are required to win a presidential election. Joe Biden and Kamala Harris were sworn in as respective President and Vice President on January 20, 2021.

The epidemic spurred global cooperation and competition for developing a vaccine, which happened in less than one year. Fifty-eight percent of Americans have been vaccinated so far. Typically, the advancement of a vaccine generally involves five to ten years of research and development. Questions surrounding the fundamental nature of the vaccine have surfaced. As of today, over seven hundred thousand Americans have died from the Coronavirus or diseases complicated by contracting the virus.

The unemployment rate in the United States has dropped notably since the gradual reopening of businesses began, almost eighteen months ago. Safety issues and additional workplace situations and circumstances that developed during the initial months of the pandemic have been addressed. This morning President Biden reported that the unemployment rate in America has dropped to 4.2 percent, which is within the normal range.

As are many Massachusetts residents, I am profoundly grateful for the steady, competent, and cooperative political leadership that Massachusetts and fellow American states have experienced during recent challenging times. As are many, I am also thankful for fellow Americans who have contributed to humanitarian efforts as first responders, including hospital personnel caring for people who are ill with the Coronavirus and employees of grocery store, hardware stores, pharmacies and the like that remained open during the lockdown, putting employees of the businesses at considerable risk for contracting the virus. As are a number of people, I am also mindful of individuals, families, and businesses that have been devastated by the circumstances and the consequences of the emerging and continuing pandemic.

Shortly after the lockdown began, perhaps in April 2020, I unexpectedly observed a brush pile containing leaves underlying a large y-shaped dead tree branch situated in a heavily shaded area of a nearby back yard. I photographed the scene, because it included fresh flowering daffodils that had sprouted forth through leaves just outside the mid-section of the y-shaped dead tree branch. Daffodils blooming amid fallen dead tree leaves are not an answer to the question of why tragedy occurs; blooming daffodils are one sign of unexplainable, unimaginable, and benevolent

Divine presence in devastating as well as victorious circumstances. Triumph springs forth from each and every tragedy.

No exceptions.

It is contenting to consider people who during recent times have cooperated positively and respectfully with political leadership and when warranted, have protested matters concerning social justice, political mandates, and governmental policies, in a dignified, thought provoking, and ennobling manner. The Bill of Rights in the American Constitution includes the inalienable right of every American to free speech.

With every freedom comes responsibility. Without accepting responsibility for choices one makes, there is no true freedom; there is trouble making, turbulence, and discontent. Properly employing the right of free speech denotes calmly, confidently, clearly, and cooperatively clarifying injustice and the circumstances surrounding injustice in addition with advocating positive changes. To fully appreciate the right of free speech, each and all accept responsibility for not spewing hatred, promoting violence, or spitefully encouraging division, on social media or anywhere else.

When the now near fully lifted lockdown in Massachusetts began in March of 2020 people were reeling from the shock of closed businesses, schools, and mounting deaths, while they were also coping with being indefinitely physically separated from loved ones, due to restrictions that were imposed amid widespread surges of the virus. Although not being a regular TV viewer, I confess that during the first two to three months that Covid-19 related lockdowns that were ongoing in the United States, I used to turn on the television almost daily, in the early afternoon, initially wishing solely to hear the calming, firm, and reassuring voices of Massachusetts governor Charlie Baker and Boston mayor Martin (Marty) Walsh, and wanting to hear the governor and the mayor as well as respective colleagues of the political leaders speak during press conferences.

The governor and the mayor held the conferences as a means of informing people about the nature and spread of the virus. They also updated Massachusetts residents about efforts in Massachusetts and in the Boston neighborhoods to slow and stop the spread of the disease; the endeavor included disseminating information about the development of a vaccine for Covid-19.

Profound internal quiet that the onset of a worldwide pandemic resulting in millions of deaths, hundreds of millions of job losses, the closure of at least forty percent of businesses, indefinite separations among loved ones, and civil unrest has also created numerous mysterious opportunities for individual and communal growth. The onset of the virus stopped the "normal" comings and goings of day to day living. After lockdown restrictions were imposed in Massachusetts in mid-March 2020, I was talking with someone who works in a nearby grocery store.

He said, "People are slowing down. I can see it. Shoppers are relaxing and reflecting in ways that they were not doing this before." Perhaps people are realizing that when one experiences being alone, one is not truly alone. Meanwhile, people appreciate being able to reconnect with one another when an opportunity to do so occurs, though most of the time doing so means wearing a face mask and remaining socially distant. Lost company profits and jobs due to Covid-19 and former social and political unrest are now steadily being recovered.

Since mind blowing and soul-searching circumstances surrounding Covid-19 began, people have universally been embracing recommendations from health professionals, including social distancing—remaining at least six feet apart from another person in all public places—wearing a mask, and frequent hand washing as being a fundamental means of stemming the potentially deadly virus, whether or not people have chosen to be vaccinated. Is it possible to do anything else?

Yes. One can engage in two additional disease prevention measures. One of the measures is learning how to use appropriate foods as medicine. The second measure is embracing some form of prayer.

Food is therapeutic. Although virtually everyone grows up believing that food is energy for the body, few people, including a number of medical doctors, were or have been taught that healthy food is good medicine. Here is an example. What would most people say about a doctor who diagnosed a patient with an illness—serious or non-serious—who then said to the patient, "Go home, eat proper amounts of fruits, beans, vegetables, and seeds every day, drink adequate amounts of water, and exercise to the extent that you can, when you can, and you will soon be well." The concept of treating food as medicine is becoming widely recognized as a longtime-tested and therefore, valid method of ending as well as preventing disease. One proponent of this medically and scientifically proven fact is Dr. Joel Fuhrman.

Shortly after the Coronavirus associated lockdown began, I unwittingly watched a public television station program in which Dr. Fuhrman presented a nutritional excellence plan that he developed, based on twenty years of food science research that he conducted with the aid of professional colleagues. The basis of the "Eat to Live" program, which Dr. Fuhrman also references as nutritional excellence, is a daily eating plan which includes the consumption of what he calls G-BOMBS, or greens, beans, onions, mushrooms, berries, and seeds. When choosing to do so, one can incorporate small amounts of protein into the plan. The plan also includes and promotes proper daily hydration and regular exercise. Dr. Fuhrman presented the plan during a public television station production called, "Food is Medicine."

"Many Americans who continually eat processed food are having an illicit affair with this food and what is really tragic, is this food does not like us," Dr. Fuhrman said.

"Eating conventionally increases stress. Emotions play a role in health for sure. Is continually eating processed foods worth that?" he added. The "Eat to Live" nutritional excellence plan is as simple as it has been successful. It promotes eating whole plant foods which are high in micronutrients— disease fighting natural chemicals in plants that give the body an abundant supply of vitamins and minerals that in turn, activate the immune system, combat disease, precipitate weight loss or management of weight, curb unhealthy food cravings, and improve overall mental, physical, and spiritual health.

Many patients of Dr. Fuhrman who have utilized the plan have been cured or have seen a substantial reduction in symptoms of major as well as minor diseases. These include heart disease, strokes, cancer, obesity, dementia, arthritis, migraine headaches and asthma. A number of people in the "Food is Medicine" television audience, which numbered about one hundred fifty people, were cured patients who utilized the nutritional excellence plan that Dr. Fuhrman developed, with the aid of associates. During the presentation, Dr. Fuhrman publicly recognized a number of patients with whom he worked who were healed from serious illnesses. Some were present at the lecture; others were depicted in large before and after pictures appearing on a screen.

Two persons that he publicly recognized are women who were previously diagnosed with symptoms of multiple sclerosis. Both of the women were suffering from side effects of prescription medication. Both were overweight by one hundred pounds. After implementing the nutritional excellence plan for one year, neither of the women displayed any symptoms of multiple sclerosis. Both women had lost one hundred pounds. One had recently finished running a half marathon. The overall mental and spiritual health of both women had also dramatically improved.

Another patient with whom Dr. Fuhrman worked is a man who had four heart attacks and had five stents in his arteries. Having faithfully utilized the nutritional excellence plan, for several years, he no longer consumes heart medication and he has not had another heart attack in four years. He also lost a noticeable amount of weight. Mr. Fuhrman indicated that many of the patients whom he has treated expressed satisfaction not only with recovering physical health, losing weight, ending the consumption of prescription medication, and experiencing increased metabolic energy, but also with embracing a renewed and genuine enthusiasm for living, a sense of mental well-being which they said they had nearly lost, before they began to use the nutritional excellence plan.

What Dr. Fuhrman says is true. After being diagnosed with a digestive system-related disorder several years ago, I started to significantly increase the amount of greens I was eating, including organic romaine lettuce, peas, roasted vegetables, and green beans.

Eliminating sugar, oils, and processed foods from the daily eating plan I utilize became as important to me as significantly restricting the amount I caffeine that I drink and reducing the amount of protein that I consume. Eating an increasing number of fruits and drinking amounts of water that are in accordance with proper daily health habits became a personal priority. Health improvement that I have experienced since I began utilizing an essentially plant based food regimen has been remarkable.

Dr. Fuhrman neither discourages nor encourages anyone who wishes to continue eating meat, pork, chicken, or fish from participating in the nutritional excellence plan. He acknowledges and respects the reality that people make decisions about food every day.

In fact, the highly praised and high selling cookbook that he wrote with the aid of associates and world-renowned chefs, entitled, *Eat to Live,* contains two hundred meal recipes that are plant-based and sixteen food recipes that incorporate small amounts of protein into plant-based meal preparation. He does advise that if one wants the "Eat to Live" nutritional excellence plan to be fully effective, it is important that the amount of protein one consumes does not exceed ten percent of daily caloric intake.

Utilizing prayer as a means of preventing and healing disease is a final suggestion. Many years of research studies have repeatedly validated a belief that people who experience true success or contentment, no matter what life circumstances arise, are people who demonstrate belief in a transcendental being, whether one references this being as God, or whether or not one is religious. True faith is not a crutch. Employing true faith involves accepting mortality. Demonstrating true faith means embracing reality.

True faith denotes acknowledging and embracing the reality that there is, was, and eternally will be unimaginable, steadying, and empowering Divine love amidst and beyond each and every life circumstance. One example of this is a Holocaust survivor, who when recently being questioned in a television interview was asked, "How could you trust God?" Readily responding the person calmly commented, "How could you *not* trust God?"

The onset of a world-wide pandemic has not and will not ever stop people from persevering and experiencing milestones. New condominium neighbors, Sabrina Nearling, Allie Chamberlain and Michael Heathrow and relatively new condominium neighbors, Jeff Thomas, Mary Ellen Goode, and I recently shared hors d'oeuvres and dinner together for the first time in several years. Nervous about socializing, I thought the dinner, which started at 5:30 p.m. on a Sunday evening would be over at 6:30 p.m. The gathering ended at 9:00 p.m. We talked, laughed, related in ways in which we had not realized we were connected, and we reminisced. We also shared some spiritual conversation.

DanceSport Boston ballroom dance school has been re-opened for about a year now. All of the staff and students wear masks and the group classes, which re-convened a number of months ago, are small in number, and are as socially distant as possible. I am fortunate to be able to continue working with DSB instructor Fabio Solinga and to have been working with instructor Jayson Palmer for a little over a year. Fabio continues to be a spirited, funny, and strict teacher. Jayson is a gifted teacher who is generally quiet in nature and who sometimes leaves me suddenly bursting into laughter.

I have been able to attend several monthly dance workshops that Alia Marie Palmer has hosted. The workshops are well attended. Instruction Alia Marie offers is lighthearted, consistent, and filled with juicy dance technique tips.

Kathy Manard, a former co-worker, with whom I used to walk dogs, became a friend as well as a supporter. We share discussions—sometimes lasting for up to six hours—about current events, medical, religious, spiritual matters, and relationship issues. Then we do not see one another for a long while, before we reconnect and "catch up" again.

Nephew Rhett Jenkins and Anna Maria Valdez–the longtime girlfriend of Rhett–bought a new home and in May of 2020, welcomed an infant son, Sammy Jenkins. Nephew Jonas Jenkins and Liane Jenkins, the wife of Jonas, welcomed a fifth child in March of this year, a son who was named Liam. Nephew Jamus Reagan will graduate from high school in June this year and will be attending a college in England this fall. Jared and Elissa and family have welcomed a new dog, named Frankie. Frankie is a Labrador retriever. He is about seven months old; he jumped up to greet me the first time we met. Niece Kristin Sullivan and family welcomed a new family member, a cat named Gibby.

Niece Grace Watson is now an attorney. She recently resigned from a law firm in New York City where she had been working, as she decided to move to Iowa and was recently hired as an attorney with a firm there. She and her longtime boyfriend Rick Schaefer— who is from Iowa and is employed as a facilities manager there—have been together for four years.

Niece Myla Watson received a master's degree in public health in May of this year. Sister Valerie Watson Malloy also received a master's degree in Divinity studies, in the same month. Stella, the white furred, pocket book-sized dog of sister Lizzie turned four years old. Meanwhile, I have not stopped sleeping aside the laptop I use to write. Maybe not doing so will help me socially.

Having been an intermittent churchgoer for decades, I recently began regularly attending church services. Significantly due to kindness, competence, and respect church leaders and congregants hav demonstrated I am learning how to face and deal with conflicts surrounding faith and therefore not to regularly and unilaterally quit churchgoing, when I see personal conflict with church beliefs, policies, or practices as insurmountable.

I have deeply missed regularly participating in imperfectly perfect church community activities and now I clearly see that not routinely doing so for over four decades was a considerable error. Falsely believing that isolation is a means of setting boundaries and developing strength in solitude when conflict arises, I did not realize that in actuality, isolation or sudden withdrawal from true community is potentially deadly behavior. Any type of conflict including church going conflict, can be resolved through quietly examining conflict in solitude or separation and through prayer, followed by re-engaging in communication with community members, until a contenting albeit incomplete resolution emerges.

Additional family members are carrying on as well, all waking up, putting one foot in front of the other, and moving forward, each and every day. We do not see or communicate with one another often. Fortunately, life is very much like watching television soap operas. Whether or not people have not been in touch with one another for days, weeks, months, or decades, spending an hour or even a few minutes together allows people to be physically reconnected, in a different manner than being connected in spirit alone. Thankfully, we are all connected with one another primarily by Providence, not by earthly circumstances. Goodbye reader. Peace. *Life Flashes: A Memoir* has ended. Promise. Good wishes.